ArtScroll Tanach Series®

A traditional commentary on the Books of the Bible

Rabbis Nosson Scherman/Meir Zlotowitz
General Editors

6/1/68
TEL-AVIV

SIMEON
ASHER.

Koheles

Dear George

May the words in this
book bring you insight,
peace of mind &
clarity of vision

All my love

Simon
xxxx

Koheles

ECCLESIASTES / A NEW TRANSLATION WITH A COMMENTARY ANTHOLOGISED FROM TALMUDIC, MIDRASHIC AND RABBINIC SOURCES.

Published by

Mesorah Publications, ltd

מגילת קהלת

Translated and compiled by

Rabbi Meir Zlotowitz

'An Overview/Eternity and Futility'

by

Rabbi Nosson Scherman

Published and distributed by
MESORAH PUBLICATIONS, LTD.,
4401 Second Ave. Brooklyn, N.Y. 11232

Distributed in Israel by
SIFRIATI / A. GITLER – BOOKS
10 Hashomer Street
Bnei Brak 51361

Distributed in Europe by
J. LEHMANN HEBREW BOOKSELLERS
20 Cambridge Terrace
Gateshead, Tyne and Wear
England NE8 1RP

Distributed in Australia & New Zealand by
GOLDS BOOK & GIFT CO.
36 William Street
Baclavia 3183, Vic., Australia

Distributed in South Africa by
KOLLEL BOOKSHOP
Shop 8A Norwood Hypermarket
Norwood 2196, Johannesburg, South Africa

FIRST EDITION

First Impression . . . September 1976
Second Impression . . . December 1976

SECOND EDITION
Revised and Corrected

First Impression . . . April 1977
Second Impression . . . January 1978
Third Impression . . . June 1979
Fourth Impression . . . June 1983
Fifth Impression . . . June 1985
Sixth Impression . . . August 1986
Seventh Impression . . . February 1988
Eighth Impression . . . November 1989
Ninth Impression . . . January 1991
Tenth Impression . . . March 1994
Eleventh Impression . . . August 1996
Twelfth Impression . . . January 1998
Thirteenth Impression . . . July 1999

THE ARTSCROLL TANACH SERIES®
KOHELES / ECCLESIASTES

ISBN

0-89906-007-2 (paperback)

KOHELES / ECCLESIASTES
0-89906-006-4 (hard cover)

THE FIVE MEGILLOS
(set of five volumes)
0-89906-010-2 (hard cover)

Typography by CompuScribe at ArtScroll Studios, Ltd.
4401 Second Avenue / Brooklyn, N.Y. 11232 / (718) 921-9000

Printed in the United States of America by Moriah Offset
Bound by Sefercraft, Quality Bookbinders, Ltd. Brooklyn, N.Y.

טוב שם משמן טוב

לזכר נשמת

פסח ב"ר יעקב יצחק נובצקי ע"ה

שנפטר ביום ב' לחג הסוכות תשל"ו

אהוב ונעים בחייו

פועל צדק והולך תמים

תומך תורה ועושה חסד

דורש טוב לעמו ולמשפחתו

שמח בחלקו ונכבד על הבריות

זכה לראות בנים ובני בנים

עוסקים בתורה ובמצוות

לפני שנלקח מאתנו במיטב שנותיו

יהי זכרו ברוך

הסכמת הגאון האמיתי שר התורה ועמוד ההוראה
מורנו ורבנו מרן ר׳ משה פיינשטיין שליט״א

RABBI MOSES FEINSTEIN
455 F. D. R. DRIVE
NEW YORK, N. Y. 10002
OREGON 7-1222

משה פיינשטיין
ר״מ תפארת ירושלים
בנוא יארק

בע״ה

הנה ידידי הרב הנכבד מאד מוהר״ר מאיר יעקב בן ידידי הרב הגאון ר׳ אהרן זלאטאוויץ שליט״א אשר היה מתלמידינו החשובים בהישיבה וכל העת מתנהג בכל הענינים כראוי לבני תורה ויראי השי״ת, כבר כתב שלשה ספרים חשובים אחד על מגילת אסתר ואחד על מגילת רות ואחד על מגילת איכה, בשפה האנגלית המדוברת ביותר במדינה זו, אשר קבץ דברים יקרים ופנינים נחמדים מספרי רבותינו נ״ע, אשר הם מעוררים לאהבת התורה וקיום המצוות וחזוק האמונה בהשי״ת, ונתקבלו אצל ההמון עם ההולכים בדרך התורה, ויש מזה תועלת לקרב לב הקוראים, אף מאלו שנתרחקו קצת, לאבינו שבשמים ולקיים מצותיו. ועתה כתב ספר כזה גם על מגילת קהלת, וכבר ראה אותו בני הרה״ג ר׳ דוד שליט״א ושבחו מאד, אשר על כן דבר טוב הוא מה שמדפיסו ומוציאו לאור עולם להגדיל אהבת השי״ת ותורתו הקדושה ואמונתנו בגאולה שהובטח לנו מהשי״ת ע״י משיח צדקנו בקרוב.

וגם אני מברך את ידידי הנכבד מאד מוהר״ר נתן שערמאן שליט״א אשר הוסיף נופך לבאר תוכן כל מגילה ומגילה במקצת לפי דברי חז״ל בפתיחת הספר בדברים המושכין את הלב לתורה ויראת השי״ת שיצליח מאד בכל מעשיו בפרט בעבודת החינוך אשר עוסק בזה בכל כחו לקדש שם שמים.
וע״ז באתי על החתום בעש״ק לסדר והיה מחניך קדוש ח׳ אלול תשל״ו.

נאום משה פיינשטיין

מכתב ברכה מאאמו״ר
הרב הגאון ר׳ אהרן זלאטאוויץ שליט״א

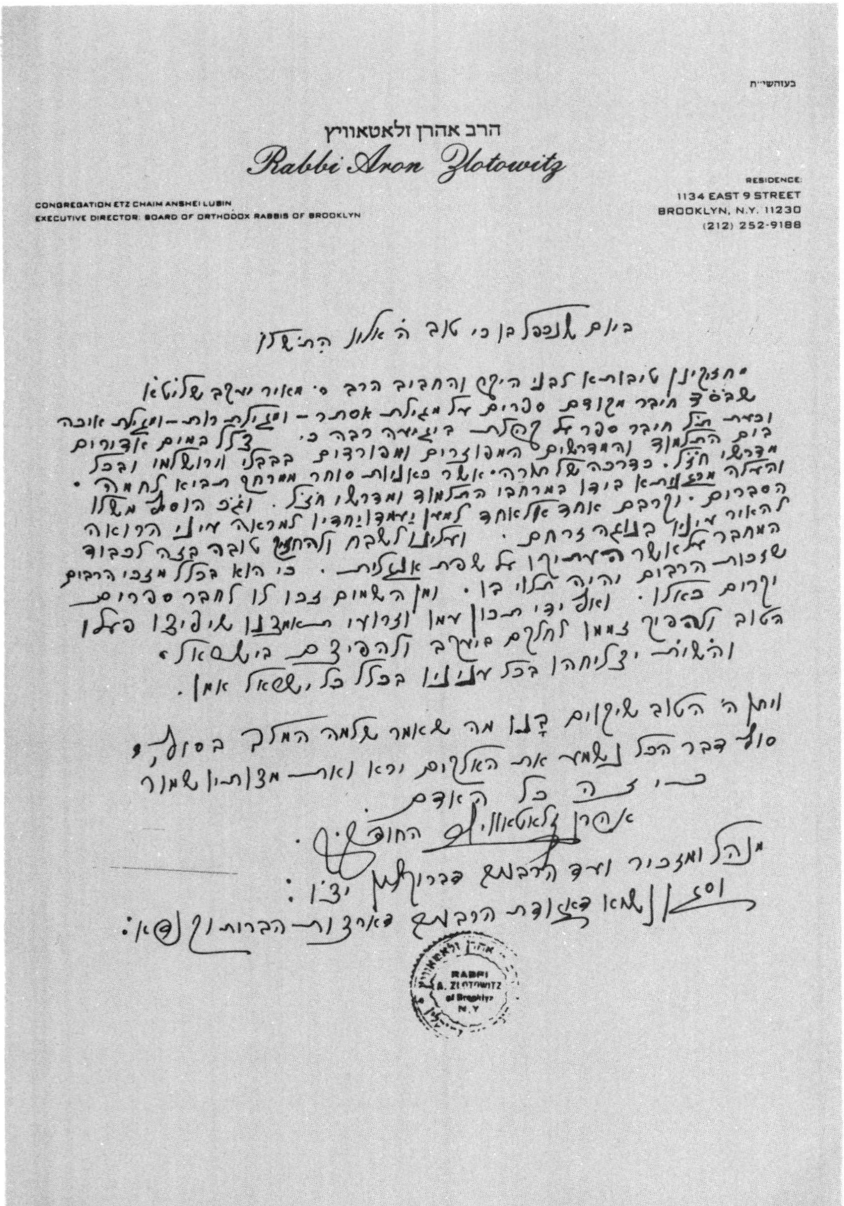

בעזהשי״ת

הרב אהרן זלאטאוויץ

Rabbi Aron Zlotowitz

CONGREGATION ETZ CHAIM ANSHEI LUBIN
EXECUTIVE DIRECTOR: BOARD OF ORTHODOX RABBIS OF BROOKLYN

RESIDENCE:
1134 EAST 9 STREET
BROOKLYN, N.Y. 11230
(212) 252-9188

ביום שנכפל בו כי טוב ה׳ אלול התשמ״ו

מחזקינן טיבותא לבני היקר והחביב הרב ר׳ מאיר יעקב שליט״א
שבס״ד חיבר מקודם ספרים על מגילת אסתר – ומגילת רות – ומגילת איכה
ובעת הנה חיבר ספר על קהלת – דיוקנא דבר בו. צלל במים אדירים
בים התלמוד והמדרשים המפוזרים ומפורדים בבבלי וירושלמי ובכל
מדרשי חז״ל. כדרכה של תורה: אשר כאניות סוחר ממרחק תביא לחמה.
והעלה מרגניתא בידו במרחבי התלמוד ומדרשי חז״ל. וגם הוסיף משלו
הסברים, וקרבם אחד אל אחד למען יתאחדו למראה עיני הרואה
להאיר עיני המחבר בנוגה זרחם. ועלינו לשבח ולהחזיק טובה בזה לכבוד
שזכות הרבים אשר המחבר על שפת אנגלית. כי הוא בכלל מזכי הרבים
וזכות הרבים יהיה תלוי בו. ומן השמים זכו לו לחבר ספרים
יקרים באלו. ואף ידי תכון עמו וזרועו תאמצנו שיפיצו פעלו
הטוב ולהפיץ צמאו לחקרם מעיינות ולהפיצם בישראל.
והשי״ת יצליחהו בכל מעשיו בכלל כל ישראל אמן.

ויתן ה׳ הטוב שיקוים בנו מה שאמר שלמה המלך בסוף,
סוף דבר הכל נשמע את האלקים ירא ואת מצותיו שמור
כי זה כל האדם.

אהרן זלאטאוויץ החותם פה
מנהל ומזכיר ועד הרבנים בברוקלין יצ״ו:
ויסד ונשיא באגודת הרבנים בארצות הברית וק[נדה]:

RABBI A. ZLOTOWITZ of Brooklyn N.Y.

Table of Contents

Preface

With the Book of Koheles the ArtScroll Tanach Series *offers its fourth publication to the Jewish public,* בעזהשי״ת*. It is done with a sense of gratitude and responsibility: gratitude because of the overwhelming response of the reading public to the books of* Esther, Ruth, *and* Eichah; *and responsibility because we are more keenly aware than ever of the need for English-language Torah translation and commentary that is completely faithful to Masorah.*

The Book of Koheles was surely the most difficult and probably the most important of the books published thus far. Unlike most books of the Scriptures, a general, superficial understanding of Koheles cannot be attained by reading it in translation. And study of it with one or two basic commentaries — the sort of study to which the typical student is limited — is far less adequate than it would be with other books. The difficulty encountered in writing this new translation and anthology of commentaries can easily be understood by even the casual reader — he need only attempt a thorough study of several verses of Koheles.

The extent to which the available English-language material on Koheles ignores Chazal *and rabbinic commentary is both shocking and distressing. Even in simple translation, most of the available work is so unfaithful to* Masorah *that it is unworthy of use by observant Jews. And the generally accepted picture of King Solomon — wisest of men and one of the holiest — is disgraceful and degrading.*

*It is instructive and important to point out a few instances — only two out of scores — where the typical reader at the mercy of the general literature is totally misled. The third verse of Koheles, "*What profit does man have for all his labor which he toils beneath the sun,*" is generally interpreted as a decadent declaration that everything is futile. But the Talmud cites it as proof that Koheles is completely "words of Torah." "Rejoice young man, in your childhood, let your heart cheer you in the days of your youth" (11:9) is rendered by English commentators as a call to young people to rejoice and enjoy the pleasures of this world while they are physically able, but the authentic Torah commentators see it as a challenge to repent. The need, then, is obvious and becomes plainer the more one attempts an independent study of the paucity of acceptable English-language material.*

In the prefaces to earlier works, we said that the purpose of the ArtScroll Tanach Series *is* לְהַחֲזִיר עֲטָרָה לְיוֹשְׁנָה*, to restore the crown of*

valid Torah interpretation to its true bearers. This goal is even more urgent in the case of Koheles. To whatever extent it has been achieved, a major service has been rendered to the Torah public.

SCOPE OF THE TRANSLATION AND COMMENTARY

The commentary is meant to appeal to a large cross section of people — from the early-teenage day school student to the Hebrew teacher; from the college student with a limited Hebrew background to the Kollel scholar who has neither access to all the sources in their original nor the time to investigate them individually. A serious attempt has therefore been made to bridge the very wide gap and fill the very unique individual needs of each reader.

The translation and commentary posed unique problems for two reasons. First, in the original Hebrew, it is often ambiguous, even incomprehensible, without commentary. Second, the division of the book into chapters (a non-Jewish division as pointed out in the prefatory remarks to Chapter 2) is often in direct opposition to the trend of the ideas as perceived by the commentaries.

As with the previously published books, we began with a new, free-flowing translation of the text — not always literal, but faithful to Rabbinic interpretation. Designed to be as readable as possible, the translation removed many of the "surface difficulties" dealt with by the Midrash, Rashi, *and* Ibn Ezra *by incorporating their interpretations into the translation. At the same time, we felt that in certain cases the ambiguity of the original Hebrew should be preserved and reflected in the translation in order to convey the richness and complexity of Koheles' language.*

The Talmud and Midrashim were consulted for selections concerned with פְּשַׁט*, the simple intended meaning of the text, which could meaningfully be incorporated into an English-language commentary.*

Next, the classic commentators, Rashi, Ibn Ezra, *and* Alshich, *as well as the major commentaries:* Rav Saadiah Gaon; Akeidas Yitzchak *by* Rav Yitzchak Arama; Nachal Eshkol *by the* Chidah; Metzudas David, Metzudas Zion *by* Rav Yechiel Altschuller; Taalumos Chachmah *by* The Lissa Gaon; Kol Yaakov *by the* Dubno Maagid, *and the commentaries of* Sforno, Rav Almosnino, Ibn Yachya, *and* Ibn Latif.

Because Koheles provided such a rich vein of thought for such ethical and philosophical masters as Rabbeinu Yonah (Shaarei Teshuvah), Rav Saadiah Gaon (Emunos V'De'os), Rav Moshe Chaim Luzatto (Mesillas Yesharim), *and* Rav S.R. Hirsch (Horeb), *we have culled these classics for elucidations of the concepts reflected in Kohele and sprinkled them through the commentary as footnotes. Enlightening selections from the* Talmud *and* Midrash *were included in the footnotes as well.*

HASHEM's NAME

Wherever the Hebrew Four Letter Name of God appears, it is translated: "HASHEM," i.e. 'THE Name' — the Holy Name of God. Where the Hebrew has Elokim, the more general and less 'personal' Name of the Diety — it is translated 'God.' Although the name of the Creator is generally written 'G-d' and not spelled out in its entirety, this Book is a portion of the Holy Scriptures and the full Four Letter Name of HASHEM appears in the Hebrew; it would have been ludicrous to abbreviate the spelling of the Name in English. אֶרֶץ יִשְׂרָאֵל, *was translated* Eretz Yisrael *(Land of Israel). Where the word 'Israel' is found, it refers to the Jewish people in general, not always specifically in distinction with the Tribes of Judah.*

A cross between the Sephardi and Ashkenazi transliteration of Hebrew words was used: Ashkenazi consonants, so to speak, with Sephardi vowels. Thus: Akeidas Yitzchak, *not* Akeidas Yitzchok; Koheles *not* Kohelet, *etc. Proper names from Scripture* that have become generally accepted have been retained. Thus: Solomon, David, Jerusalem, Moses, Judah, Isaac were retained and not changed to conform to our method of transliteration. However, when these names appear in Talmudic or Midrashic citations we have conformed to our method by using: Yitzchak, Yehudah, Yaakov, etc. Although there are several inconsistencies, the style has generally been held throughout the work.

SEVERAL WORDS OF CAUTION

There is a conflict of conscience in any work of this nature. On the one hand, there is a crying need for Torah publications in English. On the other hand, there are those equipped to study the original sources who will use the ARTSCROLL TANACH SERIES *as a means to acquire instant expertise. Neither the translation nor the commentary is meant to serve as a substitute for concentrated study of the original sources. Torah scholars who make use of this book are urged to do so as an aid to more intensive learning rather than as a substitute for it.*

It should be understood that many hundreds of pages of commentary are abridged and anthologized in this slim volume. Clearly, only highlights could be culled from the sources quoted. In the majority of cases, study of the full commentary in the original will yield much more than could be quoted in a work of this nature. Too, such study may lead the reader to different interpretations of the same commentary. This is natural and desirable, for the Torah greats of previous generations compared to us were, in the expression of the Sages, 'like angels compared to men or like men compared to donkeys.'

Far be it from the authors of the Overview and Commentary to pretend that they have done more than scratch the surface of the holy thoughts of the Torah giants.

The reader will note that the various commentaries often appear to be mutually exclusive. They are not; they complement each other just as each of the many facets of a diamond plays a part in enhancing the brilliance of a precious stone. As the Talmud says:

> The school of Rabbi Ishmael taught, *'[The word of God is] like a hammer that breaks a rock in pieces' (Jeremiah 23:29).* Just as a hammer [striking a rock] divides into many sparks, so, too, every word emanating from the mouth of the Holy One, blessed be He, divides into seventy interpretations *(Shabbos 88b).*

Every word of Torah has within it many meanings, all of them true even though they may point in different directions. Just as the myriad sparks coming from the clang of hammer against rock all come from the same source, so, too, do many varying interpretations lie within every word of Torah.

In Koheles the Sages found words of Torah and fear of God from beginning to end. It is in the Holy Scriptures because all generations must benefit from it. We can never hope to do justice to the Godly words emanating from the wisest of men. But we hope and pray that we have succeeded in transmitting some precious kernels of its abundance.

Rabbi Nosson Scherman / Meir Zlotowitz

Acknowledgements

The duty is again pleasantly mine to express my deepest feelings of gratitude to those who did not allow me to stumble over my own ignorance, and who have graciously given of their time to encourage, inspire, read and comment upon this work in its various stages:

My father HARAV HAGAON ARON ZLOTOWITZ שליט״א, *who has given of his paternal guidance and phenomenal storehouse of Torah-scholarship. I have discussed several of the selections with him before insertion, and I have benefited greatly from his sagely comments. May he and my dear mother be blessed with longevity and* נַחַת *from their children and grandchildren;*

I am indeed grateful to again have been privileged to be given free access to a group of אַנְשֵׁי־אֶשְׁכֹּלוֹת, *the most scholarly and gifted personalities*

on the American Torah scene: HARAV DAVID FEINSTEIN, *a human treasury of Torah knowledge and insight dedicated much of his precious time — as did my good friend* HARAV DAVID COHEN, *to whose scholarship and phenomenal storehouse of learning I owe much for the impetus of this project — to a meticulous and detailed critical reading and analysis of the manuscript in its evolving stages as it went from research to press.* HARAV JOSEPH ELIAS, *too, has read portions of the manuscript and made most incisive comments. Each of the three displayed his warm concern and friendship by taking time from his harried schedule to make the most profound and stimulating suggestions, noting discrepencies, and guiding me to sources and interpretations. Their mark has been left on the book, but since they have left final editorial discretion to me, they are absolved from any share of responsibility for the final product; I bear that responsibility alone.*

We are especially grateful to the Telshe Rosh haYeshivah, HAGAON HARAV MORDECHAI GIFTER *who very graciously granted us time to discuss many aspects of this undertaking. His warm encouragement and astute guidance were most valuable and immeasurably appreciated.*

We are indebted to HARAV MOSHE EISENMANN, *Mashgiach of Yeshivas Ner Israel. Upon hearing that the work was in progress, he sent us his original Hebrew manuscript on Koheles with complete freedom to use any, all, or none of it. It is a work of rare breadth and depth, and it added immeasurably to the Overview.*

The family of the late PETER NOVETSKY ז״ל, *with a profound dedication to Torah, and understanding for the need of this Series, saw in it a way to memorialize the name of a man to whom Torah was precious. They helped significantly to make this publication possible.*

Our admiration and gratitude go to RABBI YAAKOV MARCUS, *spiritual leader of the Young Israel of Staten Island for his great interest in this project. He has unselfishly assumed a leadership role in its dissemination.*

I must likewise express my appreciation to the group of long-time friends who have read the manuscript, offered suggestions, and in general encouraged me to undertake this work: MR. DAVID H. SCHWARTZ, RABBI BORUCH B. BORCHARDT, RABBI ELI MUNK, RABBI NISSON WOLPIN, RABBI YOSEF WEINBAUM, *and my brothers-in-law,* RABBI SOLOMON T. REICHEL, *and* RABBI JACOB KIFFEL. *The finished product is the best testimony to their sincere and productive contribution.*

The efforts of REB ZUNDEL BERMAN *in disseminating this volume to the B'nai Yeshivos for whom it is primarily intended, is again acknowledged.*

A special note of thanks is due my long-time friend RABBI AVIE GOLD

who undertook to meticulously proofread and check the source references in this volume. Additionally, he made valuable comments, many of which were incorporated into the final text. He has tried to assure a nearly error-free publication לְשֵׁם וּלְתִפְאֶרֶת*. The several errors which remain are due to technical reasons beyond his control.*

MRS. JUDY GROSSMAN, *too, has given of her personal time to proofread the galleys and help ensure the accuracy of the printed page. She has my gratitude.*

My sister, MRS. SHIRLEY KIFFEL, *and* MISS PEARL EINHORN *have responded with selfless devotion to this project. They have graciously given much of their own time to prepare the manuscript for the computer. That the volume was published in time for Yom Tov is due in great measure to their efforts;*

My good friend REB SHEAH BRANDER *has again risen to the need and given of his mastery of graphics and esthetic beauty to produce a visually excellent work. Were it not for Sheah's devotion, the final product would not have attained its high level of graphic excellence. Words to not adequately express my appreciation for his constant dedication.*

In closing, I would again like to share with the readers my profound recognition that the ARTSCROLL TANACH SERIES *would not have achieved its widespread acceptance were it not for the involvement of my* יְדִיד נֶכְבָּד, HARAV NOSSON SCHERMAN, *who continues to distinguish himself as a master of eloquence and clarity, presenting the most abstract Torah concepts in a manner that inspires every level of readership. By enlightening me on methodology of translating obscure phrases and concepts, he has lent the manuscript the benefit of his erudition sensitivity and flowing style;*

It is not redundant to stress that my deepest appreciation goes to my wife מנב״ת, RACHEL, *for her constant good cheer, guidance, and astute insights. The work could not have proceeded at such a pace — amidst the duties of* גִּדּוּל־בָּנִים, *domestic responsibilities — were it not for her constant encouragement. She has created an atmosphere conducive for Torah-study and turned our home into a* בֵּית וַעַד לַחֲכָמִים, *a forum for Torah scholars. May her sincere efforts for Harbatzas Torah be amply rewarded: may our children dwell in the 'tent of Torah'*

I humbly thank the רבש״ע *that He has given me the inspiration to compile this Book and that my attempts to contribute to the store of Torah knowledge have been enthusiactically received. May we merit to continue this work* לְהַגְדִּיל תּוֹרָה וּלְהַאֲדִירָהּ.

Meir Zlotowitz

Brooklyn, New York,
Rosh Chodesh Elul, 5736

An Overview —

Eternity and Futility

An Overview —
Eternity and Futility

אמר ר׳ יהודה אמר רב ... אמר אברהם לפני הקב״ה ... נסתכלתי באצטגנינות שלי ואיני ראוי להוליד בן. אמר ליה צא מאצטגנינות שלך שאין מזל לישראל

Rabbi Judah said in the name of Rav, Abraham said before the Holy One blessed be He, I have studied closely with my astrology [my knowledge of natural law] and I am incapable of giving birth to a son. [God] said to him, leave your astrology. Israel has no [dependence on] constellations (Shabbos *156a).*

מַה יִּתְרוֹן לָאָדָם בְּכָל עֲמָלוֹ שֶׁיַּעֲמֹל תַּחַת הַשָּׁמֶשׁ. ואמרו דבי ר׳ ינאי תחת השמש הוא דאין לו. קודם השמש יש לו.

What profit does man have for all his labor which he toils beneath the sun? (Koheles *1:3).*

And the academy of Rabbi Yannai said, Only [in striving for benefit in what is] under the *sun [is there] no gain, [but in striving for Torah which] preceded the sun, there is [benefit]* (Shabbos *30b).*

I. The Greatest Gift

When Solomon became King of Israel, God came to him in a dream and said: שְׁאַל מָה אֶתֶּן לָךְ, *'Ask! What shall I give you?' (I Kings 3:5).*
The young king answered,
וְנָתַתָּ לְעַבְדְּךָ לֵב שֹׁמֵעַ לִשְׁפֹּט אֶת עַמְּךָ לְהָבִין בֵּין טוֹב לְרָע כִּי מִי יוּכַל לִשְׁפֹּט אֶת עַמְּךָ הַכָּבֵד הַזֶּה.
'Give your servant an understanding heart to judge your people, to discern between

good and evil, for who is able to judge this, your difficult people?' (Ibid 9).

The Midrash likens Solomon's request to that of a royal adviser. The king wished to reward his confidante and asked him to choose whatever he would like. What should he choose?

'If I ask for gold and silver, the king will give it to me. If I ask for beautiful garments, the king will give them to me. If I ask for a luxurious palace, the king will give it to me. I will ask for one thing more precious than any of these. One thing, which will assure me of gold, silver, clothing, a palace — everything the king has to offer!'

Whereupon the servant asked for the hand of the princess in marriage.

So, concludes the Midrash, did Solomon. Rather than ask for wealth, power, or glory, he asked for one thing more precious than any of them, one thing that included them all. He asked for wisdom, for he who has wisdom gains everything (Midrash Koheles Rabba).

This is a *Midrash* that cannot be understood superficially. For, even if it were possible for an adviser to deceive his king, Solomon could not deceive God. Can we believe that his plea for wisdom was nothing more than a ploy to gain all heavenly gifts with one clever request? Or that God could praise him for ignoring all the earth's bounty in favor of wisdom when, in truth, he sought wisdom merely as a device to gain other benefits.?

At the age of twelve, when he assumed the throne, he already knew that "possible" and "impossible" are synonyms for human blindness.

No. Solomon's request revealed profound wisdom, not skillful negotiating skills. At the age of twelve, when he assumed the throne, he already knew that "possible" and "impossible" are synonyms for human blindness. He knew that the world is God's stage and that all the phenomena of nature are but tools to enact or disguise His will. He knew

that earthly goods — gold, silver, clothing, success — can always be provided if they suit God's will, if only man would open his eyes to see them.

When Eyes Open

An instance of what man can see if he is willing to look with spiritual eyes is found in the Torah. Hagar, an Egyptian princess, became the second wife of Abraham when his marriage to Sarah proved barren after many years. She gave birth to Ishmael, but after the birth of Isaac to Abraham and Sarah, Ishmael became a physical and moral danger to the young heir. Hagar and Ishmael were forced to leave the home of Abraham. Ishmael became feverish in the desert and was close to death. His distraught mother moved off into the distance to avoid watching him die. Then, a miracle happened.

וַיִּפְקַח אֱלֹקִים אֶת עֵינֶיהָ וַתֵּרֶא בְּאֵר מָיִם

And God opened her eyes and she saw a well of water (Genesis 21:19).

Note the verse closely. It does not say that a well was miraculously created; it says that Hagar's eyes were "opened"! But her eyes weren't closed. She was alone in the midst of desolation, desperately searching for water to save her son's life. Why hadn't she seen the well earlier? It was there, but she hadn't seen it because her flesh-and-blood eyes and cause-and-effect mind could focus only on the "fact" that it was "impossible" for water to flow in that burning, parched desert. When God opened her eyes, she saw more than a well, she saw the source of *all* wells. She saw behind the veils of nature; indeed, she saw that nature itself is a veil concealing the omnipotence — even the existence — of God. *Anything* can happen. The same God who commands oil to burn can command vinegar to burn *(Taanis 25),* and the same God who made the desert can transform it into a Garden of Eden.

The same God who commands oil to burn can command vinegar to burn (Taanis 25), and the same God who made the desert can transform it into a Garden of Eden.

Let us not forget that when the *Midrash* gives us a parable of a king's adviser seeking to marry a princess, it seeks to illuminate the behavior of Solomon, one of history's greatest figures. We live in

a world where all-powerful kings in the ancient sense hardly exist; where masters, lords and rulers in almost all lands are fair game for criticism and ridicule. The king in the Midrashic parable is the sort of ruler whom few if any of us have ever seen, the sort of ruler who is an earthly symbol of God Himself להבדיל. Life and death are in his hands and he is accountable to no one because everyone lives by his pleasure. Only in fairy tales do commoners believe that that sort of request could even be considered, much less honored. What could the commoner expect who dares tempt the wrath of the king by asking him for the princess — dismissal? imprisonment? execution?

The True Request

Yet the royal adviser, surely no fool, *did* make the request. Certainly not because wealth and honor were important to him — those could have been his without taking so dangerous a course. He asked for the princess because he wanted her so much that everything became insignificant by comparison; so much that he was willing to risk everything if he could not have her.

This is the parallel to Solomon.

Solomon disclaimed all the gifts of the temporal world.

Solomon knew that the sort of wisdom he sought, the ultimate depth of Torah knowledge, was beyond human power to attain. How dare he even make the request! Logically he should have contented himself with the normal wishes of kings — wealth, peace, glory, triumph. He didn't because they were meaningless to him, they were of no value in the eyes of a Solomon if they were unaccompanied by wisdom. And, indeed, the wisdom which finally became his cherished heavenly gift became the proof that he had chosen well. After becoming the wisest of men and amassing a lifetime of learning and experience, Solomon said הֲבֵל הֲבָלִים *Futility of futilities! (Koheles 1:2)* He knew when he became king that only Torah wisdom mattered; at the end of his days he would know it all the more. So Solomon disclaimed all the gifts of the temporal world. Instead

he asked for the gift that was beyond attainment, because a young man who grew up in the house of King David knew what Hagar had learned. God can open eyes to wells, and hearts to wisdom. If Solomon could have wisdom, he would have all the gold and glory he needed and more. Without wisdom, they would be fool's gold and empty vanity. *(Sfas Emes).*

God can open eyes to wells, and hearts to wisdom.

An Understanding Heart

The way he phrased his request reveals even more. He asked for לֵב שׁוֹמֵעַ, a *listening, heedful, understanding heart.* The person who desires nothing more than to listen to, to heed, and then to understand God declares that he dedicates his entire essence to Someone outside of himself. His entire being is dedicated only to the service of God. It is this desire that stamped Solomon as the master of wisdom.

For a human being can be described as the master of anything only if it is completely under his control. The leader who must tailor his every policy to suit public opinion or the satraps of his party, is truly their creature, not their leader. The businessman who always neglects himself and his family in favor of his business is truly its servant, not its owner. The human being whose life is always ordered according to the lusts and rationalizations of his heart, is a slave of his impulses and wisdom, not their possessor. Solomon wanted a heedful heart, a heart that was forever ready to listen and understand what its Creator demanded of it. Because it was that sort of wisdom that Solomon craved, because it was a wisdom always placed in the service of God, and because it was a wisdom that Solomon wanted to serve as his compass on the path of divine service, it was *his* wisdom *(Ibid).*

II. Solomon's Mission

Whose Test?

Every person has his unique mission on earth, and his tests and challenges are determined by his mission. This is seen most strikingly, of course, in the lives of the Patriarchs, but it is true, though to a much smaller extent, of every Jew.

A pivotal event in Jewish history was *Akeidas Yitzchok,* the Binding of Isaac upon an altar when Abraham was commanded to bring his beloved, only son as an offering to God *(Genesis 22).* Our prayers are filled with references to this awesome event. The courage and self-sacrifice of both father and son are inspirations and sources of merit for Jews in all generations. Abraham was bringing the offering, and Isaac was voluntarily mounting the altar prepared to give his life should that prove to be the Divine Will. Yet strangely enough, the *Talmud* and *Midrash* refer to it only as a test of Abraham. Surely, the aged father was being tested, but why should it not be regarded as a test of Isaac as well?

Surely, the aged father was being tested, but why should it not be regarded as a test of Isaac as well?

To this question, the Kotzker Rebbe answered, "It is not called Isaac's test because the Torah says of the *Akeidah* וְהָאֱלֹקִים נִסָּה אֶת אַבְרָהָם, *and God tested Abraham.*

The answer seems even harder to understand than the question. Of course, the Torah calls it Abraham's test, but that is exactly what we don't understand!

Mastery of Character

The Kotzker is right. The same event can be a test for one person but not for another. Abraham's overriding characteristic was kindness. Through kindness he won converts to his belief in the One God. Even on the third day following his circumcision, when he was in great pain, he sat in the blazing sun hoping he could spy wayfarers to invite in and serve personally.

Because he elevated mercy and generosity into a lofty means of serving God, his kindness was tested. Was he generous merely because it was his nature, or

because it was his way of serving God? What if his kind nature came in conflict with the requirements to obey God's command — what would he do then? Could he even be cruel if that was what God wanted of him?

Our Sages teach us that God is never unfair with his creatures. People are not tested with challenges beyond their capacity to endure. Abraham was great enough to master every test, therefore he was given the opportunity to surmount them all to gain merit for himself and set eternal patterns of behavior for his descendants. And all of his tests involved either cruelty or the sort of behavior that would put a distance between him and others. Could any of us send a woman with a deliriously feverish child into a burning desert without even water? Could we do it to a total stranger, much less our own wife and child? Yet Abraham was asked to dispatch his concubine, Hagar, with his sick son, Ishmael, on short notice without provisions. That divine intervention would save Ishmael's life was not known to Abraham beforehand. That was his test — would the kindest of mortals bring himself to perform an act of apparent callousness because such was the will of God?

That was his test — would the kindest of mortals bring himself to perform an act of apparent callousness because such was the will of God?

Akeidas Yitzchok was a similar test of Abraham's ability to triumph over his own nature. For a hundred years he had waited for Isaac, a son born to Sarah, a worthy scion of Abraham's ideals and mission. Now he was asked to bring him as an offering. More — Abraham had spent his entire adult life preaching that the true God did not want human sacrifice, that the God of Mercy sought to salvage human life, not destroy it. If he were to sacrifice his own beloved son, how could he ever hope to draw people close to God again? His teaching would be ridiculed; his reputation, discredited! *(Michtav Me'Eliyahu)*

Isaac's temperament was different. He represented uncompromising strength in the service of God. To him it was not difficult to give up his life if need be. For Isaac, unlike Abraham, the call to mount the altar was not a potentially traumatic test. And that is why

the Torah, in introducing *Akeidas Yitzchok,* says that *Abraham* was being tested.

Similarly, Jacob whose overriding attribute was truth, was faced with challenges to his ability to remain truthful. He had to deceive Isaac to get the Abrahamitic blessings, match wits and bargains for twenty years with Laban, and outwit Esau on his way back to Canaan. All these skirmishes with falsehood and *still* remain the master of truth — this was Jacob's test *(Ibid).*

Father and Son

David and Solomon, father and son, were the greatest kings Israel ever had, but they were very different personalities with very different missions.

David was the king who, true to the example of his forefather Judah, lived not for himself at all. He saw none of his greatness as belonging to himself; everything was at the service of his people. This attribute of unselfish majesty was a legacy of the forefather of the Davidic dynasty, Judah. He established the pattern of complete personal submersion to a mission. The name Judah— יְהוּדָה — has within it the Four-Letter Name of God. But it also has the letter ד, *dalet,* which means poverty. Judah could bear the greatness of his Creator, but, to himself, he was a pauper possessing nothing of his own. Because of this, he was king. (See *Overview* to ArtScroll edition of *Ruth*).

David remained a pauper — nothing that he had achieved was his own; all was a heavenly gift to be held in safekeeping for the people because a king belongs to the people.

His prototype descendant, David, was the same way. He, the individual, did not matter at all. He was a servant of God and the nation. The name of David begins with a ד *dalet* symbolizing his humble origins. Then comes the letter ו *vav,* a simple straight letter representing his uninterrupted spiritual ascent. But when it was all over and his greatness was acknowledged even by his bitterest enemies, his name concluded with another *dalet.* David remained a pauper — nothing that he had achieved was his own; all was a heavenly gift to be held in safekeeping for the people because a king belongs to the people *(Chidushei HaRim).*

Only once in his lifetime do we find David asking for food and drink for himself. When, after David's heartbreaking fasts and prayers, the first offspring of his union with Bathsheba died, he arose from the floor where he had been begging for Heavenly mercy, and asked that his servants bring him a meal. It was his way of showing that he accepted God's decree: כשם שמברך על הטובה כך מברך על הרעה, just as one blesses for the good, one should also bless for the bad *(Brochos 48b)* — acknowledging that, whether in our unseeing eyes God's judgment seems to be benevolent or not, we accept it with the realization, if not the understanding, that whatever He does is truly good. With the exception of that celebration of acceptance, David's life was a chain of fasting and self-denial until he could say of himself that he had killed his evil inclination with fasting *(Pri Tzaddik).*

But feasts, beauty, and wives did not affect Solomon ... and it was through his experience with them that he was able to proclaim 'Futility of futilities, all is futility

Solomon's mission was diametrically opposed. He, too, accepted God's will and subjugated his evil inclination. But his way of establishing God's kingdom within himself and Israel was to bring holiness into every aspect of luxurious living. Lavish feasts were everyday occurrences in Solomon's palace. Beauty and ostentation were the rule of the day. The harem held a total of a thousand wives and concubines. But feasts, beauty, and wives did not affect Solomon. It was through them that he proved that holiness can conquer every apparent manifestation of hedonism and it was through his experience with them that he was able to proclaim *'Futility of futilities, all is futility' (Koheles 1:2) (ibid).*

David was a man of war; as he fought his evil inclination, so he fought his enemies. For, in truth, they were both the same. Satan disguises himself in many ways: as Israel's desire and lust for sin, and as foreign enemies seeking to defeat the nation or at least weaken its spirit. As David defeated his inner enemy, his outward enemy, too, fell defeated.

Solomon had no foreign enemies. Nor had he an inner enemy. He had defeated his evil inclination, and because he had, foreign enemies became his sub-

jects. He surrounded his life with luxury — to show that it was meaningless; he seemed immersed in love — only to prove that all love belongs only to God. It is from the lavish feasts of Solomon that the Sages learn עושין סעודה לגמרה של תורה, one makes a feast upon completion of the Torah *(Midrash)*. Solomon's feasts were far from the gastronomical orgies portrayed by misreaders of Scripture; they were celebrations of Torah study, deed, and life.

True, Scripture says:

> וַיְהִי לְעֵת זִקְנַת שְׁלֹמֹה נָשָׁיו הִטּוּ אֶת לְבָבוֹ אַחֲרֵי אֱלֹהִים אֲחֵרִים וְלֹא הָיָה לְבָבוֹ שָׁלֵם עִם ה׳ אֱלֹקָיו כִּלְבַב דָּוִיד אָבִיו.
>
> *And it came to pass when Solomon was old that his wives turned away his heart after other gods, and his heart was not perfect with HASHEM his God as was the heart of David his father (I Kings* 11:4).

Thus, unquestionably Solomon fell short of what he should have been, but as the Talmud says: To say that Solomon sinned is an error; even though Scripture indicates that Solomon was actually guilty of idolatry thanks to the blandishments of his wives, he himself never worshipped idols. However, because he should have prevented his wives from continuing to serve their own foreign gods but did not, he is blamed as if he had done so himself *(Shabbos* 56b).

So great was Solomon that even an understandable, excusable lapse — the failure in his declining years to rein in wives of foreign birth and upbringing — was considered equivalent to the most grievous of all acts: idol worship. The Talmud continues that Solomon would have gladly served as a groom to swine to prevent those words from appearing in Scripture. Because he was so great, because all of the excess and luxury of his life did not affect his spiritual purity, his small lapses were so unforgivable.

Great people must hew to high standards; It is by this measuring rod alone that Solomon fell short

Great people must hew to high standards; our greatest people must adhere to standards unimaginably high by our logic. (This concept is dealt with at length in the *Overview* to the ArtScroll edition of *Ruth.)* It is by this measuring rod alone that

Solomon fell short and, therefore, spent his last years in decline. That this was so should not blind us to the awesome proportions of his greatness.

III. The Mission of the Jew

Living and Livelihood

תניא ר׳ שמעון בן אלעזר אומר מימי לא ראיתי צבי קייץ וארי סבל ושועל חנווני, והם מתפרנסים שלא בצער והם לא נבראו אלא לשמשני ואני נבראתי לשמש את קוני ומה אלו שלא נבראו אלא לשמשני מתפרנסין שלא בצער אני שנבראתי לשמש את קוני אאכו״כ? אלא שהריעותי את מעשי וקפחתי את פרנסתי

Rabbi Shimon ben Elazar said, "In all my days I have never seen a deer as a farmer, a lion as a porter, or a fox as a storekeeper. They make their living without suffering. But they were created only to serve me while I was created to serve my Maker. If they, who were created created only to serve me are supported without suffering, than surely I should be, for I was created to serve my Maker. Except that I have corrupted my deeds and thus denied myself on easy livelihood! (Kiddushin 82b)

That people can be deluded into thinking that life's goal is the acccumulation of things and comforts rather than the amassing of wisdom and goodness is a macabre tribute to the evil brilliance of the יצר הרע*, the Evil Inclination*

Man was created to live for something higher than the earning of a livelihood — that is the meaning of Rabbi Shimon's plaint. If quickness, strength, and shrewdness were necessary to earn a livelihood according to the divine plan, than the swift deer, powerful lion, and shrewd fox would find it necessary to employ their own attributes in hard, unremitting labor to earn their sustenance. Why is it only man who must be preoccupied constantly with finding the means to live? Why man? As Rabbi Shimon concludes, it is only because we have corrupted our ways that we are forced to toil in less than human pursuits. That people can be deluded into

thinking that life's goal is the accumulation of things and comforts rather than the amassing of wisdom and goodness is a macabre tribute to the evil brilliance of the יצר הרע, the Evil Inclination.

An Apt Punishment

But there is more. Rabbi Shimon makes it clear that man's battle to earn a livelihood is not a necessity; it is a punishment. It is in itself an example of מדה כנגד מדה — the Heavenly principle that the punishment must fit the crime, that it ironically resemble the crime. The person who sinned through arrogance will be punished through abject humiliation; the person who sinned through unprincipled greed will be punished with want. If man corrupts his mission by devoting his talents to the race for sustenance; by devoting his wit and guile to outsmarting others for an extra piece of earth's resources, then he is punished by being plunged ever more deeply into the maelstrom of competition for material survival. If the deer, the lion, and the fox are given their sustenance by a merciful Creator, then why not man, the object of creation?

True, even the Torah says וְאָסַפְתָּ דְגָנֶךָ, *you may gather in your grain* (*Deut.* 11:14) — the Scriptural injunction that one may work to earn a living — but that is hardly a command that a Jew devote the essence of his being to the economic fray. Rather it is a challenge that the necessary human functions of plowing, planting, and harvesting; of planning, building, and utilizing; of mining, processing, and selling, be sublimated into means toward an infinitely greater end — that of utilizing the earth's riches and man's earnings for the service of God. If man's ambition for material success becomes akin to Solomon's desire for an understanding heart (see above, I), then the gold and silver and glory that are its by-products become holy as well. Man hallows the earth which produces them just as the Temple service hallowed the utensils and clothing used in its performance — all become tools in the service of God (*Maharal*).

Man hallows the earth which produces them just as the Temple service hallowed the utensils and clothing used in its performance.

Fulfilling His Purpose

There is a familiar Talmudic saying that man was made last in the Six Days of Creation so that he could be told one of two things:

If he was virtuous and served God as he was intended to, he is told, 'Everything was created for your sake.' But if he sinned he is told, 'Even an insect preceded you.'

Man was intended to be the climax of God's work, to add a new dimension of greatness dwarfing everything that came before.

Rav Shraga Feivel Mendlowitz, the legendary pioneer of Torah *chinuch* in America, explained it this way: There are four categories in creation. In ascending order of importance, they are: דומם, צומח, חי, מדבר inanimate objects like the earth and minerals; vegetation; birds and fish; and man who has the power of speech and thought. During the days of Creation, they were fashioned in that same order. After creating the inanimate part of the universe, God went on to a higher order of existence: plant life, and so on. Man was intended to be the climax of God's work, to add a new dimension of greatness dwarfing everything that came before, just as a growing, reproducing, fruit tree dwarfs even the Rock of Gibraltar in its contribution to Creation. But if man uses his intelligence for nothing more than seeking comfort, providing food, and reproduction, then he is simply aping animal life. He is merely a two-legged animal with more intelligence than an orangutan, just as an orangutan has more intellegence than an insect. All, however, are basically the same — physical, but not spiritual. In that case, God's desire to add to the quality of the universe with each succeeding level of Creation was thwarted by man's surrender to his animal lusts and instincts. If that happens, God says to man, 'An insect preceded you. What have you added to My universe that lower orders of animal life have not already provided?'

IV. Light and Darkness

Ironic Blindness

But it cannot be denied that the earthly allures calling man to pleasure and self-indulgence are powerful. Flesh-and-blood eyes are easily blinded by the synthetic light of tinsel. How ironic that Jews who succumbed to the decadent temptations of secular humanism called their movement Enlightenment while branding the great Torah scholars as champions of Darkness. The words of our Sages are indeed prophetic: 'The Holy One, blessed be He saw that the brilliant light of Creation was too exalted for the wicked people who would emerge in the future, so He took it and hid it for the use of the righteous in the world to come *(Chagigah* 12a).' That light was spiritual. Not every manner of man is capable of seeing spiritual light; some can look at it and condemn it as 'the forces of Darkness.' They can then turn around and stare at the murkiness of spiritual perversion and applaud the 'Enlightenment.' But life retains value and the potential of holiness only because glimmers of that original light peak through — just as people can see even on the foggiest, cloudiest day because the sun is present, though invisible.

Not every man is capable of seeing spiritual light; some look at it and condemn it as 'the forces of Darkness.'

Each immersion in the 'reality' of this world casts another pall over the true light until people can stare right at it and see only darkness — so blinded have their eyes become to anything save superficial materialism. Commentators have written that the עשרה מאמרות, the ten utterances of Creation are parallel to the עשר מכות, the ten plagues that befell Egypt. (see *Avos* Chapter V). The world had become so cloaked in nature, materialism, and disbelief in the true God that Pharaoh could have the temerity to say מִי ה׳ אֲשֶׁר אֶשְׁמַע בְּקֹלוֹ, *who is this HASHEM that I should hearken to His voice? (Exodus 5:2).* As the Midrash explains, Egypt had a directory of gods, but the name of HASHEM did not even appear in it, so forgotten had the Origin of light become. The

Man has always been hyptonized by belief in strange gods whether they were called Baal, Emancipation, Liberalism, or Science.

myopia was not limited to pharaohs in ancient Egypt. Man has always been hypnotized by belief in strange gods whether they were called Baal, Emancipation, Liberalism, or Science.

From the Darkness

The ten plagues had a greater purpose than the punishment of a cruel nation. They were intended to prove that אֲנִי ה׳ בְּקֶרֶב הָאָרֶץ, *I am HASHEM in the midst of the land. (Exodus 8:18).* Israel, Egypt, and all the world had to see that all their philosophies of purpose in life were nothing but camouflage masking the existence of God and blocking the rays of His spiritual light.

Each plague peeled away one more layer of concealment. Therefore, say the commentators, ten plagues were needed to bring back the realization that God with His ten utterances brought everything into existence and remains the source of all existence. When all ten plagues were done, the realization set in once again that בְּרֵאשִׁית בָּרָא אֱלֹקִים אֵת הַשָּׁמַיִם וְאֵת הָאָרֶץ, *In the beginning God created the heavens and earth. (Genesis 1:1).*

The darkness of Egypt made the Jews see light.

The ninth plague was Darkness. It brought mankind back to the realization of the second divine utterance: יְהִי אוֹר *let there be light.* How remarkable! Egypt was bathed in blackness. While the Egyptians groped about seeing nothing, Scripture says וּלְכָל בְּנֵי יִשְׂרָאֵל הָיָה אוֹר בְּמוֹשְׁבֹתָם, *and for all the children of Israel there was light in their dwellings' (Exodus 10:23).* The darkness of Egypt made the Jews see light. The discovery that the greatest, most civilized nation on earth, for all its supposed enlightenment, was truly groping in unrelieved spiritual darkness — that in itself provided a brilliant shaft of light that made Israel know what the true light was. *Let there be light,* the Creator had said. That brilliance of spirit might be reserved for the righteous of a future day, but Israel glimpsed it then. *(Chidushei haRim).*

Solomon says in Koheles (2:13) יִתְרוֹן הָאוֹר מִן הַחֹשֶׁךְ, *(light excels darkness).* These words tell us

that the maximum benefits of light derive from previous darkness — *the excellence of light derives from darkness. (Chidushei HaRim, Resisei Layla).* A person who has always been bathed in light cannot appreciate how important it is so long as he can take it for granted; it takes an electrical blackout and hours of darkness to make one realize how vital is the light. In a deeper sense, people or nations that have been spiritually deprived *and become conscious of the deficiency,* move upward with a drive and vitality unequalled by their complacent brethren who have never known spiritual deprivation.

Therefore, במקום שבעלי תשובה עומדין צדיקים גמורים אינם עומדין, *In the place where repenters stand, even the perfectly righteous cannot stand (Berachos 34b).* The earnest repenter can surpass the righteous, thanks to his remorse over what was, and his determination to make a better future. The greater his remorse and determination, the greater his repentance. Thus the apparent paradox that the greater the sinner, the greater his potential for goodness because, once the urge to repent comes to him, it intensifies with every sin. This explains why, in the case of the most perfect repentance, sins are transformed into merits. Each sin plays a part in increasing the zeal of the repenter and in raising him to higher levels of virtue, therefore the sins themselves become part of his greatness *(Michtav Me'Eliyahu).*

Jewish history is filled with the darkness-to-light cycle. Before the giving of the Torah on Mount Sinai, there was the blackness of Egyptian exile and slavery. The impetus for the construction of the Holy Temple was the Philistine destruction of the *Mishkan* which was itself built after the sin of the Golden Calf. *Again, light emanated from darkness as the Mishkan* became an indirect product of the Golden Calf.

Source of Greatness

Greatness is not a product born of complacency; it is forged from the tension of a struggle to emerge from darkness and create light. Solomon's life's work

was to wallow in darkness that masqueraded as light; to indulge in comfort, pleasure, and luxury; to reign in peace and security — and still to recognize that the true light was spiritual, that great accomplishment was in the mind, heart, and soul; not in palaces, stables, and treasuries. He testifies in Koheles 2 that he denied himself virtually nothing. That and the astounding total of his wives paint the picture of what most people have taken to be the prototype of the oriental potentate. But Solomon was as different from that popular stereotype as is light from darkness.

Of Solomon's three sacred books — *Shir Hashirim, Mishlei,* and *Koheles* — the one whose content *seems* least sacred is *Shir Hashirim.* Yet the Midrash says that all the books of the Scriptures are holy, but that *Shir Hashirim* is holy of holies. The Sages have their own definition of holy:

בכל מקום שאתה מוצא גדר ערוה ותאוה שם אתה מוצא קדושה, *Wherever you find a barrier against immorality and lust, there you find holiness (Midrash).*

True holiness is not found in ceremonial robes, rolling eyes, and pious expressions, but in personal chastity and control.

True holiness is not found in ceremonial robes, rolling eyes, and pious expressions, but in personal chastity and control. *Shir Hashirim,* an allegorical rendering of the love between God and Israel, shows Solomon as a passionate young man; the casual reader easily sees in it the Solomon who married a thousand wives and who indulged every mortal whim. How false a vision! *Shir Hashirim* is *holy of holies!* — because its author was a man who was able to descend to the murky depths of physical indulgence and remain complete untouched and unsullied. In Jewish belief, there is no such thing as a profane person producing a holy work. A book which is holy of holies can be produced only by a man who is holy of holies — and that holiness, by definition, means abstinence from lust and obsession with pleasure. For Solomon to achieve such holiness while living the sort of life that he did, is the most eloquent testimony to the sort of human being he was — a holy of holies. His love was the antithesis of This World; it was a love that belonged purely to

A book which is holy of holies can be produced only by a man who is holy of holies.

God and it was a paramount instance of the rule that light emerges from darkness. Only a heart that has tasted the extreme of earthly darkness and from there seeks Godliness in its revulsion to the pseudo-pleasures of animal lust can taste the utmost spiritual delight of the knowledge that, in the truest sense, the delusions of material necessity, reward, and joy are but a mirage, that they have no meaningful existence at all *(Resisei Layla).*

The National Goal

For this reason, God placed Israel in every type of situation — including abject oppression. It is instinctive for human beings to flee danger, but God placed Israel in situations of extreme danger from which there was no escape. There was no escape from Egypt and there was no real escape from most of the dangers with which Jewish history has been filled up to this day. The lesson is that God wants us to find our way to Him — and hence to salvation — from the danger, the darkness, itself.

וְלֹא אָמְרוּ אַיֵּה ה׳ הַמַּעֲלֶה אֹתָנוּ מֵאֶרֶץ מִצְרָיִם הַמּוֹלִיךְ אֹתָנוּ בַּמִּדְבָּר בְּאֶרֶץ עֲרָבָה וְשׁוּחָה בְּאֶרֶץ צִיָּה וְצַלְמָוֶת.

And they did not say, Where is HASHEM Who brought us out of the land of Egypt, Who led us through the wilderness through a land of deserts and of pits, through a land of drought and of the shadow of death (Jeremiah 2:6).

In castigating his people for forgetting God, Jeremiah beseeched them to remember days when their enemies were no less powerful and dangerous than Nevuchadnezzar. 'Look back to Egypt and the forty years in the wilderness.' Israel learned then that it could call to God in any situation, that a hopeless pit could become a triumphant mountain. God promised Jacob that He would descend with him to Egypt (*Gen.* 46:4); through David he told all generations of Israel that He is with us in our every trouble (*Psalms* 91:15). All these verses and prophecies contain one central theme: every circumstance is a

What we imagine to be an evil decree ... is in reality a heavenly springboard ready to catapult us into a spiritual ascent.

product of the divine wisdom, not of chance. What we imagine to be an evil decree casting us down lower and lower into depths of hopelessness is in reality a Heavenly springboard ready to catapult us into a spiritual ascent from misery and exile just as the Egyptian exile ended in the revelation at Sinai. Every station in Israel's long trek through the desert was listed in the Torah because each wandering footstep in Jewish history can be transformed into a giant step toward the ultimate fulfillment of Israel and of the world.

Therefore, Solomon lists twenty-eight different times in Koheles (3:2-8). They represent the possible stages in life, and Israel can and must utilize all of them to reach its spiritual goal. Sometimes, Jews find the way through happiness, sometimes through tears, but every Jew must recognize that his mission is to find his own way in his own circumstances and that he can do it. Solomon found holiness in pleasure, David found it in battle, Moses found it in the fields of Midian, the Patriarchs found it in Canaan and Aram, Israel found it under the lash on the pyramids of Egypt *(Sfas Emes).*

V. Themes of Koheles

During Succos of the year 5027, Nachmanides, the *Ramban,* was preparing to leave Spain to settle in Eretz Yisrael. He parted from his students and followers with a classic sermon calling upon them to strengthen their faith in God despite the persecutions that led to the royal decree that he must go into exile in his seventies, and that eventually culminated in the Spanish Inquisition. A major topic of his sermon was Koheles. In the course of explaining many of its passages, Ramban said that there are three main themes in the book. With this writer's explanations and elaboration, they are as follows:

Pointless Striving

Because we are physical and mortal, we are born to the sensation of physical pleasures and the knowledge that there is but one short life in which to crowd them all. Our Sages taught that the יצר הרע, the Evil Inclination, is with man from birth, but the יצר טוב, the Good Inclination, comes to man at the age of *bar mitzvah.* This is no metaphysical formula, it is plain reality. An infant has no capacity to feel for others. Its only desire is to satisfy its own needs; it is a totally selfish being. Even the very young child is essentially selfish. Can the three-year old be convinced that it is wrong to wake his mother at night or to interrupt her when she is busy? In a child, this is normal. But it is precisely this inborn selfishness and disinterest in others which is the stock in trade of the Evil Inclination all through life. These animal instincts must be conquered by human understanding.

The age of responsibility is the time when a person is capable of choosing responsibility over pleasure, common good over personal benefit, long range profit over instant gratification.

The age of responsibility is the time when a person is capable of choosing responsibility over pleasure, common good over personal benefit, long range profit over instant gratification. These choices involve the employment of a developed mind and a conditioned heart. They indeed represent the Good Inclination who is a relative late-comer to his human host.

The teachers of *Mussar* perceive this concept in a verse in *Job (11:12).* וְעַיִר פֶּרֶא אָדָם יִוָּלֵד *A man is born as a wild mule* (this translation follows *Radak* and *Metzudas David).* When a human being is born, he is like a wild mule. The task of life is to turn that wild animal — slowly, painfully — into a human being.

The first lesson of Koheles is that man avoid the striving after the pleasures of this world, because — for all their allures — they are fleeting and valueless. Solomon points to himself as the one who should know this better than anyone. In Chapter 2 he speaks of his own material attainments. Homes, wealth, entertainment — whatever he desired was his, along with the respect and obeisance of the rulers and wise men of the world. Despite it all, Solomon concludes that all earthly striving is futility — הֶבֶל. *Ramban* defines *'hevel'* as a noticeable mist, like

breath turned to vapor on a cold day, or the polluted, stagnant air trapped at the bottom of a pit. One can see the vapor, feel the heavy air, but both have no substance and swiftly disappear. To use a more modern analogy, the pleasures of this world are like a mammoth fireworks display. The colors and design are dazzling, breathtaking. But in a matter of moments, they are gone.

The pleasures of this world are like a mamoth fireworks display. The colors and designs are dazzling, breathtaking. But in a matter of moments, they are gone.

Permanence of Essentials

Lest the reader conclude that if all is indeed futile, that nothing in human existence matters, then the world was created to no purpose and there is no reward or punishment, Solomon cautions (3:14) that the essentials of existence are eternal and the Creator made man to have a vital role in His master plan. What is transient and trivial is the handiwork of man. His buildings and baubles, his ambition and glory are nothing more than *'hevel':* futility, substanceless vapor. But that is not the sum total of creation.

Man's soul was not fashioned from dust as was his body, nor was it made from the other elements, or by any heavenly or earthly body that was itself part of creation. וַיִּפַּח בְּאַפָּיו נִשְׁמַת חַיִּים, *and He [God] breathed into his nostrils the breath of life.* Man's soul came directly from God, מאן דנפח מתוכיה נפח, whoever breathes, breathes from within himself *(Zohar).* Because God is eternal, the human soul is eternal; and because it is everlasting it will be called upon to answer for the deeds done while it was clothed in its earthly body. And because the only meaningful, everlasting part of man's existence is his soul and the spiritual good it brings about through man, Koheles urges that indulgence in non-essential pleasures should be disdained. Of course, physical needs must be satisfied and, each according to his own spiritual capacity, people will indulge in this-worldly pleasures. But the test must be necessity and the goal should be avoidance.

Because God is eternal, the human soul is eternal; and because it is everlasting it will be called upon to answer for the deeds done while it was clothed in its earthly body.

This goal is a characteristic of יראת אלקים, fear of God. Indeed, the Book of Koheles uses the Name

אלקים Elokim throughout. That is the Godly Name that represents judgment in contrast to the Four-Letter Name of God that represents love, mercy, and miracles. Koheles emphasizes the responsibilities of man on this world in a cause-and-effect setting. *Elokim* does not suggest miracles; on the contrary, although man is judged for his deeds — rewarded for the good ones and punished for the bad ones — the Hand of God is nowhere obvious. If man follows the commandments of the Torah, the rains will fall, his crops will be blessed, and he will enjoy good health and prosperity. If he sins, there will be drought, famine, illness, and poverty. This was the sort of relationship to God that was enjoyed by Abraham, Isaac, and Jacob. They never employed the Four-Letter Name of God. Obvious miracles were not their lot — the Plagues, Splitting of the Sea, and manna began with the coming of Moses and the formation of a Jewish nation. The Patriarchs experienced prosperity — but so did others. They fought and won victories — but so did others. they lived the life described by Koheles, disclaiming frivolity, cultivating the soul, and being rewarded and punished in their everyday lives.

This too is miraculous. For what relattionship have Sabbath observance and tefillin to abundant crops and healthy herds?

In the deeper, truer sense, this too is miraculous. For what relationship have Sabbath observance and *tefillin* to abundant crops and healthy herds? The hidden miracles of reward and punishment on earth are the raw material from which fear of God is fashioned. In urging that man's mission — his quintessential task — is fear of God, and that ultimately, both the righteous and the wicked receive their just reward and punishment, Solomon tells us that the lot of the Patriarch's *under the sun* is our lot, too. The main difference is that they saw and understood the Hand of God in every event of their lives, while we are blinded by the sun.

Suffering Righteous

One of the most serious dilemmas confronting religious thinkers throughout the ages has been how to reconcile the inconsistency of צדיק ורע לו, רשע

and Fortunate Wicked

וטוב לו, a righteous man who lives a life of suffering while a wicked sinner lives a life of good fortune. Down the centuries this question has troubled believers. Sprinkled throughout Koheles are references to it.

Solomon has two approaches to the problem. The first is that the true test of God's justice can be made only when it is complete. The righteous person's short term suffering as well as the wicked person's short term good fortune are surely both deserved — the first for his few sins and the second for his few virtues. When all is done, however, whether the final reckoning comes on this world or in the next, God's justice will be umblemished.

When all is done, however, whether the final reckoning comes in this world or in the next, God's justice will be unblemished.

In this regard, one recalls the reply of the Chazon Ish when he was questioned concerning the butchery of the holocaust and how a just and merciful God could have permitted it. He replied:

> To condemn what happened is like someone dismissing the complex commentary of *Tosefos* as illogical when he does not even know the simple meaning of the *Gemarah.* It is only after thoroughly understanding the text of the *Talmud* and the basic commentaries that one can attempt to understand the intricacies of a *Tosefos.* History is no different. We are too close to the event to understand it, its background, and its ramifications, and we don't yet know how the event blends with the other phenomena of history. At the end of days, God's plan will become plain for all to see. Then we can be confident, we will understand all of its parts.

Koheles gives a second answer, too, the same one given in Job (28:20-28). The Divine Intelligence is beyond us and God's ways are inscrutable. We simply cannot understand them all no matter how high the level of our wisdom.

וְהָיָה ה׳ לְמֶלֶךְ עַל כָּל הָאָרֶץ בַּיּוֹם הַהוּא יִהְיֶה ה׳ אֶחָד וּשְׁמוֹ אֶחָד.

And HASHEM shall be King over all the

earth; on that day HASHEM shall be one and His Name one (Zechariah 14:9).

Isn't God one now as well? Rav Acha bar Chaninah answered that This World is inferior to the World to Come. Now, we are incapable of realizing how every act of God, even the apparently tragic ones, is for the good. Now, for God's goodness we bless Him for bestowing good; for bad news we bless Him as the Judge of Truth. Because we are incapable of grasping the Oneness of all God's acts we make different blessings for different manifestations of His will. In the World to Come, whether occurrences are good or tragic, we will recognize His Oneness and perceive the goodness of His every act and bless Him as *'The Good Who Does Good' (Pesachim 50a).*

Meanwhile, we have no alternative but to accept the fact that our mortal deficiencies prevent us from understanding His ways.

Rav Acha tells us the third theme of Koheles. God is merciful and all good. It will take the coming of *Messiah* and the elevation of the world to its future state of spiritual grandeur for people to recognize His mercy in every event. Meanwhile, we have no alternative but to accept the fact that our mortal deficiencies prevent us from comprehending His ways.

VI. Koheles — Almost hidden

אמר רבי יהודה בריה דרב שמואל בר שילת משמיה דרב בקשו חכמים לגנוז ספר קהלת מפני שדבריו סותרים זה את זה ומפני מה לא גנזוהו מפני שתחלתו דברי תורה וסופו דברי תורה.

The Sages sought to hide the Book of Koheles because its statements [apparently] contradict one another. Why

didn't they conceal it? Because it commences with words of Torah and it concludes with words of Torah (Shabbos 30b).

Grounds for Concern

In spite of the fact that *Koheles* was part of the Sacred Writings, it was feared that it could be a dangerous book because, to the unlearned, it seemed to contain contradictions. The *Midrash* goes even further than does the *Talmud* — according to the *Midrash,* it was feared that unlearned people might even make heretical interpretations of parts of Koheles. Therefore, there was an opinion among the Sages that perhaps Koheles, sacred though it was, should be concealed lest it cause mistaken or heretical ideas.

It was not only Koheles that was subject to such scrutiny. There was a feeling among the Sages that even the Book of Yechezkel, though it contained only prophecies, should be concealed because some of it *appeared* to contradict the Torah *(Shabbos* 13b; *Chagigah* 13b). The Sages felt that, despite the sanctity of a book, if it presented serious dangers to the unlearned it might be wiser to conceal it. The objections to Yechezkel were answered to the satisfaction of the Sages. The conclusion concerning Koheles was that it should not be concealed because its opening and its conclusion show beyond a doubt that it is a book filled with fear of God and the spirit of Torah. Indeed there may be those who will refuse to understand it, those who will read false meanings into it. That did not frighten the Sages. The question had been asked concerning verses in the Torah itself that they lend themselves to misinterpretation. The answer of the Sages was כל הרוצה לטעות יבא ויטעה, *Whoever wishes to err, let him come and err.* They chose their words carefully. They did not say 'whoever *may* err, let him err,' they said 'whoever *wishes* to err.' It was clear to the Sages that honest, sincere people would understand or, if they didn't, that they would seek the guidance of those who did. If there should still be people who persisted in

misunderstanding the meaning of the Torah — such as those who still insist on their prattle about a literal interpretation of 'an eye for an eye' despite the Talmud's explanation that it refers to monetary compensation — then it can only be because they *wish* to err. There is no justification for criticizing the language of the Torah because it provides grist for the mills of those who wish to misunderstand. No matter how a verse could be rephrased, they would find some pretext to deny its validity if that is their wish *(Michtav MeEliyahu).*

It was clearly a statement of Torah, an exposition of fear of God. No one who read its introductory and closing statements could doubt the purity of the entire book.

The fear of those who preferred to conceal Koheles was that the text presented such difficulties that it was inevitable that people would find contraditions or worse. To this objection, the Sages cited the opening and conclusion of the book. It was clearly a statement of Torah, an exposition of fear of God. No one who read its introductory and closing statements could doubt the purity of the entire book. Contradictions? They could be only on the surface; answers could be found. Even if not, even if the most brilliant commentators of the centuries could not penetrate the entire meaning of the sacred wisdom imparted to Israel through Solomon's lips, there was no danger in allowing Koheles to become part of Israel's public legacy of fear of God. True, there will be those who choose to see in it the depression-laden testament of a decadent king — let them! 'Whoever *wishes* to err, let him come and err.'

The Proof

What are these beginning and closing verses that shed such a favorable light on a book that would otherwise have been feared? The conclusion is obvious:

סוֹף דָּבָר הַכֹּל נִשְׁמָע אֶת הָאֱלֹקִים יְרָא וְאֶת מִצְוֹתָיו שְׁמוֹר כִּי זֶה כָּל הָאָדָם.

The sum of the matter, when all has been considered: Fear God and keep His commandments, for that is man's whole duty (Koheles 12:13).

The Talmudic Sages explain further that with this

statement, Solomon tells us that the entire universe was created only for the benefit of the God-fearing person, that in importance he outweighs all the universe, that everything was created only for his convenience and companionship (*Shabbos* 30b).

But what of the opening verse that was evidence to dismiss the fears of those who would have concealed Koheles. As we look through the opening verses of the book, we fail to see it. The Talmud tells us which it is:

> מַה יִּתְרוֹן לָאָדָם בְּכָל עֲמָלוֹ שֶׁיַּעֲמֹל תַּחַת הַשָּׁמֶשׁ.
> ואמרי דבי ר׳ ינאי תחת השמש הוא דאין לו. קודם שמש יש לו.
>
> *What profit does man have for all his labor which he toils beneath the sun?* (*Koheles* 1:3)

And the academy of Rabbi Yannai said, Only [in striving for benefit in what is] *under* the sun [is there] no gain, [but in striving for Torah which] preceded the sun, there is [benefit] *(Shabbos 30b).*

This verse holds the key to Koheles. By examining its two key words אדם, *man,* and שמש, *sun,* we will go far toward understanding the message of *Koheles.* And understand it we must, because it is meant for us. Only forty-eight prophets and seven prophetesses appear in the Scriptures while Israel produced twice as many prophets as the number of those who left Egypt. Why was only such a tiny number chosen for inclusion in the Scriptures? נבואה שהוצרכה לדורות נכתבה, ושלא הוצרכה לא נכתבה, *Prophecy that was needed by future generations was written in the Scriptures, what was not needed was not written* (*Megillah* 14a).

Surely then, Solomon, who wrung light from darkness by remaining untarnished despite the attractions of his world, has perhaps more to say to us than he had to our grandparents.

Solomon's utterances were transmitted to us because we need them. No era in history has had more access to excess, more means to satisfy its lust and craving than this one. Surely then, Solomon who wrung light from darkness by remaining untarnished despite the attractions of his world, has perhaps more to say to us than he had to our grandparents.

VII. Message to Man

Without question, the most powerful force in nature is the sun. It is the source of light and energy. Without it, life would cease. There are few elements in human life more important than time: it defines our tasks and plans, our waking and retiring, our body conditioning. Time, too, is a product of the unchanging rotation of the earth around the sun. It is thus quite plain why Solomon should find man's entire existence as a creature of nature symbolized by the expression, תַּחַת הַשָּׁמֶשׁ, *under the sun.* He speaks not of a spatial concept, but of a philosophical one. We are under the sun if we consider ourselves always subject to nature and beholden by its laws.

We are under the sun if we consider ourselves always subject to nature and beholden by its laws.

In the infancy of Jewish history, Abram — before his name had been changed to Abraham — saw himself as forced to live his life 'under the sun.' He pleaded with God that no Heavenly gifts mattered to him because he realized that there was no natural way for him to have a son who would be fit to be his heir. Before God could assure him that he would indeed have an heir and that the multitudes of his descendants would be like the stars in heaven, there had to be a prerequisite.

> וַיּוֹצֵא אֹתוֹ הַחוּצָה
>
> *And God brought him outside* (*Genesis* 15:5).
>
> אמר ר׳ יהודה אמר רב אמר אברהם לפני הקב״ה נסתכלתי באצטגנינות שלי ואיני ראוי להוליד בן. אמר ליה צא מאצטגנינות שלך אין מזל לישראל.
>
> *Rabbi Judah said in the name of Rav, Abraham said before the Holy One blessed be He, I have studied closely with my astrology [my knowledge of natural law] and I am incapable of giving birth to a son. [God] said to him, leave your astrology. Israel has no [dependence on] constellations* (*Shabbos* 156a).

Abraham was right. By all the laws of nature he and Sarah could not have a son. God did not tell him that he had misread his capabilities *under the sun;* God told him that he was not bound by the laws of nature. As another *Midrash* interpretation puts it (see *Rashi*) God lifted him above the stars, symbolically showing him that the stars and their decrees held no dominion over him.

'Adam' — Man

Koheles refers to man as אדם, *adam.* This is only one of several synonyms for man, and it was not chosen at random. The term *adam* has a special meaning, one that is especially appropriate to the theme of Koheles.

The *Maharal* explains: There is a basic difference between man and all other parts of Creation, whether living earthly creatures, or the heavenly bodies and angels. All of them are created complete, perfect. Those of the heavens have a higher intelligence and holiness, those below are without human intelligence and lack holiness — but all have in common that they lack nothing upon their creation. They come into being with all the attributes they need and will ever have. Except for the natural process of animal growth they have neither the need nor the possibility of choosing good over evil and becoming better creatures. Only man is born with potential and the responsibility to realize it.

Man created from adamah is called adam. His name symbolizes his mission: he is created with potential and his usefulness depends on its realization.

In this, man is similar to *adamah,* the *earth.* It too has within it the potential to nourish and produce crops, and life is dependent on its ability to realize that potential. For that reason, man created from *adamah* is called *adam.* His name symbolizes his mission: he is created with potential and his usefulness depends on its realization.

The teachers of *Mussar* find this concept illuminated in the curse that befell the earth when Cain murdered his brother Abel and the earth soaked up the innocent victim's blood. God cursed Cain with perpetual exile and hard labor in the production of his crops. Because the earth, so to speak, became

his accomplice by swallowing Abel's blood, it, too, was cursed.

> וְעַתָּה אָרוּר אָתָּה מִן הָאֲדָמָה אֲשֶׁר פָּצְתָה אֶת פִּיהָ לָקַחַת אֶת דְּמֵי אָחִיךָ מִיָּדֶךָ. כִּי תַעֲבֹד אֶת הָאֲדָמָה לֹא תֹסֵף תֵּת כֹּחָהּ לָךְ
>
> *And now you are accursed from the earth which has opened her mouth to receive your brother's blood from your hand. When you work the earth, it shall no longer yield its strength to you.* (*Gen.* 4:11-12 see *Rashi*).

We can understand that the earth's refusal to yield its bounty would punish Cain by making his labor more difficult and less productive. But, as *Rashi* makes clear, the very earth was to be punished for its part in concealing history's first murder. How was it punished? What pain did it feel? The answer is that for any being — whether a human being or the earth — to be forbidden to realize its potential, to be foreclosed from productive activity, *is* a curse. *Adamah* was cursed by being forced to curtail its fruitful potential; *adam*, too, born of *adamah*, must grow, develop, improve, produce. That is his destiny. To the extent that he fails to do so fully, no matter how far the brilliance of his intellect or the abundance of his talent takes him, he has fallen short and failed.

Adam Under the Sun

Koheles asks what benefit there is to *adam* — man whose mission is to rise above the limitations of nature — in all of his effort if he allows himself to remain *under the sun*, under the restraints of the very conditions over which he is commanded to rise. The sun itself functions within pre-determined limits, it rules over an earth every part of which *save one* has no ability to raise itself above the conditions of its creation. *Adam*-man is superior to all of them. He is the sole member of the universe who is capable of reaching new vistas of spirituality through Torah. He can rise *above* the sun by devoting his life to Torah which preceded the sun and all its dominions.

Futility of futilities — this is Solomon's contemptuous description of any human activity that stultifies its potential by wallowing beneath the sun.

The Sages read this opening passage of Koheles and proclaimed, "These are words of Torah." The person who reads them seriously and thoughtfully will not be trapped by the difficulties of the rest of Koheles. To conceal the Book of Koheles would be to deprive Israel of the words of one of the forty-eight prophets whose teaching is needed by Israel for all time.

Then, people sacrificed their livestock and even children to the sun; today people sacrifice their souls and their spiritual potential to a sun called nature and science.

Koheles was left available to Israel among the other sacred Scriptures. In a century that conquers the moon and goes to Mars and beyond, mankind has deified the sun and all it represents to as great an extent as its worshippers of three thousand years ago. Then, people sacrificed their livestock and even children to the sun; today people sacrifice their souls and their spiritual potential to a sun called nature and science.

Soar above it! Your life belongs to Torah.

Futility of futilities, Koheles cries to us. *Adam*-man, how dare you limit your limitless potential to the strictures imposed by your stunted sun? Soar above it! Your life belongs to Torah.

אֶת הָאֱלֹקִים יְרָא וְאֶת מִצְוֹתָיו שְׁמוֹר כִּי זֶה כָּל הָאָדָם

Fear God and keep His commandments, for that is man's whole duty.

מגילת קהלת

קהלת
פרק א
א־ג

א דִּבְרֵי קֹהֶלֶת בֶּן־דָּוִד מֶלֶךְ בִּירוּשָׁלָֽם׃
ב הֲבֵל הֲבָלִים אָמַר קֹהֶלֶת הֲבֵל הֲבָלִים
ג הַכֹּל הָֽבֶל׃ מַה־יִּתְרוֹן לָאָדָם בְּכָל־עֲמָלוֹ

1. The *Talmud* notes that King Hezekiah and his colleagues 'wrote' [i.e. 'assembled' and 'committed to writing' — *(Akeidas Yitzchak)*] Isaiah's prophecies and the Books of *Isaiah, Proverbs, Song of Songs,* and *Koheles (Bava Basra* 15a).

Seder Olam Rabba [by the *Tanna,* Rabbi Yose ben Chalafta, student of Rabbi Akiva] mentions that: 'in Solomon's old age — shortly before his death — the Divine Spirit rested upon him and he "uttered" the three Books: *Proverbs, Song of Songs,* and *Koheles.*'[1]

There is a difference of opinion in the *Midrash* as to the sequence in which Solomon composed the books of *Proverbs, Song of Songs,* and *Koheles.* The dispute centers around *Proverbs* and *Song of Songs;* all agree that *Koheles* was last.

[The Sages of the *Mishnah (Shabbos* 30b*)* considered whether to conceal [לִגְנוֹז] *Koheles* in secret archives because, although its sacred nature was unquestioned, it contained *apparent* contradictions [ibid.] and *seemingly* heretical statements *(Midrash)* [i.e. expressions which ignorant people might misinterpret *(Akeidas Yitzchak).*] They decided to leave it with the Scriptures because, since its beginning and conclusion indisputably demonstrated that the entire book is dedicated to the fear of God and is an expression of His Word, the danger of misinterpretation was mitigated. (See *Overview*).

דִּבְרֵי — *The words of.* 'Wherever Scripture uses the expression דִּבְרֵי, *"the words of,"* — it introduces דִּבְרֵי תוֹכָחָה, words of reproof or admonition' *(Rashi).*

קֹהֶלֶת — *Koheles.* He was called by three names: Yedidiah [*II Samuel* 12:25], Koheles and Solomon. Why was he called Koheles? [not his proper name, but a title *(Ibn Ezra* on 12:8)] — Because his words were uttered בְּהִקָּהֵל [*b'hikahel*], *'in public assembly'* as is written אָז יַקְהֵל שְׁלֹמֹה, *'then Solomon assembled . . .' (I Kings* 8:1). In addition, droves of peoples constantly gathered to hear his wisdom *(Midrash).*

Ramban and *Ibn Ezra* note that in addition to the indisputable Talmudic tradition that Koheles is Solomon — although *'Koheles'* is not explicitly identified as Solomon — it could be no one else because Solomon was the only *'son of David'* to ascend the throne.

He was called *'Koheles'* because of the wisdom שֶׁנִּקְהֲלָה בּוֹ, 'which was assembled within him' *(Ibn Ezra),* or because שֶׁקִּיהֵל חָכְמוֹת הַרְבֵּה, 'he assembled much wisdom' *(Rashi).*

Metzudas Zion explains that the word *Koheles* is derived from קהל *'assembly', 'gathering',* and that King Solomon earned this title

[Please note: *The source for every excerpt has been documented. Whenever the author has inserted a comment of his own it is inserted in square brackets.*]

I
1-3

The words of Koheles son of David, King in Jerusalem:
2 Futility of futilities! — said Koheles — Futility of futilities! All is futile! 3 What profit does man have

because he 'gathered together' conflicting opinions and filtered out the right from the wrong.

An additional reason for the name Koheles is mentioned by *Avudraham* and others: During the *Succos* festival following שְׁמִיטָּה, the Sabbatical year, the king would gather together the people in Jerusalem [in accordance with *Deut.* 31:11] and publicly read the Book of דְּבָרִים, *Deuteronomy.* The ceremony was called הַקְהֵל, *Hakhel* ('Gathering'). Presumably, in addition to reading *Deuteronomy,* Solomon used the opportunity provided by the public assembly to deliver this sermon against preoccupation with worldly striving and possession. This accounts for the name *Koheles,* derived from *Hakhel,* and also for the custom of reading the Book in synagogues during the *Succos* festival.

בֶּן דָּוִד — *Son of David.* He was a king, son of a king; a wise man, son of a wise man; a righteous man, son of a righteous man *(Midrash).*

The *Midrash* comments: 'Happy is he who can depend on זְכוּת אָבוֹת, paternal merit. Nevertheless, personal merit is better.'

מֶלֶךְ בִּירוּשָׁלָם — *King in Jerusalem.* The city of wisdom *(Rashi).*

The city is mentioned because, as King of an illustrious city famed for its wise men, Koheles had ample opportunity to delve deeply into the knowledge of the world and to investigate his theories first hand *(Sforno, Metzudas David).* His conclusions, therefore, are worthy of great respect *(Nachal Eshkol).*

[This phrase *'king in Jerusalem'* refers to Koheles, not 'David' *(Ibn Jenach; Ramban;* and *Ibn Ezra* in reference to *'Isaiah son of Amotz the prophet')*].

'Jerusalem — the dwelling place of the Shechinah, of prophecy, and of Torah' *(Midrash Lekach Tov).*

[Jerusalem was the capital of the entire Eretz Yisrael throughout the reigns of David and Solomon.]

The *Talmud* (*Sanhedrin* 20b) — [based upon the varying descriptions of Solomon in his three books: *'King Solomon'* (*Song of Songs* 3:11), *'King of Israel'* (Proverbs 1:1), and here, *'King in Jerusalem'*]

1 The *Midrash* relates that these books were composed as the result of the Divine Spirit which rested upon Solomon when he assumed the throne at the age of twelve.

God appeared to him in Gibeon and said 'Ask what I shall give you' (I Kings 3:5). Solomon did not request silver, gold and pearls. He responded, 'Give your servant an understanding heart' (ibid. v. 9).

The Holy One, Blessed be He, said to him: 'You asked for wisdom and did not ask for riches, honor or for victory over your enemies — therefore wisdom and knowledge will be granted you and I will thereby also give you riches and possessions.'

Forthwith, the Divine Spirit alighted upon him [and later in life — (Torah T'mimah)] he composed Proverbs, Song of Songs, and Koheles.

— comments that [after his 'sin'] his kingdom was diminished. At first he was king over all, then of Eretz Yisrael only, and then only of Jerusalem *(Torah T'mimah)*.

2. הֲבֵל הֲבָלִים — *Futility of futilities!* [lit. *'breath of breaths'; vapor of vapors'* i.e. something empty of substance, utterly futile].

Koheles cries out and says that everything created during the seven days of creation is futile. The seven references in this verse to הֶבֶל, *futility* [the word הֶבֶל appears three times; and the plural הֲבָלִים, each of which connotes at least two, appears twice, making a total of seven] correspond to the seven days of creation *(Rashi; Midrash)*.[1]

All man's actions [see next verse] are inconsequential — futile and fruitless — unless they are motivated by lofty Torah ideals. Nothing will remain of man's earthly labors. Only his spiritual labor — his righteousness and Torah learning — will yield everlasting fruits *(Rabbeinu Yonah)*.

The verse refers to riches. The man blessed with wealth must view himself as a custodian whose role it is to dispense his treasures to the needy. To amass wealth selfishly, bemoans Koheles, is 'futility of futilities' *(Taalumos Chachmah)*.

Ramban and *Metzudas David* interpret הֲבֵל הֲבָלִים not as superlative nouns *'futility of futilities'* but rather as an imperative: הֲבֵל, make futile, i.e. abhor, הֲבָלִים, all futilities. Whatever is utterly futile in this world should be abhorred — i.e. Do not attempt to attach undue importance to this temporal world; all is 'futile.' [This is the interpretation adopted by most commentators for the same phrase in 12:8.]

אָמַר קֹהֶלֶת — *Said Koheles.* If someone else had declared *'futility of futilities'*, I might have said that this man, who had never owned a penny in his life, makes light of the wealth of the world and declares *'futility of futilities.'* Therefore, Koheles' name is interjected to accentuate that [not a pauper but the wise and wealthy] King Solomon — who *'made silver to be in Jerusalem like stones'* (*I Kings* 10:27) — was the one who declared *'futility of futilities' (Midrash)*.

הַכֹּל הָבֶל — *All is futile.* To dispel the notion that the world consists of *both* futile *and* enduring values — Solomon emphasizes: הַכֹּל הָבֶל, *'everything* is futile' *(Ibn Ezra)*.

Many people experience frustration, but remain convinced that others do gain real satisfaction from this world. This phrase stresses that such an assumption is but an illusion — *'all* is futile.'[2]

In the *Targum's* interpretation of these verses, Solomon, prophetically bemoans the ultimate division and destruction of the kingdom during his children's reign. 'These words of prophecy were uttered by Koheles, that is, Solomon, son of David who was king in Jerusalem. Thus envisioned Solomon, king of Israel: the kingdom of his son Rechavam would be divided with

1. The *Midrash* adds that the seven 'futilities' correspond to the seven stages of man's life: At the age of a year he is like a king seated in a canopied litter — fondled and kissed by all; at two and three he is like a pig groping in the gutters; at ten he skips like a kid; at twenty he is like a neighing horse, preening himself and seeking a wife; after marriage he [works hard for livelihood] like a donkey; when he has children he grows brazen as a dog to supply their sustenance; in old age he [loses his senses and] is like an ape.

And each of these stages is *'futility of futilities' (Torah T'mimah)*.

Jeraboam ben Nevat; Jerusalem and the Temple are destined for destruction; and his nation, the children of Israel, will be exiled. He, therefore, said: *Futility of futilities* is this world! *Futility of futilities!* Everything in which he and his father David had toiled — the kingdom, The Temple and the nation — would be shattered. *All is futile!*

3. מַה־יִּתְרוֹן לָאָדָם — *What profit* [lit. *'surplus'*] *does man have...?* i.e. 'what reward or gains' *(Rashi).*

Since all is futile, of what use to man is all his toil? *(Ibn Ezra).*

Alshich explains: 'Open your eyes and perceive! What profit or perfection can man expect to achieve by toiling in mundane and material matters on earth beneath the heavens. Better to strive to serve his Creator and immerse himself in His Torah which is loftier than the heavens. Only through the Torah and its *mitzvos* can one acquire eternal spiritual perfection.'

It is to be noted that the verse does not read מַה יִּתְרוֹן לָעוֹלָם, 'what profit does the *world* have?' Indeed the world itself *does* gain from man's physical toil; as *Rambam* notes: 'were it not for foolish people who hoard money and who build houses to last a hundred years, the earth would never be developed!' Rather the verse questions what real gain does *man himself* have from such labor? *(Kol Yaakov)*

What benefit will man realize — after he is dead — from all his toil on this world? *(Targum)*

אָדָם, *man.* Mankind in general is referred to as אָדָם, after *Adam,* the first man, who came from the אֲדָמָה, earth, and returned to the earth *(Midrash Lekach Tov).*

בְּכָל־עֲמָלוֹ — *for* [lit. *'in'*] *all his labor.* The Sages were apprehensive that the expression *'what profit does man have from all his labor'* might be misconstrued to mean that even Torah-study is unprofitable. They observed, however, that the verse emphasizes *'his* labor', i.e. labor for man's own secular pursuits. Thus it is clear to all that man should not labor for himself, for to do so is vain, but one *should* toil in the study of Torah.

תַּחַת הַשָּׁמֶשׁ — *Beneath the sun.* This translation follows most commentators. The phrase — [unique with *Koheles*] — means 'this earth **where** the sun shines' *(Metzudas David);* or, according to *Ibn Ezra, 'sun'* refers to the natural cycle of time which is governed by the rising and setting of the sun. As *Ibn Yachya* explains, man gains nothing in toiling for possessions which are subject to the limitations of time. True gain is possible only when one pursues Torah which is timeless.

Midrash Lekach Tov explains that 'sun' is used to convey that just as the sun ceaselessly follows the same daily pattern of rising and setting, so does the world relentlessly follow its futile pattern.

2. The *Dubna Maggid* cites a parable:

A group of blind beggars was in the street. A man approached one of them and said: 'Take this money and share it with the others.' But he walked away and gave the beggar nothing. The others, having overheard the conversation, demanded their share of the money which they thought he had received. A melee broke out.

Such is mankind — everyone strives for a share of the worldly pleasures they assume their neighbors have achieved. But in reality they achieved nothing — there is no true pleasure in the futilities of this world — *'all is futile.'*

ד שֶׁיַּעֲמֹל תַּחַת הַשָּׁמֶשׁ׃ דּוֹר הֹלֵךְ וְדוֹר בָּא
ה וְהָאָרֶץ לְעוֹלָם עֹמָדֶת׃ וְזָרַח הַשֶּׁמֶשׁ וּבָא
הַשָּׁמֶשׁ וְאֶל־מְקוֹמוֹ שׁוֹאֵף זוֹרֵחַ הוּא
ו שָׁם׃ הוֹלֵךְ אֶל־דָּרוֹם וְסוֹבֵב אֶל־צָפוֹן

Rashi, however interprets תַּחַת as 'instead', 'in place of.' He explains שֶׁמֶשׁ, the light of the sun, as referring to Torah which is compared to light, and translates thus: Whatever labor is undertaken תַּחַת, *in place of,* Torah-study is of no avail and yields no reward.

The *Talmud* translates תַּחַת as 'after' and renders: For his labor *'after the sun'* he has no profit' — but for his labor *'before the sun'* [i.e. in Torah which pre-existed the sun] there is profit *(Shabbos 30b).*

In the words of the *Midrash:* A man's labor is *'under the sun,'* but his treasury of reward is above the sun [i.e. in the heavenly after-life].

תַּחַת הַשָּׁמֶשׁ — *Beneath the sun.* The sun is the controlling factor in determining time and seasons. Thus, the verse refers to man's unending striving, at all times and in all seasons *(Ibn Ezra).*

4. דּוֹר הֹלֵךְ וְדוֹר בָּא — *A generation goes and a generation comes.* The *Midrash* and *Ralbag* attach this verse to the previous one and explain, *'man has no profit for all his toil under the sun' because* life and fortune on this earth are transitory — *'a generation goes and a generation comes.'* — the new generation acquires all that the former has left behind.

Rashi amplifies that whatever temporal gains are realized by the wicked from their labors of crime do not endure beyond their days, for a new generation rises up and their children lose everything as it is written (*Job* 20:10): *'His children shall seek to please the poor and his hands shall give back that which he has robbed.'*

Ibn Ezra observes that verses 4-7 refer to the four primal elements of creation: earth, fire, wind (i.e. air), and water. Earth is cited first because it is the source, the "mother" so to speak, then fire (identified with the sun); wind and water. In verse 4, Koheles says that succeeding generations, products of the earth, will come and go, eventually all returning to their earthly source. The earth itself, however, endures forever.

The *Midrash* exhorts: The generation which comes should be as esteemed by you as the generation which has passed. You should not say 'if Rabbi Akiva were now living I would study Torah under him,' etc. But the generation and sage of your days should be as the preceding generation and sage ... For whoever is the recognized Torah leader of the community, though he be lesser in stature than those of former generations, is considered equal to the most celebrated of the former generations.

וְהָאָרֶץ לְעוֹלָם עֹמָדֶת — *But* [lit. *'and'*] *the earth endures* [lit. *'stands'*] *forever,* i.e. unlike man's temporary existence wherein one generation perishes and makes room for the next, the earth itself is enduring and

for all his labor which he toils beneath the sun? [4] *A generation goes and a generation comes, but the earth endures forever.* [5] *And the sun rises and the sun sets — then to its place it rushes; there it rises again.* [6] *It goes toward the south and veers toward the north;*

does not change its routine *(Lekach Tov).*

The *Midrash* foretells: In this world one man builds a house and another has the use of it; one man plants a tree and the other eats of it. In the Hereafter, [Israel] shall not build and another inhabit, nor plant and another eat.

5. וְזָרַח הַשֶּׁמֶשׁ וּבָא הַשָּׁמֶשׁ — *And the sun rises* [lit. *'shines'*] *and the sun sets* [These verses, 5-7, elaborate on the phrase 'but the earth endures forever' by citing the daily motions of the natural world. The commentators discuss the monotonously regular course followed by the sun in order to ensure the orderly continuity of life on earth.]

[The connective ו, *also,* stresses the connection with the previous verse]: Just as the generations pass on with predictable regularity, so does the sun rise and set with the same strict discipline of regularity — rushing through the night to return to its place of rising just as each of the primal elements returns to its own source for rejuvenation. *(Cf. Rashi; Ibn Ezra, Alshich; Taalumos Chachmah).*[1]

שׁוֹאֵף — *It rushes* [lit. *pants*]. The word should be understood as 'panting breathlessly', desiring to return to its place [i.e. to fulfill its role] *(Ibn Ezra; Rashi).*

Metzudas Zion explains it as 'looking forward with earnest desire' and relates the word to *Job* 7:2 כְּעֶבֶד יִשְׁאַף־צֵל, 'as a servant *earnestly desires* the shade.'

זוֹרֵחַ הוּא שָׁם — *There it rises again* [lit. *'there it rises'*].

6. *Rashi* explains this verse as referring to רוּחַ הַשֶּׁמֶשׁ, *the 'sun's desire' to follow*] its known direction.

Ibn Ezra (in consonance with comm. to verse 4) holds that the subject of the verse is the wind [and *North* and *South* complete the four directions.]

The *Midrash,* too, holds that the wind is the subject of the verse.

הוֹלֵךְ אֶל־דָּרוֹם — *It goes toward the south* — by day *(Bava Basra* 25b; *Targum; Rashi).*

וְסוֹבֵב אֶל־צָפוֹן — *And veers* [lit. *'circles'*] towards *the north* — at night *(ibid).*

Alshich notes that הוֹלֵךְ *going* — (i.e. its true *course*] toward the

1. The *Midrash* perceives a deeper meaning in this phrase: Rav Berachiah said in the name of Rav Abba bar Kahana: Do we not know that the sun rises and sets! Rather the verse [using the rising and setting sun to symbolize the life-death cycle] tells us that before the 'sun' of one righteous man sets, He causes the sun of another righteous man to rise. On the day Rabbi Akiva died, Rabbi Yehuda haNasi was born ... Before the sun of Sarah set, He caused the sun of Rebeccah to rise. Before the sun of Moses set, He caused the sun of Joshua to rise ... and so on, generation after generation.

סוֹבֵב | סֹבֵב הוֹלֵךְ הָרוּחַ וְעַל־סְבִיבֹתָיו
ז שָׁב הָרוּחַ: כָּל־הַנְּחָלִים הֹלְכִים אֶל־הַיָּם
וְהַיָּם אֵינֶנּוּ מָלֵא אֶל־מְקוֹם שֶׁהַנְּחָלִים
ח הֹלְכִים שָׁם הֵם שָׁבִים לָלָכֶת: כָּל־
הַדְּבָרִים יְגֵעִים לֹא־יוּכַל אִישׁ לְדַבֵּר לֹא־
תִשְׂבַּע עַיִן לִרְאוֹת וְלֹא־תִמָּלֵא אֹזֶן

south — is by day. סוֹבֵב, *veering, 'circling'* — [i.e. the act of simply returning to its starting point] is at night.

וְעַל־סְבִיבֹתָיו שָׁב הָרוּחַ — *On its rounds* [i.e. its 'tracks'] *the wind returns.* Although it would like to change the monotony of its habitual course, nevertheless its desire to fulfill its natural role is constantly rejuvenated, so it continues to travel its primal course *(Metzudas David).*

Rashi understands this as referring allegorically to the wicked. Although their 'sun' shines and they seemingly prosper — their 'sun' will ultimately set and they will return to their stench. 'From filth they come and to filth they shall return.'

Midrash Leckach Tov also interprets this verse as referring to the course of the sun as manifested by the winter and summer seasons, but it adds that on a deeper level the verses refer to the Jews. Accordingly, *'south'* refers to *Eretz Yisrael,* and *'north'* to Israel's exile to the 'northern' countries. It has been dispersed throughout the four corners of the world — but it will ultimately be redeemed and return to its source.

7. [Water, the fourth primal element of creation is recalled. See *comm.* to verse 4].

וְהַיָּם אֵינֶנּוּ מָלֵא — *Yet the sea is not full.* The Talmud [*Taanis* 9b], Midrash, and commentators explain that the waters flow into the ocean which covers most of the earth, and, although it 'absorbs' the excess water, it is never full. The salty water of the ocean is then 'sweetened by the clouds' from which it returns to earth — and the cycle resumes.

Ibn Ezra explains that moisture rises from the ocean and is absorbed by the clouds which, in turn, cause rain to descend in an endless cycle.

Thus, the futility of all endeavors is stressed. The primal elements themselves are constantly engaged in a constant, futile path, unable to break away from their monotonous course. Since there is no lasting value to toil in this world, why shall man aimlessly strive for material gain *(Ibn Ezra; Sforno; Metzudas David; Taalumos Chachmah).*

Rashbam observes that the

[The same thought has been applied to the birth of Rashi which coincided with the death of Rabbeinu Gershom Meor HaGolah.]

Harav Mordechai Gifter adds that this concept is fundamental in Jewish life, and was apparent in the last generation, during the Holocaust. 'Before the sun of Europe set, He caused the sun of America to rise,' for God had prepared for the continuity of Torah.

the wind goes round and round, and on its rounds the wind returns. [7] *All the rivers flow into the sea, yet the sea is not full; to the place where the rivers flow, there they flow once more.*

[8] *All words are wearying, one becomes speechless; the eye is never sated with seeing, nor the ear filled*

process of Creation is continuous — without deviation. Only man's course is interrupted [by death], and his activity ceases.

The *Midrash* suggests, homiletically, that the verse refers to Torah. Man studies it and it enters the heart, yet the heart is never full nor the appetite ever satisfied. Even when man imparts his learning to another *'there they flow back again'* i.e. וְהָיוּ הַדְּבָרִים הָאֵלֶּה . . . עַל לְבָבֶךָ — *These words . . . shall be* [i.e. will *always* remain — even when you teach them to others —] *upon your heart* [*Deut.* 6:6].

Similarly, the Midrash explains: All Israel assembled in Jerusalem as pilgrims during the festivals — *yet the 'Sea' is not full,* i.e. they stood closely packed yet had sufficient room to prostrate themselves. [Comp. *Avos* 5:5: No one said, 'This place is too uncomfortable for me that I should lodge in Jerusalem.' This was one of the miracles associated with the Temple service.]

Rav Saadiah Gaon explains in a parable: O foolish man, why do you strive after riches? You are compared in these matters to the rivers whose waters do not remain with them but constantly flow into the sea. Your riches, too, will not remain with you. Rather acquire good deeds which are the only enduring possession.

שָׁם הֵם שָׁבִים לָלָכֶת — *There they* [*the rivers*] *flow once more,* i.e. to the sea to resume the perpetual cycle *(Rav Yosef Kara),* or according to *Midrash Lekach Tov,* the river/sea, cloud/rain cycle is here referred to.

8. כָּל־הַדְּבָרִים יְגֵעִים — *All words are wearying.* [i.e. *'cause weariness'.*] This translation follows *Rashi* who connects this verse to verse 3. If one gives up Torah study לְדַבֵּר בִּדְבָרִים בְּטֵלִים, to engage in idle talk, הֲרֵיהֶם יְגֵעִים they are wearying, and he will be unable to attain anything. If he seeks to indulge himself visually, his eyes will not be sated; if he seeks aural gratification his ears will never be satisfied.

The *Talmud* explains: One who engages in idle talk transgresses a prohibition, for it is said, *all words are wearying, man cannot* [i.e. *'ought not', 'must not'*] *speak. (Yoma* 19b).

Most commentators *(Saadiah Gaon; Ibn Ezra, Metzudas David,)* translate דְּבָרִים — *'things': 'all things* [in this world, mentioned above] lead *to weariness. . .*

לֹא־יוּכַל אִישׁ לְדַבֵּר — *One becomes speechless* [lit. *'man cannot speak'*]

לֹא־תִשְׂבַּע עַיִן לִרְאוֹת . . . — *The eye is never sated with seeing, nor the ear filled with hearing.* [lit. *'the eye will not be satisfied with seeing, and the ear will not be full with hearing.'*]

ט מִשְׁמֹעַ: מַה־שֶּׁהָיָה הוּא שֶׁיִּהְיֶה וּמַה־
שֶּׁנַּעֲשָׂה הוּא שֶׁיֵּעָשֶׂה וְאֵין כָּל־חָדָשׁ
י תַּחַת הַשָּׁמֶשׁ: יֵשׁ דָּבָר שֶׁיֹּאמַר רְאֵה־זֶה
חָדָשׁ הוּא כְּבָר הָיָה לְעֹלָמִים אֲשֶׁר הָיָה
יא מִלְּפָנֵנוּ: אֵין זִכְרוֹן לָרִאשֹׁנִים וְגַם
לָאַחֲרֹנִים שֶׁיִּהְיוּ לֹא־יִהְיֶה לָהֶם זִכָּרוֹן
יב עִם שֶׁיִּהְיוּ לָאַחֲרֹנָה: אֲנִי קֹהֶלֶת הָיִיתִי

The constant and unchanging processes of nature are beyond the powers of man to describe. His eye and ear cannot fully comprehend them *(Ralbag)*; [and thus, *'all is futile.'*]

. . . The *weariness*, i.e. monotonous activity, in the world does not stimulate man with something fresh — to satisfy his weary eye, to fill his eager ear *(Akeidas Yitzchak)*.

9. מַה־שֶּׁהָיָה הוּא שֶׁיִּהְיֶה — *Whatever has been, is what will be,* etc. *Rashi* explains that whoever pursues secular matters will find nothing new — only what has already existed since the Six Days of Creation. Only in Torah-study does one experience 'new' interpretation [see comm. end of this verse s.v. תַּחַת הַשָּׁמֶשׁ.]

Rav Saadiah Gaon comments that God's creation is perfect and complete, and lacks nothing. Whatever we view as new has already been provided for in His infinite wisdom. As part of the Creation, God created the resources, conditions, and concepts for all discoveries and inventions of succeeding generations until the end of time. Therefore when any generation witnesses an unusual phenomenon and takes it as 'new', they are mistaken; it is new only to them.

כְּבָר הָיָה לְעֹלָמִים, *it has already existed in the ages before us.* Earlier generations *have* been exposed to these phenomena.

וְאֵין כָּל־חָדָשׁ — *[And] there is nothing new.* The word כָּל [*'all'*] here means *'any'*, *'anything'* as in *Exodus* 20:10 לֹא תַעֲשֶׂה כָל מְלָאכָה — 'You shall not do *any* work' — thus, literally here: *'and there is not anything new. . .'*

תַּחַת הַשָּׁמֶשׁ — *Beneath the sun. Rav Galico* stresses that there is 'nothing new *beneath* the sun' — but *preceding* the sun [i.e. in Torah-study (see verse 3)] — 'new' explanations of halachic concepts are possible. The *Midrash* notes that 'whatever an eminent scholar will some day expound has already existed and was communicated as a halachah to Moses at Sinai'. [i.e. All later teachings were elucidations of what had already been revealed at Sinai;] and 'room' had been left for the individual to expound it *(Lekach Tov)*.]

10. יֵשׁ דָּבָר — *Sometimes there is something. Rashi* explains verses 10-11:

Sometimes something will come to you beneath the sun, of which someone might say to you *"Look, this is new!"* But it is not new; it

with hearing. 9 *Whatever has been, is what will be; and whatever has been done is what will be done. There is nothing new beneath the sun!* 10 *Sometimes there is something of which one says: 'Look, this is new!' — It has already existed in the ages before us.* 11 *As there is no recollection of the former ones; so to the latter ones that are yet to be, there will be no recollection among those of a still later time.*

already existed in the ages preceding us. Things only seem to be new because there is no recollection of what went before (also *Sforno; Metzudas David).*

רְאֵה־זֶה חָדָשׁ — *'Look, this is new!'* [All who see it will think it is totally new not realizing that it is merely a product of a re-organization of elements already in existence since Creation.]

11. *Metzudas David* and *Sforno* explains this verse as explanatory of the preceding verse: i.e. There is nothing new; it already existed in the ages before us. It appears new because *there is no recollection of these former things* for man has forgotten them.

אֵין זִכְרוֹן לָרִאשֹׁנִים — *[As] there is no recollection of the former ones.* Because they died and no longer exist. A similar fate will befall our children and their children after them because [verse 4] *'a generation goes and a generation comes' — and therefore all is futile (Rav Yosef Kara).*

Although there are some exceptions, and some former things *are* remembered, *Koheles* speaks of the majority of cases *(Ibn Yachya).*

All of the kings and mighty empires of ancient times have perished from the face of the earth with nary a trace left of them and their *'toil.'* Only *spiritual* empires retain their viability throughout eternity in the storehouse of the Hereafter *(Rav Saadiah Gaon).*

It is the *wicked* who perish from the earth. The *righteous,* however, are remembered eternally, for even though they die on this world, physically they leave behind a cherished legacy in the next *(Tuv Ta'am).* [Compare *Proverbs* 10:7]: זֵכֶר צַדִּיק לִבְרָכָה וְשֵׁם רְשָׁעִים יִרְקָב *'The memory of the just is blessed, but the name of the wicked will rot.'*

לָרִאשֹׁנִים . . . לָאַחֲרֹנִים — *Former ones . . . latter ones.* [This can refer either to *people* or *objects.*]

וְגַם לָאַחֲרֹנִים שֶׁיִּהְיוּ — *So to the latter ones that are yet to be.* i.e. Those who live after us will not be remembered by the generations that succeed them *(Rashi).*

Rav Galico comments that Solomon teaches us that the former generations who strove after futility left no remembrance after them. He cautions us not to think that we can learn from their shortcomings somehow to ensure our own eter-

יג מֶ֥לֶךְ עַל־יִשְׂרָאֵ֖ל בִּירֽוּשָׁלִָֽם׃ וְנָתַ֣תִּי אֶת־
לִבִּ֗י לִדְר֤וֹשׁ וְלָתוּר֙ בַּֽחָכְמָ֔ה עַ֥ל כָּל־אֲשֶׁ֥ר
נַעֲשָׂ֖ה תַּ֣חַת הַשָּׁמָ֑יִם ה֣וּא | עִנְיַ֣ן רָ֗ע נָתַ֧ן
יד אֱלֹהִ֛ים לִבְנֵ֥י הָאָדָ֖ם לַעֲנ֥וֹת בּֽוֹ׃ רָאִ֙יתִי֙
אֶת־כָּל־הַֽמַּעֲשִׂ֔ים שֶֽׁנַּעֲשׂ֖וּ תַּ֣חַת הַשָּׁ֑מֶשׁ
טו וְהִנֵּ֧ה הַכֹּ֛ל הֶ֖בֶל וּרְע֥וּת רֽוּחַ׃ מְעֻוָּ֖ת לֹא־

nity. Not so. The later generations — who also toil for futility — will leave no more remembrance than previous ones.

Therefore, whatever 'profit' [verse 3] transient man thinks he has gained from his toil beneath the sun is only of temporal value and is in reality vanity and worthless (Akeidas Yitzchak).

12. עַל־יִשְׂרָאֵל — *Over* [lit. *'upon'*] *Israel* — A clever and wise people. *(Metzudas David).*

בִּירוּשָׁלָםִ — *In Jerusalem.* The City of wisdom, [where there always dwelt prophets and sages (*Ibn Ezra*)] — and as such, I was always exposed to much wisdom *(Metzudas David).*

13. וְנָתַתִּי אֶת־לִבִּי — *And I applied* [lit. *'gave'*] *my mind* [lit. 'my *heart'*] The translation *'mind'* for לִבִּי [lit. *'heart'*] follows *Metzudas David.* i.e. I did not content myself merely to observe these phenomena; I diligently applied and immersed myself in their study *(Metzudas David).*

[לֵב, 'Heart' is often used in Scripture to describe the seat of emotion and intellect.]

לִדְרוֹשׁ וְלָתוּר בַּחָכְמָה — *To seek and probe by wisdom.* With whatever means I had at my disposal I sought out my desired goals as the sages proclaimed [*Megillah* 6b]: יָגַעְתִּי וְלֹא מָצָאתִי אַל תַּאֲמִין — If a man says to you 'I have labored and not found,' do not believe him . . . יָגַעְתִּי וּמָצָאתִי תַּאֲמִין, 'I have labored and found,' you may believe him' *(Sforno).*

The *Midrash* explains לָתוּר, *to probe:* 'To probe for wisdom is to become תַּיָּר, *an explorer,* of wisdom, as in *Numbers* 13:2: וְיָתֻרוּ אֶת אֶרֶץ כְּנַעַן, *'send men that they may spy out the Land of Canaan.'*

Rashi translates בַּחָכְמָה, *by wisdom,* to refer to *Torah* [i.e. to seek out and probe, using חָכְמָה, *Torah,* source of all *wisdom,* as my guide *(Kol Yaakov)*].

תַּחַת הַשָּׁמָיִם — *Beneath the sky.* All the futilites and wickedness enumerated above *(Rashi),* [and all human activities on earth].

הוּא עִנְיַן רָע — *It is a sorry* [lit. *'bad'*] *task that God has given to the sons of man with which to be concerned.* [The phrase is obscure and the translation follows *Rashi,* (who translates עִנְיַן as a form of לַעֲנוֹת = עִיוּן = involvement). In the context of the verse he translates: *I applied my mind to seek and probe the Torah* — essence of all wisdom — and through it *to comprehend the previously mentioned evils, which occur beneath the sky. And* I concluded that they are the 'evil' of

[12] *I, Koheles, was King over Israel in Jerusalem.* [13] *I applied my mind to seek and probe by wisdom all that happens beneath the sky — It is a sorry task that God has given to the sons of man with which to be concerned.* [14] *I have seen all the deeds done beneath the sun, and behold all is futile and a vexation of the*

which Moses spoke when he placed before Israel the choice between 'good and evil, life and death.' (*Deut.* 30:15). He urged Israel to choose 'good and life' by devoting itself to the service of God rather than to the vain pursuit of earthly gain.

The translation is also in consonance with the interpretation of *Ibn Ezra* who translates: 'I applied myself to probe with wisdom the inner workings of activities *although it is a sorry task that man be occupied with useless quests.'*

Taalumos Chachmah elaborates that in this verse Solomon is relating how he totally immersed himself in the study of philosophy and in material quests until he realized that the רָע, *evil,* mentioned in the Torah refers to this obsessive quest for mundanity and riches with which man is perpetually preoccupied. Although man must be involved with seeking a livelihood, it should not totally consume him to the point of exhaustion, as it is written (*Proverbs* 23:4). אַל תִּיגַע לְהַעֲשִׁיר — *'Do not wear yourself out in pursuit of wealth.'*

Other commentators, (e.g. *Targum)* translate לַעֲנוֹת, 'to be punished,' 'afflicted,' 'made subservient': *'I concluded that it is bad that God has allowed men the choice over their will so that He can punish them for their actions. For had there not been Free Will there could be no punishment (Metzudas David).*

. . . In order that mankind would be subservient to Him, God caused all man's actions to be vain *(Eiger Chumash; Rav Yosef Kara).*

[A possible translation could be: The power with which God has endowed man and which impels him to incessantly probe the actions of his fellows is a source of affliction to him.]

14. רָאִיתִי אֶת־כָּל־הַמַּעֲשִׂים — *I have seen all the deeds.* [As King I had ample opportunity to immerse myself in this quest and make the necessary observations.]

תַּחַת הַשָּׁמֶשׁ — *Beneath the sun* [see *comm.* to identical phrase in verse 3.]

וְהִנֵּה הַכֹּל הֶבֶל — *And behold all is futile* [lit. *'vanity'*]. And as a king I am qualified to make this statement *(Eiger Chumash).*

וּרְעוּת רוּחַ — *And a vexation of the spirit.* This translation follows *Rashi* and *Targum* who derive the word from רעע, to *break,* and who understand רוּחַ as spirit, i.e. 'earthly quests leave one frustrated because his desires are unfulfilled' *(Metzudas David).*

Other commentators (e.g. *Rav*

יוּכַל לִתְקֹן וְחֶסְרוֹן לֹא־יוּכַל לְהִמָּנוֹת׃
טז דִּבַּרְתִּי אֲנִי עִם־לִבִּי לֵאמֹר אֲנִי הִנֵּה
הִגְדַּלְתִּי וְהוֹסַפְתִּי חָכְמָה עַל כָּל־אֲשֶׁר־
הָיָה לְפָנַי עַל־יְרוּשָׁלִָם וְלִבִּי רָאָה הַרְבֵּה
יז חָכְמָה וָדָעַת׃ וָאֶתְּנָה לִבִּי לָדַעַת חָכְמָה
וְדַעַת הֹלֵלוֹת וְשִׂכְלוּת יָדַעְתִּי שֶׁגַּם־זֶה

Saadiah Gaon; Ibn Ezra) compare the word to רְעֶה in *Hoshea* 12:2 אֶפְרַיִם רֹעֶה רוּחַ וְרֹדֵף קָדִים — *'Ephraim shepherds the wind and chases the east wind,'* and translate our verse: *'and a grasping after wind,'* i.e. man's effort is futile and as hopeless as catching the wind. Man's life is thus spent striving after nothingness.[1]

15. מְעֻוָּת לֹא־יוּכַל לִתְקֹן — *A twisted* [or *'crooked'*] *thing cannot be made straight.* i.e. one who was *'crooked'* in his life time [and did not repent] cannot expect to 'straighten himself' after he dies *(Rav Almosnino).*[2]

The Rabbis [*Chagigah* 9a] interpret this phrase as referring to the case of one who had illicit relations and begat a *mamzer.* The result of his sin lives on, unlike one who steals and returns the theft. Alternately, the verse refers to a sage who abandoned the Torah — from a good beginning he became *'crooked'* [and the Hebrew מְעֻוָּת denotes that which has been *rendered* crooked] *(Rashi).*

The *Talmud* gives an additional application of this verse: If one [intentionally] did not recite the *Shema* or *tefilah* in its proper time, *(Berachos* 26a).

Ibn Ezra seems to interpret this verse not as a separate statement, but as a continuation of the previous two: *'All is futile . . . and a crookedness which cannot be made straight . . .'* [i.e. of what avail are our actions? We cannot redress society's wrongs; we cannot fill its deficiencies.]

וְחֶסְרוֹן לֹא־יוּכַל לְהִמָּנוֹת — *And what is not there* [lit. *'lacking,' 'absent'*] *cannot be numbered* [lit. *'counted'*] This refers to the case of one whose comrades formed a group to perform a mitzvah and he absented himself; once the mitzvah is performed he can not count himself among them to share their reward *(Rashi; Berachos 26a).*

Midrash Lekach Tov adds that one who is void of mitzvos in this world cannot expect to be counted among the righteous in the Hereafter.

Taalumos Chachmah differentiates between מְעֻוָּת, *crooked,* —

1. The *Midrash* comments that *'all is futile'* except repentance and good deeds, and compares Solomon to an old man who sat at the crossroads. Before him were two paths, one which was fine at the beginning but filled with thorns and reeds at the end, while the other began with thorns and reeds but ended evenly. He warned the passer-by about both roads . . . Should not people be thankful to him for warning them so that they should not weary themselves? Similarly, ought not people to be thankful to Solomon who sits by the gates of wisdom and warns Israel that *'all is futile and a vexation of the spirit'* — except repentance and good deeds?

I

15-17

spirit. 15 *A twisted thing cannot be made straight; and what is not there cannot be numbered.*

16 *I said to myself: Here I have acquired great wisdom, more than any of my predecessors over Jerusalem, and my mind has had much experience with wisdom and knowledge.* 17 *I applied my mind to know wisdom and to know madness and folly. I*

something which was once straight but is now bent; and חֶסְרוֹן, *lacking* — as something which had never existed.

Rav Yosef Kara translates *'there are so many deficiencies* — in the futility of man's labors — *that they cannot be numbered.'*

16. דִּבַּרְתִּי אֲנִי עִם־לִבִּי — *I said to myself:* [lit. *'I spoke with my heart'*] i.e. I reflected introspectively *(Metzudas David).* The heart is the repository of the spirit and hence synonymous with wisdom, reasoning, and creative thought *(Ibn Ezra).*

Just as physiologically, the heart pumps blood to all the organs of the body, spiritually, too, the heart influences and dispenses wisdom and compassion throughout the spiritual portions of the body *(Alshich).*

הִגְדַּלְתִּי וְהוֹסַפְתִּי חָכְמָה — *I have acquired great wisdom* [lit. *'I grew great and I added wisdom.'*] i.e. I integrated the wisdom of the ancients and added to it *(Ibn Ezra).*

עַל כָּל־אֲשֶׁר־הָיָה לְפָנַי עַל־יְרוּשָׁלָם — *More than any of my predecessors over* [lit. *'in'*] *Jerusalem.* David was his only predecessor who ruled over Jerusalem. He must therefore be referring also to the heathen kings who had ruled there in times gone by *(Metzudas David)* — [such as Malkizedek King of Salem *(Gen. 14:18).*]

The *Targum* interprets this as referring [not to his *royal* predecessors], but 'to all the *wise men* who previously lived in Jerusalem.' [Jerusalem having always been renowned as a city of wise men (see *comm.* on verse 1).]

וְלִבִּי רָאָה הַרְבֵּה — *And my mind has had much experience.* [lit. *'and my heart saw much'*] i.e. with a discerning heart I observed much wisdom and knowledge *(Metzudas David).*

17. וָאֶתְּנָה לִבִּי — *[And] I applied my mind* [lit. *'my heart'*]. After having grown great in wisdom I turned my attention to comprehending also the true nature of madness, although I knew it was a futile quest *(Ibn Ezra).*

הֹלֵלוֹת וְשִׂכְלוּת — *Madness and folly.* This translation follows *Rashi*

2. As the *Midrash* notes: This world is like the eve of Sabbath, and the Hereafter is like Sabbath; if someone does not prepare before Sabbath what will he eat on the Sabbath! The *Midrash* stresses that repentance is impossible after death, and continues: This world is like dry land and the Hereafter is like the sea. If a man does not make preparation for himself while he is on dry land, what will he eat while at sea!

יח הוּא רַעְיוֹן רוּחַ: כִּי בְּרֹב חָכְמָה רָב־כָּעַס
יח וְיוֹסִיף דַּעַת יוֹסִיף מַכְאוֹב:

[סִכְלוּת = שִׂכְלוּת, comp. 2:12.]

Ibn Ezra, following the spelling, relates it to שֵׂכֶל, 'good sense,' the opposite of madness.

Alshich interprets הֹלֵלוֹת as the mad quest for riches — as Solomon had amassed gold, horses, and earthly pleasures; and שִׂכְלוּת as the folly of having many wives — which he had also amassed for himself, somehow thinking he would nevertheless escape the temptations they placed before him. But now, in the twilight of his life, he reflected and perceived it was vanity and a vexation of the spirit.

יָדַעְתִּי *I perceived* [lit. *'I knew'*]. I established without doubt that it was valueless *(Sforno).*

שֶׁגַּם־זֶה הוּא רַעְיוֹן רוּחַ — *That this, too, is a vexation of the spirit.* i.e. that the accumulation of knowledge leads only to frustration *(Metzudas David).*

[רַעְיוֹן רוּחַ, *vexation of the spirit,* is related to רְעוּת רוּחַ in verse 14. Similarly, here too, some commentators translate *'a striving after the wind'; 'a futile quest'.*]

18. כִּי בְּרֹב חָכְמָה רָב־כָּעַס — *For with much wisdom comes much grief* [lit. *'anger'.*]

Rashi explains that Solomon had always relied heavily on his exceptional wisdom, and had always hoped that his amassing of horses would nevertheless *not* cause the people to return to Egypt and that his many wives would *not* lead him astray; [comp. *Deut.* 17:16, 17,] But in the final analysis it is recorded of him (*I Kings* 11:3) *'and his wives turned away his heart'.* When one relies too much on his own wisdom and does not keep away from prohibitions — *much grief comes to the Holy One blessed be He.* [*Rashi* thus interprets *God* as the subject of grief in this verse.]

Thus in his old age, Solomon reflects on his past actions and concludes that it would have been better for him *not* to have relied so heavily on his own wisdom, but rather to have walked humbly with God *(Tuv Taam).*

According to *Ibn Ezra,* the wise man — reflecting upon the true nature of the futility of man's labor — will always be grief stricken at the transient nature of man in this world . . .

He perceives more than the ignorant man, and he is more affected by it *(Lekach Tov).*

[The *Talmud* translates this verse: *'For much wisdom resulted from God's abundant anger'* — and comments]: Had Israel not sinned, only the Five Books of the Torah and the Book of Joshua would have been given them, [the latter] because it records the disposition of Eretz Yisrael [among the tribes — but the other books consisting mostly of the rebukes of the prophets would have been unnecessary]. From where is this known? *'For much wisdom resulted from abundant anger'* [i.e. the anger of God caused Him to send many prophets and their wise teachings.]

וְיוֹסִיף דַּעַת יוֹסִיף מַכְאוֹב — *And he who increases knowledge increases*

I
18 *perceived that this, too, is a vexation of the spirit.* 18
For with much wisdom comes much grief, and he who increases knowledge increases pain.

pain. Similarly, the extra awareness caused by increased knowledge — of the futility of mankind — will only increase the wise man's pain at this realization *(Metzudas David).*

Rav Saadiah Gaon comments that the insatiable quest for knowledge will always be a cause of grief and pain. The man who wishes to amass wisdom will never be content with what he has learned; the true scholar will always want to know more.

In his *Emunos v'De'os, Rav Saadiah Gaon* adds: 'With the increase in knowledge there are revealed to him the flaws concerning which he was fully at ease before they became evident to him.'

It is impossible for man to fathom God's method in ruling the world. The deeper man seeks to delve into esoteric problems, the more he perceives that the solution eludes him — hence be becomes frustrated and pained *(Shaar Bas Rabim).* It is therefore best to accept tradition and not delve into these restricted matters *(Kehilas Yaakov).*

[It must be noted that Solomon is not advocating that 'ignorance is bliss'. He is decrying the accumulation of רוֹב חָכְמָה *much* wisdom, as the main source of human happiness (see verse 16). As the *Kotzker Rabbi* said, *'For with much wisdom comes much grief*—וְאַף עַל פִּי כֵן, but nevertheless! It is still man's obligation to acquire wisdom.']

א אָמַרְתִּי אֲנִי בְּלִבִּי לְכָה־נָּא אֲנַסְּכָה
בְשִׂמְחָה וּרְאֵה בְטוֹב וְהִנֵּה גַם־הוּא
ב הָבֶל: לִשְׂחוֹק אָמַרְתִּי מְהוֹלָל וּלְשִׂמְחָה
ג מַה־זֹּה עֹשָׂה: תַּרְתִּי בְלִבִּי לִמְשׁוֹךְ בַּיַּיִן

II

Prefatory Remarks

[The division of the Bible into chapters is of non-Jewish origin, introduced in the Middle Ages by Christian Bible printers. Most Jewish Bibles follow these divisions for identification purposes. In Masoretic manuscripts the text is divided according to several traditional systems — some of which unfortunately have never found their way into printed editions. Most notable among them is the traditional system of פְּתוּחוֹת *[open line divisions], and* סְתוּמוֹת *[closed spaces] as found in ancient Hebrew manuscripts and* סִפְרֵי תוֹרָה, *Torah Scrolls.*

According to the Masorah, therefore, *this verse does not begin a new chapter and a new trend of thought. Rather it is a continuation of the previous verses. Hence, the commentators view this verse in the context of the verses that preceded it and so interpret it.*

Having established the futility of the pursuit of wisdom [1:13] and the futility of madness and folly [1:17], Solomon now turns to the pursuit of joy, and to the combination of several life styles while deciding which of them is worthwhile. But after experiencing every luxury life has to offer, he concludes [verse 11] that 'it was all futile and a vexation of the spirit.'*]*

1. אָמַרְתִּי אֲנִי בְּלִבִּי — *I* [*therefore*] *said to myself.* [lit. *'I said in my heart'*] [Having achieved little satisfaction with his previous pursuits, he seeks new areas of experimentation.]

לְכָה־נָּא אֲנַסְּכָה בְשִׂמְחָה — *Come, I will experiment with joy.* [He is addressing his heart; i.e. meditating and 'talking', as it were, to himself]

לְכָה, *come* [lit. *'go'*]. A form of urging, a call to action [comp. *Gen.* 37:20] *(Metzudas Zion).*

The word אֲנַסְּכָה, [from נסה, *'test'*] here translated *'will experiment'* follows *Targum,* the second interpretation in *Ibn Ezra; Metzudas Zion.*

Rashi and the first interpretation of *Ibn Ezra,* however, relate the word to מסך [=נסך] *mix* [wine], *dilute, pour out.* i.e. Solomon said: If *'wisdom yields grief'* [1:18] then I will abandon it and turn to the pleasures of joy, and indulgence in wine [see verse 3]

Alshich, also translating נסך, *dilute,* renders: 'having experienced the grief brought on by wisdom, *I decided to dilute* the grief *with joy,* — and at the same time I told my heart to be concerned, not with the intrinsic essence of joy, but בְּטוֹב, with the *goodness* [i.e. the feeling of contentment and pleasure]. But alas, this too was vanity.'

Sforno relates the word to נְסִיכוּת, *government,* and translates: *'I will conduct my kingdom and government according to the joys of pleasure.'*

וּרְאֵה בְטוֹב — *And enjoy pleasure* [lit. *and see what is good'*] This translation follows most commentators. *Targum* is more literal and translates: *'And I will see the good of this world.'*

וְהִנֵּה גַם־הוּא הָבֶל — *That, too, turned*

II
1-3

I said to myself: Come, I will experiment with joy and enjoy pleasure. That, too, turned out to be futile. 2 *I said of laughter, It is mad! And of joy, What does it accomplish!*

3 *I ventured to stimulate my body with wine —*

out to be futile [lit. *'And behold, that, too, is futile'*] Because I saw prophetically, that much evil is caused by lighthearted frivolity *(Rashi);* i.e. This obsession with wordly pleasure is itself futility *(Sforno; Metzudas David).*

2. לִשְׂחוֹק אָמַרְתִּי מְהוֹלָל — *I said of laughter, it is mad!* [or: *'to laugh, I said, is mad'*] i.e. I said of laughter born of joy that it is madness *(Metzudas David);* and it does not lead to worthwhile objectives *(Sforno).*

Most commentators relate מְהוֹלָל to הוֹלֵלוֹת, *'madness', 'senselessness'. Metzudas Zion translates it as* שִׁיעֲמוּם, *'melancholy';* and *Rashi* translates: *'mingled with cries and sighs.'*

The *Talmud,* on the other hand, relates the word to מְהוּלָל (=הלל) *praiseworthy,* and translates: *I said of laughter it is praiseworthy* — this refers to the mirth which the Holy One, blessed be He rejoices with the righteous in the world to come. *(Shabbos* 30b).

The *Midrash* derives it from מָהוּל, *mixed* [i.e. confounded or confused] and comments: How confounded is the laughter in which the heathens indulge in their circuses and theaters! *And of joy, what does it accomplish?* What cause can there be for a scholar [who has the Torah from which to derive joy] to enter such places?

וּלְשִׂמְחָה מַה־זֹּה עֹשָׂה — *And of joy, what does it accomplish?* [lit. *'And to joy, what does it do?'*] i.e. what good is it? *(Rashi);* of what value is it to man? *(Targum).* In concept it is worthless! *(Sforno).*

Taalumos Chachmah comments that Solomon says: 'I never understood what harm could come from joy — until I indulged in it and found myself succumbing to temptations induced by light-headedness.'

According to the *Talmud* this refers to שִׂמְחָה שֶׁאֵינָהּ שֶׁל מִצְוָה, joy not connected with a mitzvah. This teaches that the *Shechinah* [Divine Presence] does not rest upon man through gloom, nor through sloth, nor through frivolity, nor through levity, nor through talk nor through vain pursuits, אֶלָּא מִתּוֹךְ דְּבַר שִׂמְחָה שֶׁל מִצְוָה — only as a result of a matter of joy connected with a mitzvah *(Shabbos* 30b*).*

3. תַּרְתִּי בְלִבִּי — *I ventured.* [lit. *'I probed my heart'* (as in 1:13 וְלָתוּר בַּחָכְמָה *'and to probe wisdom')*] i.e. I resolved to attempt grasping them all: merry-making, wisdom, and folly, and to stimulate and pamper my flesh by imbibing in wine *(Rashi).*

Metzudas David explains that Solomon ventured to find a method of grasping all three divergent life styles simultaneously, thereby to ascertain which of the three was the most valid pursuit: He inbibed drink which causes physical

אֶת־בְּשָׂרִי וְלִבִּי נֹהֵג בַּחָכְמָה וְלֶאֱחֹז
בְּסִכְלוּת עַד אֲשֶׁר־אֶרְאֶה אֵי־זֶה טוֹב
לִבְנֵי הָאָדָם אֲשֶׁר יַעֲשׂוּ תַּחַת הַשָּׁמַיִם
ד מִסְפַּר יְמֵי חַיֵּיהֶם: הִגְדַּלְתִּי מַעֲשָׂי בָּנִיתִי
ה לִי בָּתִּים נָטַעְתִּי לִי כְּרָמִים: עָשִׂיתִי לִי
גַּנּוֹת וּפַרְדֵּסִים וְנָטַעְתִּי בָהֶם עֵץ כָּל־פֶּרִי:
ו עָשִׂיתִי לִי בְּרֵכוֹת מָיִם לְהַשְׁקוֹת מֵהֶם

pleasure, while his 'heart' was involved with the wisdom of the Torah — and he simultaneously indulged in external folly.

Having found pure wisdom a source of pain [1:18] and merriment futile [2:1], he resolves to explore a way of life that will combine wisdom and folly — that is, he will live a life of pleasure yet not remain neglectful of wisdom *(Ibn Ezra).*

לִמְשׁוֹךְ בַּיַּיִן — *To stimulate with wine* — an expression meaning to pamper by drinking wine. Luxurious banquets are referred to in Scripture as *'wine' (Rashi).*

The phrase therefore means: to indulge in wine-drinking which stimulates the body *(Metzudas David).*

אֶת־בְּשָׂרִי — *My body* [lit. *'my flesh.*']

וְלִבִּי נֹהֵג בַּחָכְמָה — *While* [lit. *'and'*] *my heart is involved* [lit. *'conducts'*] *with wisdom.* — Even while my body is stimulated with wine, my heart will be with wisdom and Torah observance *(Rashi).*

Ibn Ezra explains that he will pursue folly and indulge in pleasure — not with abandon, but under the guidance and restraint of wisdom, with prudent self control.

וְלֶאֱחֹז בְּסִכְלוּת — *And to grasp folly* i.e. things that seemed to be folly [the commandment of God that the heathens ridiculed. He is referring to 7:18 see *Rashi* there] *(Rashi).*

Metzudas David explains *'folly'* in this case as referring to the externalities that entice man: fine houses, musical instruments, etc. Since they do not enter the body [i.e. the body receives no direct nourishment from them] they are called *'folly'*.

Ibn Ezra explains סִכְלוּת *folly* as the craving for any earthly pleasure.

The *Midrash,* on the other hand, relates סכלות to שִׂכְלוּת and translates: *'intelligence'* [see also comm. of *Ibn Ezra* on 1:17 s.v. הֹלֵלוֹת וְשִׂכְלוּת].

עַד אֲשֶׁר־אֶרְאֶה — *Until I can discern* [lit. *'see'*]. This experiment with wine and pleasure will not be uncontrolled and indeterminate, but precise and controlled — only *until such time as I will discern to what extent man should pursue each way of life (Sforno).*

He will indulge in each of the life styles only long enough to establish its merit *(Metzudas David).*

מִסְפַּר יְמֵי חַיֵּיהֶם — *The brief span of their lives* [lit. *'the (limited) number of the days of their lives'*].

4. הִגְדַּלְתִּי מַעֲשָׂי — *I acted in grand style* [lit. *I magnified my works*] i.e. I did great things, *(Ibn Ezra)* In the

*while my heart is involved with wisdom — and to
grasp folly, until I can discern which is best for
mankind to do under the heavens during the brief
span of their lives.* 4 *I acted in grand style: I built
myself houses, I planted vineyards;* 5 *I made for
myself gardens and orchards and planted in them
every kind of fruit tree;* 6 *I constructed pools from*

following verses he enumerates what these *'works'* were *(Metzudas David).*

In order to accomplish the experiment outlined in verses 1-3, Solomon implemented his plan. Not only did he 'live like a king' he even exceeded the normal self-indulgence of royalty as the following verses relate. [He bemoans the outcome in verse 11.]

'I magnified my works' — to a greater extent than any of my ancestors *(Midrash Lekach Tov).*

בָּנִיתִי לִי בָּתִּים — *I built myself houses* — [Comp. 1 *Kings* 9:10.]

The *Midrash* notes, to Solomon's credit, that his first grand act was to build a Temple to HASHEM. [Only after the Temple was completed did he turn to this *personal* goal.]

נָטַעְתִּי לִי כְּרָמִים — *I planted* [*myself*] *vineyards.* The לִי, *'myself'*, is stressed by *Nachal Eshkol:* Solomon did not utilize the legal right of a king to expropriate his subjects' property for personal aggrandizement as the Jews were forewarned by Samuel when they asked him to appoint a king and he responded that the new king *'will take your fields and your vineyards . . .' (I Samuel* 8:14). Whatever taxes he collected went for the House of God. The grandiose schemes described in these verses were paid for with *his own property,* not with taxes expropriated from his subjects.

5. גַּנּוֹת — *Gardens* — where vegetables and flowers are planted.

וּפַרְדֵּסִים — *And orchards* — a grove where fruit trees are planted. *(Metzudas David)* [The word פַּרְדֵּס occurs again in *Nechemiah* 2:8; *Song of Songs* 4:13.]

The *Targum* adds that the gardens and orchards were outside the walls of Jerusalem because, as the *Talmud* (*Bava Kamma* 82b) notes, it was prohibited to plant gardens and orchards within Jerusalem *(Gishmei Brachah).*

עֵץ כָּל־פֶּרִי — *Every kind of fruit tree.* The *Midrash* comments that this includes even pepper [typical of the exotic plants which do not normally grow in Eretz Yisrael but which Solomon cultivated] for which Solomon imported Indian water so that the plants should be productive *(see Rashi).*

One thing led to the other. Once involved in such extravagant pursuit of luxury . . . he couldn't stop. One project led to the other . . . *(Taalumos Chachmah).*

6. בְּרֵכוֹת מָיִם — *Pools* i.e. reservoirs *(Midrash).*

ז יַעַר צוֹמֵחַ עֵצִים: קָנִיתִי עֲבָדִים וּשְׁפָחוֹת
וּבְנֵי־בַיִת הָיָה לִי גַּם מִקְנֶה בָקָר וָצֹאן
הַרְבֵּה הָיָה לִי מִכֹּל שֶׁהָיוּ לְפָנַי
ח בִּירוּשָׁלָםִ: כָּנַסְתִּי לִי גַּם־כֶּסֶף וְזָהָב
וּסְגֻלַּת מְלָכִים וְהַמְּדִינוֹת עָשִׂיתִי לִי
שָׁרִים וְשָׁרוֹת וְתַעֲנוּגֹת בְּנֵי הָאָדָם שִׁדָּה
ט וְשִׁדּוֹת: וְגָדַלְתִּי וְהוֹסַפְתִּי מִכֹּל שֶׁהָיָה
לְפָנַי בִּירוּשָׁלָםִ אַף חָכְמָתִי עָמְדָה לִּי:
י וְכֹל אֲשֶׁר שָׁאֲלוּ עֵינַי לֹא אָצַלְתִּי מֵהֶם

Rashi, in explaining the word *'pools'* notes that 'it is similar to a fishpond dug into the earth.'

7. וּבְנֵי־בַיִת — *Stewards.* [lit. *'children of the household'*] This translation follows *Targum, Midrash,* and *Metzudas David.*

According to *Ibn Ezra* they were the slave children born in the house [as distinct from slaves which *he bought*].

[Eliezer, Abraham's servant was referred to as בֶּן בֵּיתִי, *'child in my house' (Gen.* 15:3)]

[There are Scriptural references to the lavishness of Solomon's court. See, for example *I Kings* chapters 9 and 10, especially 10:5 where the Queen of Sheba is awed by the opulence of Solomon's court and his numerous attending servants.]

The *Midrash* comments that Solomon's table lacked nothing, neither relish [horseradish] in summer nor cucumbers in winter. He enjoyed them all year.

מִכֹּל שֶׁהָיוּ לְפָנַי בִּירוּשָׁלָםִ — *Than all my predecessors in Jerusalem.* [See *comm. to 1:16.]*

8. כָּנַסְתִּי לִי גַּם־כֶּסֶף וְזָהָב — *I amassed even silver and gold for myself.* [Solomon's treasure was vast, as indicated in *I Kings* 10:14: *'Now the weight of gold that came to Solomon in one year was 666 talents of gold ...'*; and *ibid.* verse 27: *'and the king made silver to be in Jerusalem like stones.'*]

The *Midrash* elaborates that these stones were huge in size — measuring eight or ten cubits. Even the weights used in the time of King Solomon were of gold.

וּסְגֻלַּת מְלָכִים — *And the treasure of kings,* the precious treasures of gold, silver, and gems which kings collect and keep guarded in their treasure houses (*Rashi,* et al).

וְהַמְּדִינוֹת — *And the provinces* — i.e. the treasures of merchants *(Rashi);* the rare treasures unique to an individual country and for which particular provinces are noted *(Ibn Ezra).*

שָׁרִים וְשָׁרוֹת — *Various musical instruments* [This translation follows *Rashi; Sforno.*]

Rav Yosef Kara, Alshich, Metzudas Zion and others translate *'singers'*; *Eiger Chumash* translates *'musicians.'*

which to irrigate a grove of young trees; 7 *I bought*
slaves — male and female — and I acquired stewards;
I also owned more possessions, both cattle and sheep,
than all of my predecessors in Jerusalem; 8 *I amassed*
even silver and gold for myself, and the treasure of
kings and the provinces; I provided myself with
various musical instruments, and with every human
luxury — chests and chests of them. 9 *Thus, I grew*
and surpassed any of my predecessors in Jerusalem;
still, my wisdom stayed with me. 10 *Whatever my*
eyes desired I did not deny them; I did not deprive

שִׁדָּה וְשִׁדּוֹת — *Chests and chests of them.* The translation follows *Rashi* and most commentators who relate it to the phrase שִׁדָּה תֵּיבָה וּמִגְדָּל, 'a chest, a box or a cupboard' [*Mishnah, Kelim* 18:3] *Rashi,* however, specifically renders: *'luxurious chariots.'*

There are many other suggestions for the meaning of this obscure phrase. *Ibn Ezra* prefers to render [from the root שָׁדַד] 'women taken by violence' — [i.e. an accumulation of many women in the royal harem.]

9. וְגָדַלְתִּי וְהוֹסַפְתִּי —*Thus, I grew and surpassed.* [A phrase similar to 1:16 (lit. *'I grew great and increased'*).]

I was greater in my own right and I exceeded them in material splendor *(Ibn Ezra),* by performing wondrous deeds *(Metzudos David)* beyond what kings usually did, as for example, [*I Kings* 10:18-20] *'And the king made a great throne of ivory . . . there was none the like made in any kingdom' (Sforno).*

[See also *ibid* verse 23: ויגדל המלך שלמה מכל מלכי הארץ לעשר לחכמה, *and King Solomon exceeded all the kings of the earth in riches and wisdom.*] The *Targum* thus translates וְהוֹסַפְתִּי: *'and I acquired wealth'.*

אַף חָכְמָתִי עָמְדָה לִּי — *Still, my wisdom stayed with me* — in good stead [guiding my steps] *(Rashi).*

[Compare the similar use of the root עמד in the Hagaddah וְהִיא שֶׁעָמְדָה לַאֲבוֹתֵינוּ 'and this is what *sustained* our fathers', etc.]

Alternately, *Rashi* and *Metzudas David* render: 'despite these vast undertakings I did not neglect wisdom *(Rashi; Sforno).*

The *Midrash,* translating אַף in its other meaning: 'anger,' 'exertion,' ['sweat of the brow'] comments homiletically: Solomon declared, of all the Torah which I learned, only the Torah I acquired through exertion [or: through the blows which my teacher gave me *(Torah Temimah)*] remained with me in my old age.

לֹא־מָנַעְתִּי אֶת־לִבִּי מִכָּל־שִׂמְחָה כִּי־לִבִּי
שָׂמֵחַ מִכָּל־עֲמָלִי וְזֶה־הָיָה חֶלְקִי מִכָּל־
יא עֲמָלִי׃ וּפָנִיתִי אֲנִי בְּכָל־מַעֲשַׂי שֶׁעָשׂוּ יָדַי
וּבֶעָמָל שֶׁעָמַלְתִּי לַעֲשׂוֹת וְהִנֵּה הַכֹּל
הֶבֶל וּרְעוּת רוּחַ וְאֵין יִתְרוֹן תַּחַת
יב הַשָּׁמֶשׁ׃ וּפָנִיתִי אֲנִי לִרְאוֹת חָכְמָה
וְהוֹלֵלוֹת וְסִכְלוּת כִּי | מֶה הָאָדָם שֶׁיָּבוֹא
אַחֲרֵי הַמֶּלֶךְ אֵת אֲשֶׁר־כְּבָר עָשׂוּהוּ׃

10. [Determined to ensure the success of the experiment, see verse 3 above, he catered to his every whim and desire, denying himself nothing.]

לֹא־מָנַעְתִּי אֶת־לִבִּי — *I did not deprive myself* [lit. *'my heart'*.]

מִכָּל־שִׂמְחָה — *of any kind of joy* i.e. from any activity that produces joy *(Metzudas David).*

This refers to the joy that comes from wealth *(Midrash).*

כִּי־לִבִּי שָׂמֵחַ מִכָּל־עֲמָלִי — *Indeed, my heart drew joy from all my activities* [lit. *'toil'*].

[i.e. I drew satisfaction from my opulent way of life.]

[עֵינַי, *my eyes,* and לִבִּי, *my heart,* are used in this verse to describe the seat of desire, as in *(Num.* 15:39) אַחֲרֵי לְבַבְכֶם וְאַחֲרֵי עֵינֵיכֶם *'after your heart and after your eyes.'*]

וְזֶה־הָיָה חֶלְקִי מִכָּל־עֲמָלִי — *And this was my reward for all my endeavors.* All these efforts yielded me nothing more than this *(Rashi);* i.e. this satisfaction, alone, was all that remained with me as reward for all my endeavors *(Ibn Ezra).*

[Solomon describes the fruits of self-indulgence as being nothing more than fleeting sensual pleasure, but there was no lasting, meaningful gain.]

11. וּפָנִיתִי — *Then I looked.* i.e. when I reflected on my endeavors I perceived that it was futile *(Ibn Ezra).*

וּבֶעָמָל שֶׁעָמַלְתִּי לַעֲשׂוֹת — *At all the things that I had done.* [lit. *'At the toil I exerted myself to do'*.]

Ibn Latif comments that Solomon prophetically foresaw that all that he wrought — The Temple and its appurtenances — were destined to be destroyed. This prompted him to declare: *'it is all futile'* [see also *comm.* to 1:2.]

וְהִנֵּה הַכֹּל הֶבֶל וּרְעוּת רוּחַ — *It was all futile and a vexation of the spirit.* Because they do not yield the eternal benefit I had expected of them.

וְאֵין יִתְרוֹן תַּחַת הַשָּׁמֶשׁ — *And there is no real profit under the sun.*

Nothing of the endeavors that I pursued was capable of yielding benefit *in this world beneath the sun (Metzudas David). [The Mishnah* in *Pe'ah* lists good deeds for which there is some reward in this world, but in all cases the

II
11-12

myself of any kind of joy. Indeed, my heart drew joy from all my activities, and this was my reward for all my endeavors.

11 *Then I looked at all the things that I had done and the energy I had expended in doing them; it was clear that it was all futile and a vexation of the spirit — and there is no real profit under the sun.*

12 *Then I turned my attention to appraising wisdom with madness and folly — for what can man who comes after the king do? It has already been*

primary reward is bestowed in the World to Come.]

12. [Having concluded the futility of all the above, Solomon sets out to establish whether there is an advantage to wisdom over folly and madness, and, as *Rashi* interprets, to contemplate in the Torah and perceive madness and folly, i.e. the punishment of sins.]

כִּי מֶה הָאָדָם שֶׁיָּבוֹא אַחֲרֵי הַמֶּלֶךְ — *For what can man who comes after the king do?* [lit. *'For what is the man who will come after the king'.*]

The phrase is ambiguous and the commentators offer several explanations:

What good will it do man to approach the king to appeal a prejudicial decree that is already in effect; he would have been better advised to consider his actions in time so that he would not be put into such a position *(Rashi).*

The matter may be likened to a human king who built a palace which all passers-by criticized saying: 'If its pillars were taller it would be more beautiful,' 'If its walls were higher it would be more beautiful'. But would someone come and say: 'If I had three hands or three eyes I would be more beautiful'? *(Midrash).*

... *Metzudas David* explains: Since God has created *folly,* how can man presume to detest it seeing that it already exists. Would, then, God have created it for naught?

Ibn Ezra, and others, translate: Coming after the king, what more could anyone hope to accomplish than the king has already done? [i.e. The king is best equipped to institute the comparison between wisdom and folly on the basis of personal experience, there is no need for anyone to follow him and repeat the experiment.]

עָשׂוּהוּ — *Has already been done* [lit. *'they have done it'.*] [The translation follows *Ibn Ezra* who regards עָשׂוּהוּ as impersonal, and adds הָעוֹשִׂים, *'the doers'* as the missing subject.]

יג וְרָאִיתִי אָנִי שֶׁיֵּשׁ יִתְרוֹן לַֽחָכְמָה מִן־
הַסִּכְלוּת כִּֽיתְרוֹן הָאוֹר מִן־הַחֹֽשֶׁךְ׃
יד הֶֽחָכָם עֵינָיו בְּרֹאשׁוֹ וְהַכְּסִיל בַּחֹשֶׁךְ
הוֹלֵךְ וְיָדַעְתִּי גַם־אָנִי שֶׁמִּקְרֶה אֶחָד
טו יִקְרֶה אֶת־כֻּלָּם׃ וְאָמַרְתִּי אֲנִי בְּלִבִּי
כְּמִקְרֵה הַכְּסִיל גַּם־אֲנִי יִקְרֵנִי וְלָמָּה
חָכַמְתִּי אֲנִי אָז יוֹתֵר וְדִבַּרְתִּי בְלִבִּי שֶׁגַּם־
טז זֶה הָבֶל׃ כִּי אֵין זִכְרוֹן לֶחָכָם עִם־הַכְּסִיל

13. [Following the theme he set forth in the previous verse], *Metzudas David* continues: 'although I realized intellectually that it is proper to detest סִכְלוּת, *folly*, nevertheless folly was not created needlessly. One can perceive the advantage of wisdom only by comparison with folly, just as one can appreciate light only by comparison with darkness.

[Following *Metzudas David*, then, the translation of this verse would be thus: *'But I perceived that the advantage of wisdom is discernable only from* (i.e. when compared with) *folly, just as the advantage of light is discernable only from darkness'.*]

כִּיתְרוֹן הָאוֹר מִן־הַחֹשֶׁךְ — *As light excels* [lit. *'as the advantage, (profit) of light'*] *over* [lit. *'from'*] *darkness.'*

Just as one can distinguish figures in the light and place perceived objects in their proper perspective, such is the intellect of the wise man *(Ibn Ezra).*

14. Solomon now elaborates on the factors that distinguish the sage from the fool *(Metzudas David).*

הֶחָכָם עֵינָיו בְּרֹאשׁוֹ — *The wise man has his eyes in his head.* i.e. high up on his body so he can see far, and he utilizes his vision by studying his route well in advance *(Metzudas David).*

He contemplates the end result of his deeds before he begins them [translating רֹאשׁ, *beginning, (Sifsei Chachomim)*] *(Rashi).*

וְהַכְּסִיל בַּחֹשֶׁךְ הוֹלֵךְ — *whereas a fool walks in darkness. Ibn Ezra* comments: The wise man clearly sees the way ahead of him and takes the most direct route to his destination, unlike the fool who goes about uncertainly as if groping in the darkness; not even knowing over what he stumbles.

[Because the wise man perceives through intellect, his vision is broad — the fool's vision is limited and narrow.]

וְיָדַעְתִּי גַם־אָנִי . . . אֶת־כֻּלָּם — *But I also realized* [lit. *'but I knew, even I.'*] *. . .them all.* Even though I praise the superiority of the wise man over the fool, nevertheless, I cannot overlook the fact that death is the fate that will overtake אֶת־כֻּלָּם, *them all,* i.e. the wise man and fool equally *(Rashi; Alshich).*

15. וְאָמַרְתִּי אֲנִי בְּלִבִּי — *So I said to myself* i.e. seeing that death is the

II
13-16

done. [13] *And I perceived that wisdom excels folly as*
light excels darkness. [14] *The wise man has his eyes in*
his head, whereas a fool walks in darkness. But I also
realized that the same fate awaits them all. [15] *So I said*
to myself: The fate of the fool will befall me also; to
what advantage, then, have I become wise? But I con-
cluded that this, too, was futility, [16] *for there is no*
comparison between the remembrance of the wise
man and of the fool at all, for as the succeeding days

common fate of all, I was in danger of questioning the advantage of remaining righteous *(Rashi),* [but see comm. below, and next verse where he became convinced that there is no comparison between the fate of the wise man and the fate of the fool.]

גַּם־אֲנִי יִקְרֵנִי — *Will befall me also.* [Although I have attained wisdom, I will die the same death as the fool.]

וְלָמָּה חָכַמְתִּי אֲנִי אָז יֹתֵר — *To what advantage then have I become wise?* i.e. of what avail, then, were all the efforts I exerted to attain wisdom? *(Ibn Ezra);* how am I superior to the fool after death — having shared a similar fate with him — for having attained wisdom during my lifetime? *(Metzudas David).*

וְדִבַּרְתִּי בְלִבִּי שֶׁגַּם־זֶה הָבֶל — *But I concluded that this, too, was futility.* i.e. But I assured myself that this type of thinking about the advantages of wisdom and about the common fate of the wise man and the fool, was futile. There is no comparison [next verse] between the way a wise man is remembered and the way a fool is forgotten *(Rashi; Metzudas David; Alshich; Taalumos Chachmah).*

Ibn Ezra and some others, interpret *'wisdom'* as the subject of this phrase; i.e. notwithstanding its advantages, the ambition to become wise is futility [because the wise man and the fool are equally forgotten after death. (But see comm. next verse).]

16. כִּי אֵין זִכְרוֹן לֶחָכָם עִם־הַכְּסִיל לְעוֹלָם — *For there is no comparison between the remembrance of the wise man and of the fool at all.* [lit. *'for there is no remembrance to the wise man with the fool forever'.*] — The wise man's memory is praised and the fool's is disgraced *(Metzudas David),* [as Solomon himself declared in *Prov.* 10:7: *'The memory of the righteous is for a blessing, but the name of the wicked shall rot.'*]

[There is a difference of opinion as to how this verse — within the context and continuity of the verses before and after it — should be translated. The above translation follows *Rashi, Midrash,* and most commentators, (see comm. previous verse).]

Ibn Ezra however, in consonance with his commentary (end of

לְעוֹלָם בְּשֶׁכְּבָר הַיָּמִים הַבָּאִים הַכֹּל
נִשְׁכָּח וְאֵיךְ יָמוּת הֶחָכָם עִם־הַכְּסִיל׃
יז וְשָׂנֵאתִי אֶת־הַחַיִּים כִּי רַע עָלַי הַמַּעֲשֶׂה
שֶׁנַּעֲשָׂה תַּחַת הַשָּׁמֶשׁ כִּי־הַכֹּל הֶבֶל
יח וּרְעוּת רוּחַ׃ וְשָׂנֵאתִי אֲנִי אֶת־כָּל־עֲמָלִי
שֶׁאֲנִי עָמֵל תַּחַת הַשָּׁמֶשׁ שֶׁאַנִּיחֶנּוּ לָאָדָם
יט שֶׁיִּהְיֶה אַחֲרָי׃ וּמִי יוֹדֵעַ הֶחָכָם יִהְיֶה אוֹ

previous verse), translates that the striving after wisdom is futile: *'For the wise man is no more remembered than the fool, for as the succeeding days roll by, both are forgotten.'*

בְּשֶׁכְּבָר הַיָּמִים הַבָּאִים הַכֹּל נִשְׁכָּח — *As the succeeding days roll by, is all forgotten?* [The phrase is understood as an incredulous question by *Metzudas David* and most commentators.] The wise man's deeds still linger on, while the deeds of the fool are forgotten *(Alshich).*

The word בְּשֶׁכְּבָר occurs only here. It is best taken as an abbreviation of בַּאֲשֶׁר כְּבָר *'inasmuch as' (Metzudas David),* or, according to *Ibn Ezra,* בְּשֶׁכְּבָר, *'as previously.'* [i.e. just as in the previous days, in succeeding days, as well.]

וְאֵיךְ יָמוּת הֶחָכָם עִם־הַכְּסִיל — *How can the wise man's death be like [lit. with] the fool's?* I.e. How can one even suggest that the deaths of the wise man and fool are similar! [The former's fame lives; the latter leaves nothing worth remembering.] *(Metzudas David; Alshich).*

The *Midrash* gives several examples of wise man and fool [Abraham / Nimrod; Moses / Balaam; David / Nebuchadnezzar.] They all died, but when adversity befalls Israel, we cry *'Remember Abraham, Isaac and Israel, Your servants'* [*Ex.* 32:13]; but do the heathen nations [in their distress] cry 'Remember the deeds of Nimrod'? [Thus the righteous are remembered; not the fools.]

According to *Rav Yosef Kara* [whose interpretation agrees with *Ibn Ezra*] אֵיךְ, *how,* is a sigh of lament [cf. אֵיכָה: *Lamentations* 1:1. *ArtScroll* edition, page 52.] The translation would then be: *'Alas! How alike in death are the wise man and the fool!'*

17. וְשָׂנֵאתִי אֶת־הַחַיִּים — *So I hated life.* [Solomon said this out of a sense of weariness, a sense of futility resulting from the frustrations he experienced from whatever he observed *'beneath the sun.'*]

'I utterly despise the life I live always having to observe the futility and frustrations of man's actions and aspirations in this world' *(Sforno).*[1]

Ibn Ezra observes that חַיִּים can

1. The *Midrash* cites a case in which *hate of life* is clearly mirrored:

A man wrote a letter to the emperor Hadrian, saying: 'If you hate the circumcised, there are also the Ishmaelites [Arabs, who practice circumcision but are not persecuted]; if you hate

II
17-19

roll by, is all forgotten? How can the wise man's death be like the fools?

17 *So I hated life, for I was depressed by all that goes on under the sun, because everything is futile and a vexation of the spirit.*

18 *Thus I hated all my achievements laboring under the sun, for I must leave it to the man who succeeds me.*
19 *— and who knows whether he will be wise or*

either be a noun [*'life'*as translated in our verse], or an adjective: [*'the living.'*]

Rashi comments that this comment was prompted by Solomon's prophetic vision of the evil generation of רְחַבְעָם, Rechaboam, his son and disappointing successor under whom the Ten Tribes of Israel defected to Jeraboam.

כִּי רַע עָלַי הַמַּעֲשֶׂה — *For I was depressed.* [lit. *'for the act is evil to me'*] i.e. distasteful, improper *(Metzudas David).*

18-23. [Koheles is further distressed by the fact that even the fruits of man's strenuous *physical* efforts to accumulate wealth, will ultimately go on to heirs whose prudence and wisdom are questionable].

עֲמָלִי — *My achievements* [this translation (lit. *'my toil'*) follows *Ibn Ezra.*]

19. וּמִי יוֹדֵעַ — *And who knows.*[2] If my heir turns out to be a wise Torah scholar who will at least utilize the inheritance to study Torah without worldly cares, I would not complain [knowing that I have a share in his

Sabbath observers, the Samaritans also observe Sabbath. You hate only *this* people [Israel] — and their God will exact punishment from you.'

Hadrian offered a reward to whomever disclosed himself as the writer of that letter.

A certain person went and identified himself as the writer of the letter, and the king ordered that he be beheaded. When the king asked the man why he wrote the letter, he answered: 'Because you free me from three evil things.' 'What are they?' he inquired.

'My appetite desires to eat morning and evening,' the man responded, 'but I have nothing to satisfy it with; and the same applies to my wife and children.'

Hadrian said: 'Since you lead such a miserable life, abandon it [and die.]'

And the man applied the text to himself *'So I hated life.'*

2. The *Midrash* comments that Rabbi Meir was a skillful scribe and used to earn three *selahs* a week. He spent one selah on food and drink, another on clothing, and the third on support of scholars.

[Noticing that he never saved any money], his disciples asked him: 'What are you doing to provide for your children?'

He answered: 'If they are righteous, then it will be as David said: *(Psalms 37:25) 'Yet I have not seen the righteous forsaken, nor his seed begging for bread'* [i.e. God will provide for them]. If they are not righteous, why should I leave my possessions to the enemies of the Omnipresent!'

סָכָל וְיִשְׁלַט בְּכָל־עֲמָלִי שֶׁעָמַלְתִּי
וְשֶׁחָכַמְתִּי תַּחַת הַשָּׁמֶשׁ גַּם־זֶה הָבֶל׃
כ וְסַבּוֹתִי אֲנִי לְיַאֵשׁ אֶת־לִבִּי עַל כָּל־
כא הֶעָמָל שֶׁעָמַלְתִּי תַּחַת הַשָּׁמֶשׁ׃ כִּי־יֵשׁ
אָדָם שֶׁעֲמָלוֹ בְּחָכְמָה וּבְדַעַת וּבְכִשְׁרוֹן
וּלְאָדָם שֶׁלֹּא עָמַל־בּוֹ יִתְּנֶנּוּ חֶלְקוֹ גַּם־זֶה
כב הֶבֶל וְרָעָה רַבָּה׃ כִּי מֶה־הֹוֶה לָאָדָם
בְּכָל־עֲמָלוֹ וּבְרַעְיוֹן לִבּוֹ שֶׁהוּא עָמֵל
כג תַּחַת הַשָּׁמֶשׁ׃ כִּי כָל־יָמָיו מַכְאֹבִים וָכַעַס
עִנְיָנוֹ גַּם־בַּלַּיְלָה לֹא־שָׁכַב לִבּוֹ גַּם־זֶה
כד הֶבֶל הוּא׃ אֵין־טוֹב בָּאָדָם שֶׁיֹּאכַל וְשָׁתָה

learning *(Sforno).*] But who can be sure that he will be a wise man? *(Alshich).*

גַּם־זֶה הָבֶל — *This, too, is futility.* That wise men should toil and fools inherit is one of the futile aspects of life *(Rashi).*

20. וְסַבּוֹתִי — *So I turned.* [In utter resignation] like one who, having given up hope of attaining his goal, turns away toward a different road *(Ibn Ezra).*

לְיַאֵשׁ — *To despair* — from toil and labor *(Rashi)* [and give up all hope.]

The *Midrash* adds 'But I reconsidered and said 'just as others toil for me, so I must toil for others'[1]

21. גַּם־זֶה הֶבֶל וְרָעָה רַבָּה — *This, too, is futility and a great evil. Akeidas Yitzchok* comments that life can be all the more futile when, as often occurs, one denies himself the satisfaction of his own needs in order to amass a greater legacy for others. Such a person has literally nothing from all his labor.

The *Midrash* explains *'man'* in this verse as an allegorical reference to God [for man was created in the *'image of God,'(Gen. 1:27)*]. The verse refers to the generation of the Flood and what it made of the world which God created with wisdom, knowledge and skill. He bequeathed it to human beings who had not toiled in it and who ultimately

1. The *Midrash* relates that the accursed Hadrian was once walking along the roads of Tiberias when he saw an old man standing and cutting down shrubs to set plants. Hadrian asked him how old he was, to which he replied: 'I am a hundred.'

'You, are a hundred years old,' the king said, 'and you stand cutting shrubs to set plants! Do you think you will eat of their fruit?'

'If I am worthy, I shall eat,' the old man replied; 'if not, just as my forefathers toiled for me, so I toil for my children.'

'By your life,' Hadrian replied, 'if you are fortunate enough to eat of their fruit, let me know.'

II
20-24

foolish? — and he will control of all my possessions for which I toiled and have shown myself wise beneath the sun. This, too, is futility. 20 *So I turned my heart to despair of all that I had achieved by laboring under the sun,* 21 *for there is a man who labored with wisdom, knowledge and skill, yet he must hand on his portion to one who has not toiled for it. This, too, is futility and a great evil.* 22 *For what has a man of all his toil and his stress in which he labors beneath the sun?* 23 *For all his days are painful, and his business is a vexation; even at night his mind has no rest. This, too, is futility!*

24 *Is it not good for man that he eats and drinks*

became a futile generation: *'and the wickedness of man was great in the earth'* [Gen. 6:5] *(Rashi).*

22. כִּי מֶה־הֹוֶה לָאָדָם — *For what has a man* i.e: what advantage, then, does man gain from all the toil and frustration he endures, finally leaving his possessions to others *(Rashi).*

רַעְיוֹן — *Stress* [or: *'vexation'*, as in 1:17.]

23. כִּי כָל־יָמָיו — *For all his days* i.e. all the waking hours during which his business endeavors are replete with pain and frustration at seeing his plans go unfulfilled *(Ibn Ezra).*

גַּם־בַּלַּיְלָה לֹא־שָׁכַב לִבּוֹ — *Even at night his mind has no rest.* His worries, even at night, allow him no sleep *(Metzudas David).*

24. ... אֵין־טוֹב בָּאָדָם שֶׁיֹּאכַל וְשָׁתָה — *Is it not good for man that he eats and drinks.* [This translation follows *Rashi* who understands the phrase interrogatively, and adds:] 'and guides his soul to perform righteousness and charity with this food and drink,' as was said to Yehoyakim [*Jeremiah* 22:15:] *'Did not your father eat and drink and do righteousness and charity, and then it was well with him?'*

Is it not proper that man be

In due course, they produced figs. The old man filled a basket with figs and went to the palace gate. 'Go and tell the king,"An old Jew whom you once met wishes to greet you," ' he told the guards.

They let him in, and he reminded the king who he was, and said: 'Behold, I have been worthy to eat of them, and these figs are the fruits they produced.'

Hadrian ordered that his basket be emptied of the figs and filled with coins.

His attendants asked him: 'You displayed all this honor to an old Jew?' He answered: 'His Creator has honored him, shall I not do so?'

פרק ב
כה־כו

כה וְהֶרְאָה אֶת־נַפְשׁוֹ טוֹב בַּעֲמָלוֹ גַּם־זֹה רָאִיתִי אָנִי כִּי מִיַּד הָאֱלֹהִים הִיא׃ כו כִּי מִי יֹאכַל וּמִי יָחוּשׁ חוּץ מִמֶּנִּי׃ כִּי לְאָדָם שֶׁטּוֹב לְפָנָיו נָתַן חָכְמָה וְדַעַת וְשִׂמְחָה וְלַחוֹטֶא נָתַן עִנְיָן לֶאֱסֹף וְלִכְנוֹס לָתֵת לְטוֹב לִפְנֵי הָאֱלֹהִים גַּם־זֶה הֶבֶל וּרְעוּת רוּחַ׃

generous with his property and not hoard it to bequeath it to others? *(Metzudas David).*

וְהֶרְאָה אֶת־נַפְשׁוֹ טוֹב בַּעֲמָלוֹ — *And shows his soul satisfaction?* [lit. *'good'*] *in his labor,* i.e. and utilizes his possessions to perform righteous and charitable deeds, thereby to attain posterity for his soul *(Metzudas David).*

כִּי מִיַּד הָאֱלֹהִים הִיא — *That it is from the Hand of God.*

Although wealth is in man's hands, I perceived that he who accumulates wealth must view himself only as its guardian who does not have permission to dispense it without Divine sanction. [i.e. Man must act only according to the ideals of charity and justice because his wealth is not simply the result of his labor; it is a gift of God *(Kol Yaakov).* For God desires that man enjoy the blessings of this earth *(Ibn Yachya),* satisfying both his physical being and his soul without being obsessed with the inevitability that his fortune will some day be bequeathed to others.]

Contrary to the previous feeling that man and beast are similar in terms of their physical, animal existence and that all striving is futile, this statement, [and verse 26] is Solomon's affirmation of Divine Providence — that all is calculated and done according to His plan *(Taalumos Chachmah).*

25. כִּי מִי יֹאכַל וּמִי יָחוּשׁ חוּץ מִמֶּנִּי — *For who should eat and who should make haste except me.* Why should I deprive myself of my own portion of food and drink. Who is more entitled to eat the fruits of my labor than I? Only the wicked have the urge to hoard all their possessions for others [next verse] *(Rashi).*

[This verse apparently modifies the previous one: If all my property will eventually pass on to strangers, is it not right that I should view my possessions as a Divine gift and perform lofty spiritual deeds with them while I am still alive? Why should only others benefit from my wealth (next verse)? This is all part of God's Master Plan.]

יָחוּשׁ — *Make haste* — to satisfy his desires *(Ibn Ezra)* by consuming my property *(Rashi).*

26. This verse modifies 24 — *'it is from the Hand of God' (Rashi).*

שֶׁטּוֹב לְפָנָיו — *Who pleases Him* [lit. *'who is good before Him'*].

II
25-26

and shows his soul satisfaction in his labor? And
even that, I perceived, is from the hand of God. — 25
For who should eat and who should make haste ex-
cept me? — 26 *To the man who pleases Him He has*
given wisdom, knowledge and joy; but to the sinner
He has given the urge to gather and amass — that he
may hand it on to one who is pleasing to God. That,
too, is futility and a vexation of the spirit.

נָתַן חָכְמָה וְדַעַת וְשִׂמְחָה — *He has given wisdom, knowledge and joy.* i.e. Has given intellect and the disposition to engage in Torah study and to rejoice in his lot by eating, drinking and donning clean garments *(Rashi; Kara)* . . . and the desire to perform good deeds *(Metzudas David).*

וְלַחוֹטֶא — *But to the sinner.* The Divine plan, on the other hand, awards the sinner with the urge to accumulate wealth which he is not permitted to enjoy and which he must ultimately bequeath to others as above in verse 21 *(Alshich).*

The *Midrash* cites an example of this doctrine in *Esther* 8:2 where the wicked Haman's lavish house was given to Mordechai.

גַּם־זֶה הֶבֶל — *That, too, is futility.* i.e. Since God will, in any event, transfer the wealth to whomever pleases Him, it is futile to strive madly for its accumulation *(Ibn Ezra).*

According to *Metzudas David* it is futile even if the wealth were eventually to go to a righteous person — because it would have been more beneficial for the wicked man to have put it to worthwhile use of his own volition.

וּרְעוּת רוּחַ — *And a vexation of the spirit* — because his wealth is thus taken from him against his will *(Metzudas David).*

פרק ג א לַכֹּל זְמָן וְעֵת לְכָל־חֵפֶץ תַּחַת הַשָּׁמָיִם:
א־ד ב עֵת לָלֶדֶת וְעֵת לָמוּת
עֵת לָטַעַת וְעֵת לַעֲקוֹר נָטוּעַ:
ג עֵת לַהֲרוֹג וְעֵת לִרְפּוֹא
עֵת לִפְרוֹץ וְעֵת לִבְנוֹת:
ד עֵת לִבְכּוֹת וְעֵת לִשְׂחוֹק
עֵת סְפוֹד וְעֵת רְקוֹד:

1-15. [Solomon elaborates on a theme that recurs throughout the Book: *'What profit does man have for all his labor which he toils beneath the sun'* — the sun symbolizes time which is governed by the rising and setting sun (see *Comm.* to 1:3). Man has no control over the laws which control the world. Moreover, he cannot fathom God's scheme for the world, nor can he change the fixed order of natural phenomena. He can only live in awe of time, witnessing the endless procession of events following one another in an unbroken circle.]

1. לַכֹּל זְמָן — *Everything has its season* [lit. *'to everything is a time'*] [i.e. Things follow a fixed order and are properly regulated.]

Rashi comments that one who has frivolously accumulated many possessions should not rejoice. For although he possesses them now, everything has its time and they will ultimately pass on to the righteous [as in 2:26.]

וְעֵת לְכָל־חֵפֶץ — *And there is a time for everything.*

Rav Almosnino differentiates between זְמַן and עֵת: עֵת is the *'point in time'* during which every event is destined to take place; and זְמַן refers to the *duration, from beginning to end,* of that particular event.

חֵפֶץ, in *Mishnaic* Hebrew means 'thing' *(Rashi).*

2-8. [Solomon illustrates his statement in verse 1, by citing juxtaposing examples from the repeated round of human experience. The examples can be interpreted literally, but the Sages have perceived deeper meanings in many of them.]

2. עֵת לָלֶדֶת — *A time to be born* — After nine months *(Rashi).*

Solomon begins by enumerating man's beginning and end — birth and death — the exact timing of which are beyond human control *(Ibn Yachya).* [It is the *natural cycle* that is being considered here; not man's capability to artificially extinguish or prolong life. (See comm. of *Rav Almosnino* to verse 3).]

The *Targum* and *Midrash* translate: *'a time to give birth'* [see next *comm.*]

וְעֵת לָמוּת — *And a time to die.* The *Midrash* notes: Is then all the wisdom which Solomon uttered simply that there is *'A time to be born and a time to die?'* Rather, the meaning is: Happy is the man whose hour of death is like the hour of his birth; just as he was pure in

Everything has its season, and there is a time for everything under the heaven:

2 A time to be born and a time to die;
a time to plant and a time to uproot the planted.
3 A time to kill and a time to heal;
a time to wreck and a time to build.
4 A time to weep and a time to laugh;
a time to wail and a time to dance.

the hour of his birth, so should he be pure in the hour of his death.

[As the *Talmud* remarks on the verse (*Deut.* 28:6): *'Blessed shall you be when you arrive, and blessed shall you be when you depart'*: Your exit from the world should be like your entry into it; just as you entered the world without sin, so may you depart from it *(Bava Metziah* 107a).]

עֵת לָטַעַת — *A time to plant* — in time of peace *(Midrash).*

Plant life, too, gives *'birth'* and is regulated by seasons *(Ibn Yatif).*

וְעֵת לַעֲקוֹר נָטוּעַ — *And a time to uproot the planted* in the time of war *(Midrash).*

3. עֵת לַהֲרוֹג — *A time to kill.* The reference is to killing in war time *(Midrash),* or according to some, to the legal execution of criminals *(Michlol Yofi).*

וְעֵת לִרְפּוֹא — *And a time to heal.* During peace time *(Midrash)*; or referring to the requirement to search for any possible way to acquit a suspect *(Michlol Yofi).*

Rav Almosnino comments: הֲרִיגָה, *'killing'*, is an artifically imposed, unnatural death caused by humans; conversely רְפוּאָה, *'healing'*, refers to the artificial prolonging of life. Thus the two concepts are juxtaposed in this verse although they are not true opposites. [מחץ, *'to wound'* would be the true antonym of רפא, *'heal'*, as noted by *Ibn Ezra.*]

עֵת לִפְרוֹץ — *A time to wreck* — during war *(Midrash).*

The inevitability of the time-determined life/death, kill/heal process extends to inanimate objects as well *(Ibn Ezra).*

וְעֵת לִבְנוֹת — *And a time to build* in time of peace *(Midrash).*

4. עֵת לִבְכּוֹת — *A time to weep.* — Tishah b'Av *(Rashi)* as it says [*Lam.* 1:2] *She* [Zion] *weeps bitterly in the night (Midrash; Lekach Tov).*

וְעֵת לִשְׂחוֹק — *And a time to laugh* — in time to come, [when Israel is redeemed] as it is written *(Psalms* 126:2) אָז יִמָּלֵא שְׂחוֹק פִּינוּ — *'Then our mouth will be filled with laughter' (Midrash; Lekach Tov).*

עֵת סְפוֹד — *A time to wail* — i.e. to eulogize the dead as a means of assuaging grief *(Metzudas David).*

וְעֵת רְקוֹד — *And a time to dance,* to

ה עֵת לְהַשְׁלִיךְ אֲבָנִים וְעֵת כְּנוֹס אֲבָנִים
עֵת לַחֲבוֹק וְעֵת לִרְחֹק מֵחַבֵּק:
ו עֵת לְבַקֵּשׁ וְעֵת לְאַבֵּד
עֵת לִשְׁמוֹר וְעֵת לְהַשְׁלִיךְ:
ז עֵת לִקְרוֹעַ וְעֵת לִתְפּוֹר
עֵת לַחֲשׁוֹת וְעֵת לְדַבֵּר:
ח עֵת לֶאֱהֹב וְעֵת לִשְׂנֹא
עֵת מִלְחָמָה וְעֵת שָׁלוֹם:

heighten the joy of an occasion, as at a wedding celebration *(Metzudas David).*

The *Midrash* interprets *'crying'* and *'wailing'* as referring to the state of mourning, and *'laughing'* and *'dancing'* to the period following mourning. *Torah Temimah* explains that Solomon thus implies the *Talmudic* dictum [*Moed Katan* 27b] that one should not display excessive grief over the dead. Rather the *time* for *crying and wailing* is limited to the period of mourning prescribed by *Halachah.* Once that period ends, public grief should not continue; it is a time to resume *'laughing'* and *'dancing.'*

5. עֵת לְהַשְׁלִיךְ אֲבָנִים — *A time to scatter stones.*

Midrash Lekach Tov explains this as prophetic reference to the Destruction of the Temple, and to the ultimate Rebuilding.

. . .As it is written [*Lam.* 4:1] *'holy stones are scattered at every street corner' (Midrash).*

וְעֵת כְּנוֹס אֲבָנִים — *And a time to gather stones.* [During the Future Redemption] as it is written [Isaiah 28:16] *'Behold I lay in Zion a stone as a foundation' (Midrash).*

Rashi also refers this to the ingathering of the exiles and cites the verse [*Zechariah* 9:16]: *'And HASHEM their God shall save them on that day as the flock of His people; for they shall be like the stones of a crown glowing over his land.'*

Ibn Ezra interprets the verse literally. Even so incidental a matter as the disposal of unused stones and the collection of them for some useful purpose is conditioned by time.

עֵת לַחֲבוֹק וְעֵת לִרְחֹק מֵחַבֵּק — *A time to embrace, and a time to shun embraces.* i.e. during periods of ritual uncleanliness *(Targum).*

The *Midrash* comments: If you see a band of righteous men standing anywhere, embrace and show them affection; but if you see a band of wicked men, maintain your distance from them and those like them.

6. עֵת לְבַקֵּשׁ וְעֵת לְאַבֵּד — *A time to seek and a time to lose.*

The *Midrash* explains this, also, as referring respectively to peacetime and war-time.

Rashi interprets: a time to seek out the scattered of Israel; and a

5 *A time to scatter stones and a time to gather stones;*
a time to embrace and a time to shun embraces.
6 *A time to seek and a time to lose;*
a time to keep and a time to discard.
7 *A time to rend and a time to mend;*
a time to be silent and a time to speak.
8 *A time to love and a time to hate;*
a time for war and a time for peace.

time when the Jews perish [אבד] in exile.

עֵת לִשְׁמוֹר — *A time to keep* [lit. *'guard'*] — when Israel does the Will of HASHEM, as it is written: [*Num. 6:24*]: יְבָרֶכְךָ ה׳ וְיִשְׁמְרֶךָ — *HASHEM bless you and keep you. — (Rashi).*

וְעֵת לְהַשְׁלִיךְ — *And a time to discard.* [when Israel acts in an evil manner, God will] *'cast them into another land'* [*Deut.* 29:27] *(Rashi).*

7. עֵת לִקְרוֹעַ — *A time to rend* — garments over the dead *(Rav Saadiah Gaon).*

וְעֵת לִתְפּוֹר — *And a time to mend* [lit. *'sew'*] — new clothes for a wedding *(Rav Saadiah Gaon).*

עֵת לַחֲשׁוֹת וְעֵת לְדַבֵּר — *A time to be silent and a time to speak.* There are times when silence bears its reward, and other situations where speech [i.e. praise of God] is called for *(Ibn Yachya).*

'The merit of attending a house of mourning lies in the silence [which must be observed until the mourner begins to speak], and the merit in attending a wedding lies in the words [of congratulations and cheer addressed to the bride and groom.]' *(Berachos 6b).*

[Compare *Job* 2:13: *'And they sat down with him on the ground for seven days and seven nights, and none spoke a word to him'*; and conversely after the Redemption (*Psalms* 126:2): וּלְשׁוֹנֵנוּ רִנָּה, *'and our tongues (will be filled) with singing.'*]

8. עֵת לֶאֱהֹב וְעֵת לִשְׂנֹא — *A time to love and a time to hate.*

Even *love/hate* is regulated by time *(Ibn Ezra)*; one may love something today and detest that same object tomorrow *(Metzudas David).*

עֵת מִלְחָמָה וְעֵת שָׁלוֹם — *A time for war and a time for peace.* There are times when a nation seeks war with its neighbor, and other times when these same two neighbors seek to dwell together in peace *(Metzudos David).*

Midrash Lekach Tov points out the word עֵת, *time,* is repeated twenty-nine times in these verses, corresponding to the days of the lunar month. The moon is 'renewed and refilled' each month as testimony of God's rule. This testifies to the existence of God and that all is under His dominion.

ט מַה־יִּתְרוֹן הָעוֹשֶׂה בַּאֲשֶׁר הוּא עָמֵל׃
י רָאִיתִי אֶת־הָעִנְיָן אֲשֶׁר נָתַן אֱלֹהִים לִבְנֵי
יא הָאָדָם לַעֲנוֹת בּוֹ׃ אֶת־הַכֹּל עָשָׂה יָפֶה
בְעִתּוֹ גַּם אֶת־הָעֹלָם נָתַן בְּלִבָּם מִבְּלִי
אֲשֶׁר לֹא־יִמְצָא הָאָדָם אֶת־הַמַּעֲשֶׂה
אֲשֶׁר־עָשָׂה הָאֱלֹהִים מֵרֹאשׁ וְעַד־סוֹף׃

9. מַה־יִּתְרוֹן — *What gain, then has the worker.* Since all is governed by seasons and time — over which man has no control — what hope is there for him to retain mastery over his efforts? *(Ibn Ezra)* The *'time,'* of the evil doer will come and all his ill-gotten gains will be forfeited *(Rashi).*

[Solomon is not simply speaking rhetorically. Having himself amassed fortunes (2:4-11) and having concluded it was all *'futility'*, he includes his *personal* experiences in this query.]

Since man is fickle, of what permanent value is his wealth today? Tomorrow he might have different values, and his toil will thus have been in vain *(Metzudas David).*

According to *Taalumos Chachmah:* All is predestined by God and regardless of man's actions, it will come to pass in its precise, appointed time as foreseen by the prophets. Therefore it would seem proper to question what man hopes to achieve by his seemingly wasted toil in Torah study and *mitzvos* when it seems not to yield results [but the following verses negate the seeming validity of this argument.]

בַּאֲשֶׁר הוּא עָמֵל — *By his toil* [lit. *'in that he toils'*.]

The *'he'* is stressed; i.e. of what avail is *man's* toil if his reward is not ordained from above?*(Targum).*

Since there are times for all things, what advantage has the laborer in his work and the honest man in his uprightness? *(Midrash).*

10. רָאִיתִי אֶת־הָעִנְיָן — *I have observed the task* i.e. I have reflected repeatedly on the toil imposed on man by God.

[See *comm.* on similar verse: 1:13.]

Upon observation, I concluded that the task — i.e. the study of Torah and performance of the commandments which God commanded us to do — posed no problem at all [as explained in the succeeding verses] *(Taalumos Chachmah).*[1]

לַעֲנוֹת בּוֹ — *To be concerned with.* [See *comm.* end of 1:13.]

Sforno translates: *'to be afflicted with'*: I perceived that God caused man to toil in order to keep him subservient lest he rebel against Him as did Adam.

11. יָפֶה בְעִתּוֹ — *Beautiful in its time.* I recognize that God created

1. According to the *Midrash,* this homiletically refers to the apparent frustration of Torah study — that a man learns Torah and forgets it. The Midrash concludes that it is good that man forgets, for if he studied Torah and never forgot it, he would occupy himself with learning for two or three years, resume his ordinary work and pay no further attention to Torah. But since he forgets, he never abandons its study.

[9] *What gain, then, has the worker by his toil?*
[10] *I have observed the task which God has given the sons of man to be concerned with:* [11] *He made everything beautiful in its time; He has also put an enigma into their minds so that man cannot comprehend what God has done from beginning to end.*

everything in its beautiful [in the sense of 'proper'] time: e.g. death in old age; and everything else in the time predestined for it by infinite wisdom *(Ibn Ezra).*

The Torah, too, was given at the proper time. The *Midrash* comments that the Torah should have been given through Adam 'the creation of My hands' so that he might occupy himself therewith.' But God said: If he was unable to fulfill the few commandments which were given to him, how much less will he be able to abide by the 613 commandments of the Torah! I will give them to his descendants.

Everything God created is beautiful, but must be utilized only in its designated time, *(Metzudas David).*

Taalumos Chachmah continues his comment [see verses 9-10] that there is no difficulty: God created everything beautiful in its time, nevertheless He did not abolish man's Free Will. In a manner that is beyond the capacity of human intellect to fathom, God allowed man to retain his freedom of choice. No decision is imposed upon him — whether to perform *mitzvos* or to transgress them is entirely in his own hands.

גַּם אֶת־הָעֹלָם נָתַן בְּלִבָּם — *He also put an enigma into their minds.* [lit. *'also the world He put into their heart.'*] This translation follows *Rashi:* Although he instilled worldly wisdom into the hearts of man, He did not instill all wisdom into all men. Rather He dispensed small amounts to each person so no one would grasp fully the workings of God, or foresee the future. This is to ensure that, not knowing when they will die or what would befall them, people will indulge in repentance.

Therefore, continues Rashi: הָעֹלָם is spelled without a *vav,* meaning הֶעֱלֵם — *hidden* — for if man knew that his day of death was near he would neither build a house nor plant a vineyard. Solomon thus exclaims that 'it is a good thing that . . . God has kept things hidden from man.'

[see *Overview* to *Esther,* Artscroll edition page 34.]

Ibn Ezra explains the verse along the same trend, but explains הָעֹלָם as *eternity*: 'God has given a sense of eternity to men and they act as if they will live forever.'

Thus, being so involved in their daily pursuits, they *'cannot comprehend what God has done from beginning to end.'*

The *Midrash* translates: *'He set in their heart a love of the world'* [i.e. to develop its resources.]

מֵרֹאשׁ וְעַד־סוֹף — *From beginning to end* [i.e.the full plan and purpose of God.]

While man is involved in the birth process he does not think of

יב יָדַעְתִּי כִּי אֵין טוֹב בָּם כִּי אִם־לִשְׂמוֹחַ
יג וְלַעֲשׂוֹת טוֹב בְּחַיָּיו׃ וְגַם כָּל־הָאָדָם
שֶׁיֹּאכַל וְשָׁתָה וְרָאָה טוֹב בְּכָל־עֲמָלוֹ
יד מַתַּת אֱלֹהִים הִיא׃ יָדַעְתִּי כִּי כָּל־אֲשֶׁר
יַעֲשֶׂה הָאֱלֹהִים הוּא יִהְיֶה לְעוֹלָם עָלָיו
אֵין לְהוֹסִיף וּמִמֶּנּוּ אֵין לִגְרֹעַ וְהָאֱלֹהִים

ultimate death; while he plants he does not think of eventual uprooting; while rejoicing, he does not consider sadness. [Man lives for the fleeting moment.][1] *(Midrash Lekach Tov).*

This is to discourage man from contemplating excessively as to what is above and below, before and after *(Chovos Halevavos).*

12. יָדַעְתִּי כִּי אֵין טוֹב בָּם — [*Thus*] *I perceived* [lit. *'I knew'*] *that there is nothing better for them,* i.e. for mankind. [This translation follows *Rashi* who interprets 'mankind' as the subject of בָּם, *them*]: 'Since [as mentioned in the previous verse] mankind's 'time of remembrance' [i.e. day of death] is hidden, there is nothing better for them than to rejoice in their lot and do what is right in God's eyes while they are yet alive.'

Sforno and Ibn Ezra interpret the *toil* and *treasures* man labors to accumulate — only to have them pass on to strangers — as the subject of this verse. [They translate: *'that there is no good in them.'*] Now that Solomon spoke of the transient nature of property and that possession is pre-determined and governed by time, he repeats that these treasures are good only *to be enjoyed and used* as tools for performing good deeds, as previously stated in 2:24.

Taalumos Chachmah translates 'there is no better in them' i.e. *the days of man's life* than the joy which man feels when having performed good deeds of his own free will, and perceiving the reward that awaits him.

In this connection, *Harav David Feinstein* points out that Jeremiah [9:22-23] prophesies that man should not praise himself for wisdom, strength, or wealth; but only for understanding and knowing God. This means that man's intelligence, strength, or wealth — because they are God-given — are not praiseworthy. It is only for harnessing his ability and resources

1. *Harav David Cohen* points out a parallel in *Rashi, Genesis* 6:6: וַיִּתְעַצֵּב עַל לִבּוֹ, *'and He [God] grieved at His heart [for having made Man on the earth.']*

In response to a heretic, Rashi cites the following *Midrash:*

A gentile asked Rav Yehoshua ben Karcha: 'Do you not admit that the Holy One, blessed be He, forsees the future?'

'Yes,' he answered.

'But it is written "He grieved at His heart"? the heretic asked. [And if God knows the future, why was He grieved?]

'Was there ever a son born to you?' Rav Yehoshua asked. 'Yes,' came the reply.

III
12-14

12 *Thus I perceived that there is nothing better for each of them than to rejoice and do good in his life.* 13 *Indeed every man who eats and drinks and finds satisfaction in all his labor — it is a gift of God.*

14 *I realized that whatever God does will endure forever: Nothing can be added to it and nothing can be subtracted from it, and God has acted so that*

and turning them toward knowledge of God — achievements that he has *earned* — that man is rightly praised.

13. וְגַם כָּל־הָאָדָם — *Indeed, every man;* even those whose good deeds and charitable use of their hard-earned treasures were not the result of rational intellect, but were inspired by natural instincts towards propriety and generosity *(Metzudas David).*

מַתַּת אֱלֹהִים הִיא — *It is a gift of God.* i.e. One should consider it a divine gift if his natural instincts so righteously motivate him *(Ibid).*

Ibn Ezra comments: Since rejoicing is regulated by time [verse 4], man must realize that he would not be able to rejoice in his lot were it not so ordained by God at the time of his birth.

14. [Unlike man's actions — which are transient and vain — God's creation is eternal, except for those changes He purposely made to instill His fear in man.]

הוּא יִהְיֶה לְעוֹלָם — *Will endure forever.* God's creation is perfect and eternal. Any changes we see are the result of God's anger at man, and His desire to instill reverent awe of Him in man's heart *(Ibn Latif).*

As the *Midrash* notes: [According to this verse that God's creations last forever] man should have lived forever. Why was the penalty of death imposed upon him? — *'God has so acted that man should stand in awe of Him.'*

עָלָיו אֵין לְהוֹסִיף וּמִמֶּנּוּ אֵין לִגְרוֹעַ — *Nothing can be added to it and nothing can be subtracted from it.* [Compare the similar phrase in *Deut.* 4:2. (לֹא תֹסִפוּ . . . וְלֹא תִגְרְעוּ — *You shall not add . . . and you shall not diminish,)* which refers to the inviolate perfection and absolute permanence of Torah. Koheles

'And what did you do?,' Rav Yehoshua asked. 'I made everyone joyous.'

'And did you not know,' Rav Yehoshua asked, 'that he would ultimately die?'

'At the time of joy, let there be joy,' said the heretic, 'and in the time of mourning, mourning.'

'So are the works of the Holy One, blessed be He,' said Rav Yehoshua. 'Even though it is revealed before Him that they would ultimately sin and be destroyed, He did not refrain from creating them for the sake of the righteous who are destined to arise from them.'

[Similarly, although one knows that the birth of an infant is imminent, one nevertheless rejoices at the moment of birth; and although one knows that death of a beloved one is imminent, one nevertheless grieves as the moment of departure.]

פרק ג
טו־יז

טו עָשָׂה שֶׁיִּרְאוּ מִלְּפָנָיו: מַה־שֶּׁהָיָה כְּבָר
הוּא וַאֲשֶׁר לִהְיוֹת כְּבָר הָיָה וְהָאֱלֹהִים
טז יְבַקֵּשׁ אֶת־נִרְדָּף: וְעוֹד רָאִיתִי תַּחַת
הַשָּׁמֶשׁ מְקוֹם הַמִּשְׁפָּט שָׁמָּה הָרֶשַׁע
יז וּמְקוֹם הַצֶּדֶק שָׁמָּה הָרֶשַׁע: אָמַרְתִּי אֲנִי

employs the phrase here to refer to the similar perfection in God's creation.][1]

וְהָאֱלֹהִים עָשָׂה שֶׁיִּרְאוּ מִלְּפָנָיו — *God has acted so that* [man] *should stand in awe of Him.* [i.e. God's eternal creation, and man's transient nature form part of God's plan to foster in man a sense of dependence, a spirit of reverence.]

Rashi enumerates many miracles by which God changed the course of nature, thereby instilling, His fear in man. Thus, concludes *Rashi,* man should involve himself in nothing but performance of *mitzvos* and fear of God.

Verily, as the *Talmud* notes, God's whole purpose in creating the world was so that man should stand in awe of Him! *(Shabbos 31b).*

15. מַה־שֶּׁהָיָה כְּבָר הוּא — *What has been already exists.* [This translation follows *Rashi* and *Rav Yosef Kara* who seem to break up the phrase מַה־שֶּׁהָיָה — *whatever has been* כְּבָר הוּא, *has already taken place previously.* i.e. history repeats itself.] *Targum* adds: 'will be.'

[The phrase follows the argument in 1:9. See *comm.* there.]

[*Rashi* explains the continuity: In the previous verse we are told of the Eternity of the world, here we are told of the Eternity of God's actions.] Jacob is the eternally oppressed, Esau the oppressor; God perpetually loves Jacob [*(Malachi 1:2-3): 'I loved Jacob and I hated Esau'*]. Egyptians pursued Israelites; the Egyptians drowned in the sea and the Israelites were victorious. וַאֲשֶׁר לִהְיוֹת *and what is still to be* — is just as it was before; God never changes His ways: *God will always seek* [i.e. be on the side of] *the pursued,* and exact retribution from the pursuer. Therefore, of what benefit are the evil ways in which one toils? He will be ultimately held to account for his deeds.

וְהָאֱלֹהִים יְבַקֵּשׁ אֶת־נִרְדָּף — *And God always seeks* [lit. *'will seek'*] *the pursued.* [Thus, *Rashi.*]

Ibn Ezra and *Taalumos Chachmah* however, understand נִרְדָּף as *'the time that has passed'* i.e. In an endless cycle *(pursuit)* of events, God repeats that which was before, because God transcends

1. *Rambam* explains in *Moreh Nevuchim*: 'This is the reason for the perpetuity, as if he meant to say that [in the human order] things are changed to supply what is wanting, or to take away what is superfluous. The works of God being most perfect, admitting no addition or deduction, must remain the same forever. It is impossible that anything should exist that could cause a change in them except what He Himself changed [by performing miracles or changing the course of nature] *'that man should stand in awe of Him.'*

III 15-17

[man] should stand in awe of Him. 15 *What has been, already exists, and what is still to be, has already been, and God always seeks the pursued.*

16 *Furthermore, I have observed beneath the sun: In the place of justice there is wickedness, and in the place of righteousness there is wickedness.* 17 *I*

time. To Him, what is, was, and will be, are the same. One thing follows the other in an endless circular motion so that every occurrence is a recurrence.

The verse is beautifully translated, in somewhat homiletic fashion, by *Amtachas Binyamin:*

Whatever happens during the year has been pre-ordained since *Rosh Hashanah.* Nevertheless, man should not say, 'Now I can act wickedly to my friend because his suffering has already been ordained. Not so— *God always* seeks the oppressed and will seek retribution from perpetrators of evil.[1]

16-22. [Koheles now enters into a discussion on corrupt practices in the administration of justice; eventual divine retribution against the wicked; and the *seeming* similarity between man and beast.]

16. תַּחַת הַשָּׁמֶשׁ – *Beneath the sun,* i.e. in this world beneath the shining sun *(Metzudas David)* [see *comm.* to 1:3.]

מְקוֹם הַמִּשְׁפָּט שָׁמָּה הָרֶשַׁע – *In the place of* [the] *justice there is* [the] *wickedness.* i.e. [In the courts of law] one expects to find justice; instead he finds injustice and perversion *(Alshich; Ibn Yachya).*

Rashi comments that רָאִיתִי, I *observed,* refers to *prophetic vision* — that Solomon foresaw the Chamber of the Hewn Stone in Jerusalem, the meeting place of the Sanhedrin, of which it was said [*Isaiah* 1:21]: *'Righteousness lodged in her, but now murders';* and he saw their retribution.

The *Midrash* amplifies: *Murders were committed there:* They slew Zechariah and Uriah [*II Chron.* 24:21; *Jer.* 26:23ff. see *comm.* to *Megillas Eichah,* 2:20; *ArtScroll* ed. page 89.]

וּמְקוֹם הַצֶּדֶק שָׁמָּה הָרָשַׁע – *And in the place of righteousness there is wickedness. Sforno* translates: *Instead of righteousness,* i.e. righteous verdicts, there are corrupt, venal judges.

הָרָשַׁע – *The wickedness.* The word is a noun, like רֶשַׁע earlier in the verse. Here it is vocalized as רָשַׁע, because, grammatically, the *segol* under the *resh:* [רֶ] becomes a

1. In human experience, it is seldom obvious who is the *true* pursuer and who is pursued. The pursuer may be seeking to avenge a grievous wrong done him by the pursued. Usually, a complex chain of circumstances obscures responsibility. God in His infinite wisdom knows which is the responsible party. Still, the verse uses the expression: 'God always *seeks'* to indicate to us that we must always investigate carefully to find the *true* victim, rather than go by superficial first impressions *(Harav David Feinstein).*

בְּלִבִּי אֶת־הַצַּדִּיק וְאֶת־הָרָשָׁע יִשְׁפֹּט
הָאֱלֹהִים כִּי־עֵת לְכָל־חֵפֶץ וְעַל כָּל־
יח הַמַּעֲשֶׂה שָׁם: אָמַרְתִּי אֲנִי בְּלִבִּי עַל־
דִּבְרַת בְּנֵי הָאָדָם לְבָרָם הָאֱלֹהִים
יט וְלִרְאוֹת שֶׁהֶם־בְּהֵמָה הֵמָּה לָהֶם: כִּי
מִקְרֶה בְנֵי־הָאָדָם וּמִקְרֶה הַבְּהֵמָה
וּמִקְרֶה אֶחָד לָהֶם כְּמוֹת זֶה כֵּן מוֹת זֶה

kamatz [ךָ] when the word appears at the end of the sentence *(Rashi).*

Ibn Ezra notes that the phrase is repeated in the verse for emphasis.

Targum however, renders it as an adjective: 'Instead of the righteous man, we find the wicked man.'

17. אָמַרְתִּי אֲנִי בְּלִבִּי — *I mused* [lit. *'I said in my heart.'*] i.e. I therefore concluded *(Rashi).*

אֶת־הַצַּדִּיק וְאֶת־הָרָשָׁע יִשְׁפֹּט הָאֱלֹהִים — *God will judge the righteous and the wicked.* The meaning, as explained by *Rashi,* is that eventually God judges all, and although judgment *appears* delayed, everyone's time comes eventually כִּי־עֵת לְכָל חֵפֶץ, *For there is a time for everything*—even for retribution—and judgment will assuredly come.

וְעַל כָּל־הַמַּעֲשֶׂה — *And for every deed* — that man does on this world, שָׁם, *there,* will he be judged *(Ibn Yachya).*

Akeidas Yitzchok, in a lengthy philosophic dissertation, discusses the question of why, if certain evil acts are pre-ordained, man is punished for committing them. [i.e. when, in effect, the perpetrator is merely carrying out God's will.] He cites the example of the Egyptians who were punished for enslaving the Jews although it was the Jews' lot to be enslaved. He concludes that God, reckons retribution *for every deed* because human beings possess free will. Neither the Egyptians nor other evil-doers were motivated by the knowledge that they were carrying out God's will. The divine plan had no effect on their actions; they committed evil because they wanted to.

[See, in this context, *commentary* to ArtScroll edition of *Megillas Eichah* 1:9 כִּי הִגְדִּיל אוֹיֵב, *'for the enemy has acted prodigiously',* which suggests that although the enemy was merely an instrument of God's will in executing Jerusalem's destruction, he is held accountable for he acted *overzealously,* and with relish, in carrying out his mission.]

שָׁם — *There.* An obvious reference to reward and punishment in the hereafter, after death *(Ibn Ezra, Rav Saadiah Gaon, et al).*

'A man can do what he pleases in this world, but in the hereafter there will be judgment and reckoning' *(Midrash).*

Rashi understands שָׁם, *there,* as 'the unspecified time which is reserved for reckoning.'

18. לְבָרָם — *Has chosen them out*

mused: God will judge the righteous and the wicked,
for there is a time for everything and for every deed,
there.
18 *Then I said to myself concerning men: 'God has*
chosen them out, but only to see that they themselves
are as beasts.' 19 *For the fate of men and the fate of*
beast — they have one and the same fate: as one dies,

[From ברר, *to sift, select,* per *Rashi.*]

The *Midrash* interprets the phrase לְבָרֵר לָהֶם – *to make manifest to them* and translates: 'God allows the wicked to revile and blaspheme, and yet prosper. For what purpose? לְבָרָם, *to make it manifest to them* what the Attribute of Judgment has in store for the wicked. *That they may see that they themselves are like beasts:* that they should recognize and demonstrate to the world that the wicked are like beasts. Just as the beast dies and does not enter the World to Come, so will the wicked die like a beast and not enter the World to Come.

וְלִרְאוֹת – *But only to see* [lit. *'and to see'.*] *Ibn Janach* translates this as a past perfect beginning a separate clause: *'And I saw'* (i.e. 'I additionally perceived).

שְׁהֶם־בְּהֵמָה הֵמָּה לָהֶם – *That they themselves are as beasts.* [This is the general sense of this ambiguous phrase (lit. *'they are a beast, they are to them').* The translation, rendering כִּבְהֵמָה, as beasts, follows *Targum* and most commentators. The sense of the verse is clear. Although men are vain about their supposed superiority, God has selected the most eminent among them to demonstrate that they are not superior at all, that even kings and officers are as selfish and shortsighted as any other animal or beast.]

According to *Rav Saadiah Gaon,* the verse, in continuation of verse 16-17, means: Then I said to myself concerning man: 'What will happen to them in the hereafter when God sifts the righteous from the wicked and makes it obvious that the difference between them is as drastic as the difference between man and beast? [The following verses are interpreted to mean that only in the futilities of life and in the actual process of death are man and beast similar. Man's purpose on this world is infinitely great; so is his reward.]

19. כִּי מִקְרֶה בְנֵי־הָאָדָם וּמִקְרֶה הַבְּהֵמָה – *For the fate of men* [lit. *'of the children of man'*] *and the fate of [the] beast.* This verse is directed to those who lack wisdom and intellect, and who, upon seeing that man seemingly shares the fate of the beast, surmise that both also share the same spirit *(Ibn Ezra).*

Therefore, since man becomes ill and dies as does the beast, man must elevate his purpose in this world and indulge in righteous acts in order to give dignity and meaning to his life *(Rav Saadiah Gaon).*

וְרוּחַ אֶחָד לַכֹּל וּמוֹתַר הָאָדָם מִן־
כ הַבְּהֵמָה אָיִן כִּי הַכֹּל הָבֶל׃ הַכֹּל הוֹלֵךְ
אֶל־מָקוֹם אֶחָד הַכֹּל הָיָה מִן־הֶעָפָר
כא וְהַכֹּל שָׁב אֶל־הֶעָפָר׃ מִי יוֹדֵעַ רוּחַ בְּנֵי
הָאָדָם הָעֹלָה הִיא לְמָעְלָה וְרוּחַ הַבְּהֵמָה
כב הַיֹּרֶדֶת הִיא לְמַטָּה לָאָרֶץ׃ וְרָאִיתִי כִּי
אֵין טוֹב מֵאֲשֶׁר יִשְׂמַח הָאָדָם בְּמַעֲשָׂיו
כִּי־הוּא חֶלְקוֹ כִּי מִי יְבִיאֶנּוּ לִרְאוֹת בְּמֶה
שֶׁיִּהְיֶה אַחֲרָיו׃

וְרוּחַ אֶחָד לַכֹּל — *And they all* [i.e. man and beast] *have the same* [lit. *'one'*] *spirit.* — For without the soul both remain lifeless cadavers *(Ibn Yachya).*

What Koheles mentioned in verse 19: *'both have the same spirit'* refers only to the similarity they share in dying; beyond that, as pointed out in verse 21, there is a very great difference between the two *(Rav Saadiah Gaon).*

וּמוֹתַר הָאָדָם מִן־הַבְּהֵמָה אָיִן — *Man has no superiority* [lit. *'gain'*] *over [the] beast.* i.e. Man's superiority is not recognizable after death, because everything reverts to nothingness by returning to dust *(Rashi).*

This applies only when man has spent his life in the futile accumulation of wealth; not if he indulged in Torah and good deeds *(Metzudas David).*

Homiletically the phrase may be translated: *'And man's superiority over beasts is: אָיִן.'* [which forms an acrostic of] אֲמִירָה יְדִיעָה נְשָׁמָה: *speech, intellect* and *soul* [by which man *does* distinguish himself over the beast.] *(Chidah).*

כִּי הַכֹּל הָבֶל — *For all is futile,* [i.e. that mankind perceives no difference between man and beast; or that the sin of Man has caused him to share the same physical death with the beast.]

20. הַכֹּל הוֹלֵךְ — *All go.* The continuity of the verses suggest that all is futile and both man and beast share the same *physical* fate: they both return to dust *(Rav Yosef Kara).*

[Comp. 12:7.]

21. מִי יוֹדֵעַ — *Who perceives* [lit. *'who knows'.*] i.e. who is of sufficient intellect to grasp ... *(Akeidas Yitzchak).*

Rav Saadiah Gaon [also *Rashi*] construes the sentence as an affirmation, like the statement מִי יוֹדֵעַ, יָשׁוּב וְנִחָם, *'he who knows will return and repent.'* [Joel 2:14] That is, 'whoever knows that he is sinning, will repent.' Likewise, here, *He who knows, understands that one soul rises upward, while the other goes down. Rav Saadiah* continues, that should anyone insist that this verse implies doubt on the part of the Sage, as the concluding verses

so dies the other, and they all have the same spirit. Man has no superiority over beast, for all is futile.
20 *All go to the same place; all originate from dust and all return to dust.*
21 *Who perceives that the spirit of man is the one that ascends on high while the spirit of the beast is the one that descends down into the earth?*
22 *I therefore observed that there is nothing better for man than to be happy in what he is doing, for that is his lot. For who can enable him to see what will be after him?*

of the chapter would seem to indicate, the Sage's final certainty is made clear by his statement *'And the spirit returns to God'* [12:7] and by his pronouncement: *'But know that for all these things God will bring you into judgment'* [11:9.]

רוּחַ בְּנֵי הָאָדָם — *The spirit of man. Rav Yosef Kara* explains 'who can know what happens to the spirit of man that ascends on high, seeing that it never returns to the living; and similarly what happens to the soul of the beast that descends down into the earth. The stress on the verse is on *'the spirit'* because the fate of *'the body'* is known: *it returns to the dust (v. 20).*

הָעֹלָה הִיא לְמָעְלָה — *is the one that ascends on high* — and, unlike the beast, must stand trial for his actions *(Rashi).*

22. וְרָאִיתִי — *And I [therefore] observed.* i.e. I concluded, based upon all of the above *(Rashi).*

מֵאֲשֶׁר יִשְׂמַח הָאָדָם בְּמַעֲשָׂיו — *For man than to be happy in what he is doing* [lit. *'in his deeds'*] i.e. in the performance of Torah and *mitzvos,* כִּי־הוּא חֶלְקוֹ, for it, Torah observance, is within man's province alone. He should concentrate on spiritual matters only, therefore, and ignore mundane matters *(Alshich).*

Rashi interprets that man is entitled to rejoice in and enjoy the products of his labor — but that he must excercise temperance and not accumulate what is not rightfully his *(Rashi).*

כִּי מִי יְבִיאֶנּוּ לִרְאוֹת — *For who can enable him to see,* what will happen to his children after he dies, and whether they will be successful with the inheritance he bequeathed them *(Rashi).*

Alshich translates literally: לִרְאוֹת מִי יְבִיאֶנּוּ, *who will bring him*—from the hereafter back to his home — *to see* what develops with his household. Only 'his righteousness endures forever' [*Psalms* 111:3] and will accompany him in the Eternal World.

פרק ד
א־ג

א וְשַׁבְתִּי אֲנִי וָאֶרְאֶה אֶת־כָּל־הָעֲשֻׁקִים
אֲשֶׁר נַעֲשִׂים תַּחַת הַשָּׁמֶשׁ וְהִנֵּה | דִּמְעַת
הָעֲשֻׁקִים וְאֵין לָהֶם מְנַחֵם וּמִיַּד
ב עֹשְׁקֵיהֶם כֹּחַ וְאֵין לָהֶם מְנַחֵם: וְשַׁבֵּחַ
אֲנִי אֶת־הַמֵּתִים שֶׁכְּבָר מֵתוּ מִן־הַחַיִּים
ג אֲשֶׁר הֵמָּה חַיִּים עֲדֶנָה: וְטוֹב מִשְּׁנֵיהֶם
אֵת אֲשֶׁר־עֲדֶן לֹא הָיָה אֲשֶׁר לֹא־רָאָה

1. וְשַׁבְתִּי ... וָאֶרְאֶה — *And I returned and contemplated* [lit. *'and I returned and I saw'*] With this verse, Solomon reverts to the thought stated in 3:16, *'in the place of justice is wickedness.'* He therefore uses the word *'returned'* i.e. *'I returned to that trend of thought;'* 'I reconsidered' *(Ibn Yachya).*

Rav Almosnino and *Ibn Ezra,* however, suggest that the continuity is with the preceding verse: I held that *'there is nothing better for man than to be happy in what he is doing'* [3:22] but then וְשַׁבְתִּי, *I returned and contemplated:* Happiness is good, but how can man be happy *'seeing all the acts of oppression that are committed beneath the sun'!*

אֶת־כָּל־הָעֲשֻׁקִים — *All the acts of oppression* — i.e. the crime and violence freely committed in the world *(Rav Yosef Kara).* Or, according to *Ibn Ezra* the corruption and graft — public officials always ready to take one's possessions by force.

וְהִנֵּה דִּמְעַת הָעֲשֻׁקִים — *Behold the tears of the oppressed* — i.e. I saw their tears flow — *they have no one to comfort them (Metzudas David).*

וּמִיַּד עֹשְׁקֵיהֶם כֹּחַ — *And their oppressors have the power* [lit. *'and from the hand of their oppressors is power'*] i.e. the oppressors abused their power and exercised it ruthlessly [taking advantage of the fact that onlookers were apathetic.] The victims are powerless to respond with anything but their own tears *(Ibn Ezra).*

וְאֵין לָהֶם מְנַחֵם — *With none to comfort them.* This phrase is repeated to stress that even under the most inhuman oppression, no one comes forth to comfort them *(Ibn Ezra).*

According to *Alshich:* Although the general public has sufficient power to save the downtrodden from the hands of their persecutors, no one does. And this is the cause of my pessimism.

Sforno translates the phrase differently: *'with none to exhort them to repent and seek divine comfort.'*

2-3. Koheles resolves, therefore, that the dead, who are no longer exposed to social injustices are more fortunate than the living. But most fortunate of all are the unborn who were never exposed to any form of human cruelty *(Rav Yosef Kara).*

וְשַׁבֵּחַ אֲנִי — *So I consider more*

*And I returned and contemplated all the acts of
oppression that are committed beneath the sun:
Behold! Tears of the oppressed with none to comfort
them, and their oppressors have the power — with
none to comfort them. 2 So I consider more fortunate
the dead who have already died, than the living who
are still alive; 3 but better than either of them is he
who has not yet been, and has never witnessed the*

fortunate [lit. *'And I praised'.*]

אֶת־הַמֵּתִים שֶׁכְּבָר מֵתוּ — *The dead who have already died* because they have found rest *(Ibn Ezra)*; and are no longer victimized *(Rav Kara).*

Ibn Ezra explains that people can accept calamity when it comes from the hand of God. However, they cannot bear to be victimized by a fellow human being. When that happens, they would rather be dead than alive.

Amtachas Binyamin homiletically explains the apparent redundancy *('dead who have already died')* in conjunction with the Rabbinic dictum: "Whoever wants to live in the World to Come should 'mortify himself' [i.e. detach himself] from This World." Thus: *I praised the 'dead'*, i.e. the righteous people שֶׁכְּבָר מֵתוּ מִן־הַחַיִּים who, even during their lifetime, disassociated themselves from This World by denying themselves its pleasures. Because they denied themselves the false allures of earthly life, הֵמָּה חַיִּים עֲדֶנָה — they are considered truly alive — because they live in the Eternal World.

The Sages offer various homiletical interpretations of the verse. Here are a few:

The *'dead'* refers to the Patriarchs and the *'living'* to Moses. When God wished to destroy Israel, Moses made countless supplications on their behalf, but he was not successful. But when he invoked the merit of Abraham, Isaac, and Jacob, God immediately relented [thus the dead are more 'praised' in the sense of more effective, than the living] *(Shabbos 30b)* .

According to the *Midrash, the 'dead'* refers to David, and the *'living'* to Solomon. When Solomon inaugurated the Holy Temple, no Heavenly fire came down to the altar despite his pleas. But when he invoked the merit of his father David, fire descended immediately.

...Another interpretation offered in the *Midrash* is that both references are to the Jews. When Ezekiel stood in the valley and commanded that the scattered dry bones come together and live again *(Ezekiel 37:4)*, they obeyed. He said to them: When you were alive you did not listen to the words of Jeremiah that you repent; now you listen!

וְטוֹב מִשְּׁנֵיהֶם — *But better than either*

אֶת־הַמַּעֲשֶׂה הָרָע אֲשֶׁר נַעֲשָׂה תַּחַת
ד הַשָּׁמֶשׁ: וְרָאִיתִי אֲנִי אֶת־כָּל־עָמָל וְאֵת
כָּל־כִּשְׁרוֹן הַמַּעֲשֶׂה כִּי הִיא קִנְאַת־אִישׁ
ה מֵרֵעֵהוּ גַּם־זֶה הֶבֶל וּרְעוּת רוּחַ: הַכְּסִיל
ו חֹבֵק אֶת־יָדָיו וְאֹכֵל אֶת־בְּשָׂרוֹ: טוֹב
מְלֹא כַף נָחַת מִמְּלֹא חָפְנַיִם עָמָל וּרְעוּת

of them [lit. *than the two of them*] — i.e. than the living or the dead *(Almosnino).*

אֲשֶׁר־עֲדֶן לֹא הָיָה — *who has not yet been* — the word עֲדֶן is a shortened form of עַד הֵנָּה, *as yet (Ibn Ezra).*

Most commentators interpret the phrase to mean: *'who have not been born.'*

There is a similar statement in the *Talmud:* The Schools of Hillel and Shammai disputed for two and a half years whether it is better for man that he was created, or whether it would have been better for man had he not been created. Finally they agreed that it would have been better had he not been created, but now that he was created, he should examine his deeds and live a righteous life *(Eruvin* 13b*).*

[The relevancy of the Talmudic dispute to the passage before us is more apparent than real.

Here in verses 1-3, Koheles speaks of man's relation with man, and he concludes that it would have been better to be unborn and thus never exposed to man's inhumanity to man. Further, in 9:4-5, Koheles speaks of man's responsibility *vis-a-vis* God and the almost inevitable sin and punishment resulting from man's inability to carry out his heavy responsibilities toward Him. There, Koheles declares that as long as there is life within him, man has the hope of serving God and repenting for transgressions.

But would it have been better not to have been born and thus be spared the agonizing responsibility?

Koheles does not discuss the question. It is that dilemma with which the Schools of Hillel and Shammai grappled in the *Talmud.*]

Rav Yosef Kara suggests that it refers to people of earlier generations, who lived before corruption became so rampant. They were spared the pain of bearing witness to it.

4. Now Koheles turns to those whose toil is not motivated by criminal motives. He concludes that even though most people are basically sincere, they are impelled by competition, greed and jealously. These factors are themselves 'futility and a vexation of the spirit' *(Ibn Latif).*

כִּי הִיא קִנְאַת־אִישׁ מֵרֵעֵהוּ — *Spring from man's rivalry with his neighbor* [lit. *'because it is a man's envy of his neighbor'*] Everyone wants to outdo his neighbor in status, living quarters, clothing, children, food, wisdom, and reputation *(Ibn Ezra).*

evil that is committed beneath the sun.
[4] *And I saw that all labor and all skillful enterprise spring from man's rivalry with his neighbor. This, too, is futility and a vexation of the spirit!* [5] *The fool folds his hands and eats his own flesh.* [6] *Better is one handful of pleasantness, than two fistfuls of labor and vexation of the spirit.*

גַּם־זֶה הֶבֶל וּרְעוּת רוּחַ — *This, too, is futility and a vexation of the spirit:* Because the drive is not a healthy one, and people will outdo themselves — often detrimentally — only in order to satisfy their competitive drive. Thus, they find themselves enslaved to their own passions *(Shaar Bas Rabim).*

5. הַכְּסִיל חֹבֵק אֶת־יָדָיו — *The fool folds ['hugs'] his hands.* The *fool,* the slothful indolent person, who abhors competition and performs no work for his own sustenance, [in contrast with the competitive workman of the previous verse] sits, *'with his arms folded'* and eats what he finds readily available *(Ibn Ezra).*

וְאֹכֵל אֶת־בְּשָׂרוֹ — *And eats his own flesh,* i.e. he destroys himself. He doesn't sustain himself and eventually dies of starvation *(Ibn Ezra).*

He allegorically 'lives off his fat' *(Metzudas David).*

Rashi translates הַכְּסִיל, *the fool,* in the sense of *'the wicked'* who does not work but supports himself with stolen goods. On the day of judgment he *'eats his own flesh'* [i.e. becomes embittered as in the English colloquialism 'eats his heart out'.][1]

6. טוֹב מְלֹא כַף נָחַת — *Better is one handful of pleasantness* i.e. It is better for man to earn less, but with pleasantness and quiet, that to earn more — handfuls more — through difficult labor and aggravation *(Metzudas David).*

Ibn Ezra places these words in the mouth of the 'fool' mentioned in the previous verse. He rationalizes *'folding his hands together'* — as if to say: 'I am satisfied with my one handful, why do I need more?'

מִמְּלֹא חָפְנַיִם עָמָל — *Than two fistfuls of labor* [Compare, for style and theme, Solomon's dictum in *Proverbs* 17:1: טוֹב פַּת חֲרֵבָה וְשַׁלְוָה־בָהּ מִבַּיִת מָלֵא זִבְחֵי־רִיב — *'Better is a dry morsel, and quietness with it, than a house full of strife'.*

1. The *Midrash* cites an example:
The matter may be likened to two men who were laboring in the Torah. One labored and improved while the other ultimately abandoned the study. The latter saw the former standing with the of righteous [in the Hereafter], whereas he stood with the band of the wicked. He folds his hands together and eats his flesh.

ז רוּחַ: וְשַׁבְתִּי אֲנִי וָאֶרְאֶה הֶבֶל תַּחַת
ח הַשָּׁמֶשׁ: יֵשׁ אֶחָד וְאֵין שֵׁנִי גַּם בֵּן וָאָח
אֵין־לוֹ וְאֵין קֵץ לְכָל־עֲמָלוֹ גַּם־עֵינָיו* לֹא־
תִשְׂבַּע עֹשֶׁר וּלְמִי | אֲנִי עָמֵל וּמְחַסֵּר
אֶת־נַפְשִׁי מִטּוֹבָה גַּם־זֶה הֶבֶל וְעִנְיַן רָע
ט הוּא: טוֹבִים הַשְּׁנַיִם מִן־הָאֶחָד אֲשֶׁר יֵשׁ־
י לָהֶם שָׂכָר טוֹב בַּעֲמָלָם: כִּי אִם־יִפֹּלוּ
הָאֶחָד יָקִים אֶת־חֲבֵרוֹ וְאִילוֹ הָאֶחָד

* עינו ק׳

7. וְשַׁבְתִּי אֲנִי וָאֶרְאֶה — *Then I returned and contemplated.* The word וְשַׁבְתִּי, *'and I returned'*, introduces a new thought *(Rav Saadiah Gaon).*

Solomon now turns from contemplating one sort of fool towards a different kind of fool: [the miser] *(Ibn Ezra).*

8. יֵשׁ אֶחָד וְאֵין שֵׁנִי — *[There is] a lone and solitary [man]* — [lit. *'there is one and not a second'*] i.e. he has no heirs *(Rav Almosnino).*

Rashi interprets the verse [as a reference to people in varying situations who share the same flaw: they do not bring companionship into their lives]: He is utterly alone. If he is a scholar, he seeks no student to be like a son and no friend to be like a brother; if a bachelor, he seeks no wife; if an entrepreneur, no partner. He goes his way alone *(Rashi).*

וְאֵין שֵׁנִי — *There is no second* — This may refer to a friend, servant or wife; probably the latter *(Ibn Ezra).*

וְאֵין קֵץ לְכָל־עֲמָלוֹ — *Yet there is no end to all his toil.* He works incessantly *(Kara)* only to accumulate needless riches *(Sforno).*

(According to *Rashi's* alternate interpretation, this refers to a scholar who studies incessantly, but — because he has no students, and no wife to give him children — he has no one to whom to transmit his knowledge).

גַּם־עֵינוֹ לֹא־תִשְׂבַּע עֹשֶׁר — *Nor is his eye ever sated with riches*—i.e. he is never satisfied with his lot *(Likutei Anshei Shem),* [*'eye'* representing the organ of desire; compare 1:8, *Numb.* 15:39.][1]

וּמְחַסֵּר אֶת־נַפְשִׁי מִטּוֹבָה — *And* [for whom] *am I depriving myself* [lit. *'my soul'*] *of goodness?* i.e. He never stops to ask why he works so hard, depriving himself of quiet and relaxation, not even having an heir to inherit his wealth *(Metzudas David).*

גַּם־זֶה הֶבֶל — *This, too, is futility* — The indolent *'fool'* in verse 5, who folds his hands, and the miser who

1. The *Talmud* relates a striking tale.
On one of his explorations, Alexander of Macedon received an eyeball as a gift. He weighed all his silver and gold against it, but the eyeball proved heavier. He said to the Rabbis: How is this?

IV
7-10

[7] *Then I returned and contemplated [another] futility beneath the sun:* [8] *a lone and solitary man who has neither son nor brother, yet there is no end to his toil, nor is his eye ever sated with riches, [nor does he ask himself], 'For whom am I toiling and depriving myself of goodness.' This, too, is futility; indeed, it is a sorry task.*

[9] *Two are better than one, for they get a greater return for their labor.* [10] *For should they fall, one can raise the other; but woe to him who is alone when he*

strives aimlessly — both are equally foolish. The proper approach is the middle path between laziness and over-aggressiveness *(Rav Galico; Ibn Ezra; Metzudas David).*

9. In this verse, Koheles addresses the fool who toils utterly alone, and advises him of the advantages of companionship, someone with whom to toil and share *(Ibn Ezra).*

טוֹבִים הַשְּׁנַיִם — *Two are better.* In every way *(Rashi).*

מִן־הָאֶחָד — *Than one.* Therefore man should find a comrade and marry a wife *(Rashi).*

The Sages give several instances illustrating the verse *'two are better than one.* Among them are:

Two who study Torah are better than one who studies alone, for if one errs, his partner will correct him *(Midrash;* see also *Makkos 10a);*

... As the *Talmud* notes: 'Knowledge of Torah can be acquired only in association with others' *(Berachos 63b);*

Mordechai and Esther helping and complementing one another accomplished what neither could have done alone *(Midrash);*

When Moses and Aaron blessed Israel together at the inauguration of the *Mishkan,* the Divine Presence rested upon the nation. When Moses alone blessed them, however, the Divine Presence did not rest upon them.

אֲשֶׁר יֵשׁ־לָהֶם שָׂכָר טוֹב בַּעֲמָלָם — *For they get a greater* [lit. *'good'*] *return* [lit. *'reward'*] *for their labor.* Two can accomplish more than one, because there are projects that an individual would never attempt alone *(Rashi).*

10. כִּי אִם־יִפֹּלוּ — *For should they fall* — physically; or should one of them err in Torah learning or in judgment, his comrade will correct

'It is the eyeball of a human being', they replied, 'which is never satisfied.'

They proved it by taking a little dust [symbolic of death] and covering the eyeball. Immediately it was outweighed; so it is written *(Proverbs 27:20) 'the eyes of man are never satiated' (Tamid 32b).*

יא שֶׁיִּפֹּל וְאֵין שֵׁנִי לַהֲקִימוֹ: גַּם אִם־יִשְׁכְּבוּ
יב שְׁנַיִם וְחַם לָהֶם וּלְאֶחָד אֵיךְ יֵחָם: וְאִם־
יִתְקְפוֹ הָאֶחָד הַשְּׁנַיִם יַעַמְדוּ נֶגְדּוֹ וְהַחוּט
יג הַמְשֻׁלָּשׁ לֹא בִמְהֵרָה יִנָּתֵק: טוֹב יֶלֶד
מִסְכֵּן וְחָכָם מִמֶּלֶךְ זָקֵן וּכְסִיל אֲשֶׁר לֹא־

him and set him on the proper path *(Rav Saadiah Gaon).*

וְאִילוֹ הָאֶחָד — *But woe to him who is alone* [lit. *'but woe to the one'*] אִילוֹ, in this case is a combination of two words: אִי לוֹ = אוֹי לוֹ *woe to him.*[1] The only other instance in Scriptures of אִי meaning אוֹי, *woe,* is in this Book [10:16] אִי־לָךְ אֶרֶץ, *woe is to you o earth' (Ibn Ezra).*

Targum, however, renders: וְאִילוּ = וְאִילוּ, *'but if.'*

11. [Solomon cites another example of the benefits of association.]

גַּם אִם־יִשְׁכְּבוּ שְׁנַיִם וְחַם לָהֶם — *Also if two sleep together they keep warm* — two companions huddling together in wintry weather *(Rashbam).*

Alshich explains the verse in a spiritual sense: if two people fall into spiritual slumber and neglect their religious observance, their hearts will stir within them with the 'fire of God' and each one will 'warm the heart' of his comrade to 'awaken' and serve God in the proper manner.

12. [And the final example of mutual security:]

וְהַחוּט הַמְשֻׁלָּשׁ לֹא בִמְהֵרָה יִנָּתֵק — *A three-ply cord is not easily* [lit. *'soon'*] *severed!* If the companionship of one friend yields such benefits, (above, verse 10-11) imagine the value of *two* companions! A three-ply cord is stronger than one or two plies! [i.e. as if to say: *Two are better than one; but three are better than two.*]

Rashi refers to the *Talmudic* dictum [*Bava Metzia* 85a]: If someone is a scholar, and his son and grandson are scholars as well, the Torah will nevermore cease from his seed as it is written [*Isaiah* 59:21]: *'My words . . . shall not depart from your mouth, nor from the mouth of your seed . . . nor of your seed's seed [i.e. three generations].'* These three generations of scholarship are alluded to by the strength of the *three-ply cord* in our verse. Henceforth, *(Kesubos 62b)* the Torah 'seeks its home' [i.e. the family which has been its host for three generations.][2]

The *Midrash* sums up verses 9-

1. When the *Sfas Emes* was stricken with his final illness, the *Avnei Nezer,* the Rabbi of Sochatchov, came to visit. Seeing how serious the illness was, the *Avnei Nezer* went into a room to pray. He was overheard repeating over and over: 'Woe to him who is alone when he falls and there is no one to raise him!'

Later the Rav explained what he meant: When a great man is ill, prayers for his recovery must be offered by someone of equal stature. But when someone as great as the *S'fas Emes* is so gravely ill, *'there is no one to raise him'* — no one of equal stature to pray on his behalf.

IV 11-13

falls and there is no one to raise him! 11 *Also, if two sleep together they keep warm, but how can one be warm alone?* 12 *Where one can be overpowered, two can resist attack: A three-ply cord is not easily severed!* 13 *Better is a poor but wise youth, than an old and foolish king who no longer knows how to*

12: *Two are better* [vs. 9] when they study Torah together, *than one* who labors alone. *For should they fall* [vs. 10] i.e. should one of them forget a *halachah, one can raise the other:* the other can restore it to him. *And a three-ply cord is not readily severed* [vs. 12]: this refers to a pair of scholars that has a third as a teacher who corrects their mistakes for them.

Pri Tzaddik notes that the Patriarchs: Abraham, Isaac and Jacob, are considered a three-ply cord which endures forever. They achieved this eminence with the birth of Jacob because he constituted the third generation of greatness. It is for this reason that Jacob is referred to in *Midrash Breishis* as בְּחִיר שֶׁבְּאָבוֹת, *the chosen one of the Patriarchs.* He combined within himself the virtues of Abraham, the virtues of Isaac, and his own virtues — *a three-ply cord.*

13. [Solomon now proceeds to extol the reign of wisdom, but concludes that it, too, is impermanent and ultimately futile.]

טוֹב יֶלֶד מִסְכֵּן וְחָכָם — *Better is a poor but wise youth* [lit. *'good is a child, poor and wise.'*] The verse compares the youth to a king and juxtaposes: youth / old, poor / king, wise / foolish. 'Youth' is here to be understood in the sense of an open-minded man [even though he lacks experience of the world *(Almosnino)*] who is susceptible to wise counsel, in contrast to the foolish, willful old king [who has life-experience but, being foolish, lacks the intellect to relate his observations to everyday situations] *(Ibn Ezra).*

The *Midrash* assigns a deeper meaning to the verse: The poor but wise child is the יֵצֶר הַטּוֹב, Good Inclination, which is referred to as *'youth'* — because it comes to a person only at the age of thirteen; [when a Jew reaches the age of responsibility for his deeds; see *Overview*] *'poor'* — because all do not obey it; *'wise'* — because it teaches the right way. The *old and foolish king* refers to the יֵצֶר הָרַע, Evil Inclination. It is referred to as *'king'* — because all obey it; *'old'*

2. The *Midrash* comments: There are various kinds of families: A family of scribes produces scribes; a family of Torah scholars produces Torah scholars; a family of rich men produces rich men. But, the objection was raised: 'Behold there is a certain wealthy family which became reduced and ceased to be wealthy.'

He replied: Is it written 'A threefold cord [representing three generations] is *never* severed'? It is written: 'Is not *readily* severed'! If a generation is harsh with Torah scholars, [i.e. it does not support them] it ceases to be rich.

יד יָדַע לְהִזָּהֵר עוֹד׃ כִּֽי־מִבֵּית הָסוּרִים יָצָא
טו לִמְלֹךְ כִּי גַּם בְּמַלְכוּתוֹ נוֹלַד רָשׁ׃ רָאִיתִי
אֶת־כָּל־הַחַיִּים הַמְהַלְּכִים תַּחַת הַשָּׁמֶשׁ
טז עִם הַיֶּלֶד הַשֵּׁנִי אֲשֶׁר יַעֲמֹד תַּחְתָּיו׃ אֵין־
קֵץ לְכָל־הָעָם לְכֹל אֲשֶׁר־הָיָה לִפְנֵיהֶם
גַּם הָאַחֲרוֹנִים לֹא יִשְׂמְחוּ־בוֹ כִּי־גַם־זֶה

because it clings to man from his earliest youth [thus becoming part of man many years before the Good Inclination]; *'foolish'* — because it teaches the way of evil.

אֲשֶׁר לֹא־יָדַע לְהִזָּהֵר עוֹד — *Who no longer knows how to take care of himself.* [lit. *'who no longer knows how to beware'*] He is so set in his folly that he spurns wise counsel *(Ibn Yachya).*

Some explain it as 'He did not know how to exercise proper precautions and guard his throne, thus enabling the youth to depose him *(Ibn Latif).*

The *Midrash* interprets: *'Who no longer knows how to receive admonition,'* and comments: 'Because man does not realize how much trouble and suffering come upon him, therefore he does not learn from them' [i.e. the purpose of suffering is to teach the victim that his ways are in error, but few learn the lesson.]

14. כִּי־מִבֵּית הָסוּרִים יָצָא לִמְלֹךְ — *Because from the prison-house he emerged to reign.* [This is the literal translation. The verse further describes Solomon's allegory and explains why he feels that the wise young child is superior to the old king]: Because such a wise youth would manage to find his way to the throne even if he were imprisoned *(Ibn Ezra).*

Rashi notes that the story is reminiscent of Joseph in Egypt who emerged from the dungeon to become viceroy.

(The word בֵּית הָסוּרִים = בֵּית הָאֲסוּרִים; prison-house. It lacks the א, *alef.*)

כִּי גַּם בְּמַלְכוּתוֹ נוֹלַד רָשׁ — *While even in his reign he was born* [or, *Rashi: 'has become'*] *poor.* [The translation is literal and illustrates the ambiguity of the subject and verb. The commentators suggest possible renderings for this difficult phrase]:

Rashi [holds that 'the youth' is the subject]: He was proper and worthy to assume the throne, because even during his reign he acted humble as a pauper before the Sages.

Metzudas David: 'He was fit to be king because all acclaimed him: Behold, this pauper was born for royalty — eligible to be king as if he were born king.'

Ibn Ezra [interprets the 'old king' as the subject:] 'Even the old king was born poor';

Rav Almosnino: 'Even during his reign, the old king was turned into a pauper' [by being deposed.]

Rav Yosef Kara translates the

take care of himself; 14 *because from the prison-house he emerged to reign, while even in his reign he was born poor.* 15 *I saw all the living that wander beneath the sun throng to the succeeding youth who steps into his place.* 16 *There is no end to the entire nation, to all that was before them; similarly the ones that come later will not rejoice in him. For this, too, is futlity and a vexation of the spirit.*

verse: A wise youth —even one who was imprisoned — will be successful in attaining a throne as was Joseph — but the foolish old king will be made poor; even in the midst of his reign. He will be deprived of his power because of his foolishness, as was רְחַבְעָם, Rechaboam, most of whose provinces seceded *(1 Kings 12:16).*

Sh'nos Chaim translates בֵּית הָסוּרִים — 'prison-house' as referring to the mother's womb: i.e. *'the youth was fit to reign as soon as he went forth from his mother's womb;* unlike the old foolish king, who *even in royalty was born a pauper,* i.e. a pauper in wisdom.'

15-16. [The structure of these two verses is difficult and ambiguous, but the theme comes through: Although droves of people flocked around this new young king, he himself ultimately fell into disfavor because popularity is short lived and is itself *futility, and a vexation of the spirit.*]

15. רָאִיתִי אֶת־כָּל־הַחַיִּים — *I saw all the living* [A poetic exaggeration denoting the populace of that particular kingdom.]

עִם הַיֶּלֶד הַשֵּׁנִי — *Throng to the succeeding youth* [lit. *'with the second youth'*] — i.e. the *'second'* in succession to the foolish king mentioned earlier *(Rav Yosef Kara).*

Or, according to *Metzudas David* this is the *'second youth'* i.e. the supplanter of the first youth. After deposing the old king, the wise youth ultimately lost popularity and was himself dethroned [next verse.]

Ibn Ezra suggests an entirely different interpretation: הַיֶּלֶד הַשֵּׁנִי, *the succeeding generation:* 'I contemplated all these — the members of this generation — living and inhabiting the earth; along with the succeeding generation which will follow them . . .'

16. אֵין־קֵץ לְכָל־הָעָם — *There is no end to the entire nation, to all that was before them.* [The phrase, literally translated, is ambiguous.] As culled from the commentaries, the meaning is:

There was a great multitude of people who grew disenchanted with the old, foolish monarch and replaced him with the wise youth. But, alas, גַּם הָאַחֲרוֹנִים לֹא יִשְׂמְחוּ־בוֹ, *similarly the ones that come later,*

פרק ד יז הֶבֶל וְרַעְיוֹן רוּחַ: שְׁמֹר רַגְלְיךָ* כַּאֲשֶׁר
יז תֵּלֵךְ אֶל־בֵּית הָאֱלֹהִים וְקָרוֹב לִשְׁמֹעַ
* רַגְלְךָ ק׳ מִתֵּת הַכְּסִילִים זָבַח כִּי־אֵינָם יוֹדְעִים
לַעֲשׂוֹת רָע:

i.e. the succeeding generation, *will not rejoice in him* i.e. will not continue the enthusiastic support. The rigors of just government are awesome and no policies can be universally popular. He will never be able to lead the people on the right path and, at the same time, satisfy everyone. Ultimately, they will grow disenchanted, for popularity is transient and wisdom is relative in the perspective of endless generations.

Solomon bemoans this series of events — commonplace even in our day, as *futility and a vexation of the spirit!*

17. [Having stated the main theme of his philosophy, *Koheles* now turns to a more optimistic series of thoughts. Having remonstrated against the futilities of life, Solomon now turns to the proper path a man should take in this world. In the following verses he exhorts man to serve God with dignity and respect — even in such commonplace acts as walking and talking. He begins with prayer, man's most intimate form of communication with God, and concludes that hearkening to God's Word is preferable to insincere sacrifice.]

שְׁמֹר רַגְלְךָ — *Guard your foot,* i.e. *'watch your step' (Ibn Ezra).* Guard yourself from all forms of sin when you go to the House of God *(Kara).* Avoid the obligation to go to the Temple with a required offering to atone for a sin. It is far better not to sin than to come with a sin-offering *(Metzudas David).*

וְקָרוֹב לִשְׁמֹעַ — *Better to draw near and hearken* [lit. *'and near to listen'*] This is a parenthetical phrase which some [*Rashi, Targum, Lekach Tov*] interpret as an infinitive implying a command: *'draw near to listen'* [to the Word of God; to the Teaching of the Prophets and the Sages.']

Our translation follows *Ralbag, Ibn Yachya* and *Metzudas David* who translate *'and closer* to God, i.e. preferable in His eyes, *is one who heeds . . .'*

Ibn Ezra: For God is closer and therefore more ready to listen to those who call upon Him in a spirit of sincerity, than to those who pray insincerely like fools offering sacrifice.

[Compare *1 Sam.* 15:22: *Has HASHEM as great delight in burnt offerings and sacrifices as in obedience to the voice of HASHEM?*]

מִתֵּת הַכְּסִילִים זָבַח — *Than to offer the sacrifices of fools* [lit. *than the fools' giving sacrifices*] — who sin and then use their transgression as an excuse for offering sacrifices, thinking that God delights in their offerings *(Ralbag).*

כִּי־אֵינָם יוֹדְעִים לַעֲשׂוֹת רָע — *For they* [i.e. *'the fools'*] *do not consider that*

IV
17

[17] *Guard your foot when you go to the House of God; better to draw near and hearken than to offer the sacrifices of fools, for they do not consider that they do evil.*

they do evil. The literal translation is: *For they do not know to do evil,* [so *Rashi.*] They do not even attempt to comprehend the implications of their evil. In their foolishness they think that God is pleased when they sin and offer a sacrifice in expiation *(Metzudas David).*

Ibn Ezra offers two interpretations: 'they know how to do *only* evil'; or: 'they haven't even the intelligence to do evil.'

[A similar thought is expressed of the Ninevites *(Jonah* 4:11): אֲשֶׁר לֹא־יָדַע בֵּין־יְמִינוֹ לִשְׂמֹאלוֹ *'Who cannot discern between his right and left hand'*]

Perhaps the best understanding of this verse lies in the *Talmudic* interpretation:

What is the meaning of the verse *'Guard your foot when you go to the House of God'*? Guard yourself from sinning, but in case you do sin bring an offering before Me ... *'Better to draw near and hearken'*; Be ready to hearken to the words of the wise who, if they sin, bring an offering and repent. *'But do not offer the sacrifices of fools'*: Do not be like fools who sin and bring an offering, but do not repent. *'For they do not know to do evil'*: How can that be? [If they have no knowledge of evil, then] they are righteous? It means this: Do not be like the fools who sin and bring an offering, [but do not repent and feel no remorse for what they have done. Because their offering is a meaningless ritual they] do not know whether they bring it for a good action or a bad action. Says the Holy One, blessed be He: They do not distinguish between good and evil, yet they bring an offering before Me *(Berachos* 23a).

Alshich paraphrases the verse: Guard your foot when you go to the Synagogue to pray and repent your sins. Do not turn to leave quickly as one who divests himself of a load for God is near to respond to your prayers — nearer than He is to receive the sacrifices of fools, for they, lacking knowledge of Torah, do not comprehend that they have sinned.

פרק ה

א אַל־תְּבַהֵל עַל־פִּיךָ וְלִבְּךָ אַל־יְמַהֵר
לְהוֹצִיא דָבָר לִפְנֵי הָאֱלֹהִים כִּי הָאֱלֹהִים
בַּשָּׁמַיִם וְאַתָּה עַל־הָאָרֶץ עַל־כֵּן יִהְיוּ
ב דְבָרֶיךָ מְעַטִּים׃ כִּי בָּא הַחֲלוֹם בְּרֹב עִנְיָן
ג וְקוֹל כְּסִיל בְּרֹב דְּבָרִים׃ כַּאֲשֶׁר תִּדֹּר
נֶדֶר לֵאלֹהִים אַל־תְּאַחֵר לְשַׁלְּמוֹ כִּי אֵין
ד חֵפֶץ בַּכְּסִילִים אֵת אֲשֶׁר־תִּדֹּר שַׁלֵּם׃ טוֹב
אֲשֶׁר לֹא־תִדֹּר מִשֶּׁתִּדּוֹר וְלֹא תְשַׁלֵּם׃

א־ד

1. אַל־תְּבַהֵל עַל־פִּיךָ — *Be not rash* [lit. *'hasten'*] *with your mouth.* i.e. do not be hasty to comment *(Metzudas David)* without thinking first *(Ibn Latif).*

לְהוֹצִיא דָבָר לִפְנֵי הָאֱלֹהִים — *To utter a word before God* i.e. to speak critically of Him *(Rashi).*

When man suffers, let him not speak irreverently against his Creator, as is recorded of Job: *'In all this Job did not sin with his lips'* [*Job* 2:10] *(Midrash Lekach Tov).*

כִּי הָאֱלֹהִים בַּשָּׁמַיִם וְאַתָּה עַל־הָאָרֶץ — *For God is in heaven and you are on earth.* i.e. God rules the world, and lowly man cannot presume to fathom His method of ruling His creatures *(Lekach Tov).*

Rashi quotes the *Midrash*: 'If the weak one is above and the strong one below, the fear of the weak one is upon the strong one; how much more so when it is the strong One [God] Who is above and the weak one [mortal man] below [we should surely be in awe of Him and not speak rashly of Him.']

[As the Prophet said (*Isaiah* 55:9) *'For as the heavens are higher than the earth, so are My ways higher than your ways and My thoughts than your thoughts'.*]

עַל־כֵּן יִהְיוּ דְבָרֶיךָ מְעַטִּים — *So let your words be few. Rashbam* and *Ibn Ezra* interpret this as an exhortation against long prayer: When you pray, do not needlessly multiply words before God, for He is exalted and must be approached with reverence rather than with verbosity.

. . . As did Moses when he prayed for his sister with a prayer composed of only five words [*Num.* 12:13]: אֵל נָא רְפָא נָא לָהּ, *Please God, please heal her* , and as did the High Priest on Yom Kippur when he recited a concise prayer [*Yoma* 52b] *(Rav Galico).*

2. כִּי בָּא הַחֲלוֹם בְּרֹב עִנְיָן — *For a dream comes from much concern.* [Solomon employs the simile of dreams to lend cogency to the earlier exhortation against excess verbiage.]: Dreams reflect an overabundance of [unrelated] fleeting thoughts, and overanxiety in practical affairs. Similarly, excessive use of words [often as incoherent and unrelated as in a dream *(Akeidas Yitzchak)*] betrays the fool. Therefore *'let your words be few' (Rashi).*

V
1-4

Be not rash with your mouth, and let not your heart be hasty to utter a word before God; for God is in heaven and you are on earth, so let your words be few. 2 *For a dream comes from much concern, and foolish talk from many words.* 3 *When you make a vow to God, do not delay paying it, for He has no liking for fools; what you vow, pay.* 4 *Better that you not vow at all, than that you vow and not*

3. כַּאֲשֶׁר תִּדֹּר נֶדֶר לֵאלֹהִים — *When you make a vow to God,* to perform a righteous deed *(Metzudas David).*

[Quoted almost verbatim from *Deut.* 23:22.]

Just as you are exhorted to guard your tongue in the House of God, and speak little, so should you exercise caution in every utterance you make before Him [as when you make vows] and not be like the fools for whom He has no use *(Ibn Ezra).*

אַל־תְּאַחֵר לְשַׁלְּמוֹ — *Do not delay paying it. Alshich* cautions that one who made a vow to give charity as a result of being subjected to great suffering, should fulfill the vow immediately without waiting for the suffering to end. Proper belief in God dictates that the vow be discharged immediately.

כִּי אֵין חֵפֶץ בַּכְּסִילִים — *For He has no liking for fools* [lit. *'for there is no desire in fools'*.] The translation follows *Rashi, Targum* and most commentators: 'There is no wish before the Holy One, blessed be He, for wicked men who vow but do not fulfill.'

Metzudas David translates: חֵפֶץ as *'desire', 'will'*: there is no consistent will in fools. At one moment they will desire something, but in the next moment they want it no longer. Whoever vows is considered a fool [because a vow is made in a moment of exultation, often to be ignored later.] Therefore, *'do not delay in paying it'*, because the fervor may evaporate with time and with it the inclination to pay. Therefore: אֵת אֲשֶׁר־תִּדֹּר שַׁלֵּם, *what you vow, pay* — immediately and without delay.

4. טוֹב אֲשֶׁר לֹא־תִדֹּר — *Better that you not vow at all.* As in the verse of the Torah [*Deut.* 23:23]: *'then no sin will be upon you'*[1] *(Ibn Ezra).*

Rav Meir said: Preferable to both [i.e. vowing and not paying, and even vowing and paying] is not to vow at all. Rather let the man bring his lamb to the Temple [without previously making a vow to bring it], dedicate it, and have it offered *(Midrash).*

If you don't have the money, why vow? Wait until the money is

1. From the commentary of *Rav S.R. Hirsch* on *Deut. 23:23:*

Making vows is not only in itself nothing meritorious, but actually belongs to the sphere of the sinful. 'Everybody who vows, although he keeps his vow, is called a sinner,' is a principle

פרק ה ה אַל־תִּתֵּן אֶת־פִּיךָ לַחֲטִיא אֶת־בְּשָׂרֶךָ
ה־ו וְאַל־תֹּאמַר לִפְנֵי הַמַּלְאָךְ כִּי שְׁגָגָה הִיא
לָמָּה יִקְצֹף הָאֱלֹהִים עַל־קוֹלֶךָ וְחִבֵּל
ו אֶת־מַעֲשֵׂה יָדֶיךָ: כִּי בְרֹב חֲלֹמוֹת

in your hand and give it then *(Ibn Yachya).*

[However, in time of trouble, it is commendable to make vows for charity, or vows to do good deeds, as we find *'and Jacob vowed a vow' (Gen.* 28:20; *Tosafos, Chullin* 2b). It is also commendable to make a vow to strengthen one's resolve to perform good deeds *Nedarim* 8a).].

מִשֶּׁתִּדּוֹר וְלֹא תְשַׁלֵּם — *Than that you vow and do not pay.*

[Hence the praiseworthy custom of saying 'בְּלִי נֶדֶר', *'without a vow.'* Thereby, although the speaker still obligates himself to keep his word, he avoids the transgression of breaking a vow in the event he is unable to do so.]

Also implied by this verse is that one should pay his personal debts before vowing to give to charity: *Better that you not vow at all than vow and not pay others* the debt you owe them. Charity is meaningful when it is given from one's *own* money, not from money he owes to others *(Shevet Reuven).*

5. אַל־תִּתֵּן אֶת־פִּיךָ — *Let not your mouth.* By uttering a vow *(Rashi).*

לַחֲטִיא אֶת־בְּשָׂרֶךָ — [*to*] *bring guilt on* [or: *'to'*] *your flesh.* The *Midrash* comments: 'let not one organ [your mouth] bring punishment upon all your organs.' i.e. Do not let vain promises made with your mouth, bring sin and punishment upon your whole person *(Ibn Ezra; Alshich).*

[As it is written [*Deut.* 23:22]: כִּי דָרֹשׁ יִדְרְשֶׁנּוּ ... מֵעִמָּךְ וְהָיָה בְךָ חֵטְא *For HASHEM your God will surely demand payment of it from you, and there would be sin upon you.*]

The *Talmud,* however, [and many commentators], interprets *'flesh'* as "the members of one's family": 'For all the transgressions in the Torah the sinner alone is punished, but here both he and his family may be punished, for it is said, *"Do not let your mouth bring guilt on your flesh"*; and "flesh" means "near relative," as in the verse [*Isaiah* 58:7] וּמִבְּשָׂרְךָ לֹא תִתְעַלָּם, *"And from your own* flesh *do not hide yourself." (Shevuos* 39a*).*

In consonance with this, *Rashi* translates *'children'*; [see excerpt from *Talmud,* tractate *Shabbos* 32b, quoted next page.]

וְאַל־תֹּאמַר לִפְנֵי הַמַּלְאָךְ — *And do not tell the messenger.* The representative of the congregation who comes to collect the proceeds of the vow *(Midrash; Rashi; Kara).*

Alshich and *Ibn Ezra* understand

of our sages. It would have been more right if the good deed had been done without its having been vowed, for it says: 'But if you refrain to make vows then no sin will be upon you' — hence if you have not refrained there is sin (Nedarim 77b). 'Making vows is similar to erecting a בָּמָה, *bama' [altar] — at the time when such alters are forbidden [Deut. 12:13; see*

pay. 5 *Let not your mouth bring guilt on your flesh, and do not tell the messenger that it was an error. Why should God be angered by your speech and destroy the work of your hands?* 6 *In spite of all*

the term מַלְאָךְ in its Biblical sense: *Angel of God* — 'whose role it is to keep a record of all man's utterances' *(Ibn Ezra)* and will one day act as God's messenger to exact punishment from man for his delinquency *(Alshich).*

Sforno, on the other hand, explains the word here as referring to the 'messenger' i.e. the scholar who will be called upon to annul the vow.

כִּי שְׁגָגָה הִיא — *That it was an error.* — i.e. that the vow was made in error with the intention of paying it *(Kara),* but the the vower does not have the funds *(Metzudas David).*

Or, as *Midrash Lekach Tov* translates: *It is an error!:* I am doubtful whether I ever did, in fact, utter the vow.

לָמָּה יִקְצֹף הָאֱלֹהִים — *Why should God be angered?* i.e. Why should you act this way and provoke God's anger *(Metzudas David).*

עַל־קוֹלֶךָ — *By your speech* [lit. *'at your voice'*] — at the voice with which you uttered the violated vow *(Midrash).*

וְחִבֵּל אֶת־מַעֲשֵׂה יָדֶיךָ — *And destroy the work of your hands* — God brings a curse on the few מִצְוֹת, *pious acts,* which are in the hands of that man, and causes them to be lost to him *(Rashi; Midrash).*

Man is blessed in all his endeavors through the merit of charity. Conversely, when he publicly vows and then withholds payment of charity, his endeavors are destroyed *(Metzudas David).*

In the *Talmud 'works of the hands'* refers to *'children':* For the sin of [unfulfilled] vows one's children die young, as it is written: *'. . . and destroy the work of your hands.'* What is the work of a man's hands? — It is a man's sons and daughters *(Shabbos* 32b*).*

This illustrates the importance of *'letting your words be few.'* Not only with reference to mundane talk, but even concerning a meritorious act, one should limit one's speech. What is the purpose of vowing in advance? When you have the money — give it immediately without first vowing.' *(Taalumos Chachmah).*

6. כִּי בְרֹב חֲלֹמוֹת . . . — *In spite of all dreams, futility, and idle chatter, rather: Fear God* [lit. *'for in a multitude of dreams and futilities and much words (or: 'things') fear God]*

The verse is difficult in syntax and the translation follows most commentators who counsel that one should ignore all contrary influences (dreams, vain prophets,

Zevachim 112b]. Both are sins of similar nature, both perpetrators think they can do something special to please God, something beyond what He has commanded us to do [*Ran to Nedarim 22a.*]

וַהֲבָלִים וּדְבָרִים הַרְבֵּה כִּי אֶת־הָאֱלֹהִים
ז יְרָא: אִם־עֹשֶׁק רָשׁ וְגֵזֶל מִשְׁפָּט וָצֶדֶק
תִּרְאֶה בַמְּדִינָה אַל־תִּתְמַהּ עַל־הַחֵפֶץ כִּי
גָבֹהַּ מֵעַל גָּבֹהַּ שֹׁמֵר וּגְבֹהִים עֲלֵיהֶם:
ח וְיִתְרוֹן אֶרֶץ בַּכֹּל הִיא* מֶלֶךְ לְשָׂדֶה נֶעֱבָד:

* הוא ק׳

and idle chatter) and, instead, Fear God.[1]

The *Midrash* advises: 'If you see ill-omened dreams and ill-omened, confusing visions of which you are afraid, take hold of three things and you will be delivered from them: . . . prayer, charity and repentance . . . Likewise a change of name and a change of conduct' [or: a change of profession *(Torah Temimah)*] annul evil decrees. Some add: Also a change of place [residence.]

According to *Sforno:* Rash vows must often be inspired by bad dreams and other external, misleading factors. Hence, the admonition of this verse that preoccupation with these matters will give rise to many words (careless vows) — let the fear of God dispel such vain fears; vows are unnecessary.

כִּי אֶת־הָאֱלֹהִים יְרָא — *Rather: Fear God!* [The translation *'rather'*, (אֶלָּא) for כִּי *('but')* follows *Rashi;*] — and He will guard you from all evil *(Metzudas David).*

7. בַּמְּדִינָה — *In the State.* i.e. open and brazen oppression, rather than stealthy and clandestine *(Ibn Ezra).*

אַל־תִּתְמַהּ עַל־הַחֵפֶץ — *Do not be astonished at the fact* [or: *'at the Will'*] i.e. Do not be astonished that God *seems* to approve of this, and is 'slow' in exacting retribution *(Almosnino).*

כִּי גָבֹהַּ מֵעַל גָּבֹהַּ — *For* [have faith that]: *there is One higher than high* [lit. *'because Higher upon Higher'*] i.e. God. Do not despair at the impunity and freedom from retribution with which unscrupulous wielders of power oppress the helpless. Know that the most august of all beings, God, who is *Higher than High,* sees what they do and will avenge the victims when the proper time comes *(Rav Saadiah Gaon; Sforno; Kara; Taalumos Chachmah; Ralbag).* Or according to others *(Midrash; Midrash Lekach Tov; Ibn Ezra;): Higher than high* refers to the angels [who are 'higher than man'.]

שֹׁמֵר — *Who watches,* i.e. who waits patiently — As in *Gen.* 37:11 וְאָבִיו שָׁמַר אֶת הַדָּבָר — *But his father kept the matter in mind* [i.e. שָׁמַר, waited patiently for the result]. God waits, but He will punish them in the proper time *(Rashi; Saadiah; Kara; et al.)*

1. The *Midrash* relates that when Hezekiah fell ill, God said to Isaiah, 'Go and tell him, *Set your house in order, for you shall die and not live'* [*Isaiah* 38:1.]

Isaiah went and told him and Hezekiah answered: 'Isaiah, it is usual for a person visiting an invalid to say to him "May mercy be shown you from Heaven," and the physician prescribes a diet for him. Even when the visitor sees him near death, he does not say to him, 'Set your house in order,' that his mind not be upset. You, however, tell me, *'Set your house in order,*

dreams, futility and idle chatter, rather: Fear God!

7 *If you see oppression of the poor, and the suppression of justice and right in the State, do not be astonished at the fact, for there is One higher than the high Who watches and there are high ones above them.*

8 *The advantage of land is supreme; even a king is indebted to the soil.*

[As it is written above 3:17: *God will judge the righteous and the wicked for there is a time for every event and every deed.*]

וּגְבֹהִים עֲלֵיהֶם — *And [there are] high ones above them.* According to the first view cited above [*Rav Saadiah,* et al and *Rashi:*] this refers to the angels whom God appointed to eventually punish the oppressors [and who are 'higher' than the oppressed. According to the latter view *(Midrash, et al)* this high One is the Holy One, blessed be He Himself. (The plural גְּבוֹהִים — suggests the royal plural, as in *Joshua. 24:19* כִּי אֱלֹהִים קְדֹשִׁים הוּא — [*Midrash Lekach Tov*]).

8. וְיִתְרוֹן אֶרֶץ בַּכֹּל הִיא — *The advantage of land* [i.e. of agriculture] *is supreme* [lit. *'the advantage of land is in everything'*] even a king is indebted [i.e. subject] *to the soil.* The phrase is obscure and the translation follows *Ibn Ezra* who comments: Having discoursed on the fear of God, Solomon reverts to the theme of which occupation is best, and most sin-free. Agriculture yields the most reward. Even a king is sustained by the soil. . . .

And whoever tills the land, living a righteous life and providing honestly for his own sustenance, is assured a life of dignity likened to a king, who must himself be sustained by the produce of the earth. The miser in the next verse, however, loves money — rather than honest work — and steals to satisfy his lust for it. לֹא־יִשְׂבַּע כֶּסֶף — *he will never be* satisfied with money *(Alshich).*

The *Midrash,* too, ties this verse to the following and translates: *'Moreover the profit ['advantage'] of the earth is in all things,'* and comments:

'Even things which you deem superfluous in the world are essential parts of its composition, e.g. palm-fibre for the making of ropes, and twigs for the formation of garden-hedges are essential parts of the world's composition . . .

for you will die and not live!' I ignore what you say, and I will not heed your advice. I accept only what my ancestor [David] said: Even if a sharp sword rests upon a man's neck he should not desist from prayer ... and what my ancestor [Solomon] said: *"In spite of ... much words . . fear God!"* '

Immediately [next verse] *'Hezekiah turned his face to the wall [and prayed to* HASHEM*] and said "Remember now,* HASHEM*, I beseech, You, how I have walked before You in truth and*

פרק ה ט אֹהֵב כֶּסֶף לֹא־יִשְׂבַּע כֶּסֶף וּמִי־אֹהֵב
ט־יב י בֶּהָמוֹן לֹא תְבוּאָה גַּם־זֶה הָבֶל׃ בִּרְבוֹת
הַטּוֹבָה רַבּוּ אוֹכְלֶיהָ וּמַה־כִּשְׁרוֹן
ראות ק׳ יא לִבְעָלֶיהָ כִּי אִם־רְאִית עֵינָיו׃ מְתוּקָה
שְׁנַת הָעֹבֵד אִם־מְעַט וְאִם־הַרְבֵּה יֹאכֵל
יב וְהַשָּׂבָע לֶעָשִׁיר אֵינֶנּוּ מַנִּיחַ לוֹ לִישׁוֹן׃ יֵשׁ

Similarly, flies, fleas, and gnats are an essential part of the world's constitution.

A king makes himself servant to the field: Even if a king has dominion, from one end of the earth to the other, he is enslaved to the soil. If the field produces, he can achieve something, but if the soil is unproductive he can achieve nothing (*Midrash;* [see also *comm.* of *Midrash* on next verse]).

9. אֹהֵב כֶּסֶף לֹא־יִשְׂבַּע כֶּסֶף — *A lover of money* [lit. *'silver'*] *will never be satisfied with money* [*'silver'*]. [For as the *Midrash* notes (above, on 1:13) 'He who has a hundred wants two hundred, and he who has two hundred wants four hundred.']

Akeidas Yitzchak notes: *'He will never be satisfied with money'* — i.e. money will never still a rich man's hunger, for who can eat money?

The *Talmud (Makkos 10a)* interprets this verse as a homiletical reference to Moses: One who loves good deeds never has his fill of good deeds. Although Moses knew he would not live to designate the three cities of refuge in *Eretz Yisrael* proper, he nevertheless did not let the opportunity slip by and he designated the first three cities on the eastern side of the River Jordan.

וּמִי־אֹהֵב ... — *A lover of abundance has no wheat* [lit. *'and who loves abundance, no wheat.'*] i.e. he who surrounds himself with an abundance of non-productive servants in order to impress his friends will *'have no wheat'* i.e. will not be able to feed and sustain them and, what is more, he will have nothing left for himself as explained in the next verse *(Kara; Lekach Tov; Sforno; Metzudas David).*

Rashi comments, he who loves to accumulate [inedible] money, rather than nourishing *wheat, indulges in futility.*

[The *Midrash,* continues its commentary to the preceding verse, extolling the importance of agriculture, as opposed to the fleeting nature of coin. Abundance of money without agricultural produce is futile — ephemeral and uncertain. The *Midrash* thus translates]: *Nor he that loves an abundance* [of money] *without*

with a perfect heart, and have done that which is good in Your sight." And Hezekiah wept grievously.' (ibid. verses 2-3*).*]

Forthwith, *the word of* H*ASHEM came to Isaiah saying: 'Go and say to Hezekiah . . . I have heard your prayer. . .'*

'Lord of the Universe', said Isaiah, 'at first You tell me one prophecy and now another? How can I go and tell him this?'

9 *A lover of money will never be satisfied with money; a lover of abundance has no wheat. This, too, is futility!* 10 *As goods increase, so do those who consume them; what advantage, then, has the owner except what his eyes see?* 11 *Sweet is the sleep of the laborer, whether he eats little or much; the satiety of the rich does not let him sleep.*

[earth] *produce: this also is futility.* If someone is greedy and covetous of money, but has no land, what benefit does he derive?

10. בִּרְבוֹת הַטּוֹבָה רַבּוּ אוֹכְלֶיהָ — *As goods increase, so do those who consume them.* A wealthier household acquires a larger stock of food and supplies and attracts more relatives, friends, and paupers. The owner sees before him a larger supply of provisions, speedily to be consumed. Thus, he is often in a worse position than he was before *(Ibn Yachya; Rav Yosef Kara; Ibn Latif).*

וּמַה־כִּשְׁרוֹן לִבְעָלֶיהָ — *What advantage, then, has the owner* [following *Ibn Ezra; Metzudas David;* or: *What good is the owner's 'skill'*, as כִּשְׁרוֹן is translated in 2:21.]

The *Midrash* homiletically comments: when those destined to eat good things increase in number [i.e. when the population of the world increases] the good things are increased in quantity [God provides more sustenance to the world to meet the need. An appropriate response to those advocates of zero population growth!]

11. מְתוּקָה שְׁנַת הָעֹבֵד — *Sweet is the sleep of the laborer.* The man who is not indolent, and does not work only in order to hoard riches, but who tills the ground earnestly to support his family is extolled in this verse. Such a man has his concerns. He has no large estates or fortunes over which to worry constantly. Whether he eats little or much, he is able to sleep undisturbed by business worries *(Rav Yosef Kara).*

וְהַשָּׂבָע לֶעָשִׁיר אֵינֶנּוּ מַנִּיחַ לוֹ לִישׁוֹן — *The satiety of the rich does not let him sleep.* [Koheles does not refer to physical satiety; that would affect the rich and poor man alike:] The reference is to the abundant possessions of the rich *(Ibn Ezra)*: It fills him with worry and anxious cares which deprive him of his sleep *(Rashi; Lekach Tov).*

The Sages similarly expounded this concept in the *Mishnah* [*Avos* 2:7]: מַרְבֶּה נְכָסִים מַרְבֶּה דְאָגָה, 'the more possessions the more worry' *(Rav Yosef Kara).*

'Hezekiah is a humble man,' replied Hashem*, 'He will accept it from you. Furthermore, the report has not yet gone out'* [to the ears of the people, who might find it difficult to understand the two different messages brought in the name of God.]

When *Isaiah* went to him with the second message, Hezekiah exclaimed: 'Did I not tell you, *In spite of ... much words ... indeed, Fear God!' (Berachos 10a; Midrash)*

רָעָה חוֹלָה רָאִיתִי תַּחַת הַשָּׁמֶשׁ עֹשֶׁר
יג שָׁמוּר לִבְעָלָיו לְרָעָתוֹ: וְאָבַד הָעֹשֶׁר
הַהוּא בְּעִנְיַן רָע וְהוֹלִיד בֵּן וְאֵין בְּיָדוֹ
יד מְאוּמָה: כַּאֲשֶׁר יָצָא מִבֶּטֶן אִמּוֹ עָרוֹם
יָשׁוּב לָלֶכֶת כְּשֶׁבָּא וּמְאוּמָה לֹא־יִשָּׂא
טו בַעֲמָלוֹ שֶׁיֹּלֵךְ בְּיָדוֹ: וְגַם־זֹה רָעָה חוֹלָה
כָּל־עֻמַּת שֶׁבָּא כֵּן יֵלֵךְ וּמַה־יִּתְרוֹן לוֹ
טז שֶׁיַּעֲמֹל לָרוּחַ: גַּם כָּל־יָמָיו בַּחֹשֶׁךְ יֹאכֵל

12-13. רָעָה חוֹלָה — *A sickening* [lit. *'sick'*] *evil* [i.e. an unusually grievous injustice.] This verse continues extolling the benefits of owning real property rather than money *(Ibn Ezra).*

עֹשֶׁר שָׁמוּר לִבְעָלָיו לְרָעָתוֹ — *Riches hoarded* [lit. *'guarded'*] *by their owner to his misfortune.* According to *Ibn Ezra* the translation is: riches hoarded not *by* the owner but, by a guardian *for* their owner. Thus, next verse, when the riches are lost it is a double catastrophe.

His wealth frequently jeopardizes his personal safety, as when robbers kidnap and even slay him *(Sforno).*

Rashi cites as an example, the wealth of Korach which led to his unrealistic ambitions and his eventual downfall [see *Numbers 16].*

[An example of such a *'sickening evil'* is given in the following verse]:

וְאָבַד הָעֹשֶׁר הַהוּא בְּעִנְיַן רָע — *And he loses* [lit. *'lost'*] *those riches in some* [unlucky] *bad venture.* He loses his [or another's — (see *Ibn Ezra* above)] riches by some misfortune and has nothing left to bequeath to his heirs *(Ibn Yachya).*

— The result is that all his sleepless nights worrying about his treasures [verse 11] were totally in vain *(Rav Yosef Kara).*

וְהוֹלִיד בֵּן — *If he begets a son* [lit. *'and he begat a son'*]. The further irony is that when he possessed the treasure he had no heir; only now that he is penniless is a child born *(Akeidas Yitzchak).*

14. עָרוֹם יָשׁוּב לָלֶכֶת כְּשֶׁבָּא — *Naked will he return as he had come.* [The translation follows the punctuation which has a minor pause (זָקֵף קָטוֹן) after מִבֶּטֶן אִמּוֹ — *his mother's womb,* and attaches עָרוֹם to the second clause. It is also in consonance with a parallel verse in *Job* 1:21: *'Naked I came out of my mother's womb and naked I shall return there.'*]

Metzudas David, connecting עָרוֹם, *naked,* to the first clause, translates: *'As he had come naked from his mother's womb, so will he return, as he had come.'* The *'nakedness'* of the return is a figure of speech meaning *'he can salvage nothing from his labor . . . '*

This verse is to be understood, not as a separate thought, but as a description of the son mentioned in the preceding verse *(Rav Saadiah Gaon).*

וּמְאוּמָה לֹא־יִשָּׂא בַעֲמָלוֹ שֶׁיֹּלֵךְ בְּיָדוֹ —

12 *There is a sickening evil which I have seen under*
the sun: riches hoarded by their owner to his misfor-
tune, 13 *and he loses those riches in some bad ven-*
ture. If he begets a son, he has nothing in hand. 14 *As*
he had come from his mother's womb, naked will he
return, as he had come; he can salvage nothing from
his labor to take with him. 15 *This, too, is a sickening*
evil: Exactly as he came he must depart, and what did
he gain by toiling for the wind? 16 *Indeed, all his life*
he eats in darkness; he is greatly grieved, and has

He can salvage nothing from his labor to take with him. When a person enters this world his hands are clenched as if to say: 'The whole world is mine, I shall inherit it'; but when he takes leave of the world, his hands are spread open as if to say: 'I have inherited nothing from the world.' *(Midrash).*[1]

15. וְגַם־זֹה רָעָה חוֹלָה — *This, too, is a sickening evil* i.e. that mentioned in verse 14: *'as he came — naked, so will he return' (Ibn Latif).*

כָּל־עֻמַּת שֶׁבָּא כֵּן יֵלֵךְ — *Exactly as he came he must depart.* i.e. *'naked'* in elaboration of the preceding verse *(Ibn Ezra); or, according to Rashi:* 'just as the money came, it will depart'.

The *Midrash* comments: 'As man comes into the world so weak that he must be fed cereal, so when he goes, in his feeble old age, he must be fed cereal.'

שֶׁיַּעֲמֹל לָרוּחַ — *By toiling for* [lit. *'to'*] *the wind.* [i.e. toiling hopelessly, seeking something without substance. See *commentary* to 1:14 s.v. וּרְעוּת רוּחַ.]

Although, in essence, man does not actually 'lose' in this world, because he arrived here naked and penniless, and can never leave with less, nonetheless, people should evaluate their lives as they would a business. In commerce, a concern that shows no profit, is considered a losing business. So, too, with a life. Unless someone can show significant achievement, he should feel dissatisfied *(Imrei Shefer).*

16. גַּם כָּל־יָמָיו בַּחֹשֶׁךְ יֹאכֵל — *Indeed, all his life he eats in darkness.* Being obsessively overcome with accumulating riches, he sits down to eat only at night. He thus lives a life of rigorous self-denial, fear of robbery, and exposes himself to many trying experiences *(Ibn Ezra; Akeidas Yitzchak; Metzudas David).*

Ibn Janach translates: *'in miserliness'* [sitting 'in darkness' being the epitome of poverty and the ultimate parsimony of the miser.]

1. The *Midrash* illustrates this with a parable:

A fox once came upon a vineyard that was entirely fenced in except for one opening too small for it to enter through. So he fasted three days until he became lean enough to squeeze through the hole. He ate of the grapes and regained his former size so that when he wished to exit, he discovered to his dismay that he was too large to fit through.

He fasted another three days, became lean and emaciated, and went out. When he was out-

יז וְכָעַס הַרְבֵּה וְחָלְיוֹ וָקָצֶף: הִנֵּה אֲשֶׁר־
רָאִיתִי אָנִי טוֹב אֲשֶׁר־יָפֶה לֶאֱכוֹל־
וְלִשְׁתּוֹת וְלִרְאוֹת טוֹבָה בְּכָל־עֲמָלוֹ |
שֶׁיַּעֲמֹל תַּחַת־הַשֶּׁמֶשׁ מִסְפַּר יְמֵי־חַיָּו*
יח אֲשֶׁר־נָתַן־לוֹ הָאֱלֹהִים כִּי־הוּא חֶלְקוֹ: גַּם
כָּל־הָאָדָם אֲשֶׁר נָתַן־לוֹ הָאֱלֹהִים עֹשֶׁר
וּנְכָסִים וְהִשְׁלִיטוֹ לֶאֱכֹל מִמֶּנּוּ וְלָשֵׂאת
אֶת־חֶלְקוֹ וְלִשְׂמֹחַ בַּעֲמָלוֹ זֹה מַתַּת
יט אֱלֹהִים הִיא: כִּי לֹא הַרְבֵּה יִזְכֹּר אֶת־יְמֵי
חַיָּיו כִּי הָאֱלֹהִים מַעֲנֶה בְּשִׂמְחַת לִבּוֹ:

*חַיָּיו ק׳

וְחָלְיוֹ — *And has illness* [an abbreviation of two words: וְחוּלִי לוֹ, *sickness is his,* as *Genesis* 22:24 וּפִלַגְשׁוֹ = וּפִלֶגֶשׁ לוֹ *(Ramban)*]

Sforno interprets this as the 'sickness of wealthy people': miserliness, and the desire to die.

17.-18. These two verses are essentially a restatement of the conclusion Solomon reached in earlier discourses: (2:24; 3:12,22). Since man must depart exactly as he came, I concluded that financial pursuits are worthless. Let man rather involve himself in Torah pursuits *(Rashi),* and let him eat of God's bounty and be content *(Ibn Yachya; Ibn Ezra).*

לֶאֱכוֹל וְלִשְׁתּוֹת — *To eat and drink.* Note the *Midrash:* All the eating and drinking mentioned in this Book, refers to Torah and good deeds. The most clear proof is 8:15. Do, then, food and drink accompany man to the grave? What does accompany him? Torah and good deeds.

וְלִרְאוֹת טוֹבָה — *And enjoy pleasure* [lit. *'and see good';* comp. 2:1] i.e. indulge in Torah study and be satisfied with his lot *(Rashi).*

בְּכָל־עֲמָלוֹ — *With all one's labor* — i.e. with the fruit of one's labor that he accumulated in this world *(Metzudas David).*

מִסְפַּר יְמֵי־חַיָּו — *During the brief span of his life* [comp. 2:3].

כִּי־הוּא חֶלְקוֹ — *For that is his lot.* i.e. God bequeathed these few pleasures to man so it is only proper that man harness them and, by utilizing them for the proper spiritual goals, lift himself up to the greater service of God *(Almosnino).*

[See *comm.* to similar phrase on 3:22.]

נָתַן־לוֹ הָאֱלֹהִים עֹשֶׁר וּנְכָסִים — *To whom God has given riches and possessions.* [To approach the essence of this verse I quote from a passage in *Horeb* on *Tzedakah* by *Rav S.R. Hirsch*]: 'Why should God give you more than you need

side, he turned his face and gazing at the vineyard, said: 'Vineyard, Vineyard! You are beautiful and your fruit is sweet. But what benefit does one have from you? As one enters you so he leaves.' Such is this world.

illness and anger.

[17] *So what I have seen to be good is that it is suitable to eat and drink and enjoy pleasure with all one's labor that he toils beneath the sun during the brief span of his life that God has given him, for that is his lot.* [18] *Furthermore, every man to whom God has given riches and possessions and has given him the power to enjoy them, possess his share and be happy in his work: this is the gift of God.* [19] *For he shall remember that the days of his life are not many, while God provides him with the joy of his heart.*

unless He intended to make you the administrator of this blessing for others, the treasurer of His treasures? Every penny you can spare is not yours, but should become a tool for bringing blessing to others. Would you close your hand on something that is not yours?'

וְהִשְׁלִיטוֹ לֶאֱכֹל מִמֶּנּוּ — *And has given him the power to enjoy* [lit. *'eat'*] *them* i.e. gave him the merit [and desire *(Metzudas David)*] to derive joy from it *(Sforno)*, during his own lifetime *(Rashi)*, rather than hoard it *(Alshich)*.

וְלָשֵׂאת אֶת־חֶלְקוֹ — [*And*] *possess* [lit. *'carry'*] *his share* after death *(Rashi)*. i.e. to perform meritorious deeds with his treasure so that he can 'carry' his merit along with him to the Hereafter [Treasure does not accompany man; only the merit of the good deeds he performs with his resources.] *(Almusnino)*.

מַתַּת אֱלֹהִים הִיא—*This is the gift of God.* This applies only to a select group in whom God especially delights *(Midrash)* for only a small minority of those who are blessed with wealth, earn the additional blessing of partaking of it themselves in the Hereafter by virtue of their good deeds *(Sforno)*.

כִּי לֹא הַרְבֵּה יִזְכֹּר אֶת־יְמֵי חַיָּיו — *For he shall [himself] remember that the days of his life are not many.* [lit. *'for not much will he remember the days of his life'*]. The words are out of order and the translation follows most commentators: *Alshich; Ibn Ezra; Rashi; and Kara* who adds: and therefore he will be sure to enjoy his possessions while still alive.

כִּי הָאֱלֹהִים מַעֲנֶה בְּשִׂמְחַת לִבּוֹ — *While God provides him* [i.e. *'responds'*] *with the joy of his heart.* — while constantly remembering that it is *God* Who provided him with this means of rejoicing *(Galico)*, and it is only fitting that he therefore utilize his happiness in the most idealistic manner *(Tuv Taam)*.

Thus when man properly utilizes *God's gift,* God stands up, as it were, and מַעֲנֶה, *bears witness* for him that He is the source of his happiness and that He specifically bequeathed it to him to enable him to derive joy from His works *(Rav Yosef Kara)*.

א יֵשׁ רָעָה אֲשֶׁר רָאִיתִי תַּחַת הַשָּׁמֶשׁ וְרַבָּה
ב הִיא עַל־הָאָדָם: אִישׁ אֲשֶׁר יִתֶּן־לוֹ
הָאֱלֹהִים עֹשֶׁר וּנְכָסִים וְכָבוֹד וְאֵינֶנּוּ
חָסֵר לְנַפְשׁוֹ | מִכֹּל אֲשֶׁר־יִתְאַוֶּה וְלֹא־
יַשְׁלִיטֶנּוּ הָאֱלֹהִים לֶאֱכֹל מִמֶּנּוּ כִּי אִישׁ
ג נָכְרִי יֹאכְלֶנּוּ זֶה הֶבֶל וָחֳלִי רָע הוּא: אִם־
יוֹלִיד אִישׁ מֵאָה וְשָׁנִים רַבּוֹת יִחְיֶה וְרַב |
שֶׁיִּהְיוּ יְמֵי־שָׁנָיו וְנַפְשׁוֹ לֹא־תִשְׂבַּע מִן־
הַטּוֹבָה וְגַם־קְבוּרָה לֹא־הָיְתָה לּוֹ

1. [Solomon now bemoans those who have wealth, but whom God has denied the opportunity of enjoying it. In contrast to the case in 5:12-14 of a man who begat children but lost his wealth — here the verse describes a man who has everything but is prevented by circumstances from enjoying it.]

יֵשׁ רָעָה — *There is an evil* [in the sense of: *'there is an injustice'*.]

וְרַבָּה הִיא עַל־הָאָדָם — *And it is prevalent among mankind.* The translation follows *Rashi. Ibn Ezra* translates: *'It is great upon man'*; while *Metzudas David* renders: *'it bears heavily upon man.'*

2. וְכָבוֹד — *And honor,* from his fellow man. This sort of recognition makes one rejoice and feel gratified *(Metzudas David).*

וְלֹא־יַשְׁלִיטֶנּוּ הָאֱלֹהִים לֶאֱכֹל מִמֶּנּוּ — *Yet God did not give him the power,* i.e. the capacity, *to enjoy it.* Instead, He instilled in him miserly tendencies *(Metzudas David)* [in contrast to 5:18.]

כִּי אִישׁ נָכְרִי יֹאכְלֶנּוּ — *Instead, a stranger will enjoy it. Alshich* suggests the case of a man who dies without close heirs. Because his estate is uncontested, it remains with his widow and eventually goes to her second husband.

Or, the case of a childless bachelor whose estate passes on to a complete stranger *(Ralbag).*

זֶה הֶבֶל וָחֳלִי רָע הוּא — *This is futility and an evil disease.* i.e. this accumulation of wealth — with no benefit accruing to is owner — is wasted and futile, and causes great pain to the observer *(Metzudas David).*

3. [According to most commentators, this verse introduces a new case in distinction to the previous one of a childless person whom *'a stranger will inherit.'* Here Solomon describes the futility of someone blessed with a large family, longevity, and every opportunity to enjoy goodness. But he lacks the capacity to derive joy from his blessings, and ultimately dies without even proper burial. A stillborn, declares Solomon, is better than he.]

*There is an evil I have observed beneath the sun,
and it is prevalent among mankind:* 2 *a man to
whom God has given riches, wealth and honor, and
he lacks nothing that the heart could desire, yet God
did not give him the power to enjoy it; instead, a
stranger will enjoy it. This is futility and an evil disease.* 3 *If a man begets a hundred children and lives
many years — great being the days of his life — and
his soul is not content with the good — and he even is
deprived of burial; I say: the stillborn is better off*

אִם־יוֹלִיד אִישׁ מֵאָה — *If a man begets a hundred [children].*

[The word *'children'* is not in the Hebrew but is implied by the context and is supplied by *Rashi* in his commentary.]

'One hundred' like 'ten', 'thousand' or occasionally 'seven' are arbitrary numbers used in Scriptures *(Ibn Ezra).*

[The exaggerated figure of a hundred children is intended to suggest the extent of the Heavenly blessing of a large family.]

וְשָׁנִים רַבּוֹת יִחְיֶה — *And lives many years.* To a ripe old age *(Ibn Ezra).* [Thus, he has numerous progeny and longevity, two of the greatest blessings of God: see *Psalms* 128:3-4,6: *'Your wife shall be as a fruitful vine . . . your children like olive plants . . . Thus shall the man be blessed who fears* HASHEM *. . . and you shall see your children's children.'*]

וְרַב שֶׁיִּהְיוּ יְמֵי־שָׁנָיו — *Great being the days of his life.* [This is close to a literal translation, following *Metzudas David* who translates *'great' 'honorable,' are days of his life.*]

Rashi translates: רַב as meaning *'sufficient'*: i.e. he has ample opportunity to partake of goodness during his lifetime. According to *Ibn Ezra,* רַב implies *'greater than usual'* — i.e. he lives a longer life than is usual.

וְנַפְשׁוֹ לֹא־תִשְׂבַּע מִן־הַטּוֹבָה — *And his soul is not content with the good.* [Although he is so blessed, he lacks the capacity to rejoice in the good with which he is blessed. To the contrary:] He was not satisfied with his lot and gains no pleasure from his possessions *(Rashi).*

וְגַם־קְבוּרָה לֹא־הָיְתָה לּוֹ — *And he is even deprived of burial.* [lit. 'and also burial he did not have.']

In addition to never enjoying life, he was denied the final honor given even to the most impoverished — burial *(Ibn Yachya).*

This refers to a case of one who was devoured by dogs *(Rashi)*; or drowned at sea *(Kara)* — and was never buried.

According to *Ibn Ezra* קְבוּרָה refers to תַּכְרִיכִין, the garments of the dead, [i.e. he did not even have a proper funeral]. According to *Sforno* the phrase means 'he did not die yet' — and thus continues his

פרק ו ד אָמַרְתִּי טוֹב מִמֶּנּוּ הַנָּפֶל: כִּי־בַהֶבֶל בָּא
ד־ו וּבַחֹשֶׁךְ יֵלֵךְ וּבַחֹשֶׁךְ שְׁמוֹ יְכֻסֶּה:
ה גַּם־שֶׁמֶשׁ לֹא־רָאָה וְלֹא יָדָע נַחַת
ו לָזֶה מִזֶּה: וְאִלּוּ חָיָה אֶלֶף שָׁנִים פַּעֲמַיִם
וְטוֹבָה לֹא רָאָה הֲלֹא אֶל־מָקוֹם אֶחָד

joyless existence.[1]

אָמַרְתִּי טוֹב מִמֶּנּוּ הַנָּפֶל — *I say: the stillborn is better off than he.* As explained in the next verse *(Ibn Yachya).*

At least the stillborn was spared the tribulations of life on this world *(Almosnino).*

4. כִּי־בַהֶבֶל בָּא — *Though its* [i.e. the stillborn] *coming is futile* [lit. *'because it came in futility'*] — from a putrid drop *(Alshich);* with no purpose *(Metzudas David).*

וּבַחֹשֶׁךְ יֵלֵךְ — *And it departs in darkness* — to the grave [comp. 11:8] *(Alshich);* unnoticed *(Metzudas David);* without public mourning *(Almosnino).*

וּבַחֹשֶׁךְ שְׁמוֹ יְכֻסֶּה — *though its very name is enveloped in darkness.* It departs unnoticed and never achieved status worthy of a name *(Sforno).* Because it was stillborn, it is not referred to by name; its parents cannot even say: 'we had a child by such and such a name' *(Alshich).*

[According to *halachah* an infant that died before being named 'is given a name as a remembrance so that he will evoke compasssion from Heaven and will arise with the Resurrection of the Dead. He will thereby be enabled to identify his father' *(Tur, Beis Yosef* 263) Thus, the verse implies, not that the child is unnamed, but that the name is unused and therefore remains in obscurity.]

The subject of this verse, according to most commentators (including *Rashi, Sforno*) is the stillborn.

Rabbeinu Yonah and Rav Yosef Kara suggest that the subject described in this verse is the *man* of the previous verses. Man, explains *Rabbeinu Yonah* is created for three purposes: to live in this world; gain merit for the World to Come, and earn a good name by virtue of the goodness he does for others. The man described previously lacks these requirements: *his coming* — into this world — *was futile; he departs* — to the Hereafter — *in darkness; and his very name is enveloped in darkness* — for his deeds did not earn him a good reputation.

5. גַּם־שֶׁמֶשׁ לֹא־רָאָה וְלֹא יָדָע — *Though* [lit. *'also'*] *it never saw the sun nor knew.* i.e. the stillborn who never experienced the 'light of day' [idiomatic for the state of living] and knew nothing — never having reached the consciousness of being

1. An interesting interpretation is offered by *Alshich:* Even if a man has a hundred children and lives many years, *'and moreover he has no burial'* — i.e. not a single death occurred in his family to bring sorrow upon him — his life can be futile if he always creates worries and fails to rejoice in life.

VI
4-6

than he. 4 *Though its coming is futile and it departs*
in darkness, though its very name is enveloped in
darkness, 5 *though it never saw the sun nor knew; it*
has more satisfaction than he. 6 *Even if he should live*
a thousand years twice over, but find no contentment
— do not all go to the same place?

— has at least one comfort. It has never toiled in mundane affairs, unlike the rich man [in verse 3] who *did* experience life and is aware that he had no peace, but toiled without reward in both worlds *(Ibn Ezra).*

נַחַת לָזֶה מִזֶּה — *It has more satisfaction than he.* [The stillborn, from this perspective of quiet and freedom from care, has the advantage over the frustrated rich man. Compare 4:3 for a similar concept.]

The stillborn does not anguish over what he never had, unlike the wealthy man who *'begat a hundred children,* etc.' but now grieves because everything was taken from him *(Metzudas David).*[1]

The *Alshich* removes the pause after וְלֹא יָדָע, nor knew, and translates: It never saw the sun nor did it know to distinguish whether there is more satisfaction to having been in this world or to never having seen it, for as the Sages concluded 'it would have been better for man never to have been created.' [see comm. to 4:2-3]

6. [The subject of this verse is again the rich man described in verse 3.] Even if he lives to two thousand years [more than twice as old as anyone recorded in the Bible (cf. Mesushelach lived 969 years — *Gen.* 5:27)], of what benefit is this longevity to him since וְטוֹבָה לֹא רָאָה *'he found no contentment'*? Ultimately he will return to the dust just like all paupers! *(Rashi).*

אֶלֶף שָׁנִים פַּעֲמַיִם — *A thousand years twice over* i.e. two thousand years *(Metzudas David),* a hyperbolic figure [used to strengthen the illustration *(Ibn Ezra* on verse 3).]

In his comments to this verse, *Ibn Ezra* interprets the phrase אֶלֶף שָׁנִים פַּעֲמַיִם to mean: 'a thousand years multiplied by itself, i.e. a million.'

Nachal Eshkol interprets: 'And if he lived a thousand years *and then relived his life* — starting over as a youth and living another thousand years, again *finding no contentment* and performing no righteous acts — then his double existence was a waste. To the place [i.e. death] where he was before he will return, *for do not all go to the same place?'*

1. *The matter may be likened to two men who were sailing on a ship. When it reached the harbor one of them went ashore and saw food, drink, peace and contentment. When he returned to the ship his comrade asked him, 'What did you see there?'*

'I saw much food, drink, peace and contentment,' he replied.

'Did you enjoy any of it?' he inquired.

'No,' was the answer.

'Then it was better,' he retorted, 'that I did not go ashore and did not see it!' (Midrash).

So, too, in our verse, the stillborn babe who never saw the allures of this world is more fortunate than those who went through life seeing its allures, but not savoring them *(Torah Temimah).*

פרק ו ז הַכֹּל הוֹלֵךְ: כָּל־עֲמַל הָאָדָם לְפִיהוּ וְגַם־
ז־י ח הַנֶּפֶשׁ לֹא תִמָּלֵא: כִּי מַה־יּוֹתֵר לֶחָכָם
מִן־הַכְּסִיל מַה־לֶּעָנִי יוֹדֵעַ לַהֲלֹךְ נֶגֶד
ט הַחַיִּים: טוֹב מַרְאֵה עֵינַיִם מֵהֲלָךְ־נָפֶשׁ
י גַּם־זֶה הֶבֶל וּרְעוּת רוּחַ: מַה־שֶּׁהָיָה כְּבָר

אֶל־מָקוֹם אֶחָד הַכֹּל הוֹלֵךְ — *All go to the same place. All* — [i.e. the still-born as well as the long-lived] *go to the same place* — the grave *(Ibn Ezra).*

7-9. [Man labors incessantly to satisfy his cravings which, alas, remain unappeased. What, then, is the advantage of wisdom, especially when, despite intelligence and ability, one remains poor? It is of no advantage. Better is enjoyment of what we can enjoy than the futile quest of unsatisfied longing.]

7. לְפִיהוּ — *for his mouth* — i.e. man toils to satisfy his hunger and wants, and to sustain himself in this world and the next. Our subject, in contrast, never had contentment in his life *(Rashi).*

וְגַם־הַנֶּפֶשׁ לֹא תִמָּלֵא — *Yet his wants* [lit. *'soul'*] *are never satisfied* [lit. *'full'*] According to *Rashi* and *Kara,* for all his striving, he did not succeed in satisying even a fraction of his earthly lust. If so, continues verse 9, *what advantage* has the magnate over the pauper?

Man's toils are for *'his mouth'* i.e. affording only momentary joy. Man's eternal soul cannot be satiated from such transient, fleeting pleasure as food and drink *(Alshich).*

In a different vain, *Rav Galico* explains that whatever evils descend upon man are a result of *his mouth* — i.e. eating forbidden foods and indulging in improper speech, creating, as it were, a separation between man and God. At the same time וְגַם־הַנֶּפֶשׁ לֹא תִמָּלֵא, even the soul is deterred from reaching fulfillment.

The *Midrash* notes: Man's quest for good deeds is for *his mouth* and not for the mouth of his son or daughter. [A persons good deeds can earn rewards in the Hereafter only for himself, not for his children *(Torah Temimah)*]. *Yet the soul is not satisfied* because it knows that whatever it earns is for itself — and therefore never has enough of Torah and good deeds. This is likened to a villager who married a princess. Though he may bring her all his earthly possessions, they are not esteemed by her, because she is of royal lineage [and accustomed to luxury beyond the imagination of a mere villager.] So it is with the soul; though you bring it all the luxuries in the world, they are valueless to it. Why? Because it is of heavenly origin [and its values are spiritual; infininitely higher than earthly goods.]

8. מַה־יּוֹתֵר לֶחָכָם — *What advantage then* has the wise man from his wisdom, מִן הַכְּסִיל, over what he would have if he were a fool? *(Rashi).*

Of what value is the wisdom to achieve wealth if it does not pro-

[7] *All man's toil is for his mouth, yet his wants are never satisfied.* [8] *What advantage, then, has the wise man over the fool? What [less] has the pauper who knows how to conduct himself among the living?* [9] *Better is what the eyes see than what is imagined. That, too, is futility and a vexation of the spirit.*

vide contentment. What advantage has the 'hungry' wise man over the fool who has not the capacity to accumulate wealth and as a result also starves [i.e. for whatever reason, both suffer deprivation.] *(Rav Yosef Kara).*

[A rhetorical question. There is no advantage to the wise. Both must toil for what they achieve. The difference lies in how the fruits of the labor are utilized and appreciated.]

מַה־לֶּעָנִי יוֹדֵעַ לַהֲלֹךְ נֶגֶד הַחַיִּים — *What* [less] *has the pauper who knows how to conduct himself among the living?* A difficult phrase, the translation of which follows *Rashi, Kara, Ibn Ezra:* i.e. how is a pauper who has the intelligence to get along in this world worse off than the wise man who has wealth but finds no contentment?

[For a similar phrase נֶגֶד הַחַיִּים, *among* (lit. *'against') the living,* compare *Gen.* 33:12 וְאֵלְכָה לְנֶגְדֶּךָ which *Rashi ad. loc.* translates *'equally with you.'*]

The *Midrash* asks: What is a poor man to do regarding business transactions? Is he to sit idle? Let him learn a handicraft and the Holy One blessed be He, will support him with a livelihood.

9. טוֹב מַרְאֵה עֵינַיִם מֵהֲלָךְ־נָפֶשׁ — *Better is what the eyes see than what is imagined.* [lit. *'Better the sight of the eyes than the path of the soul'.*]

The intent of this verse is that man should utilize the little that is available to him *('that which he sees'),* rather than yearn in vain for riches that may elude him *(Rav Saadiah Gaon; Almosnino).*

Rav Yosef Kara and *Rashi,* however, view this verse as the rationale of the miser: It is a great evil that many people would rather gaze upon a treasury full of gold and silver, enjoying *what the eyes see* and contenting themselves with that lustful vision, than to diminish their wealth by investing it to nourish their souls. Such a trait, is *'futility and a vexation of the spirit.'*

גַּם־זֶה הָבֶל — *This, too, is futility* — Man may long for certain goals, but the quest is in vain: he will achieve only what was predestined for him at birth *(Sforno).* Whatever 'extra' man *does* manage to acquire will only pass on to others *(Almosnino).*

Metzudas David explains the verse differently: It would be preferable for man to perceive מֵהֲלָךְ־נָפֶשׁ, *the path, and destiny of evil souls,* and thus improve his conduct. This is futile, however, because he would then be serving the Creator only out of fear. Since his service of God would be based on selfish interests and not true love of God, this, too, *'is futility and a*

נִקְרָא שְׁמוֹ וְנוֹדָע אֲשֶׁר־הוּא אָדָם וְלֹא־
יא יוּכַל לָדִין עִם שֶׁהַתַּקִּיף* מִמֶּנּוּ: כִּי יֵשׁ־
דְּבָרִים הַרְבֵּה מַרְבִּים הָבֶל מַה־יֹּתֵר
יב לָאָדָם: כִּי מִי־יוֹדֵעַ מַה־טּוֹב לָאָדָם
בַּחַיִּים מִסְפַּר יְמֵי־חַיֵּי הֶבְלוֹ וְיַעֲשֵׂם כַּצֵּל

* שֶׁתַּקִּיף ק׳

vexation of the spirit' (*Metzudas David*)

Sforno comments that, rather than strive after unattainable philosophical goals, it is better to be content with tangible, material assets. But because such possessions are pre-ordained, excessive striving after them is futile.

10. [The verse cautions that man should perceive the limits of his essence as predetermined by God. He is אָדָם, *mortal man,* and his limitations as a human being have been imposed on him from Creation. He cannot contend with his Creator who formed him thus (*Ibn Latif*). But he should be thankful for however God formed him (*Midrash Lekach Tov*). Nor can he hope to overpower the angel of death i.e. he should submit to his mortality.]

Rashi (as amplified by *Metzudas David*) explains the verse differently. Man's greatness was established and well known during his lifetime. His death, however, makes it manifestly clear that he is essentially אָדָם, mortal. Ultimately he dies, unable to resist the angel of death, who is more powerful than he.

Several additional interpretations and amplifications follow:

מַה־שֶּׁהָיָה כְּבָר נִקְרָא שְׁמוֹ — *What has been was already named.* Man's destiny has already been determined by God (*Ibn Yachya*) and it has been established whether he will be rich, poor, or otherwise (*Sforno*).

[As in *Isaiah* 40:26, *'He brings out their host by number, and calls them by name.'*]

וְנוֹדָע אֲשֶׁר־הוּא אָדָם — *And it is known that he is* [*but*] *a man* — and not God [i.e. mortal and not Eternal] (*Rashi; Midrash*).[1]

[*'But'* is not in the Hebrew. It is, however, implied according to most commentators.]

עִם שֶׁתַּקִּיף מִמֶּנּוּ — *With one who is mightier than he.* i.e. the angel of death (*Rashi*), or according to *Sforno* and others [see above]: with God, i.e. man cannot change what God willed.

He should therefore leave a legacy of good deeds on this world (*Rav Yosef Kara*).

11. כִּי יֵשׁ־דְּבָרִים הַרְבֵּה מַרְבִּים הָבֶל — *There are many things that increase futility.* There are many activities with which man gets involved during his lifetime [such as the ac-

1. It may be likened to a king and a governor who were seated in a chariot. The populace wished to greet the king but did not know which of the two he was. What did the king do? He pushed the other out of the chariot and then everyone knew which was king. Similarly, when God created the first man, the ministering angels thought he was divine and wanted to proclaim before him, 'Holy!' What did God do? God cast a sleep upon him and all knew he was man, and He said to him: (*Gen.* 3:19) *You are dust and to dust will return.* (*Midrash*).

10 *What has been was already named, and it is known that he is but a man. He cannot contend with one who is mightier than he.* 11 *There are many things that increase futility; how does it benefit man?* 12 *Who can possibly know what is good for man in life, during the short span of his futile existence*

cumulation of wealth, power, or pleasures *(Ibn Ezra)*]. Later he realizes that they were futile *(Kara; Rashi).*

Akeidas Yitzchak, in his view of the continuity of the verses, translates דְּבָרִים, *words,* and comments that man cannot contend with God. It is futile for him to express his views on what he thinks is best suited for man's temperament. Thus: *'Many words add to the futility'.*

מַה־יֹּתֵר לָאָדָם — *How does it benefit man?* [lit. *'what is there more to man?'*] i.e. How, then — by virtue of his intellect — is man superior to other beings? *(Metzudas David).*

Or according to *Rashi: After his death* [what endures of man's futility?]

12. כִּי מִי — *Who can possibly* [lit. *'for who'*] i.e. only a small minority have the intellect to comprehend which is the proper course for man to take during his short life *(Metzudas David).*

Even though a particular course might seem proper in one period of life, who can be certain whether it yields true goodness in the greater perspective of a full lifetime? *(Sforno)*

. . .And whether it will bring him goodness in the Hereafter *(Rashi).*

Rav Pinchas said: since the days of man's life are in vain, few in number and like a shadow, what benefit has he from his existence? Let him, then, occupy himself with words of Torah which are called 'Life' *(Midrash).*

מִסְפַּר יְמֵי־חַיֵּי הֶבְלוֹ — *During the short span of his futile existence* [lit. *(the limited) 'number of the days of his futile life' (Rashi).* compare 2:3; 5:17.]

וְיַעֲשֵׂם כַּצֵּל — *Which* [lit. *'and'*] *he should consider like a* [*mere*] *shadow. Rashi, Metzudas David, Sforno,* refer this to the transitory significance of man's actions in this world.

Ibn Ezra, Alshich, Ibn Yachya, Ralbag interpret this to modify *'the short span of his futile existence.'* [i.e. which is of no substance and vanishes like shadows.][1]

[Solomon employs the phrase without explaining what kind of shadow is meant. If life is like the shadow cast by a wall or by a date-palm there is some substance to it! (because it is not so fleeting and affords some protection from the sun as compared to the shadow cast by a bird which lasts only a moment

1. Some interpret this phrase homiletically:
One should live his life like a shadow; just as a shadow imitates man's actions, so does God imitate man's actions. If man acts with compassion, God treats him compassionately, as it is written [*Psalms* 121:5] ה׳ צִלְּךָ, *God is your shade.* Socially, too, as one acts towards his comrades, so they act toward him *(Kedushas Levi).*

פרק ו אֲשֶׁר מִי־יַגִּיד לָאָדָם מַה־יִּהְיֶה אַחֲרָיו
תַּחַת הַשָּׁמֶשׁ:

פרק ז א טוֹב שֵׁם מִשֶּׁמֶן טוֹב וְיוֹם הַמָּוֶת מִיּוֹם
א־ב ב הִוָּלְדוֹ: טוֹב לָלֶכֶת אֶל־בֵּית־אֵבֶל מִלֶּכֶת

(Torah Temimah). David, in *Psalms* 144:4 already explained it: *'His days are like a shadow that passes away'* in a fleeting moment; life is thus fleeting and of no substance.]

מַה־יִּהְיֶה אַחֲרָיו תַּחַת הַשָּׁמֶשׁ — *What will be after him beneath the sun.* i.e. how to assure that the fortune which he accumulated unjustly will endure with his children on this world *(Rashi).*

[Koheles displays the same intellectual remorse which he developed in 2:3-21, and with which he culminated 3:22 regarding the uncertainty of the future.]

The best course, therefore, is to store up *spiritual fortunes* which will definitely live on beyond him *(Alshich)* — as the *Midrash* concludes: I will tell you what is best of all [next verse] טוֹב שֵׁם מִשֶּׁמֶן טוֹב *a good name is better than good oil.*

VII

1. As the *Midrash* notes at the end of the last chapter, these verses might be, in part, Solomon's own answer to the question (6:12) *'Who knows what is good for man in life?' (Midrash Lekach Tov).*

טוֹב שֵׁם מִשֶּׁמֶן טוֹב — *A [good] name is better than good oil* — i.e. a fine reputation — acquired with diligence and good deeds *(Sforno)* — is a more valuable possession than precious oil *(Rashi)* [which was used in ancient times to preserve the body from disintegration.] Thus, notes the *Alshich,* a fine reputation will preserve the dead more effectively than precious oils.

The meaning of this statement is that a good name is better than good oil, for a fine reputation travels much further than the scent of fine oil. But a good name is not an essential and ultimate good of the soul. Therefore, the day of death, when a man has attained his complete knowledge, is better than the day of his birth; for on the day of death, he has already actualized the potential of his intellect. On the day of birth, however, his physical being has developed to the point where it can independently sustain life, but his spiritual, intellectual being — the perfection of the soul — has only the potential of existence *(Sefer Ha-Ikkarim).*

'It has been taught: A man is called by three names: one which his father and mother call him, a second which other persons call him, and a third by which he is

VI *which he should consider like a shadow; who can tell a man what will be after him beneath the sun?*

VII
1-2
A good name is better than good oil, and the day of death than the day of birth.

2 *It is better to go to the house of mourning than to*

designated in the book of the generation of his creation [i.e. the name which he gains for himself as the result of his conduct in life.]' *(Midrash).*

'The end of man is to die, and the end of the beast is to be slaughtered, and all are doomed to die. Happy is he who was brought up in the Torah and whose labor was in the Torah and who has given pleasure to his Creator and who grew up with a good name and departed the world with a good name; and of him Solomon said *"A good name is better than good oil, and the day of death than the day of birth"' (Berachos* 17a*).*

וְיוֹם הַמָּוֶת מִיּוֹם הִוָּלְדוֹ — *And the day of death* [is better] *than the day of birth.*

Because the man who has lived an exemplary life and acquired a *good name*, views his death as a culmination of a life well spent and as a transition to the World of Peace and Reward. Unlike the time of his birth 'for man is born to toil' when he is uncertain of how his life will unfold *(Akeidas Yitzchak; Ibn Ezra).*[1]

The righteous are born obscurely, but when they die, everyone feels it: When Miriam was born, nobody knew her; but when she died the בְּאֵר, *well,* [created by God in honor of Miriam to accompany the Jews and supply them with water on their journeys *(Taanis* 9a*)*] ceased to exist [and everyone felt the loss.] Similarly, when Aaron died the עַנְנֵי הַכָּבוֹד, *clouds of glory,* departed; and when Moses died the מָן, *manna,* ceased to descend *(Rashi).*

The reverse is true of the wicked man, however. Indeed, the day of his birth which is unblemished with sin is better than the day of his death when he looks back on his sinful life *(Rav Yosef Kara).*

2. טוֹב לָלֶכֶת אֶל־בֵּית־אֵבֶל — *It is better to go to the house of mourning.* [The commentators explain that by visiting the house of mourning and listening to the eulogies and lamentations, thoughts of the beauty of life will stimulate one to resolve to lead a religiously observant life, and he will repent his ways. For at that time — when the virtues of the deceased are re-

1. The *Midrash* observes that when a man is born there is much rejoicing, when he dies all weep. Yet, logically, it should be the reverse. When a person is born there should be no rejoicing over him because his record of good deeds is clouded in mystery and there is reason to be apprehensive. But when he dies there is cause for rejoicing if he departs with a good name and leaves the world in peace.

It is as if there were two ships. The one leaving the harbor attract shouts of joy, and the ship

פרק ז
ג־ד

אֶל־בֵּית מִשְׁתֶּה בַּאֲשֶׁר הוּא סוֹף כָּל־
ג הָאָדָם וְהַחַי יִתֵּן אֶל־לִבּוֹ: טוֹב כַּעַס
ד מִשְּׂחוֹק כִּי־בְרֹעַ פָּנִים יִיטַב לֵב: לֵב
חֲכָמִים בְּבֵית אֵבֶל וְלֵב כְּסִילִים בְּבֵית

counted — man is reminded that the only thing of value is a good reputation. Anyone present will resolve to assure himself an untarnished name by the time he dies and others visit *his* house of mourning.]

מִלֶּכֶת אֶל־בֵּית מִשְׁתֶּה — *Than to go to a house of feasting* — [where frivolity and even immorality preclude wholesome meditation.]

My father, *Harav Aron Zlotowitz* שליט״א brought to my attention that the *Maharsha* in his commentary to *Kesubos* 72a points out that *'feasting'* here refers only to מִשְׁתֶּה שֶׁל רְשׁוּת, a feast not associated with the performance of a precept, because *halachically* a מִשְׁתֶּה שֶׁל מִצְוָה, a feast required by precept, such as a wedding feast, takes precedence, as in the Talmudic dictum [*Kesubos* 17a]: 'A bridal procession takes precedence over a funeral procession.' [Comp. *comm.* to 8:15.]

בַּאֲשֶׁר הוּא סוֹף כָּל־הָאָדָם — *For that is the end of all man* — i.e. death is the inevitable fate of everyone and if he does not attend the funeral now, when then? A feast is different — if a person could not attend one celebration, he will be able to attend another in that family at some later time *(Rashi).*

וְהַחַי יִתֵּן אֶל־לִבּוֹ — *And the living should take it to heart.* i.e. Do a kindness so that one will be done to you; attend a funeral so that people should attend your funeral; mourn for others so that others should mourn for you; bury so that others should concern themselves with your burial; act benevolently so that benevolence should be done to you *(Midrash).*

And thereby recognize that the inevitable end of all men is death *(Ibn Ezra)* and be moved to repent *(Kara).*

3. טוֹב כַּעַס מִשְּׂחוֹק — *Grief is better than gaiety.* [כַּעַס, in this context is understood by many commentators not in its usual sense of *'anger'*, but as the *grief* aroused by the laments in the *'house of mourning.'*] Such 'grief' brings about רֹעַ פָּנִים, *'a sad face,'* i.e. a brooding, reflective countenance; which in turn יִיטַב לֵב, will cause *'his heart to be improved'*, i.e. turn his heart to better his ways — because this reflecting will cause him to take stock of his own situation. He will repent and thus bring on his own redemption. שְׂחוֹק, *'gaiety'*, however, is not conducive to such

entering the harbor attract a minimal amount of attention.

The reverse should be the case. There is no cause to rejoice over the departing ship because no one knows what seas and storms it may encounter. Indeed it is a time for concern. The returning vessel that has reached the harbor safely deserves the shouts of joy.

Similarly, when a person dies all should rejoice and offer thanks that he departed from the world with a good name and in peace.

go to a house of feasting, for that is the end of all man, and the living should take it to heart.
3 *Grief is better than gaiety — for through a sad countenance the heart is improved.* 4 *The thoughts of the wise turn to the house of mourning, but the thoughts of fools to the house of feasting.*

serious contemplation *(Rav Yosef Kara).*[1]

Additionally, several commentators quote the *Talmud* and *Midrash* which refer this verse to the anger of God: Preferable is the anger which God displays to the righteous in this world than the 'laughter' which He displays to the wicked *(Shabbos* 30b*)* for when God's anger is manifested, man is inspired to mend his ways. Similarly, *(Taalumos Chachmah)* had He been vexed at the sins of the Generation of the Flood and the men of Sodom [and not let them stoop to their low level of degeneration] it would have been better for them than the 'laughter' [i.e. over-indulgence] in which He 'engaged' with them. Had He shown them a 'sad face' they would have repented *(Rashi).*

Binyan Ariel understands this verse in its literal sense and comments that כַּעַס, *'anger'* is an undesirable trait and is to be frowned upon [see verse 9]. Nevertheless, in comparison with שְׂחוֹק, *gaiety, laughter* [frivolity and unrestrained hedonism, 2:2] *'anger'* is the lesser of the two evils, for as the Sages proclaimed *(Avos* 3:13*)*: שְׂחוֹק וְקַלּוּת רֹאשׁ מַרְגִּילִין אֶת־הָאָדָם לְעֶרְוָה, 'Laughter and levity accustom man to immorality.'

4. לֵב חֲכָמִים בְּבֵית אֵבֶל [Therefore] *the thoughts of the wise turn to the house of mourning* [lit. *'the heart of the wise is in the house of mourning'*] The translation follows *Rashi* who comments: Their thoughts are concentrated on the day of death.

. . . So their desires will be subordinated and they will avoid sin *(Metzudas David).* Thus influencing their perspective of life *(Ibn Latif).*

Rav Yitzchak said: It may be likened to one who said to his servant, 'Go and bring me a desirable object.' 'Where can I find a desirable object?' he asked. 'If you find many people going to a place, a desirable object is likely to be there' [i.e. death being common, men are constantly going to a house of mourning, and precious spiritual truths are to be learned there] *(Midrash).*

This verse tells that even when the wise don't physically enter a house of mourning [verse 2], the house of mourning is always within them *(Ibn Ezra).*

וְלֵב כְּסִילִים בְּבֵית שִׂמְחָה — *But the thought of fools to the house of*

1. [The *Midrash* interprets כַּעַס in the usual sense of *'anger'* and explains this verse as a moral lesson in child-rearing. A parent should be stern when disciplining his children. He should show them anger (tempered with mercy) and should not always display levity]:

'Solomon said: If my father had displayed anger to Adonijah it would have been better for him [and the latter would have been spared execution as a traitor (see *I Kings* 2:23)] . . .Why?

ה שִׂמְחָה: טוֹב לִשְׁמֹעַ גַּעֲרַת חָכָם מֵאִישׁ
ו שֹׁמֵעַ שִׁיר כְּסִילִים: כִּי כְקוֹל הַסִּירִים
תַּחַת הַסִּיר כֵּן שְׂחֹק הַכְּסִיל וְגַם־זֶה
ז הָבֶל: כִּי הָעֹשֶׁק יְהוֹלֵל חָכָם וִיאַבֵּד אֶת־
ח לֵב מַתָּנָה: טוֹב אַחֲרִית דָּבָר מֵרֵאשִׁיתוֹ
ט טוֹב אֶרֶךְ־רוּחַ מִגְּבַהּ־רוּחַ: אַל־תְּבַהֵל

feasting. [lit. *'and the heart of fools is in the house of feasting'*] [The fool, on the other hand, is only concerned with frivolity and extravagant physical pleasure. There is no place in his philosophy of life for serious contemplation. He lives for the moment; the future is of no concern to him.]

5. טוֹב לִשְׁמֹעַ גַּעֲרַת חָכָם — *It is better to listen to the rebuke of a wise man* — although criticism hurts, it is beneficial because it brings about moral improvement *(Metzudas David).*

מֵאִישׁ — *Than for one* [lit. *'than a man'*] i.e. even though he considers himself an אִישׁ, a man of high caliber, and he thinks that the revelries of the fools will not affect him *(Alshich).*

שֹׁמֵעַ שִׁיר כְּסִילִים — *to listen* [lit. *'who listen'*] *to the song of fools.* Although these songs make the heart joyous, they are composed by foolish revelers and in a short time will inspire levity in the hearts of all who hear them *(Metzudas David).*

6. כִּי כְקוֹל הַסִּירִים תַּחַת הַסִּיר — *For like the crackling of thorns under a pot.* Thorns crackle and flare up into a roaring blaze and quickly subside, barely heating the pot *(Kara).*

כֵּן שְׂחֹק הַכְּסִיל — *So is the laughter of the fool.* It, too, makes a momentary uproar and expires, disclosing no useful purpose *(Akeidas Yitzchak).*

Just as the crackling of thorns blacken the pot, so the revelries of fools blacken the heart *(Alshich).*

וְגַם־זֶה הָבֶל — *And this, too,* [i.e. the revelry of fools *(Ibn Ezra)*] *is futility.*

For what lasting value does this revelry provide? *(Alshich).*

Rav Yosef Kara takes the phrase to refer to both *the crackling of thorns* and *the laughter of fools:* both are futile.

7. כִּי הָעֹשֶׁק יְהוֹלֵל חָכָם — *For oppression makes the wise foolish.* The provocations with which fools provoke *(Metzudas David)* the wise — such as the taunts of Dathan and Abiram against Moses — cause the wise man's wisdom to depart from him — and they eventually provoke the Holy One, blessed be He *(Rashi; Midrash).*

Thus the wise man should keep far away from 'the song of fools' because by involving himself in much discussion with fools, his

For through a sad countenance the heart is gladdened'. Had David shown him a sad [i.e. displeased] countenance, it might have led him to mend his ways. Instead, it is written [*ibid.* 1:6] *'And his father had never grieved him at any time saying: Why did you do so?.'*

5 *It is better to listen to the rebuke of a wise man than for one to listen to the song of fools,* 6 *for like the crackling of thorns under a pot, so is the laughter of the fool;* 7 *for oppression makes the wise foolish, and a gift corrupts the heart.*

8 *The end of a matter is better than its beginning; patience is better than pride.* 9 *Do not be hastily up-*

own wisdom will suffer *(Metzudas David).*

וִיאַבֵּד אֶת־לֵב מַתָּנָה — *And a gift corrupts* [lit. *'loses'*] *the heart.* This is the literal translation and follows *Ibn Ezra* who translates this phrase in consonance with the verse in *Proverbs* 15:27: וְשׂוֹנֵא מַתָּנֹת יִחְיֶה *'and he that hates gifts shall live.'*

Rashi, Sforno, Metzudas Zion and others translate this phrase as the result of the beginning of the verse: as a result of the provocation of wicked fools, wise men *'will forfeit the heart* [i.e. intellect] *which is the gift of God to man,'* as it is written [*Proverbs* 2:6]: ה׳ יִתֵּן חָכְמָה, *'for HASHEM gives wisdom.'*

8. טוֹב אַחֲרִית דָּבָר מֵרֵאשִׁיתוֹ — *The end of a matter is better than the beginning* — since only by the outcome can a matter be properly evaluated *(Rashi).*

A wise man should thus always try to foresee the result of every one of his actions and act accordingly *(Ibn Ezra).*

The *Midrash* quotes Elisha ben Abuyah telling Rabbi Meir that Rabbi Akiva explained the verse: 'Good is the end of a thing when it was good from its inception' i.e an act which was initially undertaken לְשֵׁם שָׁמַיִם, for the name of Heaven, will in the end be successful.

טוֹב אֶרֶךְ־רוּחַ מִגְּבַהּ רוּחַ — *Patience is better than pride.* Similarly, one who controls his temper and is not provoked to anger easily (because he looks ahead to the outcome of his anger and not just to the provocation), is better than the quick-tempered individual who is easily provoked but will regret his outburst afterward *(Rashi, Metzudas David; Kara).*[1]

An example of such restraint is that of King David who restrained his anger and did not punish Shim'i [*II Samuel* 16]; ultimately, Mordechai descended from Shim'i [*Megillah* 13a; see *Overview* to ArtScroll edition of *Megillas Esther* p. xxx] *(Michlol Yofi).*

9. אַל־תְּבַהֵל בְּרוּחֲךָ לִכְעוֹס — *Do not be hastily upset* [lit. *do not be hasty with your spirit to be angry;* i.e. 'do

1. A Persian came to Rav and said to him, 'Teach me the Torah; (I wish to convert.)'

He [consented, and, pointing to the first letter of the alphabet], told him, 'Say *Aleph.*' The man remarked, 'Who says that this is *Aleph?* There may be others who say that it is not!'. 'Say *Beth*', to which he remarked, 'Who says that this is *Beth?*' Rav rebuked him and drove him out in anger.

He went to Shmuel and said to him, 'Teach me the Torah.' He told him, 'Say *Aleph.*' The man remarked, 'Who says that this is *Aleph*?' 'Say *Beth,*' to which he remarked, 'Who said this is *Beth?*'

בְּרוּחֲךָ לִכְעוֹס כִּי כַעַס בְּחֵיק כְּסִילִים
י יָנוּחַ: אַל־תֹּאמַר מֶה הָיָה שֶׁהַיָּמִים
הָרִאשֹׁנִים הָיוּ טוֹבִים מֵאֵלֶּה כִּי לֹא
יא מֵחָכְמָה שָׁאַלְתָּ עַל־זֶה: טוֹבָה חָכְמָה
יב עִם־נַחֲלָה וְיֹתֵר לְרֹאֵי הַשָּׁמֶשׁ: כִּי בְּצֵל

not display an uncontrollable bad temper,' in continuation of the previous verse, 'patience is better than pride'.]

כִּי כַעַס בְּחֵיק כְּסִילִים יָנוּחַ — *For anger lingers in the bosom of fools* eager to burst forth for all to see at the slightest provocation *(Sforno).*

Thus the Sages teach us in *Avos* 2:10: אַל תְּהִי נוֹחַ לִכְעוֹס, 'Be not easily angered.' It is well known that anger is a very bad thing, but by nature men are drawn to it. That is why Rabbi Eliezer says: 'Since against your wish you will sometimes become angry, beware not to be angered easily . . . weigh the matter wisely: is it worth getting angry over?' And if you find any excuse to dismiss anger, dismiss it. Then when there is reason to be genuinely angry, your anger will not fail you . . .*(Rabbeinu Yonah).*

Our Sages warned against indulgence in anger even for a worthy cause. Even a teacher should not display anger toward his pupil, nor a father toward his child. This does not mean that they should never reprove; when they do, however, they should do so without anger, but with a view only to correction. The anger which they display should be more assumed than real *(Shab.* 105b; see *Midrash* quoted to verse 3). In the words of Solomon "Do not be hastily upset; for anger lingers in the bosom of fools" *(Mesillas Yesharim).*

10. This verse cautions the wise to be satisfied with their lot. If they suffer an adverse turn of fortune they should not complain about their lot and be jealous of those who are better and attribute their decline to a changing world. Everyone of understanding is aware that life remains the same — man is given whatever has been ordained for him *(Ibn Ezra).*

הָרִאשֹׁנִים הָיוּ טוֹבִים מֵאֵלֶּה — *That former times* [lit. *'days'*] *were better than these. Rashi* explains that one should not wonder that the generations of the desert, of Joshua, and of David were recipients of more goodness than the current generation . . .

כִּי לֹא מֵחָכְמָה שָׁאַלְתָּ עַל־זֶה — *For that is not a question prompted by wisdom* [lit. *'for not from wisdom did you ask about this.'*] — i.e. it is a foolish question; the answer is obvious *(Metzudas David)* all depends on the merit of each generation *(Rashi).*

The *Talmud* remarks that one

The teacher pulled his ear and the man exclaimed, 'My ear! my ear!' Shmuel asked him, 'Who said that this is your ear?' He answered, 'Everybody knows that this is my ear!' The teacher retorted, 'In the same way everybody knows that this is *Aleph* and that is *Beth.*' Immediately the Persian was silenced and accepted the instruction.

VII
10-12

set, for anger lingers in the bosom of fools.

10 *Do not say, 'How was it that former times were better than these?' For that is not a question prompted by wisdom.*

11 *Wisdom is good with an inheritance, and a boon to those who see the sun,* 12 *for to sit in the shelter of*

should not deprecate the leaders of his time by comparing them to great personalities of the past. Rather Jerubaal in his generation is like Moses in his generation . . . Yiftach in his generation is like Samuel in his . . . one must be content with the judge who is in his days, and not look back at former times *(Rosh Hashanah* 25b*)*.

The *Kobriner Rebbe* said: Some people feel that 'Nowadays it is difficult to serve God. In former times it was easier; there were more *tzadikim* whose example could be imitated.'

This is absurd. Has anyone every endeavored to seek God without avail? Endeavor to seek him in the manner of those in former days and you too will find Him, just as they did.

11. טוֹבָה חָכְמָה עִם־נַחֲלָה — *wisdom is good with an inheritance.* It is good for the scholar to be self-supporting and free from financial worries so he can immerse himself in his studies — and furthermore his wisdom is a *boon to all mankind,* who will thus benefit from his wise counsel *(Alshich).*

Wisdom is good when there is an inheritance together with it. As we learned in *Avos* 2:2: יָפֶה תַּלְמוּד תּוֹרָה עִם דֶּרֶךְ אֶרֶץ, 'Excellent is Torah-study together with a worldly occupation' *(Midrash).*

Another explanation given in the *Midrash*: Wisdom is good when it is an inheritance [i.e. wisdom transmitted from teacher to student or from father to son for several generations is the superior kind for any possible errors will have been sifted out over a period of many years. (Compare *comm.* to 4:11).]

Wisdom is good when it is accompanied by זְכוּת אָבוֹת, ancestral merit [which is acquired by 'inheritance' *(Torah Temimah)*] *(Rashi).* Happy is one when the merit of his ancestors abides with him and illumines him *(Midrash).*

וְיֹתֵר לְרֹאֵי הַשָּׁמֶשׁ — *A boon to those who see the sun.* i.e. such wisdom benefits all mankind. רֹאֵי הַשָּׁמֶשׁ, *'those who see the sun'* is an all-encompassing phrase embracing all those who benefit from the sun and not only those with sight *(Rashi).*

...[As in the *Talmud*]: הַנּוֹדֵר מֵרוֹאֵי חַמָּה, 'he who vows (not to benfit) from the seers of the sun is forbidden from the blind, too' *(Mishnah, Nedarim* 30b*).*]

12. כִּי בְּצֵל הַחָכְמָה בְּצֵל הַכָּסֶף — *'For*

Hence, *'patience is better than pride'* — better is the forbearance which Shmuel displayed toward the Persian than the impatience which Rav showed him, for with Rav's way, the Persian might have returned to his heathenism. [*Midrash;* a somewhat similar incident is related in the Talmud, *Shabbos* 31a, of *Hillel* and *Shammai.*]

הַחָכְמָה בְּצֵל הַכָּסֶף וְיִתְרוֹן דַּעַת
יג הַחָכְמָה תְּחַיֶּה בְעָלֶיהָ׃ רְאֵה אֶת־מַעֲשֵׂה
הָאֱלֹהִים כִּי מִי יוּכַל לְתַקֵּן אֵת אֲשֶׁר
יד עִוְּתוֹ׃ בְּיוֹם טוֹבָה הֱיֵה בְטוֹב וּבְיוֹם רָעָה
רְאֵה גַּם אֶת־זֶה לְעֻמַּת־זֶה עָשָׂה

(to sit) in the shelter of wisdom (is to sit) in the shelter of money' — because wisdom will ensure eventual wealth *(Rashi).* As we see of Solomon, when God said *'Ask, what shall I give you?' [I Kings* 3:5], he did not request riches, but asked for wisdom, because *'to sit in the shelter of wisdom is to sit in the shelter of money.'* All is included in wisdom *(Rabbeinu Yonah;* see footnote *comm.* to 1:1, and *Overview).*

וְיִתְרוֹן דַּעַת הַחָכְמָה תְּחַיֶּה בְעָלֶיהָ — *And the advantage of knowledge* is that wisdom [or: *'and the advantage of knowing* that wisdom'] *preserves the life of its possessors.* i.e. this is the additional advantage of wisdom over wealth *(Rashi).* Wisdom is spiritual and not subject to physical death *(Ibn Ezra).*

. . . For wisdom can be the means of saving a man's life [and the *Midrash* cites several examples of how the lives of wise people were saved by their ingenuity]. Wealth, however, might be the cause of the owner's death at the hands of robbers *(Metzudas David;* comp. 5:12*).*

13. Man must contemplate why God gave him life. Obviously, only to perform His commandments and act righteously — for who can right his wrongs after death? Therefore submit to God and accept the vicissitudes of life *(Tuv Taam).*

רְאֵה — *Observe,* [i.e. consider], accept graciously *(Kara).*

אֶת־מַעֲשֵׂה הָאֱלֹהִים — *God's doing.* i.e. Consider God's creation — His scheme of the world. Man's lot is predetermined since the Six Days of Creation *(Ibn Ezra).*

Everything is prepared according to man's actions: Gan Eden for the righteous and Gehinnom for the wicked. Consider to what you should cling during your lifetime *(Rashi).*

If you see punishment come upon your generation, be submissive — for who can negate God's Will? *(Kara).*

אֵת אֲשֶׁר עִוְּתוֹ — *What He has twisted?* This refers to Adam. Who can rectify the punishment of death brought about by the Evil Inclination which caused him to eat of the Tree of Knowledge? *(Alshich).*

As the *Midrash* comments: When the Holy One, blessed be He, created the first man, He took him and led him around all the trees of the Garden of Eden, and said to him, 'Behold My works, how beautiful and commendable they are! All that I have created, I created for your sake. Pay heed that you do not corrupt and destroy My universe; for if you corrupt it there is no one to repair it after you!'

14. בְּיוֹם טוֹבָה הֱיֵה בְטוֹב — *Be pleased when things go well* [lit. *'on a day of goodness be good'*] enjoy

*wisdom is to sit in the shelter of money, and the ad-
vantage of knowledge is that wisdom preserves the
life of its possessors.*

13 *Observe God's doing! For who can straighten
what He has twisted?* 14 *Be pleased when things go
well, but in a time of misfortune reflect: God has
made the one as well as the other so that man should*

the good that is granted you and derive pleasure to your heart's content *(Metzudas David)*, seeking to acquire eternal perfection which is the greatest 'good' *(Sforno)*. But while enjoying the good, וּבְיוֹם רָעָה רְאֵה, anticipate [lit. 'see'] the inevitability of bad times, and act accordingly *(Ibn Ezra)*. Contemplate why God punished you, and strive to correct your ways, thrust off your sins and repent *(Almosnino)*.

As *Pesikta d'Rav Kahana* comments: When a day for doing a good deed arrives, do it at once; but when facing a day on which you have done evil, consider how best to repent, so as to be spared from the punishment of the Day [of Judgment.]

Rashi interprets the phrase: when you are in a position to do good, be among those who do good — וּבְיוֹם רָעָה רְאֵה, and when evil comes upon the wicked, be among the observers only, not among the afflicted.

Sefer Chassidim 715 alludes to this verse: 'On a day that you hear good news, be cheerful and do not indulge in fasting and eulogizing; and on an evil day when a scholar dies, do not spend your time strolling about.'

גַּם אֶת־זֶה לְעֻמַּת־זֶה עָשָׂה הָאֱלֹהִים — *God has made the one as well as the other* [i.e. one to parallel the other] — good, with its reward, and evil with its ensuing punishment *(Rashi)*.

God's punishment is never greater than that merited by the seriousness of the transgression, the manner of the punishment corresponds to the sin *(Sforno)*. [One of the classic examples of the above concept is that for the crime of drowning Jewish male infants, the Egyptians themselves were subsequently drowned at the Splitting of the Sea.]

Rabbi Meir said: For everything that God created on this world, He created its counterpart. He created lofty mountains and low hills. He created broad oceans and narrow rivers (*Chagigah* 15a). This concept can be extended to all of creation which is replete with opposite extremes. The size of the universe with its stars, galaxies, and outer cosmos, is virtually infinite; we find that the minuteness of atoms and their component particles are beyond imagination. The orbits of stars and planets are similar to the orbits of electrons around the nuclei of atoms. Most matter is charged with opposite electrical charges, positive and negative. Magnetism has opposite poles. There is matter that exists for

הָאֱלֹהִים עַל־דִּבְרַת שֶׁלֹּא יִמְצָא הָאָדָם
טו אַחֲרָיו מְאוּמָה: אֶת־הַכֹּל רָאִיתִי בִּימֵי
הֶבְלִי יֵשׁ צַדִּיק אֹבֵד בְּצִדְקוֹ וְיֵשׁ רָשָׁע
טז מַאֲרִיךְ בְּרָעָתוֹ: אַל־תְּהִי צַדִּיק הַרְבֵּה
יז וְאַל־תִּתְחַכַּם יוֹתֵר לָמָּה תִּשּׁוֹמֵם: אַל־

millenia and particles whose existence lasts the barest fraction of a second. Science does not yet know the extremes of hot and cold. There are holy and profane, male and female, light and darkness, giver and receiver, influencer and influenced — all examples of זֶה־לְעֻמַּת זֶה the parallel nature of creation *(Rabbi Yaakov Kiffel).*

עַל דִּבְרַת — *So that* [or: *'in order that'.*]

שֶׁלֹּא יִמְצָא הָאָדָם אַחֲרָיו מְאוּמָה — *Man should 'find' nothing after Him* — i.e. Man can have no cause to complain to God because all punishment is clearly in response to man's deeds *(Rashi; Ibn Ezra; Alshich; Sforno).*

Rav Yosef Kara explains the verse differently: God causes both good and evil to descend upon man interchangeably so that man will *find* what will happen *afterwards* to *himself.* With both good and evil always present in the world, man will have no foreknowledge of his destiny — nor will he presume to fathom God's scheme. He will thus submit righteously to his fate [see 3:11].

15. אֶת־הַכֹּל רָאִיתִי — *I have seen everything.* I have contemplated all phenomena in this world in order to perceive their true meaning *(Metzudas David).*

בִּימֵי הֶבְלִי — *During my futile existence* [lit. *'in the days of my futility'.*]

יֵשׁ צַדִּיק אֹבֵד בְּצִדְקוֹ — *Sometimes a righteous man perishes for all his righteousness;* i.e. in spite of his righteousness. God will be more exacting with him and punish him immediately for a minor infraction. Were he not righteous, he might not have been punished at all because better behavior could not be expected of him *(Metzudas David).* [See *Overview;* and *Overview* to ArtScroll edition of *Ruth,* pp. 23-26.]

Rashi explains the verse: even if his death is imminent, he will maintain his righteousness up to the last moment.

וְיֵשׁ רָשָׁע מַאֲרִיךְ בְּרָעָתוֹ — *And sometimes a wicked man endures for all his wickedness. Alshich* explains this as the paradox of צַדִּיק וְרַע לוֹ רָשָׁע וְטוֹב לוֹ — *righteous people who suffer while wicked are fortunate.* God deals strictly with the righteous on earth to atone for their sins so that they will not require punishment in the Hereafter, but He is seemingly lax in punishing the wicked. In reality, however, He is waiting for them to repent.

...[As God says *(Ezek.* 18:32): *'For I have no pleasure in the death of him that dies ... rather repent and live.'*]

find nothing after Him.

15 *I have seen everything during my futile existence: Sometimes a righteous man perishes for all his righteousness, and sometimes a wicked man endures for all his wickedness.* 16 *Do not be overly righteous or excessively wise: why be left desolate?*

The *Midrash* comments: As long as man lives, God looks to him to repent, but when he is dead the hope of doing so is gone . . . For three reasons does God show forbearance to the wicked in this world: perhaps they will repent, perhaps they will perform some precepts for which God can reward them in this world [rather than the Hereafter], and perhaps righteous children will issue from them. Thus we find that He showed forbearance with Ahaz [by allowing him to reign for 16 years *(II Kings* 16:2)] because Hezekiah issued from him; similarly Mordechai issued from the wicked Shim'i [I Kings 2:8; see *comm.* to verse 8.]

Sforno comments that a righteous man will be punished for his sins despite all his good deeds. Only repentance, not good deeds, can atone for sins. Conversely, the wicked are rewarded for their good deeds no matter how outnumbered they may be by sins.

16. אַל־תְּהִי צַדִּיק הַרְבֵּה — *Do not be overly righteous.* Be not more righteous than your Creator, as was Saul who tried to display righteousness but misdirected his mercy on the wicked [I *Sam.* 15:8,9; see *Overview* to *ArtScroll* edition of *Esther* page 28] *(Rashi; Midrash).*

[There is a special term in the *Talmud* for one who is overly righteous: חָסִיד שׁוֹטֶה, *a pious fool.* The classic example is given in the *Talmud:* What is a pious fool like? — for example, a woman is drowning in the river and he says, 'It's improper for me to look upon her and rescue her' (and in his 'piety' he lets her drown; *Sotah* 21b).]

Or: Do not view yourself as being excessively righteous and therefore unworthy of the punishments being thrust on you *(Midrash Lekach Tov).*

וְאַל־תִּתְחַכַּם יוֹתֵר — *Or [do not be] excessively wise.* i.e. [do not presume to be wiser than the Creator or wiser than the Sages] by vowing upon yourself self-imposed, unrequired restrictions *(Sforno).*

As *Rambam* codified in *Hilchos De'os* 3:1: . . . The Sages accordingly enjoined that we should only refrain from that which the Torah has expressly withdrawn from our use. And no one should, by means of vows and oaths, inhibit to himself the use of things permitted. "Do not the prohibitions of the Torah suffice", say our sages, "that you add others for yourself?" In this condemnation, are included those who make a constant practice of fasting; they too are not walking in the right way; our wise men prohibited self-mortification by constant fasting. And concerning

פרק ז
יח־כ

תִּרְשַׁע הַרְבֵּה וְאַל־תְּהִי סָכָל לָמָּה תָמוּת
יח בְּלֹא עִתֶּךָ: טוֹב אֲשֶׁר תֶּאֱחֹז בָּזֶה וְגַם־
מִזֶּה אַל־תַּנַּח אֶת־יָדֶךָ כִּי־יְרֵא אֱלֹהִים
יט יֵצֵא אֶת־כֻּלָּם: הַחָכְמָה תָּעֹז לֶחָכָם
כ מֵעֲשָׂרָה שַׁלִּיטִים אֲשֶׁר הָיוּ בָּעִיר: כִּי
אָדָם אֵין צַדִּיק בָּאָרֶץ אֲשֶׁר יַעֲשֶׂה־טּוֹב

this and similar excesses Solomon exhorts us, *"Do not be overly righteous, nor overly wise. Why be left desolate?"*

Amtachas Binyamin notes that the verse does not say אַל־תְּהִי חָכָם הַרְבֵּה – *Do not be very wise.* Wisdom is a virtue and much wisdom is commendable. The verse cautions אַל־תִּתְחַכַּם יוֹתֵר 'be not *excessively* wise', i.e. do not go beyond your capabilities of wisdom by acting conceitedly, thinking yourself wiser than the Torah.

לָמָּה תִּשּׁוֹמֵם – *Why be left desolate?* – alienated from your friends because of your excessive piety *(Metzudas David).* According to the *Midrash* which refers this phrase to Saul, the meaning of the phrase is: *Why bring about your own doom?*

17. אַל־תִּרְשַׁע הַרְבֵּה – *Be not overly wicked.* Even if you have done something wicked, do not persist in your wickedness [mistakenly thinking that there is no hope of repentance] *(Rashi).*

וְאַל־תְּהִי סָכָל – *Nor be a fool.* Do not, upon realizing that excessive wisdom is a cause of desolation, take the opposite course and become a fool! *(Kara).*

לָמָּה תָמוּת בְּלֹא עִתֶּךָ – *Why die before your time?* As did Saul [*I Chronicles* 10:13] *'who died for his transgressions which he transgressed against HASHEM'.*

[The concept that evil and death are intertwined is found throughout Scriptures. On the verse [*Deut.* 30:15]: וְאֶת הַמָּוֶת וְאֶת הָרָע – *'The death and what is bad'. Rashi* comments: 'If you do good you will have life; but if you do evil you will have death.' See also *Psalms* 37:34 בְּהִכָּרֵת רְשָׁעִים תִּרְאֶה, *'and you will see when the wicked are cut off.'*

18. טוֹב אֲשֶׁר תֶּאֱחֹז בָּזֶה וְגַם־מִזֶּה . . . – *It is best to grasp one and not let go of the other.* [lit. *'it is good that you grasp onto this, and from this you do not release your hand.'*] *Rashi* explains that one must grasp both good and 'evil' – i.e. if a prophet tells you to do something which appears to be evil, you must have confidence and obey him.

Ibn Ezra comments that one should grasp onto both worlds – the spiritual and physical – and scrupulously follow the ideals of the Torah.

According to *Rav Yosef Kara,* the verse reverts to *'righteousness'* and *'wisdom'* in verse 16, and advises that one should tread a middle path between these two virtues and cling to both.

VII
17-20

17 *Be not overly wicked nor be a fool: why die before your time?* 18 *It is best to grasp the one and not let go of the other; he who fears God performs them all.*
19 *Wisdom strengthens the wise more than ten rulers who are in the city.* 20 *For there is no man so wholly righteous on earth that he [always] does good and never sins.*

כִּי־יְרֵא אֱלֹהִים יֵצֵא אֶת־כֻּלָּם — *For he who fears God performs* [i.e. *accomplishes* lit. *'will go forth'*] *them all.* i.e. both traits will blend in him to form a God-fearing way of life *(Ibn Yachya).*

[יֵצֵא — *performs* is translated in the *Talmudic* sense: 'fulfill one's obligations'.]

19. הַחָכְמָה תָּעֹז לֶחָכָם — *Wisdom strengthens the wise* — Having recommended that excessive, conceitful wisdom be shunned, Solomon adds that, nevertheless, wisdom in its proper measure — neither carried to extremes nor obsessive — is one's surest protection [because it leads him to repent *(Rashi)*] — *(Ibn Ezra).*

מֵעֲשָׂרָה שַׁלִּיטִים אֲשֶׁר הָיוּ בָּעִיר — *More than ten rulers who are in the city.* i.e. superior even to the protection that comes to a city from its governing powers ['ten' being a general number standing for *'many'* — see *comm.* to 6:3] *(Ibn Ezra).*

Wisdom *'strengthens'* the wise — enabling intellect to conquer lust. It is more powerful than the ten major organs of man: eyes, ears, hands, feet, mouth and heart which cause man to stray *(Sforno).*

20. No man is so righteous that he can dispense with the aid of wisdom *(Ibn Latif).*

כִּי אָדָם אֵין צַדִּיק בָּאָרֶץ — *For there is no man so wholly righteous on earth.* This verse connects with verse 16: *Do not be overly righteous,* and advises that *complete righteousness* is an impossible goal. Man must succumb to sin in some form — whether by act, speech, or thought *(Ibn Ezra).*

[The phrase is clearly reminiscent of Solomon's prayer at the Dedication of the בֵּית הַמִּקְדָּשׁ, Holy Temple *(I Kings* 8:46): כִּי אֵין אָדָם אֲשֶׁר לֹא־יֶחֱטָא *'for there is no man who does not sin.'*]

The phrase בָּאָרֶץ, *on earth* is stressed because it is the אַרְצִיּוּת, *mundanity,* of this earthly existence, that draws man to sin *(Yavetz).*

אֲשֶׁר יַעֲשֶׂה־טּוֹב וְלֹא יֶחֱטָא — *Who [always] does good and never sins.* [The translation follows *Ibn Ezra;* literally the Hebrew translates: *'who will do good and not sin.'*]

Therefore the wise man should not be over-confident. Even Moses sinned! *(Michlol Yofi)* Let him rather search out and improve his ways *(Rashi).*[1]

1. It is self-evident that, being aware of his shortcomings, a man should be humble. It is impossible for any man to be altogether without faults which may be due to nature, to heredity, to accidents, or to his own doings. *"For there is not a man wholly righteous on earth who*

פרק ז כא וְלֹא יֶחֱטָא: גַּם לְכָל־הַדְּבָרִים אֲשֶׁר
כא־כה יְדַבֵּרוּ אַל־תִּתֵּן לִבֶּךָ אֲשֶׁר לֹא־תִשְׁמַע
כב אֶת־עַבְדְּךָ מְקַלְלֶךָ: כִּי גַּם־פְּעָמִים רַבּוֹת
יָדַע לִבֶּךָ אֲשֶׁר גַּם־אַתְּ* קִלַּלְתָּ אֲחֵרִים:
כג כָּל־זֹה נִסִּיתִי בַחָכְמָה אָמַרְתִּי אֶחְכָּמָה
כד וְהִיא רְחוֹקָה מִמֶּנִּי: רָחוֹק מַה־שֶּׁהָיָה
כה וְעָמֹק | עָמֹק מִי יִמְצָאֶנּוּ: סַבּוֹתִי אֲנִי וְלִבִּי
לָדַעַת וְלָתוּר וּבַקֵּשׁ חָכְמָה וְחֶשְׁבּוֹן
וְלָדַעַת רֶשַׁע כֶּסֶל וְהַסִּכְלוּת הוֹלֵלוֹת:

* אַתָּה ק׳

Therefore, if you see a *'righteous man who perishes for all his righteousness,'* [verse 16] know that his punishment is probably the result of some infraction for which he received retribution in this world, because *'no man is so righteous on earth that he never sinned' (Rav Saadiah Gaon).*

21.-22. גַּם לְכָל־הַדְּבָרִים אֲשֶׁר יְדַבֵּרוּ — *Moreover, pay not attention to everything [men] say.* Do not be receptive to the evil talk of others about yourself *(Rashi).*

אֲשֶׁר לֹא־תִשְׁמַע אֶת־עַבְדְּךָ מְקַלְלֶךָ — *Lest you hear your [own] servant disparaging you.* If you pay attention to what others say about you, you will discover that even your own servant speaks disparagingly of you. Therefore, ignore such talk and spare yourself anger and vexation *(Ibn Ezra; Kehilas Yaakov).*

The translation מְקַלְלֶךָ, *'disparaging'*, follows *Rashi* who comments [on *Deut.* 21:23] that the term קְלָלָה in Scriptures always denotes treating lightly or acting disparagingly.

אֲשֶׁר גַּם־אַתְּ קִלַּלְתָּ אֲחֵרִים — *That you yourself disparaged others* — and being guilty of the same misdeed why should you grow angry when you hear it from others? *(Sforno).*

23. כָּל־זֹה נִסִּיתִי בַחָכְמָה — *All this I tested with wisdom.* The truth of the above reflections — and that which follows — I tested with wisdom *(Ibn Ezra)* of the Torah *(Rashi).*

וְהִיא רְחוֹקָה מִמֶּנִּי — *But it is beyond me.* I could not master the kind of wisdom that would enable me to solve the deeper perplexities of life *(Ibn Yachya).*

Although wisdom was beyond me, I persisted until I acquired it *(Ibn Ezra).*

The *Midrash* points out that in his wisdom Solomon perceived the

always does good; and never sins". . . There is no one so learned that he does not make mistakes, or who is not in need of learning from his equals, and at times even from his disciples. How, then, shall a man dare to boast of his learning?

The man of understanding will, upon reflection, realize that there is no justification for pride even if he was privileged to become very learned. A man of understanding who has acquired more knowledge than the average person, has accomplished nothing more than what

[21] *Moreover, pay no attention to everything men*
say, lest you hear your own servant disparging you,
[22] *for your own conscience knows that many times*
you yourself disparged others.
[23] *All this I tested with wisdom; I thought I could*
become wise, but it is beyond me. [24] *What existed is*
elusive; and so very deep, who can find it? [25] *So I*
turned my attention to study and probe and seek
wisdom and reckoning, and to know the wickedness
of folly, and the foolishness which is madness:

meaning of all the ordinances of the Torah, 'but the chapter of the פָּרָה אֲדוּמָּה, *Red Heifer,* I was unable to fathom. When I labored therein, *I thought I could become wise, but it is beyond me.'* [The commentators point out that the numerical value of וְהִיא רְחוֹקָה, *but it is beyond* [= 341] equals פָּרָה אֲדוּמָּה, *Red Heifer.*]

24. רָחוֹק מַה־שֶּׁהָיָה וְעָמֹק עָמֹק מִי יִמְצָאֶנּוּ — *What existed is elusive, so very deep, who can fathom it.* [lit. *'for that which has been; and deep, deep, who can find it?'*]

[Everything is elusive: what pre-existed creation; what is above and below, who can fathom? Man is helpless — in his limited intellect — before the infinite greatness of God's Creation.]

Furthermore, man is not permitted to delve into these metaphysical matters of 'what is above and below, before and after' *(Rashi).*

The crux of the matter is that although one can conceivably reach a state of Belief by intellectual means, he should not rely solely on wisdom, for often it can cause man to stray from the proper path. Only if the intellect is permeated with Belief and Torah ideals will it stand him in good stead *(Rav Saadiah Gaon).*

25. סַבּוֹתִי אֲנִי וְלִבִּי — *So I turned my attention* [lit. *'I turned, I and my heart'*] i.e. I totally and intensively immersed myself — body and soul —into this quest *(Ibn Latif; Metzudas David).*

וְחֶשְׁבּוֹן — *And reckoning* i.e. reason and perception *(Metzudas David).* [In verse 29 it has the meaning of 'contrivance' *(Sforno).*]

Rav Yosef Kara explains the verse differently: 'When it became clear to me that comprehension of the deeper workings of the world was beyond my intellectual grasp סַבּוֹתִי אֲנִי וְלִבִּי — *I shifted my attention* to pursuing my observations on life as they flowed from the practical wisdom at my command. He concentrated on perceiving

his nature impelled him to do, as it is the nature of the bird to fly, or of the ox to pull with all its strength. Hence if a man is learned, he is indebted to natural gifts which he happens to possess . . . For indeed we are like the servants of a household. Everyone of us is appointed to some task and is expected to remain at his post and do the work of the household as well as possible. In the scheme of life there is no room for pride *(Mesillas Yesharim).*

כו וּמוֹצֶא אֲנִי מַר מִמָּוֶת אֶת־הָאִשָּׁה אֲשֶׁר־
הִיא מְצוֹדִים וַחֲרָמִים לִבָּהּ אֲסוּרִים יָדֶיהָ
טוֹב לִפְנֵי הָאֱלֹהִים יִמָּלֵט מִמֶּנָּה וְחוֹטֵא
כז יִלָּכֶד בָּהּ׃ רְאֵה זֶה מָצָאתִי אָמְרָה קֹהֶלֶת
כח אַחַת לְאַחַת לִמְצֹא חֶשְׁבּוֹן׃ אֲשֶׁר עוֹד־
בִּקְשָׁה נַפְשִׁי וְלֹא מָצָאתִי אָדָם אֶחָד
מֵאֶלֶף מָצָאתִי וְאִשָּׁה בְכָל־אֵלֶּה לֹא
כט מָצָאתִי׃ לְבַד רְאֵה־זֶה מָצָאתִי אֲשֶׁר
עָשָׂה הָאֱלֹהִים אֶת־הָאָדָם יָשָׁר וְהֵמָּה
בִקְשׁוּ חִשְּׁבֹנוֹת רַבִּים׃

which is the worst of all evils and most foolish of all folly, the result of which he reveals in the following verses.

26. וּמוֹצֶא אֲנִי מַר מִמָּוֶת — *And I have discovered* [lit. *'and I find'*] *more bitter than death.* Because she demands of man things which are beyond his power she ultimately kills him with a bitter death *(Midrash).* Given a choice, one should prefer death *(Metzudas David).*

[It is abundantly clear that Solomon refers only to evil, licentious women, who erotically trap man into evil ways. This is not a wholesale condemnation of all women. His praise of the God-fearing women in *Proverbs* 18:22 מָצָא אִשָּׁה מָצָא טוֹב, *'he who has found a wife found good'*; ibid. 31:10 ff, (the famous *'Aishes Chayil'*); and his statement in 9:9 leave no room for doubt.]

The *Talmud* notes that they used to ask a man who had just gotten married, thus: מָצָא, *'Matza?'* or מוֹצֵא, *'Motzei?'* [i.e. 'is your wife good or evil?'] because in *Prov. 18:22 the word 'matza'* is used in connection with a good wife, and in our verse *'motzei'* is used in connection with a bad wife *(Berachos* 8a).

אֶת־הָאִשָּׁה אֲשֶׁר־הִיא מְצוֹדִים וַחֲרָמִים לִבָּהּ — *The woman whose heart is snares and nets* [or: *'who is snares, and her heart nets.'*] — always eager to ensnare *(Ibn Yachya).*

אֲסוּרִים יָדֶיהָ — *Her arms are chains* — No one can escape her clutches *(Rashi).* [or: *Her hands are tied* — she performs no useful task, and becomes indolent.]

טוֹב לִפְנֵי הָאֱלֹהִים יִמָּלֵט מִמֶּנָּה — *He who is pleasing to God* — like Joseph [*Gen.* 39:13] *(Midrash)* — *escapes her.*

27. [Solomon assures us that he formulated this discovery only after a minute investigation.]

אָמְרָה קֹהֶלֶת — *Said Koheles* — the verb here is in the feminine form. *Rashi* explains that here *Koheles* means *'a collection of wisdom'* rather than the name of Solomon. Thus, the word *Koheles,* in this sense is feminine.

26 *And I have discovered more bitter than death:
the woman whose heart is snares and nets; her arms
are chains. He who is pleasing to God escapes her but
the sinner is caught by her.*
27 *See, this is what I found, said Koheles, adding
one to another to reach a conclusion,* 28 *which yet my
soul seeks but I have not found. One man in a thousand I have found, but one woman among them I
have not found.* 29 *But, see, this I did find: God has
made man simple, but they sought many intrigues.*

Metzudas David holds that the subject of the verse is the 'soul' (a feminine word) of the gatherer of conflicting ideas.

אַחַת לְאַחַת לִמְצֹא חֶשְׁבּוֹן — *Adding one to another* [lit. *'one to one'*] *to reach a conclusion.* Just as one who is involved with a great mathematical problem begins with 'one', so did Solomon proceed according to the disciplines of logic in his quest *(Kara).*

28. אֲשֶׁר עוֹד־בִּקְשָׁה נַפְשִׁי וְלֹא מָצָאתִי — *Which yet my soul seeks but I have not found* — besides the quests described above, he strove for one more thing but was as yet unsatisfied *(Rashi).*

אָדָם אֶחָד מֵאֶלֶף מָצָאתִי — *One man in a thousand I have found* — I was able to find a small number of worthy men, aloof from sin; who could collaborate in my investigation; *but one woman among them* — i.e. from all my thousand wives [700 wives, 300 concubines (*I Kings* 11:3] *I could not find (Kara; Ralbag)* because Solomon was ultimately led into sin by his wives *(Ibn Yachya).*

Metzudas David says that, generally speaking, people can be considered good only relative to others who are inferior to them. Very few are so eminent that they would be regarded as exceptional even without comparing them to others. Solomon says that among men he has occasionally found such a person, but among all his thousand wives he found not one.

[It is clear, as was pointed out earlier, that Solomon is not suggesting that righteous women did not exist at all — but, in his personal experience they were even a greater rarity than righteous men.]

29. לְבַד רְאֵה־זֶה מָצָאתִי — *But, see, this I did find* — something which is also more bitter than death *(Alshich);* and which brought about a stumbling-block before the world *(Rashi).*

אֲשֶׁר עָשָׂה הָאֱלֹהִים אֶת־הָאָדָם יָשָׁר — *God has made man simple* [lit. *'upright'*], i.e. God created Adam perfectly upright *(Rashi).*

וְהֵמָּה — *But they,* i.e. when Eve was created from the body of Adam, and he became two people *(Midrash; Rashi).*

בִקְשׁוּ חִשְּׁבֹנוֹת רַבִּים — *Sought many intrigues* [lit. *'reckonings'*] and Adam then lost his uprightness and

פרק ח א מִי כְּהֶחָכָם וּמִי יוֹדֵעַ פֵּשֶׁר דָּבָר חָכְמַת
א־ד ב אָדָם תָּאִיר פָּנָיו וְעֹז פָּנָיו יְשֻׁנֶּא: אֲנִי פִּי־
מֶלֶךְ שְׁמוֹר וְעַל דִּבְרַת שְׁבוּעַת אֱלֹהִים:
ג אַל־תִּבָּהֵל מִפָּנָיו תֵּלֵךְ אַל־תַּעֲמֹד בְּדָבָר
ד רָע כִּי כָּל־אֲשֶׁר יַחְפֹּץ יַעֲשֶׂה: בַּאֲשֶׁר
דְּבַר־מֶלֶךְ שִׁלְטוֹן וּמִי יֹאמַר־לוֹ מַה־

sinned *(Midrash).*

Many commentators apply this verse to mankind as a whole: *God created mankind upright* — i.e. with a perfect nature capable of high attainments. Man's perversions spring from his own devices, which, in turn, cause his downfall *(Rambam).*

[God has provided man with all his needs — but man is not satisfied; he always tries to 'improve' nature. He thus causes his own complications] ...

Not only does man seek out one intrigue — he seeks *many* intrigues; i.e. he delves into areas which are beyond him and tries to become overly wise. This results in man losing the simplicity which is innately his *(Akeidas Yitzchak).*

VIII

1. מִי כְּהֶחָכָם — *Who is like the wise man?* [A rhetorical question]: Who in this world is as important as the man of wisdom? *(Rashi).*

Who is as wise as that one man in a thousand that I found? [7:28] *(Sforno).*

וּמִי יוֹדֵעַ פֵּשֶׁר דָּבָר — *And who knows what things mean?* i.e. the solution of things *(Rashi).*

According to *Metzudas David,* the comparative prefix כְּ ['like'] of the first phrase refers to this phrase as well. Thus: וּמִי כְּיוֹדֵעַ, and who is like the one who knows what things mean? [No one equals the man of wisdom and insight.]

חָכְמַת אָדָם תָּאִיר פָּנָיו — *A man's wisdom lights up his face.* Because of his wisdom man gains the admiration of all who know him. This gladdens one's heart and causes his countenance to beam *(Metzudas David).*

See the difference between wealth and wisdom. Wealth increases anxieties and robs one of his sleep [2:23]; wisdom, however, brightens his face *(Kara).*

According to the *Midrash,* this verse refers to the scholar who knows how to expound his learning. His *'wisdom makes his face shine'* — when he is asked a question and is able to answer.

וְעֹז פָּנָיו יְשֻׁנֶּא — *And the 'boldness of his face' is transformed* i.e. wisdom refines one's countenance *(Metzudas David).*

2. אֲנִי — *I counsel you.* [The Hebrew has only *'I'.* The words *'counsel you'* are supplied following the commentaries of *Ibn Ezra; Metzudas David).*

VIII
1-4

Who is like the wise man? and who knows what things mean? A man's wisdom lights up his face, and the boldness of his face is transformed.
2 I counsel you: Obey the king's command, and that in the manner of an oath of God.
3 Do not hasten to leave his presence, do not persist in an evil thing; for he can do whatever he pleases.
4 Since a king's word is law, who dare say to him, 'What are you do-

פִּי־מֶלֶךְ שְׁמֹר — *Obey the king's command* [lit. *'guard the king's mouth'.*] The commentaries differ which *'king'* is referred to: the King of the Universe or a mortal king. *Rashi* offers both interpretations.

Shaar Bas Rabim interprets this as referring to a mortal king whom we are required to obey. He quotes, in support, the dictum in *Avos* 3:2: 'Pray for the peace of the government.'

וְעַל דִּבְרַת שְׁבוּעַת אֱלֹהִים — *And that in the manner of an oath of God.* [An ambiguous phrase which can be variously interpreted]: Because of the oath of allegiance to God's commandments that we took at Horeb *(Rashi);*

Obey the king's orders if only because of the oath of allegiance taken in God's Name at the time of coronation *(Kara)* [and because of the injunction against uttering שְׁבוּעַת שָׁוְא, an Oath in God's Name, in vain.]

The king's command must be obeyed — but only when his command is in consonance with the שְׁבוּעַת אֱלֹהִים, the Oath to God, i.e. that his requests are not contrary to the Laws of the Torah *(Metzudas David).*

3. אַל־תִּבָּהֵל מִפָּנָיו תֵּלֵךְ — *Do not hasten to leave his presence.*

[The translation follows *Ibn Ezra* who interprets תֵּלֵךְ not as an isolated word: *'Go!'*, but as if it were שֶׁתֵּלֵךְ or לָלֶכֶת.]

Do not throw off your allegiance to the king *(Akeidas Yitzchak).*

Do not be hasty and say that you intend to flee from His Presence to a spot where he does not reign. He reigns everywhere *(Rashi).*

אַל־תַּעֲמֹד בְּדָבָר רָע — *Do not persist* [lit. *'stand'*] *in an evil thing,* i.e. something that is evil in his eyes, for he can do as he pleases [and exact retribution] *(Ibn Ezra).*

Rav Yosef Kara comments: Do not associate with those who would rebel against him.

Ethically, the verse is interpreted: *Do not persist in an evil thing;* when you have done something evil, do not continue, but withdraw and repent immediately *(Me'am Loaz).*

This phrase is cited as the reason that in the Synagogal reading of the Torah, the reader does not conclude an individual *aliyah* with an inauspicious phrase, because אַל־תַּעֲמֹד, בְּדָבָר רָע 'Do not stand [i.e. pause] during a bad thing [an inauspicious verse]' (cf. *Midrash; Poras Yosef).*

4. בַּאֲשֶׁר דְּבַר־מֶלֶךְ שִׁלְטוֹן — *Since a king's word is law* [lit. *'is power'*].

פרק ח

ה תַּעֲשֶׂה: שֹׁמֵר מִצְוָה לֹא יֵדַע דָּבָר רָע
ו וְעֵת וּמִשְׁפָּט יֵדַע לֵב חָכָם: כִּי לְכָל־חֵפֶץ
יֵשׁ עֵת וּמִשְׁפָּט כִּי רָעַת הָאָדָם רַבָּה
ז עָלָיו: כִּי־אֵינֶנּוּ יֹדֵעַ מַה־שֶּׁיִּהְיֶה כִּי
ח כַּאֲשֶׁר יִהְיֶה מִי יַגִּיד לוֹ: אֵין אָדָם שַׁלִּיט
בָּרוּחַ לִכְלוֹא אֶת־הָרוּחַ וְאֵין שִׁלְטוֹן
בְּיוֹם הַמָּוֶת וְאֵין מִשְׁלַחַת בַּמִּלְחָמָה

The translation of בַּאֲשֶׁר, *since,* follows *Rashi. Targum* and *Ibn Ezra* render it as a geographical connotation: *wherever* the king's dominion extends, he rules over you, and no one dares contradict him. If this applies to a human king, how much more to the True King whose glory is omnipresent! *(Ibn Ezra).*

[This verse thus sums up the futility of rebelling against royalty.]

5.-6. שׁוֹמֵר מִצְוָה — *He who obeys the commandment* [i.e. the מִצְוֹת, precepts of HASHEM (according to most commentators).]

לֹא יֵדַע דָּבָר רָע — *Will know no evil. Ibn Ezra* translates: will not seek to know of anything evil [thus harmonizing the verse with the apparent contradictions in 7:15 and 8:14.]

[Or, if the verse refers to mortal kings, the meaning is obvious: No harm will come to one who is obedient to the king.]

וְעֵת וּמִשְׁפָּט יֵדַע לֵב חָכָם — *A wise mind* [lit. *'heart'*] *will know time and justice.* i.e. a wise man will perceive that there is a predetermined time during which God will exact justice from the wicked *(Rashi).*

[לֵב, *heart,* is used interchangeably throughout Scriptures to represent the seat of intellect and emotion.]

כִּי לְכָל־חֵפֶץ יֵשׁ עֵת וּמִשְׁפָּט — *For everything has its time and justice* — and retribution is sure to come *(Ibn Latif).*

'For everything has its time' and every time has its thing. As man wishes so can he act in this world; but there will be a judgment and reckoning *(Midrash).*

כִּי־רָעַת הָאָדָם רַבָּה עָלָיו — *For man's evil overwhelms him* — and man is the cause of his own punishment *(Divrei Chefetz).*

Rashi interprets כִּי, *when,* and renders: when *man's evil becomes exceedingly overwhelming* [in God's eyes] and their 'measure overflows' meaning that their measure of sins goes beyond God's forbearance, then punishment is heaped upon them *(Rashi).* [This description of sin and punishment is similar to the sequence found concerning the Generation of the Flood (*Gen* 6:5, 7): *'And HASHEM saw that the wickedness of man was great in the earth'* . . .(and then) . . . *'HASHEM said, I will destroy man.'*]

The moral is that man should therefore be wary of his ways and avoid punishment *(Kara).*

ing?' 5 He who obeys the commandment will know no evil; and a wise mind will know time and justice. 6 For everything has its time and justice, for man's evil overwhelms him. 7 Indeed, he does not know what will happen, for when it happens, who will tell him?

8 Man is powerless over the spirit — to restrain the spirit; nor is there authority over the day of death;

7. כִּי־אֵינֶנּוּ יֹדֵעַ מַה־שֶּׁיִּהְיֶה — *Indeed, he does not know what will happen.* The future is closed to man and he cannot foresee specific future events except in general, vague terms *(Ibn Ezra).*

A clear comprehension of potential events is closed to man unless he completely immerses himself in these matters. Then his intellect will allow him to perceive 'the time and justice' *(Metzudas David).*

Rashi explains the phrase that when the wicked person sins *he does not give thought to the outcome, and to the resulting punishment,* and 'woe to him for this!'

כִּי כַּאֲשֶׁר יִהְיֶה מִי יַגִּיד לוֹ — *For when it happens who will tell him?* When he performs a potentially destructive act, who will forewarn him of the consequences so he can be more cautious in the future? *(Sforno).*

Or, according to *Rashi:* When the time for punishment has come, who will discuss the matter with him and first ask permission? Punishment will descend suddenly and without warning.

8. אֵין אָדָם שַׁלִּיט בָּרוּחַ — *Man is powerless over the spirit,* i.e. even if man were to know his day of death, how would it avail him? He has no control over the will of God's emissary [the Angel of Death who is referred to as a 'spirit' *(Midrash)*], לִכְלוֹא אֶת־הָרוּחַ, *to restrain the spirit,* i.e. to lock his soul within his body where it is 'imprisoned' and not release it *(Rashi, Ibn Ezra, Metzudas David).*

וְאֵין שִׁלְטוֹן בְּיוֹם הַמָּוֶת — *Nor is there* [i.e. *'nor has he'*] *authority over the day of death,* as the *Midrash* comments: A man cannot say to the Angel of Death 'Wait for me until I finish my business and then I will come.'

Rashi and *Ibn Ezra* translate: Royalty is of no avail on the day of death [i.e. kings, too, are subject to death and their royalty is not recognized by the Angel of Death]. As *Rashi* observes, David is referred to throughout Scripture as הַמֶּלֶךְ דָּוִד, King David. When his approaching death was mentioned, however, he is called merely 'David' [*I Kings* 2:1]: וַיִּקְרְבוּ יְמֵי דָוִד לָמוּת, *'and the days of David drew near to die'.* His kingship is ignored.

וְאֵין מִשְׁלַחַת בַּמִּלְחָמָה — *Nor discharge* [i.e. *'embassy', 'dispatch'*] *in war.* A man cannot say [when engaged in this battle with the Angel of Death *(Kara; Torah Temimah)*], 'Here is my son, or my slave, or a member of my household

ט וְלֹא־יְמַלֵּט רֶשַׁע אֶת־בְּעָלָיו: אֶת־כָּל־זֶה
רָאִיתִי וְנָתוֹן אֶת־לִבִּי לְכָל־מַעֲשֶׂה אֲשֶׁר
נַעֲשָׂה תַּחַת הַשָּׁמֶשׁ עֵת אֲשֶׁר שָׁלַט
י הָאָדָם בְּאָדָם לְרַע לוֹ: וּבְכֵן רָאִיתִי
רְשָׁעִים קְבֻרִים וָבָאוּ וּמִמְּקוֹם קָדוֹשׁ
יְהַלֵּכוּ וְיִשְׁתַּכְּחוּ בָעִיר אֲשֶׁר כֵּן־עָשׂוּ גַּם־

instead of me' *(Midrash; Rashi).*

Ibn Ezra and *Metzudas Zion* translate מִשְׁלַחַת: weapons, and render: 'neither will weapons be of avail to provide immunity from death in war-time.'

וְלֹא־יְמַלֵּט רֶשַׁע אֶת־בְּעָלָיו — *And wickedness cannot save the wrong-doer* [lit. *'its owner'*] i.e. Evil-doers will not escape punishment for their deeds — their *wickedness* will not be their salvation, [as Solomon declared in *Proverbs* 10:2, 11:4]: וּצְדָקָה תַּצִּיל מִמָּוֶת, 'and it is *righteousness* that saves from death' *(Kara).*

Many commentators *(Ibn Ezra; Sforno; Lekach Tov)* explain רֶשַׁע as referring to 'riches' — the bulk of which man acquires through evil means: wealth will not save its owner from punishment; only repentance and good deeds will.

. . . *Torah Temimah* explains the above interpretation: By changing the order of a word's letters, a different word is often formed. This new word suggests a deeper meaning in addition to the simple interpretation. . .[He cites many Talmudic examples such as וישחטו וישטחו *(Yoma 75b);* פרש־שרף *(Yevamos 16b, Maharsha);* ויצף ויפץ: בעמלו־בעולמו *(Midrash).*] Thus רֶשַׁע, *'wickedness',* when inverted becomes עֹשֶׁר *riches.* The above interpretation is suggested by another of Solomon's utterances [*Prov.* 11:4]: לֹא יוֹעִיל הוֹן בְּיוֹם עֶבְרָה —*'Riches are of no avail in the day of wrath.'*

[Man must thus strive to live righteously; nothing else can help him on the day of death.]

9. אֶת־כָּל־זֶה רָאִיתִי — *All this have I seen* i.e. perceived by actual experience *(Sforno).*

Rashi takes this phrase to refer to the previous verses and interprets it as a concluding remark.

Metzudas David understands it to be an introductory remark i.e. whatever follows, I personally experienced and set my mind to comprehend.

וְנָתוֹן אֶת־לִבִּי — *and I applied* [lit. *gave*] *my mind* [lit. *'my heart'.*]

[Again *'heart'* is used to depict the seat of intellect and emotion.]

עֵת אֲשֶׁר שָׁלַט. . . — *There is a time when one man rules over another to his detriment.* [The translation follows *Rashi* and *Sforno.*] One person can attain dominion over another, but will ultimately be punished for his acts of domination. Amalek attacked Israel, but was later doomed. Egypt enslaved Israel only to be decimated *(Rashi, Sforno).*

*nor discharge in war; and wickedness cannot save the
wrong-doer.*
9 *All this have I seen; and I applied my mind to
every deed that is done under the sun: there is a time
when one man rules over another to his detriment.*
10 *And then I saw the wicked buried and newly
come while those who had done right were gone from
the Holy place and were forgotten in the city. This,*

According to *Metzudas David*, the object of the sentence is not the oppressor, but the oppressed: *'One man rules over another to his* (the victim's) *detriment.*

Rav Yosef Kara explains the verse: I realized that when man feels that the time is auspicious he will persecute his comrade, rob and steal from him, and rationalize that there is no Law and no Judge. He does not realize that his actions are detrimental to him because *'God defends the pursued'* [3:15] and he will be punished.

10. וּבְכֵן רָאִיתִי — *And then I saw.* [This is one of the most semantically difficult verses in the entire book and several interpretations are offered. In translation, perhaps a paraphrase does it the most justice. Our translation, which presents the meaning of the words following the written text is based on *Ibn Ezra.* The subject of the verse is the wicked of the previous verse 'who rule over their fellow man' — and קְבֻרִים, are buried peacefully in their graves as in *Psalms* 74:4, i.e. who die without anguish. He understands וָבָאוּ as meaning 'they came into the world a second time (i.e. their children succeed and perpetuate them)...

The phrase וּמִמְּקוֹם קָדוֹשׁ יְהַלֵּכוּ, *while those who were gone from the holy place* refers to the righteous, 'the holy ones' who, because they die without children, become forgotten in the city where they were ...

And these [ironically] are the ones אֲשֶׁר כֵּן־עָשׂוּ who had acted righteously (כֵּן meaning 'right' as in *Numbers* 27:7 כֵּן בְּנוֹת צְלָפְחָד דֹּבְרֹת *The daughters of Zelafchad speak right).*

The anomaly is how the good deeds of the righteous are forgotten, but the wicked die peacefully and leave a legacy of evil behind them. This is a great futility.]

According to *Rashi* קְבֻרִים, *buried,* refers to the wicked who were held in contempt by the nations of the world and were worthy of being buried in the dust. Though a despicable nation, they would one day conquer the Holy City and dwell in the Holy Temple. Upon returning home they would be brazen enough to pride themselves in their ugly deeds.

וּמִמְּקוֹם קָדוֹשׁ יְהַלֵּכוּ — *Were gone from the holy place.* This phrase, as explained, refers to the righteous whose every action leads from one sanctity to another *(Metzudas David).*

Midrash Lekach Tov interprets

יא זֶה־הָבֶל: אֲשֶׁר אֵין־נַעֲשָׂה פִתְגָם מַעֲשֵׂה
הָרָעָה מְהֵרָה עַל־כֵּן מָלֵא לֵב בְּנֵי־הָאָדָם
יב בָּהֶם לַעֲשׂוֹת רָע: אֲשֶׁר חֹטֶא עֹשֶׂה רָע
מְאַת וּמַאֲרִיךְ לוֹ כִּי גַּם־יוֹדֵעַ אָנִי אֲשֶׁר
יִהְיֶה־טּוֹב לְיִרְאֵי הָאֱלֹהִים אֲשֶׁר יִירְאוּ
יג מִלְּפָנָיו: וְטוֹב לֹא־יִהְיֶה לָרָשָׁע וְלֹא־
יַאֲרִיךְ יָמִים כַּצֵּל אֲשֶׁר אֵינֶנּוּ יָרֵא מִלִּפְנֵי

the entire phrase as referring to the wicked: They live out their lives and new ones spring up after them, imitating their ways. וּמִמְּקוֹם קָדוֹשׁ יְהַלֵּכוּ, they always keep away from holy places — synagogues and study-houses, וְיִשְׁתַּכְּחוּ בָעִיר אֲשֶׁר כֵּן־עָשׂוּ, and their evil deeds are ultimately forgotten without anyone having learned a moral lesson from their evil ways. This is futility.

11. [Koheles attributes the flourishing of wickedness to the delay in retribution which tends to strengthen the tendency toward evil.]

פִּתְגָם — *Sentence* [lit. *'decree'* as in *Esther* 1:20.]

מְהֵרָה — *Quickly* i.e. A man sins and the מִדַּת הַדִּין, Attribute of Justice, does not overtake him *(Midrash).*

מָלֵא לֵב בְּנֵי־הָאָדָם בָּהֶם — *Men are encouraged* [lit. *'the heart of man is full in them.'*] They lose all fear of retribution *(Rabbi Eliezer of Worms)* and rationalize that there is no justice in the world. Therefore, they sin with impunity *(Ralbag).*

They assume that because punishment does not befall them immediately after their sin, they will escape altogether. What they do not realize, however, is that, *at that moment*, some merit of theirs protected them from retribution. But it will not shield them indefinitely. Punishment will come *(Torah Temimah).*

12.-13. [These verses continue the thought of the previous verse. They elaborate on what the wicked see that encourages them to sin with impunity. Nevertheless, Solomon disavows this evidence and affirms his faith in the Divine Justice which rewards the righteous and punishes the sinner.]

עֹשֶׂה רָע מְאַת — *Does what is wrong a hundred times* (so *Ibn Ezra);* incalculable times in multiples of a hundred *(Rashi);* or 'did wrong to a hundred people' *(Metzudas David).*

וּמַאֲרִיךְ לוֹ — *And [God] is patient with him.* [lit. *'and He extends to him'*] i.e. מַאֲרִיךְ לוֹ אַף, *withholds His anger (Metzudas David)* [אֶרֶךְ אַפַּיִם, *Slow to Anger,* being one of the Attributes of God *(Ex.* 34:6)][1]

1. In this connection I quote *Rav S.R. Hirsch's* comment on *Exodus* 34:6:
As אֶרֶךְ אַפַּיִם, Who has Patience, [God] is forbearing and gives time for the powers which He has granted, and grants again and again, to bear the intended fruit of moral development of

VIII
11-13

too, is futility! 11 *Because the sentence for wrong-doing is not executed quickly — that is why men are encouraged to do evil,* 12 *because a sinner does what is wrong a hundred times and He is patient with him, yet nevertheless I am aware that it will be well with those who fear God that they may fear Him,* 13 *and that it will not be well with the wicked, and he will not long endure—like a shadow—because he does not fear God.*

[The wicked therefore interpret this forbearance as permission to continue their evil ways, rather than understanding it as part of God's master plan of the world.][2]

כִּי גַם־יוֹדֵעַ אָנִי — *Yet nevertheless I, am aware* [lit. *'for also I know'*]. Let no one think that I [Koheles] share the sinner's view. Just as every man of intellect perceives God's justice, so do I know that in the Eternal World it will go well only for those who fear Him, and that in the Hereafter the wicked will find no goodness, but their souls will be cut off *(Metzudas David).*

Even to the righteous He is 'patient' in granting his reward, but just as I believe that in the end the sinner will receive his due, I also believe that the righteous will ultimately receive his reward *(Tuv Taam).*

Although God does not hurry to exact retribution from the wicked and make a distinction between the righteous and the wicked, nevertheless I know that ultimately everyone will receive his just reward and it will go well with those who fear Him *(Rashi).*

וְטוֹב לֹא־יִהְיֶה לָרָשָׁע — *And that it will not be well with the wicked* — in the Hereafter, and his soul will be cut off *(Metzudas David).*

כַּצֵּל — *Like a shadow* — [which is non tangible and unenduring.]

life — Who gives patient consideration to the moral weakness — which are just what give the possibility of moral greatness — of those of his creatures who are called upon to give free-willed obedience. Who has pleasure in waiting and waiting until the Godly freedom in Man has gained the upper hand in the fight against the temptations of the senses, and in this expectation keeps up even those who are still ignoble and incomplete with His strength-giving, never ending, maintaining love (אֶרֶךְ אַפַּיִם); or, where the gifts granted expand faithfully in accordance with the object for which they were given.

2. Much enlightenment on this subject is provided in the *Sefer haIkkarim.* I quote at length:

Benefits may come to the wicked for their own sake or for the sake of the righteous. For their own sake they are sometimes well treated so as to harden their hearts that they may not repent after having rebelled against and grieved His holy name and committed great wrong. This is what the Rabbis mean when they say that God withholds the ways of repentance from the wicked. Or the opposite, namely that God is kind and prolongs their days in order that they may repent.

A wicked man may also be prosperous for the sake of the righteous in order to increase the reward of his righteous contemporaries who, despite the example of the wicked man's prosperity, continue in their innocence and integrity. For if the wicked man were punished as

יד אֱלֹהִים: יֶשׁ־הֶבֶל אֲשֶׁר נַעֲשָׂה עַל־הָאָרֶץ
אֲשֶׁר | יֵשׁ צַדִּיקִים אֲשֶׁר מַגִּיעַ אֲלֵהֶם
כְּמַעֲשֵׂה הָרְשָׁעִים וְיֵשׁ רְשָׁעִים שֶׁמַּגִּיעַ
אֲלֵהֶם כְּמַעֲשֵׂה הַצַּדִּיקִים אָמַרְתִּי שֶׁגַּם־
טו זֶה הָבֶל: וְשִׁבַּחְתִּי אֲנִי אֶת־הַשִּׂמְחָה
אֲשֶׁר אֵין־טוֹב לָאָדָם תַּחַת הַשֶּׁמֶשׁ כִּי
אִם־לֶאֱכֹל וְלִשְׁתּוֹת וְלִשְׂמוֹחַ וְהוּא יִלְוֶנּוּ
בַעֲמָלוֹ יְמֵי חַיָּיו אֲשֶׁר־נָתַן־לוֹ הָאֱלֹהִים
טז תַּחַת הַשָּׁמֶשׁ: כַּאֲשֶׁר נָתַתִּי אֶת־לִבִּי

14. [The following verses until 9:12 form a cohesive unit discussing the dilemma presented by the prosperity of the wicked and the suffering of the righteous.]

יֶשׁ־הֶבֶל—*There is a futility* which confounds mankind *(Rashi).*

עַל־הָאָרֶץ — *On earth,* i.e. in this world *(Metzudas David).*

יֵשׁ צַדִּיקִים — *Sometimes there are righteous men,* etc. The יֵשׁ, *'there is'* in this context implies a rare occurrence *(Ibn Ezra* on 7:3*).*

[The meaning is that sometimes the wicked prosper and the righteous suffer — the lot of the righteous and the lot of the wicked are seen to sometimes reverse. See *Overview*]

שֶׁגַּם־זֶה הָבֶל — *This, too, is vanity.* My initial reaction was that both the righteous and the wicked led a futile existence and I almost stooped to a level reminiscent of *Psalms* 73:2-3 *'my feet had almost turned away'* [i.e. I nearly wavered from the proper path; . . . *'I was envious of those who seemed resplendent when I saw the prosperity of the wicked. . .'*]

The maintenance of Free Will — a necessary ingredient of God's plan — requires a certain amount of suffering for the righteous and prosperity for the wicked. For, if all wickedness were to be punished immediately, there would be no room for choice and everyone would be righteous .Thus, the wicked often prosper, but they misinterpret this prosperity as sanction to continue their wicked ways. They should realize that it is futility — that in reality there is justice, but that God allows them to flourish in order to confuse mankind *(Me'am Loez).*

soon as he commits a wrong act, the righteous men who serve God from love would not receive their due credit, for one might suspect that their worship of God was due not to love, but to the fear of punishment which they see coming upon the wicked. But when one sees that the wicked are not punished as soon as they do evil, he thinks that they will never be punished, and hence everyone does as he pleases.

Solomon calls attention to this in Ecclesiastes: *"Because the sentence for wrongdoing is not executed quickly — that is why men are encouraged to do evil."*

In these words Solomon expresses the problem. Why is it, he says, that the wicked man is not punished as soon as he does an evil deed? This surely leads to men's hearts being fully set

14 *There is a futility that takes place on earth: Sometimes there are righteous men who are treated as if they had done according to the deeds of the wicked; and there are wicked men who are treated as if they had done the deeds of the righteous. I declared, this, too, is vanity.*

15 *So I praised enjoyment, for man has no other goal under the sun but to eat, drink and be joyful; and this will accompany him in his toil during the days of his life which God has given him beneath the sun.*

15. וְשִׁבַּחְתִּי אֲנִי אֶת־הַשִּׂמְחָה — *So I praised enjoyment.* [Not enjoyment for its own sake] but שֶׁיְּהֵא שָׂמֵחַ בְּחֶלְקוֹ, that a person should be *satisfied with his lot* and be involved in performing 'righteous precepts which gladden the heart' [*Psalms* 19:9] from that which God has bestowed upon him *(Rashi).*

[The *Talmud* discusses the apparent discrepancy between this verse where Solomon praises joy, and verse 2:2 *'And of joy,* (I said,) *what does it accomplish'?*] — 'There is no difficulty: . . . this verse refers to שִׂמְחָה שֶׁל מִצְוָה, *the joy of a precept* [the celebration of the performance of a precept, e.g. a marriage]; ... verse 2:2 refers to שִׂמְחָה שֶׁאֵינָהּ שֶׁל מִצְוָה, joy which is not in connection with a precept *(Shabbos* 30b*).*

לֶאֱכֹל וְלִשְׁתּוֹת וְלִשְׂמוֹחַ — *To eat, drink and be joyful.* The *Midrash* notes that all 'eating and drinking' mentioned in this Book signify Torah and good deeds [for just as eating and drinking sustain the body, Torah and good deeds sustain the soul *(Torah Temimah* based on *Zohar).*]

The proof of this [continues the *Midrash*] is this verse: *this will accompany him in his toil during the days of his life* — to the grave. בַּעֲמָלוֹ, *in his toil* should be homiletically read בְּעָלְמוֹ, in his world [see *comm. of Torah Temimah* above on verse 8.] Are there, then, food and drink which accompany man to the grave? —It means Torah and good deeds which a man performs.

16.-17. כַּאֲשֶׁר נָתַתִּי אֶת־לִבִּי — *When I set my mind* [lit. *'my heart'*] Solomon proceeds to explain why

in them to do evil. Then he answers the question by saying that their are two reasons, as we said, for this situation:

"Because a sinner does what is wrong a hundred times and He is patient with him." What he means to say is that, the reason God prolongs the wicked man's life is either in order that he may repent, or in order that he may not, as we said before. Then he says that there is another reason:

"Yet nevertheless I am aware that it will be well with those who fear God that they may fear him." i.e. the reason for prolonging their life is also in order to benefit those who fear God, that they may fear Him and serve Him from love and not from fear of punishment.

פרק ח

לָדַעַת חָכְמָה וְלִרְאוֹת אֶת־הָעִנְיָן אֲשֶׁר
יז נַעֲשָׂה עַל־הָאָרֶץ כִּי גַם בַּיּוֹם וּבַלַּיְלָה
יז שֵׁנָה בְּעֵינָיו אֵינֶנּוּ רֹאֶה: וְרָאִיתִי אֶת־
כָּל־מַעֲשֵׂה הָאֱלֹהִים כִּי לֹא יוּכַל הָאָדָם
לִמְצוֹא אֶת־הַמַּעֲשֶׂה אֲשֶׁר נַעֲשָׂה תַחַת־
הַשֶּׁמֶשׁ בְּשֶׁל אֲשֶׁר יַעֲמֹל הָאָדָם לְבַקֵּשׁ
וְלֹא יִמְצָא וְגַם אִם־יֹאמַר הֶחָכָם לָדַעַת
לֹא יוּכַל לִמְצֹא:

פרק ט

א כִּי אֶת־כָּל־זֶה נָתַתִּי אֶל־לִבִּי וְלָבוּר אֶת־
א כָּל־זֶה אֲשֶׁר הַצַּדִּיקִים וְהַחֲכָמִים
וַעֲבָדֵיהֶם בְּיַד הָאֱלֹהִים גַּם־אַהֲבָה גַם־

he came to the conclusion set forth in the last verse praising enjoyment: When I immersed myself in the quest of gaining insight into the nature of things — mustering up every ounce of the superior wisdom with which God endowed me — in order to understand why the righteous suffer while the wicked prosper — even to the extent of going without sleep day and night, I became convinced that man cannot fathom these matters and although he feels he has nearly grasped it, he will ultimately fail in his quest. It is beyond the realm of his intellect. *(Divrei Chefetz; Kara; Rashi; Ralbag; Taalumos Chachma).*

כִּי גַם בַּיּוֹם וּבַלַּיְלָה ... — *For even day or night its eyes see no sleep.* בְּעֵינָיו, *'its eyes'* refers to [the 'eyes' of] *'my heart'* — i.e. I was so engrossed in this quest that even sleep eluded me *(Ibn Ezra).*

Research thus consumes a man's total being. It even robs him of his sleep *(Kehilas Yaakov).*

אֶת־כָּל־מַעֲשֵׂה הָאֱלֹהִים — *And I perceived all the work of God* — i.e. I delved into those of God's works [i.e. plans regarding His Providence of the world] which He allowed man to comprehend *(Rashi),* nevertheless I concluded that mortal man cannot comprehend God's reasons for rewarding the wicked. Not that they are without reason or consistency [God forbid!]; God's purpose is definitely well defined, but is beyond mortal comprehension. Therefore it is best to leave these matters in God's hand and not investigate them *(Alshich).*

לֹא יוּכַל הָאָדָם לִמְצֹא — *He cannot fathom it* [lit. *'to find it'*]. Even Moses could not comprehend it as it is written *(Exodus* 33:13): הוֹדִעֵנִי נָא אֶת דְּרָכֶךָ — *'Show me now Your way' (Rashi).*

VIII 16-17

16 *When I set my mind to know wisdom and to observe the activity which takes place on earth — for even day or night its eyes see no sleep. —* 17 *And I perceived all the work of God. Indeed man cannot fathom the events that occur under the sun, inasmuch as man tries strenuously to search, but cannot fathom it. And even though a wise man should presume to know, he cannot fathom it.*

IX 1

For all this I noted and I sought to ascertain all this: that the righteous and the wise together with their actions are in the Hand of God; whether love or hate

Therefore, I praised enjoyment [as defined above in verse 15], for any other quest is fruitless *(Metzudas David).*

[For though Koheles opened this chapter implying that the wise man *'knows what all things mean,'* — he concludes that certain divine matters remain hidden even to the wisest of men.]

IX

1. [Solomon continues his theme of the righteous and wicked, Divine Providence and Fate, and affirms that his conclusion that God's plan of governing the universe is unfathomable by mortal man who bases his conclusions on empirical observations alone.]

כִּי אֶת־כָּל־זֶה *For all this.* I.e. the matters discussed above in chapter 8 *(Metzudas David).*

וְלָבוּר — *Sought to ascertain* from ברר, *to sift, select (Rashi).*

. . . For we see slaves rise to great heights and wise men descend to great depths. The reason for this is not revealed to man; it is in God's hand *(Kara).*

גַּם־אַהֲבָה גַּם־שִׂנְאָה אֵין יוֹדֵעַ הָאָדָם — *Whether love or hate, man does not know.* Man cannot even comprehend what inspires him to love or hate something *(Metzudas David).* The final determination of the true success of man's efforts is in God's hand. Often one achieves what he seeks — only to find that the object of his love is detrimental to him, or that the object of his hate would have been beneficial to him. The execution of the desire itself however, is in the realm of man's Free Will *(Ibn Latif).*

שִׂנְאָה אֵין יוֹדֵעַ הָאָדָם הַכֹּל לִפְנֵיהֶם:
ב הַכֹּל כַּאֲשֶׁר לַכֹּל מִקְרֶה אֶחָד לַצַּדִּיק
וְלָרָשָׁע לַטּוֹב וְלַטָּהוֹר וְלַטָּמֵא וְלַזֹּבֵחַ
וְלַאֲשֶׁר אֵינֶנּוּ זֹבֵחַ כַּטּוֹב כַּחֹטֶא הַנִּשְׁבָּע
ג כַּאֲשֶׁר שְׁבוּעָה יָרֵא: זֶה | רָע בְּכֹל אֲשֶׁר־

Similarly, man does not comprehend why God sometimes guides man to love or hate, as, for example, in the desire of Judah for Tamar, David for Bathsheba, or the hatred of the brothers for Joseph. None of those powerful emotions were designed by them, but all were created in order to carry out God's plan which pre-existed them *(Taalumos Chachmah*; see *Overview* to ArtScroll ed. of *Ruth)*.

Rav Yosef Kara comments: There are cases where God grants man goodness and man cannot comprehend whether the goodness was granted as a reward out of God's love for him, or if God granted it to him out of hate in order to give him a fleeting moment of gratification so that he will be subject to the agony of later losing it to someone else.

Rashi interprets this *vis-a-vis* man's relationship to God: Ordinary people [except for the righteous and wise *(Sifsei Chachamim)*] do not have the intellect to perceive by what means they can become *beloved*, or, conversely, *hated* by God.

הַכֹּל לִפְנֵיהֶם — *All preceded them.* i.e. all was decreed before they were born *(Targum; Ibn Ezra; Taalumos Chachmah)* and is arranged as a matter of Divine Providence *(Akeidas Yitzchok)*.

[According to *Rashi* לִפְנֵיהֶם (lit. 'before them')in this context does not mean 'before them,' 'preceding them,' in time, but rather 'in their presence.' He therefore renders the phrase]: *'all is before them'* — i.e. before the righteous and wise. [They have the intellect to perceive what God loves and what He hates.]

Rav Yosef Kara's rendering of the phrase is similar to *Rashi*. But he explains that although everything is laid out before man — man still does not have the intellect to comprehend God's ways.

And as *Ibn Ezra* comments: For the righteous and wise cannot tell when the things they love or hate will come to them; both are before them though they have no perception.

2. הַכֹּל כַּאֲשֶׁר לַכֹּל — *All things come alike to all* [lit. *'the all as to all'*.]

. . . מִקְרֶה אֶחָד — *The same* [lit. *'one'*] *fate awaits them all.* i.e. everyone knows that death, the common equalizer, is the fate that awaits all men in this world. Nevertheless [those with intellect] choose to take the proper path because they realize that there is a distinction between good and evil people in the Hereafter *(Rashi)*.

[*'Fate'* is clearly not to be understood as some 'haphazard' event. As *Rashi* notes to 3:19 *'death'* is alluded to, and within the context of

man does not know; all preceded them.
2 *All things come alike to all; the same fate awaits the righteous and the wicked, the good and the clean and the unclean, the one who brings a sacrifice and the one who does not. As is the good man so is the sinner, as is the one who swears, so is the one who fears an oath.*

these verses all is guided by Providence. (See *comm. of S.R. Hirsch* quoted in *ArtScroll ed.* of *Ruth* 2:3, page 88) s.v. וַיִּקֶר מִקְרֶהָ.]

לַצַּדִּיק וְלָרָשָׁע — *The righteous and the wicked* [These nouns as well as most of the nouns throughout this verse are preceded with the prefix ל = *'to'* but it is dropped in the translation for idiomatic reasons].]

Rashi, following the *Midrash,* provides examples of actual diverse personages in Scripture who are illustrative of the descriptions in this verse and who shared common fates. For example, righteous - wicked is a description of Noah and Pharaoh-Necho both of whom were injured in the course of their lives, as noted in the *Midrash,* and died with a limp.

לַטּוֹב וְלַטָּהוֹר וְלַטָּמֵא — *[To] the good, [and to] the clean and [to] the unclean.* Those who do good with others; those who have pure thoughts; and those who concentrate on impure thoughts and levity *(Metzudas David).*

[The terms are thus explained by the commentators as having both a ritual and moral connotation.]

Rashi refers *'good'* to Moses; *'the clean'* — to Aaron; and *'unclean'* — to the מְרַגְּלִים, *Spies.* Moses and Aaron praised Eretz Yisrael and the Spies deprecated it, yet they all shared a common fate: neither of them entered the Land *(Rashi).*

וְלַזֹּבֵחַ וְלַאֲשֶׁר אֵינֶנּוּ זֹבֵחַ — *[to] The one who brings a sacrifice* [lit. *'shall slaughter'*], and [to] the one who does not [*bring a sacrifice,* lit. *'does not slaughter'*]

— יֹאשִׁיָּהוּ, Josiah, who offered sacrifices [II *Chron.* 35:7] and Ahab who abolished the pilgrimages to the Temple; both were killed by arrows [*I Kings* 22:34; *II Chron.* 35:23.] *(Rashi).*

כַּטּוֹב כַּחֹטֶא — *As is the good man so is the sinner* — i.e. they are completely identical *(Ibn Ezra).*

— David and Nebuchadnezzar. The former was responsible for building the Temple and the latter destroyed it, but each reigned for 40 years *(Rashi).*

הַנִּשְׁבָּע כַּאֲשֶׁר שְׁבוּעָה יָרֵא *[As is] the one who swears so is the one who fears an oath.* i.e. the one who swears [i.e. takes an oath] rashly and is not concerned with his ability to fulfill it, and conversely the other who refrains from swearing out of apprehension that he may unintentionally be taking the name of God in vain *(Metzudas David).*

— Zedekiah, who swore falsely to Nebuchadnezzar [*II Chron.* 36:13]; and Samson [who gave credence to oaths by trusting the oath of the

פרק ט

נַעֲשָׂה תַּחַת הַשֶּׁמֶשׁ כִּי־מִקְרֶה אֶחָד לַכֹּל
ד וְגַם לֵב בְּנֵי־הָאָדָם מָלֵא־רָע וְהוֹלֵלוֹת
בִּלְבָבָם בְּחַיֵּיהֶם וְאַחֲרָיו אֶל־הַמֵּתִים: כִּי־ ד
מִי אֲשֶׁר יְבֻחַר* אֶל כָּל־הַחַיִּים יֵשׁ בִּטָּחוֹן
כִּי־לְכֶלֶב חַי הוּא טוֹב מִן־הָאַרְיֵה הַמֵּת:

* יְחֻבַּר ק׳

members of the tribe of Judah (*Judges* 15:12)]; both died by having their eyes gouged out [*Judges* 16:21; *II Kings* 25:7] (*Rashi*).

Ibn Ezra explains that the five opposites listed in the verse refer to five facets of human behavior and thought: righteous / wicked, *to deed*, impure / pure, *in body*; one who offers / one who doesn't offer, *to the use of resources*; good / sinful, *in heart [thought rather than deed]*; and swearing / fearful of swearing, *to speech*.

3. זֶה רָע — *This is an evil.* i.e. the most grievous evil in the world (*Metzudas David*); and nothing is more difficult than this (*Ibn Ezra*).

כִּי־מִקְרֶה אֶחָד לַכֹּל — *That the same fate awaits them all.* [i.e. that תַּחַת הַשֶּׁמֶשׁ, *in this world*, death comes to all, and no distinction is made 'beneath the sun' between the righteous and the wicked, all distinction awaiting the Hereafter.]

This is what confuses the wicked (*Taalumos Chachmah*).

בְּנֵי־הָאָדָם מָלֵא־רָע — *Therefore the heart of man is full of evil* i.e. as a result of the above man is emboldened to presume that there is no Providence and no justice (*Metzudas David*)[1] they attribute everything to blind chance, benefitting sometimes the righteous and sometimes the wicked (*Rashi*).

The diminutive term בְּנֵי־הָאָדָם *'sons' of man* is used here because 'smaller' people, because of their limited intellect, find this problem even more perplexing (*Ibn Ezra*).

וְהוֹלֵלוֹת בִּלְבָבָם בְּחַיֵּיהֶם — *And*

1. As the *Midrash* relates of the Sage Elisha ben Abuyah:

He once saw a man climb to the top of a palm-tree on the Sabbath, take the mother-bird with the young [in violation of the Sabbath and of *Deut* 22:7], and descend in safety. After the Sabbath, he saw a man who was told by his father to climb to the top of a tree, and bring down young birds, and he ascended, dismissed the mother-bird, took the young, and on the way down fell and was killed.

Elisha exclaimed: Of both these precepts [honoring parents (*Deut.* 5:16); and sending away the mother-bird (*ibid* 22:7)] it is written: *'that it may go well with you and that your days may be prolonged.' Where is the well-being of this man and where is the prolonging of his days!*

He was unaware of how Rabbi Akivah explained it: *'that it may go well with you'* — in the World [to come] which is wholly good, *'and that your days may be prolonged'* — for the world which is unending. [Both refer to the next world, not to this, and thereby emphasize that reward comes only then, but not in this world. Elisha, on the other hand, interpreted it literally as referring to this world, and seeing that the promise was not fulfilled, turned unbeliever.]

Others say that the cause for his losing his faith was that he saw the tongue of Chutzpis the interpreter [a great sage, one of the martyrs in the Hadrianic persecutions] dragged along by a dog, and he exclaimed: 'The mouth that uttered pearls licks the dust! If so there is no reward for the righteous!' He then went on to sin. (see also *Kidd.* 39b).

[It was thus the eternal question of why the righteous suffer (see *Overview*) that led him to religious apostasy.]

[3] *This is an evil about all things that go on under the sun: that the same fate awaits all. Therefore, the heart of man is full of evil; and madness is in their heart while they live; and after that, they go to the dead.*

[4] *For he who is attached to all the living has hope, a live dog being better than a dead lion.* [5] *For the liv-*

madness is in their heart [i.e. *'mind'*] while they live. i.e. during their lifetime they are preoccupied with melancholic conflicting thoughts *(Metzudas David)* [and, unrestrained by the the fear of retribution, they give rein to their desires and wild passions.]

וְאַחֲרָיו אֶל־הַמֵּתִים — *And after that* [*they go*] *to the dead — i.e. their melancholy accompanies them throughout life (Metzudas David),* until ultimately they go to Gehinnom *(Rashi),* and the wicked are stripped of their eternity *(Taalumos Chachmah).*

To quote *(Rav Saadiah Gaon:* 'The translation of this verse is to the effect that the hearts of the sons of men are full of evil and that there is insanity in their hearts while they are alive, as well as afterward when they are dead.'

The last phrase is interpreted by *Rav Yosef Kara* as a separate clause: 'Another reason that *man's heart is full of evil* is that during life the wicked think that אַחֲרָיו אֶל־הַמֵּתִים, his ultimate destination is to join the dead, and he therefore becomes a fatalist and loses faith.'

4. כִּי־מִי אֲשֶׁר יְחֻבַּר . . . — *For he who is attached to all the living has hope.* As long as he lives there is hope that even the sinner will repent *(Rashi).*

Ibn Ezra comments that this verse is a citation of the common rationale of mankind: 'While there is life there is hope.' [see prefatory comment to verse 7.]

To all the living — even if he attaches himself to the wicked; there is still hope of eventual repentance *(Metzudas David).*

For once he dies all hope has ended as is written (*Ezek.* 37:11) *'our bones are dried, our hope is lost' (Kara).*

The כְּתִיב, *written text,* has יִבָּחֵר, *'will choose,'* to suggest that only those who can 'choose' have hope; and the dead can no longer choose; for them all hope is lost *(Ibn Ezra).*

כִּי־לְכֶלֶב חַי . . . — *A live dog being better than a dead lion* — ['Dog' in Scriptures is a term of contempt (*I Sam.* 17:43); while the lion, is *'the mightiest among beasts'* (*Prov.* 30:30). Nevertheless the despised dog — who is alive — is better than the mighty lion — who is dead.]

1. Life in this world is praised because it affords the opportunity for repentance, the performance of mitzvos, and the attainment of high spiritual states. This constitutes the hope that exists for one who is joined to life. The meaning of "... *for a living dog* ..." is that the lowliest person alive can grow spiritually — something that the wisest, most righteous dead cannot do. Elsewhere, however, Koheles belittled and demeaned this world in respect to the acquisition of its pleasures and its honor, saying, "What profit hath man of all his labor

ה כִּי הַחַיִּים יוֹדְעִים שֶׁיָּמֻתוּ וְהַמֵּתִים אֵינָם
יוֹדְעִים מְאוּמָה וְאֵין־עוֹד לָהֶם שָׂכָר כִּי
ו נִשְׁכַּח זִכְרָם: גַּם אַהֲבָתָם גַּם־שִׂנְאָתָם
גַּם־קִנְאָתָם כְּבָר אָבָדָה וְחֵלֶק אֵין־לָהֶם
עוֹד לְעוֹלָם בְּכֹל אֲשֶׁר־נַעֲשָׂה תַּחַת
ז הַשָּׁמֶשׁ: לֵךְ אֱכֹל בְּשִׂמְחָה לַחְמֶךָ וּשְׁתֵה

5. כִּי הַחַיִּים ... וְהַמֵּתִים — *For the living . . . but the dead.* i.e. the living — even if they are fools — recognize that death is inevitable. The dead, however — even if they were wise in life — perceive nothing, nor have they any goal — they cease to function *(Almosnino).*

Man should constantly bear in mind the day of death and remember that he was sent into this world only to observe His Torah and perform *mitzvos.* He must not grow neglectful and his hands not weaken in the service of the Blessed One . . . There are those who allow no time for their souls, who do not set aside times for the understanding of their end, occupied as they are with the affairs of the world. Thus they die without having learned to understand their end, to perfect their souls, and to store up provisions for their way, as it is written: *(Deut.* 32:29) לוּ חָכְמוּ יַשְׂכִּילוּ זֹאת יָבִינוּ לְאַחֲרִיתָם, *'If they were wise, they would understand this, they would discern their latter end' (Rabbeinu Yonah).*

וְהַמֵּתִים אֵינָם יוֹדְעִים מְאוּמָה — *But the dead know nothing at all* — and even if they were to have perception, of what avail is it? They are dead and it is too late for regret! *(Metzudas David).*

וְאֵין־עוֹד לָהֶם שָׂכָר — *There is no more reward for them.* Once they die they no longer perform mitzvos worthy of reward, and 'he who has not prepared on the eve of Sabbath what shall he eat on Sabbath?' *(Rashi)*

[Compare comm. of *Midrash* cited in footnote to 1:15].

כִּי נִשְׁכַּח זִכְרָם — *Their memory is forgotten.* At least the living man who repented is remembered for good. The dead, however, cannot change their reputations *(Metzudas David).*

6. [According to *Rashi:* the verse refers to *the dead* who died without having repented, and whose memory is forgotten.]

גַּם אַהֲבָתָם — [Also] *Their love* — in that they loved foolishness and mockery; גַּם־שִׂנְאָתָם, [also] *their hate:* in that they hated knowledge; גַּם־קִנְאָתָם, [also] *their jealousy* — in having provoked God's wrath by

wherein he laboreth under the sun?" [1:3], and, "Wherefore I praised the dead that are already dead more than the living that are yet alive" [4:2].

[Thus, here he views death as evil, symbolizing the end of man's hope. In 4:2-3 where he *praised the dead and glorified the unborn, it was not life per se,* but misspent life — and man's suffering at the hand of his fellow man — that vexed his spirit.]

Our Sages of blessed memory said, [*Avos* 3:1] "Consider three things and you will not enter into transgression: Where do you come from — from a putrefying drop. Where are you

*ing know that they will die, but the dead know
nothing at all; there is no more reward for them, their
memory is forgotten.* 6 *Their love, their hate, their
jealousy have already perished — nor will they ever
again have a share in whatever is done beneath the
sun.*
7 *Go, eat your bread with joy and drink your wine*

their evil deeds *(Rashi).*

כְּבָר אָבָדָה — *Have already perished.* i.e. with their death their lifetime loves and hates cease to have importance *(Metzudas David).*

וְחֵלֶק אֵין־לָהֶם עוֹד לְעוֹלָם — *Nor will they ever again have a share* — and with their death they are henceforth and forever excluded from the process of the living *(Ibn Yachya).*

7-10. [There is a difference of opinion among the commentators concerning the interpretaion of verses 3-10. In general, we follow the interpretaion of *Rashi* and most commentators who understand these verses as describing the evil of wicked man's inability to perceive beyond what his empirical experience allows him to comprehend. He therefore becomes a fatalist and feels that all is governed by chance. The wicked thus become emboldened to sin. Solomon bemoans this fact and praises life, for while life exists there is hope that the wicked will repent. Once they reach the grave, however, it is too late for regrets.

Now (in verses 7-10) Solomon advises the righteous — whose deeds God has already approved, and who are destined for the World to Come — to enjoy what God has granted them and not fear death but rather *'wear white'* i.e. do good deeds and always stand in spiritual readiness for eventual death and its imminent reward, and in general, spend life in the lofty service of God.

Rav Saadiah Gaon, Ibn Ezra, and *Taalumos Chachmah* however, interpret these verses as being Solomon's description of the *discredited* hedonistic rationales of sinners. According to the wicked, only the living have any importance; everyone shares the same fate and there is no Judgment — so why not indulge in sensuality and sin? Thus the wicked man's philosophy becomes: Spend your life eating and drinking and enjoying this world because God enjoys such employment of His earthly bounty.

But, according to these commentators, Solomon rebuffs these philosophies in verse 11: שַׁבְתִּי (which *Ibn Ezra* explains as): *'I reconsidered; reevaluated'.*]

7. לֵךְ אֱכֹל בְּשִׂמְחָה לַחְמֶךָ — *Go eat*

going — to a place of dust, worms, and maggots. And before whom will you be called upon to give an accounting — before the King of Kings, the Holy One Blessed be He." When you consider where you come from, you will grow humble in spirit and despise pride. When you remember where you are going, you will discount the world and recognize that it has no preeminence, and you will occupy yourself with it only in the service of the blessed Creator before whom you will be called to account *(Mesillas Yesharim).*

בְּלֶב־טוֹב יֵינֶךָ כִּי כְבָר רָצָה הָאֱלֹהִים
ח אֶת־מַעֲשֶׂיךָ: בְּכָל־עֵת יִהְיוּ בְגָדֶיךָ לְבָנִים
ט וְשֶׁמֶן עַל־רֹאשְׁךָ אַל־יֶחְסָר: רְאֵה חַיִּים
עִם־אִשָּׁה אֲשֶׁר־אָהַבְתָּ כָּל־יְמֵי חַיֵּי
הֶבְלֶךָ אֲשֶׁר נָתַן־לְךָ תַּחַת הַשֶּׁמֶשׁ כֹּל יְמֵי
הֶבְלֶךָ כִּי הוּא חֶלְקְךָ בַּחַיִּים וּבַעֲמָלְךָ

your bread with joy etc. *Alshich* stresses the possessive nouns *'your* bread, *your* wine': true happiness is present when you eat *your own* bread — the bread you toiled for with the sweat of your own brow [cf. *Psalms 128:2*] even when it is only *'bread'*, i.e. the basic necessities of life rather than luxuries. Similarly, your wine should be drunk בְּלֵב טוֹב, with a *'glad'* [lit. *'good'*] heart', i.e. at the behest of the יֵצֶר טוֹב, Good Inclination, in the performance of the commandments such as for *kiddush* and *havdallah* on the Sabbath, the Four Cups at Passover, and the Purim feast. Also, the wine should be 'your own' and drunk in moderation, not to the point of drunkenness, and only *after* רָצָה הָאֱלֹהִים אֶת־מַעֲשֶׂיךָ, *God has already approved your deeds,* because you have repented from sin. Only then do you have the right to partake of God's joy on this world.

Rav Yosef Kara attaches this verse to 2:24-25 and 5:18 and comments that when man perceives that God has allowed him to derive *true* joy from His Creation, he is assured that *'God has already approved his deeds.'*

The *Midrash* comments that when Abraham was about to sacrifice Isaac and the angel said: *'Abraham, Abraham do not lay your hand upon the lad* [*Gen.* 22:12] Abraham felt some uneasiness and thought, 'Perhaps there was some disqualification in my son and for that reason he was not accepted.' A בַּת קוֹל, Heavenly Voice, issued forth and said to him 'Abraham, Abraham. *Go, eat your bread with joy . . . God has already approved your deeds;* He has accepted your sacrifice . . .'

Similarly the verse may be interpreted as referring to Rosh Hashanah and Yom Kippur . . . On Yom Kippur all fast and God remits to them their sins. As the *Midrash* states, A Heavenly Voice proclaims: *'Go, eat your bread with joy* — your prayer has been heard.'

8. בְּכָל־עֵת יִהְיוּ בְגָדֶיךָ לְבָנִים — *Let your garments always be white.* [The *Talmud* interprets this verse allegorically that one should always be in a state of spiritual preparedness.][1]

וְשֶׁמֶן עַל־רֹאשְׁךָ אַל־יֶחְסָר — *And your head never lack oil.* [White garments were worn on festive occa-

1. Rav Eliezer said: 'Repent one day before your death.' His disciples asked him, 'Does then one know on what day he will die?'

'Then all the more reason that he repent today,' he replied, 'lest he die tomorrow. Thus his whole life is spent in repentance.' And Solomon, too, said in his wisdom, *'Let your garments always be white; and let your head never lack oil.'*

with a glad heart, for God has already approved your deeds. [8] *Let your garments always be white, and your head never lack oil.*

[9] *Enjoy life with the wife you love through all the fleeting days of your life that He has granted you beneath the sun, all of your futile existence; for that is your compensation in life and in your toil which*

sions. It was the symbol of purity *(Isaiah* 1:18), and the garments of *priests (Lev.* 6:3). Oil, too, bespoke the festive mood (*Psalms* 45:8).]

In a very beautiful homiletical interpretation of this verse, *Ol'los Ephraim* comments that a white garment stains easily and even a small spot is readily noticeable, and hard to remove...

Therefore, Solomon exhorts man to conduct his life constantly as if he were wearing white garments and carrying a full pitcher of oil on his head. He must therefore concentrate on keeping his balance and not approach anything which can soil the whiteness of his garments. Man must live a life of spiritual and moral purity, always on guard lest he besmirch himself with a careless sin, for man, like a white garment, is easy to soil and hard to cleanse.

9. רְאֵה חַיִּים — *Enjoy life* [lit. *'see life'* as in וּרְאֵה בְטוֹב *'see good'*, 2:1] i.e. see (experience) the good life *(Targum);* see to it that your 'life' is fulfilling *(Ibn Yachya).*

The *Talmud (Kiddushin* 30b) interprets the phrase *'see to a livelihood'*, i.e. learn a trade, for a livelihood will ensure domestic tranquility *(Me'am Loez).*

עִם־אִשָּׁה אֲשֶׁר־אָהַבְתָּ — *With the* [lit. *'a'*] *wife you love.* Only if he enjoys life with his own wife and does not stray after strange women *(Ibn Latif).*

And a man who has no wife lives without good, help, joy, blessing and atonement. He lives without peace . . . and lives without life, as it is written: *'enjoy life with the wife you love' (Midrash).*

[There is no contradiction between this verse and Solomon's harsh estimate of women in 7:26, 28. There he condemns *'the woman whose heart is snares and nets'*; here his sober admonition is directed to *'the wife you love'*.]

כִּי הוּא חֶלְקְךָ בַּחַיִּים — *For that* [lit. *'he'*] *is your compensation* [lit. *'portion'*] *in life* i.e. this alone is of any avail during your life *(Metzudas David).*

And according to *Rashi* [in consonance with the metaphoric *Midrashic* interpretation: The synthesis of a life of Torah and worldly occupation] . . . will provide sustenance in this world and next, for labor in the two of them makes sin forgotten [cf. *Avos* 2:2].

Rav Yochanan ben Zakkai said: This may be compared to a king who summoned his servants to a banquet without appointing a time. The wise ones adorned themselves and sat at the door of the palace, for they said, 'Is anything lacking in a royal palace? [i.e. little or no time is needed for preparation; everything is always stocked up in a royal palace.] The summons to enter may come at any moment.'

י אֲשֶׁר־אַתָּה עָמֵל תַּחַת הַשָּׁמֶשׁ: כֹּל אֲשֶׁר
תִּמְצָא יָדְךָ לַעֲשׂוֹת בְּכֹחֲךָ עֲשֵׂה כִּי אֵין
מַעֲשֶׂה וְחֶשְׁבּוֹן וְדַעַת וְחָכְמָה בִּשְׁאוֹל
יא אֲשֶׁר אַתָּה הֹלֵךְ שָׁמָּה: שַׁבְתִּי וְרָאֹה
תַחַת־הַשֶּׁמֶשׁ כִּי לֹא לַקַּלִּים הַמֵּרוֹץ וְלֹא
לַגִּבּוֹרִים הַמִּלְחָמָה וְגַם לֹא לַחֲכָמִים
לֶחֶם וְגַם לֹא לַנְּבֹנִים עֹשֶׁר וְגַם לֹא
לַיֹּדְעִים חֵן כִּי־עֵת וָפֶגַע יִקְרֶה אֶת־כֻּלָּם:

[It may be inferred from the vocalization in *Targum:* הִיא *'she'* — that he interprets the subject to be 'your wife'; i.e. *she* is your compensation.]

וּבַעֲמָלְךָ — *And in your toil* [i.e. 'and this is your compensation in your toil'.]

10. כֹּל אֲשֶׁר תִּמְצָא יָדְךָ לַעֲשׂוֹת בְּכֹחֲךָ עֲשֵׂה — *Whatever you are able to do with your might, do it.* [This translation follows *Rashi.*] *Targum,* following the Masoretic punctuation *('trop')* translates more literally: *'Whatever you are able to do,* בְּכֹחֲךָ עֲשֵׂה, *do with all your might.*]

Rashi: Whatever you are able to do — in fulfilling the Will of your Creator — *while you still possess your strength, do it.*

Repent while you have the ability. While the wick is still lit, add oil to keep it kindled. Once the light is extinguished, oil no longer helps *(Yalkut Shimoni).*

Therefore take advantage of this life in achieving eternity while it is within the realm of תִּמְצָא יָדְךָ, within the reach of your own hand, i.e. in your own power, to do so *(Sforno).*

Ibn Ezra, who views this verse as a continuation of the discredited hedonistic view of sinners [see prefatory remark to verse 7] interprets this as the rationale of sinners who exclaim: Indulge in pleasure while you can; in the grave all activity stops, and death is the common fate of all.

כִּי אֵין מַעֲשֶׂה וְחֶשְׁבּוֹן . . . — *For there is neither doing, nor reckoning . . . in the grave where you are going.* i.e. there is no action which can justify you once you are dead, and if you led a righteous life you need not have any reckonings [recriminations] about death. *(Rashi).*

Once the soul leaves the body, all activity stops *(Kara).*

11. [According to the thematic interpretation of *Rashi* and others as discussed in the prefatory remarks to verse 7, the verses are to be understood as Solomon's affirmation of his principles that this world is transitory and man is governed by God.

The fools, however, went about their work, saying, 'Can there be a banquet without preparations?' [i.e. we have plenty of time until the banquet is arranged; we can dress after being called.]

Suddenly, the king desired the presence of his servants: the wise entered adorned, while the

you exert beneath the sun.
10 *Whatever you are able to do with your might, do it. For there is neither doing nor reckoning nor knowledge nor wisdom in the grave where you are going.*
11 *Once more I saw under the sun that the race is not won by the swift; nor the battle by the strong, nor does bread come to the wise, riches to the intelligent, nor favor to the learned; but time and death will happen to them all.*
12 *For man does not even*

Even according to the interpretation of *Ibn Ezra,* with this verse Solomon no longer cites the hedonistic philosophies of the sinners. He responds that joy and attainment of pleasure in this world is ephemeral at best — it is not always man's exceptional talent that gives him success: the swift sometimes lose; the strong are sometimes defeated.]

שַׁבְתִּי וְרָאֹה — *Once more I saw.* According to *Ibn Ezra: 'I reconsidered and perceived.'*

... That man's destiny is not controlled exclusively by man's prowess; God's Will determines the result of human endeavor *(Sforno; Ibn Ezra; Metzudas David).*

כִּי לֹא לַקַּלִּים הַמֵּרוֹץ — *The race is not won by the swift* [lit. *'for not to the swift is the race,'* etc. and similarly in the following phrases.]

Swiftness doesn't always help the swift one escape his pursuer *(Metzudas David). Rashi* refers this verse to the incident of Asahel [*II Samuel* 2:18-23]: *'Who was as light of foot as a wild gazelle'* and nevertheless Abner slew him.[Thus when man's time comes his attributes can be the cause of his downfall. The very swiftness of Asahel enabled him to catch up with Abner who, in turn, killed him.

וְלֹא לַגִּבּוֹרִים הַמִּלְחָמָה — *Nor the battle by the strong.* As in the verse [*Psalms* 33:16]: *'A mighty man is not saved by great strength' (Ibn Ezra).*

וְגַם לֹא לַחֲכָמִים לֶחֶם — *Nor does bread come to the wise.* One would think that the wise man would rule over fools. But the matter is usually reversed *(Ibn Ezra).* Being wise does not guarantee one food *(Metzudas David).*

וְגַם לֹא לַיֹּדְעִים חֵן *Nor favor to the learned* — Knowledge does not always win one the acclaim of his fellow man *(Metzudas David),* or the respect of the government that they should defer to his knowledge.

An example of unappreciated knowledge is give in verses 14-17 *(Kara).*

כִּי־עֵת וָפֶגַע יִקְרֶה אֶת־כֻּלָּם — *But* [lit. *'for'*] *time and death will happen to them all.* To *the swift, the strong,*

fools entered soiled. The king rejoiced at the wise but was angry with the fools.

'Those who adorned themselves for the banquet,' the king ordered, 'let them sit, eat and drink. But those who did not adorn themselves for the banquet, let them stand, watch, . . . and hunger' *(Shabbos* 153a).

יב כִּי גַּם לֹא־יֵדַע הָאָדָם אֶת־עִתּוֹ כַּדָּגִים
שֶׁנֶּאֱחָזִים בִּמְצוֹדָה רָעָה וְכַצִּפֳּרִים
הָאֲחֻזוֹת בַּפָּח כָּהֵם יוּקָשִׁים בְּנֵי הָאָדָם
יג לְעֵת רָעָה כְּשֶׁתִּפּוֹל עֲלֵיהֶם פִּתְאֹם׃ גַּם־
זֹה רָאִיתִי חָכְמָה תַּחַת הַשָּׁמֶשׁ וּגְדוֹלָה
יד הִיא אֵלָי׃ עִיר קְטַנָּה וַאֲנָשִׁים בָּהּ מְעָט
וּבָא־אֵלֶיהָ מֶלֶךְ גָּדוֹל וְסָבַב אֹתָהּ וּבָנָה
טו עָלֶיהָ מְצוֹדִים גְּדֹלִים׃ וּמָצָא בָהּ אִישׁ
מִסְכֵּן חָכָם וּמִלַּט־הוּא אֶת־הָעִיר
בְּחָכְמָתוֹ וְאָדָם לֹא זָכַר אֶת־הָאִישׁ

the wise, etc. *(Metzudas David).*

[And their swiftness, strength, wisdom, etc. will not save them from God's plan.] Therefore whoever advocates hedonistically that 'whatever one is able to do with his might, do it' — is a fool *(Ibn Ezra).*

The translation of פֶּגַע [*'occurrence'*] as 'death' follows *Metzudas Zion* who relates it to *II Samuel* 1:15: גַּשׁ פְּגַע־בּוֹ, *'approach, slay him.*

12. And this, too, I saw . . . *(Sforno).*

אֶת־עִתּוֹ — *His hours.* The time when misfortune shall suddenly descend upon him *(Rashbam);* so he can take precautions against it *(Sforno).*

This is a rebuke to men who always postpone repentance by rationalizing that death is far off, with the result that even if they live to seventy it does not suffice — death will still catch them unprepared *(Alshich).*

בִּמְצוֹדָה רָעָה — *A fatal net.* Following *Metzudas Zion:* A *'painful'* net. *Rashi:* an inferior net. A damaged net which is nevertheless usable *(Kara).* [To be trapped and killed by an inferior net is especially heartbreaking.]

The *Midrash* asks: Is there, then, an evil net and a good net? — It denotes a fish-hook [which is the *'bad'* i.e. 'painful' way of being caught as compared with the net.]

כָּהֵם יוּקָשִׁים בְּנֵי הָאָדָם לְעֵת רָעָה — [*Like them*] *So are men caught in the moment of disaster.* Just as fish who cause their own death, and later attribute it to the bait, to the hook hidden within, so men attribute their death to sickness, not to their sins *(Alshich).*

[Thus, man — with all his intellect, power and skill — is not even superior to fish when it comes to knowing his life span; all Creation is subject to God's government of the Universe.]

13. גַּם־זוֹ רָאִיתִי חָכְמָה תַּחַת הַשָּׁמֶשׁ — *This, too, have I observed* [*about*] *wisdom beneath the sun.* Having earlier deprecated wisdom, [verse 11] Solomon now relates a story

know his hour: like fish caught in a fatal net, like birds seized in a snare, so are men caught in the moment of disaster when it falls upon them suddenly.

13 *This, too, have I observed about wisdom beneath the sun, and it affected me profoundly:*

14 *There was a small town with only a few inhabitants; and a mighty king came upon it and surrounded it, and built great siege works over it.*
15 *Present in the city was a poor wise man who by his wisdom saved the town. Yet no one remembered that*

complimentary to wisdom *(Ibn Ezra; Sforno; Metzudas David).*

Athough a wise man 'has no bread' of his own, his wisdom can be instrumental in saving an entire town, because *'wisdom is better than might'* although *'a poor man's wisdom is despised.'*

וּגְדוֹלָה הִיא אֵלָי — *And it affected me profoundly* [lit. *and it is great for me.* i.e. I learned a great lesson from it.]

[Some commentators relate this story to the incident in *II Sam.* 20:15. See comm. to verse 16.]

14. עִיר קְטַנָּה ... — *There was a small town with only a few inhabitants.* Thus it was vulnerable to attack on account of its small size and lack of populace *(Kara).*

וּבָא־אֵלֶיהָ מֶלֶךְ גָּדוֹל — *And a mighty king came upon it.* — With a large army *(Metzudas David).*

וּבָנָה עָלֶיהָ מְצוֹדִים גְּדֹלִים — *And built great siege works over it.* The city was low and the towers were built overlooking it. From these towers they could catapult boulders and destructive materials at the populace. Their victory was virtually certain *(Ibn Ezra; Metzudas David).*

But it did not work out that way *(Ateres Shmuel).*

15. וּמָצָא בָהּ אִישׁ מִסְכֵּן חָכָם — *Present in the city* [lit. *'he found (or: 'encountered') there'*] *was a poor wise man.* He was poor, and could not even sustain himself [as in verse 1] but his wisdom proved more effective than strength *(Ibn Latif).*

Compare 4:13 where Solomon also extols a poor but wise youth over an old and foolish king *(Akeidas Yitzchak).*

וּמִלַּט־הוּא אֶת־הָעִיר בְּחָכְמָתוֹ — *[And] Who by his wisdom saved the town.* By negotiating with the king and assuaging his anger *(Leket Shoshanim).*

לֹא זָכַר אֶת־הָאִישׁ ... — *No one remembered that poor man.* i.e. before the wise man saved the city no one held him in esteem — and everyone questioned what good he was to society — because he was poor *(Rashi; Ibn Yachya; Ralbag).*

Ibn Ezra translates: 'the man was never mentioned,' i.e. before he saved the city.

Had he been previously renowned for his wisdom, he would

טז הַמִּסְכֵּן הַהוּא׃ וְאָמַרְתִּי אָנִי טוֹבָה חָכְמָה
מִגְּבוּרָה וְחָכְמַת הַמִּסְכֵּן בְּזוּיָה וּדְבָרָיו
יז אֵינָם נִשְׁמָעִים׃ דִּבְרֵי חֲכָמִים בְּנַחַת
יח נִשְׁמָעִים מִזַּעֲקַת מוֹשֵׁל בַּכְּסִילִים׃ טוֹבָה
חָכְמָה מִכְּלֵי קְרָב וְחוֹטֶא אֶחָד יְאַבֵּד
טוֹבָה הַרְבֵּה׃

have been famous and his act of diplomacy could have been attributed in part to his fame and reputation. But he was poor and obscure, so his feat can be attributed to wisdom only; this is the moral of the story *(Ibn Latif; Metzudas David).*

According to the *Talmud* [*Nedarim* 32b]; *Midrash;* and many commentators *(Alshich; Lekach Tov; Taalumos Chachmah;* also quoted by *Rashi* and *Ibn Ezra)* the story is an allegory:

There was a small town, refers to the body; *with only a few inhabitants:* the limbs; *and a mighty king surrounded it:* the יֵצֶר הָרַע Evil Inclination; — Why is it called *'mighty'?* Because it is thirteen years older than the יֵצֶר הַטּוֹב Good Inclination [see *comm.* to 4:13 and *Overview*]; *And built great siege works over it:* guiding it to do evil. *Present was a poor wise man:* The Good Inclination — Why is it called *'poor'?* Because most people ignore it; *who by his wisdom saved the town:* for whoever obeys the Good Inclination escapes punishment. *Yet no one remembers that poor man:* no one holds the Good Inclination in any kind of esteem, and when the Evil Inclination gains dominion, no one remembers the Good Inclination.

Nevertheless, in the next verses, according to this interpretation, Solomon praises the Good Inclination, as being superior to the Evil Inclination.

16. טוֹבָה חָכְמָה מִגְּבוּרָה — *Wisdom is better than might.* Although the wisdom of a poor man is despised and deprecated and he himself is ignored — in an emergency the wise can accomplish more than the mighty — as illustrated by this story where his simple wisdom, not enhanced by esteem, saved the whole town from the might of the king *(Rashi; Ibn Ezra; Metzudas).*

According to *Midrash Lekach Tov* this entire sequence of events in verses 14-16 refers to the incident related in *II Samuel* 20, when Yoav came to pursue Sheva ben Bichri who had rebelled against David and a certain wise woman saved the town. Her wisdom was thus better than might.

17. דִּבְרֵי חֲכָמִים בְּנַחַת נִשְׁמָעִים . . . — *The gentle words of the wise are heard above the shouts of a king over fools.* This translation follows *Ibn Ezra* who attaches בְּנַחַת to דִּבְרֵי: *'The words of the wise spoken quietly are heard.' Metzudas David* comments: Although the words of the wise are soft-spoken and not shouted, they are heard and accepted.

Rashi attaches בְּנַחַת to נִשְׁמָעִים

poor man. 16 *So I said: Wisdom is better than might, although a poor man's wisdom is despised and his words go unheeded.*

17 *The gentle words of the wise are heard above the shouts of a king over fools,* 18 *and wisdom is better than weapons, but a single rogue can ruin a great deal of good.*

and translates: *'The words of the wise are received with pleasure by people.'*

מִזַּעֲקַת מוֹשֵׁל בַּכְּסִילִים — *Above* [lit. *'than'*] *the shouts of a king over fools.* The sagely advice of the wise is often more effective than the military orders — shouted in a hopeless situation — of a boisterous ruler to an underequipped militia *(Kara).* For very often the ruler of fools is himself a fool *(Midrash Lekach Tov).*

Similarly, Moses departed from this world long ago, yet his decrees are accepted by the Jews; yet how many kings have issued decrees and their words did not endure! *(Rashi).*

18. טוֹבָה חָכְמָה מִכְּלֵי קְרָב — [*And*] *wisdom is better than weapons.* [As related here; and] the incident in *II Sam.* 20 *(Rashi).*

Wisdom is more effective than weapons, too, — because more people benefit from wisdom than do warriors from armor *(Ibn Latif).*

וְחוֹטֶא אֶחָד יְאַבֵּד טוֹבָה הַרְבֵּה — *But a single rogue* [lit. *'sinner'*] *can ruin a great deal of good.* As in the case of Achan [*Joshua* chapter 7] *(Sforno).*

In the ethical perspective, man must view himself as being the deciding factor in the world's righteousness or guilt. Thus if Israel were equally divided between righteousness and guilt, one rogue alone could tip the scales and condemn the whole world. *(Rashi; Rambam; Taalumos Chachmah).*[1]

Similarly, if even one from among a group of wise men becomes a sinner, many people will recoil from wisdom. Thus, as effective as wisdom is, even a single sinner can cause a distaste for wisdom and a cessation of much good *(Metzudas David).*

1. Our Rabbis taught: A man should always regard himself as though he were half guilty and half meritorious: if he performs one precept, happy is he for weighting himself down on the scale of merit; if he commits one transgression, woe to him for weighting himself down in the scale of guilt, for it is said, *'but a single sinner can ruin a great deal of good.'* i.e., on account of the commission of a single sin, much good is lost to him. Rav Eleazar son of Rav Shimon said: Because the world is judged by its majority, and an individual, too, is judged by the majority of his deeds, good or bad, if he performs one good deed, happy is he for turning the scale both for himself and for the whole world on the side of merit; if he commits one transgression, woe to him for weighting himself and the whole world in the scale of guilt, for it is said, *'but a single sinner,'* etc. — on account of the single sin which this man commits, he and the whole world lose much good. *(v. Kiddushin* 40b).

פרק י
א־ד

א זְבוּבֵי מָוֶת יַבְאִישׁ יַבִּיעַ שֶׁמֶן רוֹקֵחַ יָקָר
ב מֵחָכְמָה מִכָּבוֹד סִכְלוּת מְעָט: לֵב חָכָם
ג לִימִינוֹ וְלֵב כְּסִיל לִשְׂמֹאלוֹ: וְגַם־בַּדֶּרֶךְ
כְּשֶׁהַסָּכָל* הֹלֵךְ לִבּוֹ חָסֵר וְאָמַר לַכֹּל
ד סָכָל הוּא: אִם־רוּחַ הַמּוֹשֵׁל תַּעֲלֶה עָלֶיךָ
מְקוֹמְךָ אַל־תַּנַּח כִּי מַרְפֵּא יַנִּיחַ חֲטָאִים

* כְּשֶׁסָּכָל ק׳

1. [This verse continues the theme of the last verse: *'A single rogue can ruin a great deal of good.'*]

זְבוּבֵי מָוֶת — *Dead flies. Ibn Ezra* notes that although the plural is used, the meaning is: even one dead fly can putrefy the perfumer's oil.

Rashi renders the phrase: *'dying flies'* and comments: 'In the wintertime, flies have no strength and are near death, but if only one falls into the perfumer's ointment, it putrefies the entire mixture. A fly is insignificant, yet it spoils a precious article. So, too, even a minor sin can outweigh much wisdom and honor. Should even one transgression be committed by someone whose virtues and sins are equally balanced, it inclines the scales to guilt.

יַבְאִישׁ יַבִּיעַ — *Putrefy* [lit. *'putrefy, effervesce'* i.e. create אֲבַעְבֻּעוֹת, *'bubbles' (Rashi, Ibn Ezra).*]

Rav Saadiah Gaon understands יַבִּיעַ as a noun: A container of oil, and would thus render: As dying flies — who have strength for nothing else — can putrefy the container of perfumer's oil, so do fools, also incapable of anything else, counterbalance wisdom and honor.

יָקָר מֵחָכְמָה מִכָּבוֹד סִכְלוּת מְעָט — *A little folly outweighs wisdom and honor.* i.e. all the wisdom and honor a man possesses can be nullified in the eyes of men by one foolish act, just as one sin can outweigh much good *(Ibn Ezra).*

[The translation of יָקָר, *'outweighs'* follows *Rashi.*]

2. [There follows a series of one-sentence proverbs.]

לֵב חָכָם לִימִינוֹ — *A wise man's mind* [lit. *'heart'*] *[tends] to his right.* His wisdom is always prepared to lead him in the correct path for his benefit *(Rashi);* and his intellect is always at hand when he needs it *(Metzudas David).*

Some interpret: *'A wise man's intellect is at his right hand',* just as an artisan keeps his most needed tools and materials at his right hand, always ready for use, and less needed items at his left hand. The allegory is that a wise man uses his intellect often and keeps it at the ready, so to speak, whereas the fool to whom other things are more important, keeps his intellect in a secondary position *(Divrei Chefetz).*

Ibn Ezra interestingly notes: 'a left-handed person should not feel slighted because the allegory here refers to the majority of people.'

וְלֵב כְּסִיל לִשְׂמֹאלוֹ — *While a fool's mind* [lit. *'heart'*] *[tends] to his left.* Always eager to drive him off the proper path *(Rashi).*

And is not ready and expeditious in time of need *(Metzudas David).*

X
1-4

Dead flies putrefy the perfumer's oil; a little folly outweighs wisdom and honor.
2 *A wise man's mind tends to his right; while a fool's mind tends to his left.* 3 *Even on the road as the fool walks, he lacks sense, and proclaims to all that he is a fool.*
4 *If the anger of a ruler flares up against you, do not leave your place, for deference appeases great offenses.*

וְגַם־בַּדֶּרֶךְ כְּשֶׁסָּכָל הֹלֵךְ— *Even on the road as the fool walks.* The fool, by his every action, manifests his lack of good sense *(Ibn Ezra).* Even if he doesn't tarry long in one place his foolishness is still obvious to all *(Metzudas David).*

לִבּוֹ חָסֵר — *He lacks sense* [lit. *'his heart is lacking'*] *Alshich* interprets this verse as an allegorical reference to 'the path of Torah'. Even when the fool walks the path of Torah and performs *mitzvos,* his ignorance shines forth and his 'heart' lacks the proper appreciation of the significance of the precepts. His actions proclaim his ignorance.

וְאָמַר לַכֹּל סָכָל הוּא — *And [he] proclaims to all that he is a fool* i.e. his actions make it so plain that it is as if he had shouted to all passers-by that he is a fool *(Ibn Ezra).*

The *Midrash* interprets the phrase: 'The fool thinks that all people are fools like himself. He does not realize that he is the fool and the others are wise.'

. . . The fool thinks himself wise and brands as a fool anyone who fails to conform to his ways *(Akeidas Yitzchak).*

4. אִם־רוּחַ הַמּוֹשֵׁל תַּעֲלֶה — *If the anger of a ruler flares up against you.* The translation of רוּחַ *anger* follows *Metzudas David* and most commentators.

Ibn Ezra suggests that this verse is directed toward the wise man who has risen to high positions of government. He should not forget his earlier lower status and become haughty. Rather, he should continue his quest for wisdom as he did before he became powerful..

Chovos haLevavos understands רוּחַ in its usual sense: *spirit,* desire: If you feel inclined to become a ruler [i.e. to domineer], do not do so; keep humble.

מְקוֹמְךָ אַל־תַּנַּח — *Do not leave your place* — Because if you flee, you will just compound the ruler's anger *(Metzudas David).*

כִּי מַרְפֵּא יַנִּיחַ חֲטָאִים גְּדוֹלִים — *For deference* ['weakness'] *appeases great offenses.* Deference to his rule — rather than flagrant flight from him — will make him more kindly disposed towards clemency and will avoid a penalty for great offenses *(Ibn Yachya).*

Harav David Feinstein notes, in this context, the contrast between the responses of Saul and David when each was accused of sinning. When Samuel confronted Saul in the matter of Amalek, Saul first at-

ה גְּדוֹלִים׃ יֵשׁ רָעָה רָאִיתִי תַּחַת הַשָּׁמֶשׁ
ו כִּשְׁגָגָה שֶׁיֹּצָא מִלִּפְנֵי הַשַּׁלִּיט׃ נִתַּן הַסֶּכֶל
בַּמְּרוֹמִים רַבִּים וַעֲשִׁירִים בַּשֵּׁפֶל יֵשֵׁבוּ׃
ז רָאִיתִי עֲבָדִים עַל־סוּסִים וְשָׂרִים הֹלְכִים
ח כַּעֲבָדִים עַל־הָאָרֶץ׃ חֹפֵר גּוּמָּץ בּוֹ יִפּוֹל
ט וּפֹרֵץ גָּדֵר יִשְּׁכֶנּוּ נָחָשׁ׃ מַסִּיעַ אֲבָנִים
י יֵעָצֵב בָּהֶם בּוֹקֵעַ עֵצִים יִסָּכֶן בָּם׃ אִם־

tempted to justify his actions, and only later did he confess and say *'I have sinned.'* But it was too late, *'HASHEM had rejected him from being king over Israel' (I Sam.* 15:23). David, on the other hand, when confronted by the prophet Nathan in the matter of Bathsheba, *immediately* confessed and said *'I have sinned against HASHEM'* [*II Sam.* 12:13]. David's display of deference might have been one the reasons that he received clemency, as the verse concludes: *'HASHEM has commuted your sin.'*

Rashi interprets the verse as referring to God's anger: If the anger of the Ruler of the Universe flares up against you do not set aside your striving for good deeds and say 'of what avail is my righteousness?' For suffering, מַרְפֵּא, *will heal* your transgressions and will atone for your great sins.

5. כִּשְׁגָגָה — *As if it were an error.* I.e. like a royal decree made in error, which is irreversible, so are the Heavenly decrees described in verses 6 and 7 *(Rashi).*

Ibn Ezra and *Metzudas David* comment that this verse continues the thought in verse 4 in describing the potential evils of a rise to power. A ruler sometimes finds it politically expedient to commit an injustice and say it was done in error.

[Others regard the prefix כ of כִּשְׁגָגָה not as the comparative *'like'*, but rather: *'Indeed'*, 'for.' Man must be cautious regarding the words that emanate from his mouth. One word uttered by a king can cause irreparable damage. And, as the *Talmud (Moed Katan* 18a*)* notes: בְּרִית כְּרוּתָה לִשְׂפָתַיִם 'a covenant has been made with the lips', i.e. the way in which a thing is expressed may contain a portent for the future, so it behooves man to choose his words carefully.]

In this context the *Midrash* notes that Rachel's death ensued because of Jacob's words [*Gen.* 31:32] . . . and that Samuel's sons did not succeed their father because of what Eli said to him.[*I Sam.* 3:17; 4:11; 8:1ff].

6. נִתַּן הַסֶּכֶל בַּמְּרוֹמִים רַבִּים — *Folly is placed on lofty heights.* This is one of the evils referred to in the previous verse: The rich who presumably deserve honor are arbitrarily shunted, while fools are elevated to high positions. It appears to be an error from On High. But it is no error [it is part of God's unrevealed plan of governing the Universe] *(Metzudas David).*

X
5-9

[5] *There is an evil which I have observed in the world as if it were an error proceeding from the ruler:* [6] *Folly is placed on lofty heights, while rich men sit in low places.* [7] *I have seen slaves on horses and nobles walking on foot like slaves.*

[8] *He who digs a pit will fall into it, and he who breaks down a wall will be bitten by a snake.* [9] *He who moves about stones will be hurt by them; he who splits logs will be endangered by them.*

7. רָאִיתִי עֲבָדִים עַל־סוּסִים — *I have seen slaves on horses.* [This verse repeats the point made in the preceding one. The respective positions of slaves/rulers are reversed like those of the rich man/fool in the earlier verse.]

8. [In the following proverbs *Koheles* enjoins care in all undertakings. These verses may also be interpreted as additional examples of the 'evils' described in vss. 6-7, in the sense that man should not place his faith in his control of events: Every act is the result, not of human planning, but of Divine Providence *(Alshich).*]

חֹפֵר גּוּמָּץ בּוֹ יִפּוֹל — *He who digs a pit will fall into it.* The verse is understood by many commentators in its literal sense. *Rashi* and *Metzudas David* understand it as a parable: He who plots against his fellow man, will himself fall into the trap.

וּפֹרֵץ גָּדֵר יִשְּׁכֶנּוּ נָחָשׁ — *And he who breaks down a wall will be bitten by a snake.* [This clause repeats the point made in the earlier clause]: Whoever breaches a wall so that his neighbor's field will lay exposed to robbers, will himself be bitten by snakes and be unable to enter that field *(Alshich).* Or, whoever breaks open a wall so that snakes who nestle between the crevices may roam about and bite others, will himself be bitten *(Metzudas David).*

Rashi (following the *Talmud, Avodah Zarah* 27b) applies this verse to those who break through the 'legal fences' [i.e. Rabbinic ordinances] which serve to safeguard the Torah and are smitten with death at the hand of Heaven.

9. מַסִּיעַ אֲבָנִים יֵעָצֵב בָּהֶם — *He who moves about stones will be hurt by them* [following *Alshich* and *Metzudas David*:]Whoever scatters rocks to trip others will himself be tripped and hurt by them.[1]

1. Our Rabbis taught: A man should not remove stones from his ground to public ground. A person was removing stones from his ground onto public ground when a pious man met him and admonished him: 'Fool! Why do you remove stones from ground which is not yours to ground which is yours?'

[Not understanding the message of the pious man] he laughed at him.

After some time that man became improverished and was forced to sell his field, and when he was walking on that public ground he tripped over those very stones. He then exclaimed 'well had that pious man spoken when he said to me "why do you remove stones from ground which is not yours to ground which is yours?"' *(Bava Kamma* 50b*).*

קֵהָה הַבַּרְזֶל וְהוּא לֹא־פָנִים קִלְקַל
יא וַחֲיָלִים יְגַבֵּר וְיִתְרוֹן הַכְשֵׁיר חָכְמָה׃ אִם־
יִשֹּׁךְ הַנָּחָשׁ בְּלוֹא־לָחַשׁ וְאֵין יִתְרוֹן
יב לְבַעַל הַלָּשׁוֹן׃ דִּבְרֵי־פִי־חָכָם חֵן
יג וְשִׂפְתוֹת כְּסִיל תְּבַלְּעֶנּוּ׃ תְּחִלַּת דִּבְרֵי־

Rashi translates: He who quarries rocks will be fatigued by them . . . So, too, one who perpetuates evil will reap evil.

יִסָּכֶן בָּם — *Will be endangered by them.* He might have planned to fell the timber on someone else, but he himself is in primary danger *(Alshich).*

Metzudas David notes that the verses repeat the same theme to stress how commonplace these occurrences are.

These verses teach that the fool in his foolishness will place himself in danger, while the wise man will guard himself. Also, nothing in this world is acquired without toil and some inherent danger *(Ibn Ezra).*

10. This verse is semantically difficult. The translation follows *Rashi:*

If an axe (sword) lost its sharpness and its blade is not polished, it is still a potent weapon that helps make its bearers strong and victorious. Great mental ability is even more potent than weapons. The allegory is that if a sage's face is blackened by hunger [i.e. has become dulled with hunger], and you see him sitting like a poor man among the rich, realize that many 'soldiers' are strengthened by his merit [i.e. he is still a potent force.].

Ibn Ezra explains קלקל as a double form of נְחֹשֶׁת קָלָל, *'burnished brass'* [*Ezekiel* 1:7.]

Rav Yosef Kara explains that a utensil is effective only if it is prepared first. Therefore, preparation is more important than the metal itself. Similarly, initiative and effort are necessary to achieve maximum benefit from a good mind.

The *Meiri* translates as follows: If an axe is dull and it has not been sharpened then more power must be exerted in using it to compensate for its dullness. Similarly, if there is dullness of intellect one must strive harder to compensate for the handicap.[1]

11. אִם־יִשֹּׁךְ הַנָּחָשׁ בְּלוֹא־לָחַשׁ — *If the snake bites because it was not charmed* [lit. *'whispered'*] But had it been charmed it would not have bitten *(Metzudas David).*

וְאֵין יִתְרוֹן לְבַעַל הַלָּשׁוֹן — *Then there is no advantage to the charmer's art* [lit. *'to the master of the tongue'.*] i.e. there is no advantage in knowing how to exercise a charm and not making use of it *(Rashbam).*

Similarly, there is no advantage

1. The *Talmud* interprets the verse as referring to one's studies:
'If you see a student to whom his studies are hard as iron, it is because he failed to systematically memorize his studies. As it is said והוא לא פָּנִים קִלְקַל he did not know his studies because he did not memorize the laws correctly. What is his remedy? Let him spend more time in Yeshivah, as it is said *he must exert more strength; but wisdom is more profitable to exert.* [The latter words indicate]: How much more profitable would his efforts be if he had

10 *If an axe is blunt and one has not honed the edge, nevertheless it strengthens the warriors. Wisdom is a more powerful skill.*
11 *If the snake bites because it was not charmed, then there is no advantage to the charmer's art.*
12 *The words of a wise man win favor, but a fool's lips devour him.*
13 *His talk begins as*

to wisdom if, while his fellow men sin the wise man maintains his silence, and does not teach them Torah *(Rashi).*

Alshich comments: If a snake killed someone because his charmer did not prevent him from doing so, then what is the difference between the charmer and the snake? The charmer shares the moral guilt. Similarly, man's tongue is like the charmer's snake. He who allows his tongue to slander is guilty because man's speech often causes death and destruction to all who hear his foolishness, both in This World and the Hereafter.

The *Midrash* interprets לַחַשׁ, *'incite'*, and comments: 'Never does a serpent bite unless it has been incited [נִלְחַשׁ לוֹ] from Above, nor does a lion rend its prey unless it has been incited from Above,nor does a government interfere with men unless it has been incited from Above.'

12. דִּבְרֵי פִי־חָכָם חֵן — *The words of a wise man win favor.* To all who hear him *(Rashi),* because all are impressed with his wisdom and they rally around him *(Ibn Latif).*

Ibn Ezra [obviously concerned that the verse might be misinterpreted to mean 'many words by a wise man are favorable'] comments: 'God forbid that the wise man should be a man of many words! The intent of the verse is that whatever emanates from the mouth of the wise is favorable; but the fool will destroy himself with his words.'

וְשִׂפְתוֹת כְּסִיל תְּבַלְּעֶנּוּ — *But a fool's lips devour him* — i.e. will lead to his own destruction *(Ibn Yachya).*

According to the *Midrash*: *'The words of a wise man win favor'* [lit. *are gracious*] — this refers to Cyrus who permitted the rebuilding of the Temple [*Ezra* 1:2,3]; *'but the lips of a fool are swallowed up'* — this refers to Ahasuerus who swallowed his words and ordered the work on the rebuilding of the Temple to stop [*Ezra* 4:17 see *Overview* to ArtScroll edition of *Esther,* p. xvii] *(Midrash Lekach Tov).*

Seder haYom comments that the wise man must exercise great care in his every utterance. Whatever he says as a result of wise deliberation, wins great favor, but *the very same thoughts* expressed by the fool will wreak destruction.

originally systematized his studies. Thus, for example *Resh Lakish* would systematically review his studies forty times corresponding to the forty days during which the Torah was given and only then would he come before Rav Yochanan. Rav Adda bar Ahava made it his practice to systematically review his studies twenty-four times coresponding to [the 24 Books of] Scripture and only then would he come before Rava *(Taanis* 8a).

פִּיהוּ סִכְלוּת וְאַחֲרִית פִּיהוּ הוֹלֵלוּת
יד רָעָה: וְהַסָּכָל יַרְבֶּה דְבָרִים לֹא־יֵדַע
הָאָדָם מַה־שֶּׁיִּהְיֶה וַאֲשֶׁר יִהְיֶה מֵאַחֲרָיו
טו מִי יַגִּיד לוֹ: עֲמַל הַכְּסִילִים תְּיַגְּעֶנּוּ אֲשֶׁר
טז לֹא־יָדַע לָלֶכֶת אֶל־עִיר: אִי־לָךְ אֶרֶץ
שֶׁמַּלְכֵּךְ נָעַר וְשָׂרַיִךְ בַּבֹּקֶר יֹאכֵלוּ:

13. [This verse amplifies the latter part of the preceding verse.]

תְּחִלַּת דִּבְרֵי־פִיהוּ סִכְלוּת — *His talk begins as foolishness* [or: *the start of his talk is foolishness*] i.e. There is no sense to the fool's words from beginning to end *(Ibn Ezra)* — they start out as foolishness and end in madness, they are utterly engulfed in nonsense and melancholy *(Metzudas David)*.

The fool does not cease from uttering foolishness until ultimately it ends as evil madness and he causes harm unto himself *(Kara)*.

As soon as the fool opens his mouth it is obvious to all that his words are foolish; but as he continues he utters folly that is evil even in the eyes of God *(Akeidas Yitzchak)*.

הוֹלֵלוּת רָעָה — *Evil madness* [i.e. words of utter and unredeeming madness and folly — evil in the sight of man and God.]

14. וְהַסָּכָל יַרְבֶּה דְבָרִים — *The fool prates on and on* [lit. *'and the fool increases words'*].

[Not only does the fool speak nonsense, as mentioned in the previous verse, but he *constantly* chatters, discussing all subjects, even those of which man is ignorant, such as the events of the future.]

Rav Yosef Kara explains: the fool presumes to boast 'I will do such and such' — as if the performance of the act were entirely within his control. But, as the verse continues to expound, people are not masters of their acts.

לֹא־יֵדַע הָאָדָם מַה־שֶּׁיִּהְיֶה — *But man does not know what will be.* He does not even know what the morrow will bring, and וַאֲשֶׁר יִהְיֶה מֵאַחֲרָיו מִי יַגִּיד לוֹ, *what shall be after that* (in the more distant future) *who can tell him?* [Only a fool will presume to make irresponsible plans for the near or distant future.]

Several commentators *(Alshich; Ibn Yachya; Tuv Taam)* interpret this phrase are a direct quote of the fool's prattling. He goes about misleading people by saying: 'Man does not know his destiny and who can tell man what the Hereafter is like?' He thus incites people to become unbelievers.

וַאֲשֶׁר יִהְיֶה מֵאַחֲרָיו מִי יַגִּיד לוֹ — *And who can tell him what will be after him?* [i.e. beyond the immediate future; or in the Hereafter. Compare 6:12 and 8:7 for similar thoughts.]

Rashi translates מֵאַחֲרָיו 'in back of him', i.e. behind him: Not only can man not perceive what is ahead

X
14-16

foolishness and ends as evil madness. [14] *The fool prates on and on, but man does not know what will be; and who can tell him what will happen after him?*

[15] *The toil of fools exhaust them, as one who does not know the way to town.*

[16] *Woe to you, O land, whose king acts as an adolescent, and whose ministers dine in the morning.*

of him — even for what is already behind him in the past, he needs clarification.

15. עֲמַל הַכְּסִילִים תְּיַגְּעֶנּוּ — *The toil of fools exhaust them.* Why should fools busy themselves with complex and mysterious matters when they lacks comprehension of the simplest and most obvious things. They are thus compared to those who wish to go to the city but do not know the way. They stumble trying to find the proper road and weary themselves without achieving their end *(Kara, Ibn Ezra).*

On a philosophical level this verse refers to one who follows a system of thought and then abandons it because he has discovered some flaw in it. He transfers to another system and yet another, giving each one up in turn because something has made it reprehensible to him. Such a person may be compared to one who wishes to go to a certain city but does not know which road leads to there; consequently he tries many roads *(Rav Saadiah Gaon).*

[The additional irony is that a traveler could be guided properly were he to ask directions. Conversely, the fool persists in his folly to the point of exhaustion because he refuses to consult with the wise and seek proper guidance.]

16. אִי־לָךְ אֶרֶץ — *Woe to you, o land.* The word אִי has the same meaning as אוֹי, *'woe!'* It appears in Scriptures with this meaning only here and above in 4:10: אִילוֹ.

שֶׁמַּלְכֵּךְ נָעַר — *Whose king acts as an adolescent* [lit. *'that your king is a youth'.*] This translation follows *Rashi, Metzudas David* [עוֹשֶׂה מַעֲשֵׂה נַעֲרוּת, 'who acts childlishly'] and is in harmony with other commentators who all agree that the reference is not simply to a 'youthful' king [or else he would have used the word יֶלֶד 'boy'. *(Akeidas Yitzchak).*

Similarly, *Ibn Yachya* translates: *'whose king is devoid of wisdom and is enslaved to folly and madness;'* and according to *Ramban:* 'inexperienced and foolish.'

Several commentators *(Ralbag; Alshich; Almosnino)* interpret נָעַר allegorically as one who is enslaved to his youthful lusts, and translate: Woe to the person who is a slave to pleasure and, like a rebellious youth, will not heed sage advice. Instead, he gives way to material yearnings [*'whose ministers dine'* (on material pleasures) *in the 'morning'* (i.e. the *'morning'* = apex of their youth)] unlike the next verse which praises the *'free man'*, i.e. one who serves the Creator free

פרק י

יז אַשְׁרֵיךְ אֶרֶץ שֶׁמַּלְכֵּךְ בֶּן־חוֹרִים וְשָׂרַיִךְ
יז־כ בָּעֵת יֹאכֵלוּ בִּגְבוּרָה וְלֹא בַשְּׁתִי:
יח בַּעֲצַלְתַּיִם יִמַּךְ הַמְּקָרֶה וּבְשִׁפְלוּת יָדַיִם
יט יִדְלֹף הַבָּיִת: לִשְׂחוֹק עֹשִׂים לֶחֶם וְיַיִן
כ יְשַׂמַּח חַיִּים וְהַכֶּסֶף יַעֲנֶה אֶת־הַכֹּל: גַּם

of the dictates of his Evil Inclination.

[The verse as interpreted by the commentators does not contradict 4:13. There *'youth'* refers to age, here it refers to the level of maturity.]

וְשָׂרַיִךְ בַּבֹּקֶר יֹאכֵלוּ — *And whose ministers dine in the morning.* Because their prime concern is not the welfare of the state but their own satiety. They indulge in revelry when they should attend to the duties of state *(Ibn Latif).*

[The commentators explain that late afternoon or evening was the usual time for kings to dine; whereas the morning hours were reserved for judging the people (cf. *Jeremiah* 21:12). This is evident from the *Talmud, Shabbos* 10a where this verse is translated to mean that the judges do not eat a large meal early in the morning but sit and judge until the proper time for eating — so, that, as the next verse concludes, they will judge in the strength of the Torah and not in the drunkenness of wine.]

17. In contrast:

אַשְׁרֵיךְ אֶרֶץ שֶׁמַּלְכֵּךְ בֶּן חוֹרִים — *Happy are you, O land, whose king is a man of dignity* [lit. *'a free man'*] i.e. one who is master of his passions, and acts with dignity; [as חוֹרִים, *'nobles'* in *Nech.* 2:16 *(Metzudas Zion);* 'those who act in the manner of the truly great.' [בֶּן־חוֹרִים is thus in this sense the antonym of בֶּן בְּלִיַּעַל, *irresponsible scoundrel. (Ibn Ezra).*]

וְשָׂרַיִךְ בָּעֵת יֹאכֵלוּ — *And whose ministers dine at the proper time.* For 'they eat to live rather than live to eat' *(Ibn Yachya).*

בִּגְבוּרָה וְלֹא בַשְּׁתִי — *'In strength' and not in drunkenness.* They engage in the vigorous pursuit of wisdom and understanding rather than in drinking wine *(Rashi).*

Ibn Ezra explains 'strength' in this context: they eat as they require the strength-giving energy of food; with restraint, to satisfy a need.

Their true strength is that they control their passions [*Avos* 4:1.] Unlike the wicked who dine in the morning, they do not judge the people vindictively while under the influence of alcohol *(Ibn Yachya).*

18. בַּעֲצַלְתַּיִם יִמַּךְ הַמְּקָרֶה — *Through slothfulness the ceiling* [or: *'beam'*] *sags.* This dual proverb, though it deals with a house which has become dilapidated through the laziness and stinginess [וּבְשִׁפְלוּת יָדַיִם] of its owner, forms a continuity in the context of the previous verses. The house is regarded as a simile for the state. Those kings 'who dine in the morning', neglect their duties to the state, hence, like a neglected house, the state will deteriorate *(Ibn Ezra).*

[17] *Happy are you, O land, whose king is a man of dignity, and whose ministers dine at the proper time — in strength and not in drunkenness.*

[18] *Through slothfulness the ceiling sags, and through idleness of the hands the house leaks.*

[19] *A feast is made for laughter, and wine gladdens life, but money answers everything.*

וּבְשִׁפְלוּת יָדַיִם — *And through idleness* [lit. *'lowliness'*] *of the hands.* i.e. letting down the hands and not lifting them up to do work *(Metzudas David).*

Ibn Ezra translates: poverty, deprivation.

Alshich homiletically renders 'humbleness of the hand' i.e. due to readiness to dispense charity, 'rains of blessing' descend with such force that they 'leak' into the home.

19. [Many commentators explain that joyous occasions — such as weddings — are celebrated with banquets and guests gladden their hearts with wine. Without money such celebrations could not be held. Thus, this verse continues the urging against slothfulness and idleness by saying that without industrious labor, even the permitted joys of life cannot be properly enjoyed.

According to others, this refers to the pleasure-loving princes of the previous verses who spend their days in hedonistic wine-feasts — not to give nourishment to the body but to engage in sport and pleasure.

These are the same rulers who in the previous verse 'neglect their house' and their duties to the State.]

Thus they squander the public treasury: money sufficient to answer all needs *(Poras Yosef).*

לֶחֶם — *A feast* [lit. *'Bread'*] *'Bread'* refers to *'meal,' 'feast'* as in *Daniel* 5:1 *'Belshazzar the king made* לְחֶם רַב, *a grand feast,' (Rashi);* and *I Sam.* 20:27 — *'Why does the son of Yishai not come* אֶל־הַלָּחֶם, *to the meal . . .' (Kara).*

וְהַכֶּסֶף יַעֲנֶה אֶת־הַכֹּל — *But* [lit. *'and'*] *money answers everything* i.e. money is needed by all and makes everything possible. In the previous verse slothfulness is deprecated, here man is encouraged toward industry. Lazy people do not earn the money required for living *(Rashi; Metzudas David).*

[According to the alternate interpretation, the reference is to the money kings extort from their subjects to finance their lavish feasts.]

Yalkut haGershuni comments that יַעֲנֶה can be related to עִינוּי, *affliction:* 'money afflicts all.' [Its abundance as well as its absence causes the heart of man to be afflicted.]

Hoarding of vast amounts of money is forbidden; the acquisition of *necessary* financial assets for living and performing charitable acts is encouraged *(Ibn Yachya).*

On an ethical level, the verse is interpreted: 'money makes everyone respond' — for money, everyone will accede to your every request *(Kedushas Levi).*

פרק י

בְּמַדָּעֲךָ מֶלֶךְ אַל־תְּקַלֵּל וּבְחַדְרֵי מִשְׁכָּבְךָ
אַל־תְּקַלֵּל עָשִׁיר כִּי עוֹף הַשָּׁמַיִם יוֹלִיךְ
אֶת־הַקּוֹל וּבַעַל הַכְּנָפַיִם יַגֵּיד דָּבָר׃

* כְּנָפַיִם ק׳

פרק יא

א־ב

א שַׁלַּח לַחְמְךָ עַל־פְּנֵי הַמָּיִם כִּי־בְרֹב
ב הַיָּמִים תִּמְצָאֶנּוּ׃ תֶּן־חֵלֶק לְשִׁבְעָה וְגַם

20. גַּם בְּמַדָּעֲךָ מֶלֶךְ אַל־תְּקַלֵּל — *Even in your thoughts do not curse a king.* Although Koheles criticizes the extravagance of profligate kings, he counsels extreme caution against voicing displeasure toward a ruler or governor of the land. He even warns against *thinking* these criticisms, because ultimately they will be verbalized *'and a bird of the skies may carry the sound' (Ibn Latif).*

[The translation of בְּמַדָּעֲךָ, *thoughts,* follows the majority of commentators who relate it to מַדָּע, *knowledge,* — i.e. the mind; seat of knowledge.]

וּבְחַדְרֵי מִשְׁכָּבְךָ אַל־תְּקַלֵּל עָשִׁיר — *And in your bed-chamber do not curse the rich* — i.e. even in the privacy of your own bedroom where you are certain no one hears you *(Metzudas David)* because 'the walls have ears' *(Midrash).*

'Rich' implies members of an influential ruling class who, because of their wealth, gain high status and are usually most vindictive *(Ralbag).*

כִּי עוֹף הַשָּׁמַיִם יוֹלִיךְ אֶת־הַקּוֹל — *For a bird of the skies may carry the sound.* An idiomatic phrase to imply that your utterance will quickly spread and reach the ears of government officials *(Metzudas David).*

Midrash Psalms explains that the matter will be found out by divination of the flight of birds [an ancient form of sorcery used by magicians of non-Jewish kings which determined events from the manner and formation of flying birds. Thus the phrase may be understood literally: The birds of the air will convey to the king —by divinations — that you reviled against him.]

וּבַעַל כְּנָפַיִם יַגֵּיד דָּבָר — *And some winged creature may betray* [lit. *'tell'*] *the matter.* Literally this phrase conveys similar ideas to the one preceding it. *Rashi,* however, comments that it refers to people who flurry to and fro. One must be apprehensive that perhaps someone overheard his curses and will betray him.

XI

1. שַׁלַּח לַחְמְךָ עַל־פְּנֵי הַמָּיִם — *Send your bread upon the waters.* [Most commentators explain this verse as urging that charity be given even to

X
20 ²⁰ *Even in your thoughts do not curse a king, and in your bed-chamber do not curse the rich, for a bird of the skies may carry the sound, and some winged creature may betray the matter.*

XI
1-2 *Send your bread upon the waters, for after many days you will find it.* ² *Distribute portions to*

strangers who will never be seen again. The generosity will not go unrewarded; the favor will be repaid.][1]

[The *Midrash, Shmos Rabba* 27 remarks: 'Are men so foolish as to throw their bread upon water? Rather,] the verse is to be understood allegorically to refer to one like יִתְרוֹ, Jethro, who told his daughters to invite the stranger, Moses — whom he thought was an Egyptian and whom he never expected to ever see again — to dinner. As it turned out, Moses became his son-in-law; the 'King of Israel'; he eventually brought Jethro under the 'Wings of the Shechinah'; with the result that Jethro's descendants later served in the Sanhedrin *(Rashi).*

The *Midrash* does, however, relate an incident of a man who actually used to throw a loaf of bread into the sea every day. One day he bought a fish. On cutting it open, he found a beautiful object inside. People said of him: 'This is the man whose loaf stood him in good stead' and they applied to him the verse: *'send your bread upon the waters.'*

This verse follows the theme of the previous verse. In 10:20 man is cautioned against cursing the rich and rationalizing that word of it will never reach them because they are far away. No, *'a bird of the skies will carry the sound.'* Here, too, man is warned about a different kind of complacency. A person might be tempted to say of giving constantly to charity: 'Why should I send my bread upon the waters? Will I ever find it? — The verse assures us: 'After many days you *will* find it' *(Me'am Lo'ez).*

Alshich explains that one of the highest forms of charity [as enumerated by *Rambam*] is when the giver and recipient are unknown to each other. Solomon alludes to this concept with his parable: When one lets bread float on water, and further downstream a hungry person picks it up and eats it, it is a classic example of the giver and recipient remaining unknown to each other. Ultimately the man will

1. *Rabbi Akiva said: When I was traveling at sea, I saw a ship which had been wrecked and I was greatly concerned about a rabbinical scholar who had been on board and went down with the ship. On arriving at the province of Cappadocia, however, I noticed him sitting before me and asking questions.*

'My son,' I said to him, 'how did you come up out of the sea?'

He replied, 'Rabbi, thanks to your prayer on my behalf, one wave tossed me to another, and

פרק יא

לִשְׁמוֹנָה כִּי לֹא תֵדַע מַה־יִּהְיֶה רָעָה עַל־
ג הָאָרֶץ: אִם־יִמָּלְאוּ הֶעָבִים גֶּשֶׁם עַל־
הָאָרֶץ יָרִיקוּ וְאִם־יִפּוֹל עֵץ בַּדָּרוֹם וְאִם
בַּצָּפוֹן מְקוֹם שֶׁיִּפּוֹל הָעֵץ שָׁם יְהוּא:

be rewarded as the Sages proclaimed [*Shabbos* 119a]: עַשֵּׂר בִּשְׁבִיל שֶׁתִּתְעַשֵּׁר — 'give tithes so that you may become wealthy.' [Generally man is not permitted to 'test' God by trying to see if there will be a reward for performance of a commandment. The case of tithes and charity , however, are exempted from this prohibition as evidenced by the verse in *Malachi* 3:10 that urges people to test God by giving tithes *(Taanis 9a)*.]

Taalumos Chachmah refers this verse to one who reproves his neighbors in vain. It advises him not to become frustrated. After a period of time his exhortations *will* yield the desired results and enter the hearts of the sinners.

The words כִּי־בְרֹב הַיָּמִים תִּמְצָאֶנּוּ are homiletically interpreted to mean that in reward of charity, one will merit to *find* רֹב יָמִים, longevity *(Alshich).*

Rav Yosef Kara, however, explains the verse not figurateively, but as literal advice to a farmer: Sow your seeds *'upon the waters'* — i.e. at the edge of the water — i.e. in a moist area. Then, even if rain does not descend and crops fail, yours will thrive. *'For after many days',* i.e. at harvest time, *'you will find it'* i.e. you will reap abundantly (also *Midrash Lekach Tov).*

2. [The commentators explain this verse, also, as referring to charity, specifically its wider distribution.]

לְשִׁבְעָה וְגַם לִשְׁמוֹנָה — *To seven, or even to eight* i.e. abundantly, without pause *(Ralbag).*

Ibn Ezra comments that *'seven'* refers primarily to seven days of the week, and *'eight'* to the first day of next week. Thus, *eight* is a reference to constancy: after doing something for an entire week (seven days), begin the next week (the eighth day) by continuing it. Thus, the verse admonishes: Give charity constantly.

[For the similar phrase נְתַן חֵלֶק see 2:21. On the indefinite number 'seven' see *comm.* to 6:3.]

Dispense charity to whomever needs it and don't cry, 'Enough!' *(Rashi).*

Rav Yosef Kara explains that this verse refers to financial advice: Divide your money among many associates [i.e. 'do not put all your eggs in one basket'] because if one of your investments fails or is confiscated, then there will be others

so on until they brought me ashore.'

I asked him, 'My son, what good deeds do you possess [which caused your rescue from drowning]?'

'When I went aboard the ship', he answered, 'a poor man accosted me and cried, "Help me," and I gave him a loaf of bread. He then said to me, "As you have restored my life to me by your gift, so will your life be restored to you."'

Rabbi Akiva added: I applied to him the verse: 'Send your bread upon the waters' (Midrash).

seven, or even to eight, for you never know what
calamity will strike the land.
3 *If the clouds are filled they will pour down rain*
on the earth; if a tree falls down in the south or the
north, wherever the tree falls, there it remains. 4 *One*

with whom your money will be safe. [Note: *Rav Kara's* published commentary to Koheles ends with this verse.]

The *Midrash* comments: Devote one portion in seven [i.e. one day of the week: Sabbath] to God and rest thereon. *Devote the eighth,* homiletically refers to circumcision which is the eighth day *(Rashi).*

Avudraham quotes the *Midrash* that this verse alludes to *Succos,* a seven day festival followed by *Shmini Atzeres,* the eighth festival day. This may be why Koheles is read on Succos.

כִּי לֹא תֵדַע — *For you never know what calamity* [lit. *'evil'*] *will strike the land.* If you are thrust into poverty and require the assistance of others, you will be saved by virtue of your former charitable acts *(Rashi).*

Rav Chiyyah said to his wife: When a poor man comes be quick to offer him bread, so that others may be quick to offer it to your children ... because poverty is a 'wheel' that revolves in the world [coming to all people or their descendants.] ... and he who is merciful to others, mercy will be shown to him by Heaven, while he who is not merciful to others, mercy is not shown to him by Heaven *(Shabbos* 151b).[1]

3. אִם־יִמָּלְאוּ הֶעָבִים — *If the clouds are filled.* A lesson is to be learned: Clouds filled with rain-water do not keep it to themselves, but they beneficently pour it upon the earth. In turn, the earth receives moisture which by the natural cycle, returns to the clouds [cf. 1:7]. Similarly a man who is blessed by God and 'filled' with wealth is bidden not to hoard his wealth for himself, but to 'pour forth' his wealth as charity to those less fortunate. If the wheel turns and he finds himself in need, he will be sustained by others *(Metzudas David).*

Rashi comments: If clouds send rain to earth, one can be sure that the results will be seen in vegetation and crops. So, too, if a wise, righteous man lives in a city, his presence will be felt in improved moral and intellectual life.

[The word יָרִיקוּ, *pour down,* is related to the word וַהֲרִיקוֹתִי in *Malachi* 3:10: וַהֲרִיקֹתִי לָכֶם בְּרָכָה עַד בְּלִי דָי, *'And I will pour down for you a blessing until it is immeasurable'.*]

And conversely:
וְאִם־יִפּוֹל . . . שָׁם יְהוּא — *If a tree falls down . . . there it remains.* i.e. if a tree is uprooted by a southerly or northerly gale *(Ralbag).*

Once a tree does not bear fruit no

1. I quote from Rav S.R. Hirsch on the topic of *Tzedakah:*
A poor man comes to you, and in him God sent you His creature that you shall clothe and feed, look after and care for, and that it shall bring you greater blessings than you give. But when pity, or rather the voice of duty, opens your hand to give or to lend, do not let the cold,

פרק יא ד שֹׁמֵר רוּחַ לֹא יִזְרָע וְרֹאֶה בֶעָבִים לֹא
ד־ו ה יִקְצוֹר: כַּאֲשֶׁר אֵינְךָ יוֹדֵעַ מַה־דֶּרֶךְ הָרוּחַ
כַּעֲצָמִים בְּבֶטֶן הַמְּלֵאָה כָּכָה לֹא תֵדַע
אֶת־מַעֲשֵׂה הָאֱלֹהִים אֲשֶׁר יַעֲשֶׂה אֶת־
ו הַכֹּל: בַּבֹּקֶר זְרַע אֶת־זַרְעֶךָ וְלָעֶרֶב אַל־

one tends it. Wherever it lies, it will remain indefinitely. So, man who does not dispense charity and righteousness will find himself in need with no one to help him: There he will lie *(Metzudas David).*

Sforno interprets *'rain'* as the subject of *'fall'*. The clouds give rain . . . wherever the tree is, there the rain falls.

The *Talmud* explains the phrase שָׁם יְהוּא 'there shall its *fruits* be!' [The teachings of the wise are preserved in the place where they lived] *(Avodah Zarah* 31a); *Torah Temimah* explains that this is inferred from the fact that the plural יְהוּא, 'there *they* shall be' rather than the singular יִהְיֶה is used. Also, the verse implies the 'fruits of a scholar, his children, will tend to be of equal stature and greatness to their father.'

4. [One must perform the tasks required of him and have faith that God will bless his works.]

שֹׁמֵר רוּחַ לֹא יִזְרָע — *One who watches the wind will never sow.* i.e. one who forever waits for ideal conditions will never get his work done *(Ibn Latif).* Similarly in matters of dispensing charity one should not be over-suspicious and over-prudent; he should follow his inclination and dispense it as it is required *(Nachal Eshkol).*

Alshich explains the phrase as referring to the performance of *mitzvos* (with which one 'plants' in this world): Someone may say, 'I cannot perform good deeds until רוּחִי, *'my spirit, induces me'* — such a person will never 'plant.'

וְרֹאֶה בֶעָבִים לֹא יִקְצוֹר — *And one who keeps his eyes on* [lit. *'sees'*] *the clouds will never* [lit. 'not'] *reap.* One who dreads that rain will fall and therefore does not harvest — will never be able to harvest because of constant fear *(Rashi).*

5. כַּאֲשֶׁר אֵינְךָ יוֹדֵעַ — *Just as you do not know* . . . Following the theme of the previous verse, man is cautioned against 'watching the wind and the clouds,' for man cannot fathom God's intricate ways any more than man can know the sex or distinguishing characteristics of an embryo in its mother's womb *(Metzudas David; Rashi).*

בְּבֶטֶן הַמְּלֵאָה — *In a pregnant* [lit. *'full'*] *stomach* [interpreting הַמְּלֵאָה as an adjective modifying stomach], or: 'The stomach of the pregnant

unreasonable voice that you believe is clever calculation close it once more in the act of charity, while you ponder whether you will ever get back your loan, or reflect whether the gift will make you poorer. Is what you hold then really yours? Has not God a right to your all? And when He makes demand on you for His creature, will you close your hand ... from dispensing that which is His? ...

The law says that tzedakah is a high duty, and the repudiation of this duty can bring heavy consequences, even death. Nobody becomes poor through tzedakah, and God has proclaimed

who watches the wind will never sow, and one who keeps his eyes on the clouds will never reap. 5 *Just as you do not know the way of the wind, nor the nature of the embryo in a pregnant stomach, so can you never know the work of God who makes everything.* 6 *In the morning sow your seed and in the evening do*

woman' [הַמְּלֵאָה, 'the full one,' being a noun referring to the woman] *(Ibn Ezra).*

אֶת־מַעֲשֵׂה הָאֱלֹהִים — *The work of God.* Similarly, God's decrees concerning wealth and poverty are sealed to man. Therefore, one must never recoil from charity out of fear that he will lose his estate and become poor; nor refrain from Torah study out of fear that he will neglect his business and grow poor; nor rationalize that he should not marry because he will then have to support children *(Rashi).*

[Rather תָּמִים תִּהְיֶה עִם ה' אֱלֹהֶיךָ, *'Be whole-hearted with* HASHEM *your God' (Deut.* 18:13), upon which *Rashi* comments: 'Walk with Him in whole-heartedness and depend on Him and don't probe into the future. Whatever befalls you accept whole-heartedly . . .']

6. בַּבֹּקֶר זְרַע אֶת־זַרְעֶךָ — *In the morning sow your seed.* The words בַּבֹּקֶר, *in the morning,* and לָעֶרֶב, *in the evening,* imply 'always' *(Ibn Ezra)* — i.e. plant without regard to climatic conditions *(Metzudas David).*

In the *Midrash,* Rabbi Eliezer interprets the verse in the literal sense: If you have sown in the early season, sow also in the late season, because you do not know which will succeed for you: the early or the late sowing.

[The other Sages explain the verse metaphorically: *'morning',* i.e. 'the morning of life', youth; *'evening',* i.e. old age:]

Rabbi Yehoshua said: If you are married in your youth and your wife died, marry again in your old age. If you had children in your youth [i.e. *'planting seed'* is metaphorically understood as procreation] have them also in your old age — 'for you cannot know which will succeed': which set of children will be better, or whether both are equally good (also *Yevamos* 62b).

Rabbi Akivah said: If a man studied Torah in his youth, he should also study it in his old age [because we cannot know which knowledge will endure, whether that of the youth or the old age *(Midrash)*]; if he had disciples in his youth, he should also have disciples in his old age *(Yev.* 62b*).*

The *Midrash* goes on to relate that Rabbi Akivah had 24,000 disciples all of whom died a violent death during his lifetime between

that 'Never will tzedakah become the cause of any grave suffering of misfortune.' To him who has compassion for the poor, Hashem will also show compassion — as you wish God to hear your prayers, so shall you listen to the prayers of the poor. Give, and neither to your children nor to your grandchildren, nor even to your remote descendants will help be refused when they are in need; for riches and poverty come round in their circle, and there is never an entire succession of generations that entirely escapes poverty. It is your finest deed ... (Horeb).

פרק יא
ז־ט

תַּנַּח יָדֶךָ כִּי אֵינְךָ יוֹדֵעַ אֵי זֶה יִכְשַׁר הֲזֶה
ז אוֹ־זֶה וְאִם־שְׁנֵיהֶם כְּאֶחָד טוֹבִים: וּמָתוֹק
הָאוֹר וְטוֹב לַעֵינַיִם לִרְאוֹת אֶת־הַשָּׁמֶשׁ:
ח כִּי אִם־שָׁנִים הַרְבֵּה יִחְיֶה הָאָדָם בְּכֻלָּם
יִשְׂמָח וְיִזְכֹּר אֶת־יְמֵי הַחֹשֶׁךְ כִּי־הַרְבֵּה
ט יִהְיוּ כָּל־שֶׁבָּא הָבֶל: שְׂמַח בָּחוּר

Passover and Shavuos [the semi-mourning of the *Sefirah* period commemorates their death.] It was the students whom he acquired later in life who succeeded him and disseminated Torah throughout the land.

Others translate the verse as allegorically referring to charity: In the *'morning'* while you are affluent, utilize your wealth and dispense charity; and in the *'evening'* —if you fall into difficult straits — *'do not be idle'* [lit. *'do not withhold your hand'*] from dispensing whatever you can. You can never be certain which act is more pleasing to God: the abundant generosity of your affluence, or the meager amount you give in your own time of need; or if it is the combination of both that sustains you *(Derech Chaim).*

Rabbi Yehoshua used to say: If you have given a coin to a poor man in the morning and another poor man comes to you in the evening, give him, too. Do not tell him, 'I already gave in the morning' for you do not know which of the acts is better: the morning or the evening one; or whether it is the combination of both that will stand you in good stead *(Avos deRabbi Nosson).*

כִּי אֵינְךָ יוֹדֵעַ . . . הֲזֶה אוֹ־זֶה — *For you cannot know which will succeed: this or that.* [In the plain sense of the verse, referring to agriculture], one can never be certain which endeavor — the sowing in the morning or the evening; or perhaps the combination of both of them — was the one that yielded results *(Metzudas David).*

[Man should thus not delve into the unknown. He should not postpone his labor waiting for especially favorable weather conditions. He should simply work diligently and confidently and seek God's blessing.]

7. וּמָתוֹק הָאוֹר — *Sweet is the light.*

Metzudas David explains that 'light' refers metaphorically to life: Sweet is the life of man while he is still permitted to enjoy the light of day! In the second part of the verse, the thought is rephrased forming an effective parallel.

Ibn Ezra notes that light is not edible and cannot be 'sweet' in the true sense of the word; nevertheless, it is common to use a word that is relevant to one sense when referring to another sense. [i.e. 'sweet' in this context must be allegorical because literal sweetness cannot refer to light.] Compare for example רְאֵה רֵיחַ בְּנִי —*'See* the odor of my son' (*Gen.* 27:27); רֹאִים אֶת־הַקּוֹלֹת *'Saw* the thunderings' (*Ex.* 20:15)... *Ibn Ezra* therefore concludes that verse 6 urged constant preoccupation with good deeds. The result,

not be idle, for you cannot know which will succeed: this or that; or whether both are equally good.

7 Sweet is the light, and it is good for the eyes to behold the sun! 8 Even if a man lives many years, let him rejoice in all of them, but let him remember that the days of darkness will be many. All that comes is futility. 9 Rejoice young man, in your childhood let

this verse says, will be the satisfaction of *'sweet is the light.'*

וְטוֹב לַעֵינַיִם לִרְאוֹת אֶת־הַשָּׁמֶשׁ — *And it is good for the eyes to behold the sun.* [As explained above, this refers to the love of life. On the subject of farming, in the previous verses, it is perhaps possible to translate the verse as refering to the need for diligence in working as long as the sun shines. Obviously the verse cannot be taken literally: looking directly into the sun is certainly *not* 'good for the eyes'!]

The *Midrash* explains 'light' as Torah: 'Sweet is the light of Torah . . . and happy is he whose study enlightens him like the sun [leaving him free of doubts and perplexities.] . . . Rav Acha said: Sweet is the light of the World to Come, happy is he who is worthy to behold that light!'

8. בְּכֻלָּם יִשְׂמָח — *Let him rejoice in all of them.* i.e. let him be satisfied with what God has granted him *(Rashi).*

וְיִזְכֹּר אֶת־יְמֵי הַחֹשֶׁךְ — *But let him remember the days of darkness.* But at the same time it is imperative that he keep in mind the transitory nature of this world and strive to improve his ways, for *the days of darkness* — an allusion to death and the judgment of the wicked — *'will be many.'* Those days are more eternal than the short duration of life on this world *(Rashi).*[1]

[*'Remember'* in this case does not mean 'recall' but 'ponder'.]

כָּל־שֶׁבָּא הָבֶל — *All that comes is futility* [This translation follows most commentators.] *Rashi,* however, comments that הֶבֶל in this verse does not mean *futility* as it does throughout Koheles, but *punishment, trouble.*

According to *Ibn Ezra,* the verse is to be rendered as follows: Even if man were to know that he will live many years and rejoice in them all, once he recalls how eternal will be the days in the grave the 'light' referred to previously will become bitter. Man must also perceive that *all that comes into this world* — in the sense of *'a generation goes and a generation comes'* [1:4] — is futile.

Metzudas David explains the last phrase as referring to punishment in the Hereafter: *All that will come,* i.e. all punishment that man will receive in the Hereafter, *is futile* [see

1. *If a man would consider that after all his greatness he will return to dust and be food for worms, surely, then, his pride would be humbled and his arrogance forgotten. Of what good is his pride or his greatness, since he is bound to end in shame and derision?*

Again, let man picture himself being summoned before the Great Tribunal of the heavenly host and standing in the presence of the King of Kings, the Holy One, blessed be He, who is

פרק יא

בְּיַלְדוּתֶיךָ וִיטִיבְךָ לִבְּךָ בִּימֵי בְחוּרוֹתֶיךָ
י וְהַלֵּךְ בְּדַרְכֵי לִבְּךָ וּבְמַרְאֵי* עֵינֶיךָ וְדָע כִּי
עַל־כָּל־אֵלֶּה יְבִיאֲךָ הָאֱלֹהִים בַּמִּשְׁפָּט:
י וְהָסֵר כַּעַס מִלִּבֶּךָ וְהַעֲבֵר רָעָה מִבְּשָׂרֶךָ

*וּבְמַרְאֵה קרי

Rashi above.] In this world, suffering deters sin and causes one to search his ways and repent. But in the grave it is too late to examine one's ways and repent. Therefore, let man consider this and correct his conduct on this world while he is still alive.

This verse is reminiscent of an incident recorded in the *Talmud:*

Rav Chisda's daughter asked him if he wished to take a nap. He answered: The time will come when there will be long days in the grave where Torah study and observance will be impossible. We will sleep much there. Meanwhile, we must exert ourselves and be involved with Torah and the commandments *(Eruvin* 65a).

9. שְׂמַח בָּחוּר בְּיַלְדוּתֶךָ — *Rejoice, young man, in your childhood.* [As evidenced by the end of the verse this is in no way to be interpreted as a hedonistic *carte-blanche* to run amok with one's passion.] It is clearly to be understood as words of warning to those rebellious youths who wallow in sin [and who would not accept his words if they were said in such negative terms as: 'Do not rejoice ... do not follow your heart.'] Rather Solomon said: I know full well that fools tend to sin in their youth, but beware! Judgment is forthcoming *(Midrash Lekach Tov).*

Rashi comments that this is similar to a man telling his servant and child: Go on, persist in your iniquities. But realize that you will be punished in one blow for all your sins!

Ibn Ezra puts the phrase into a perspective which we can comprehend when he compares it to *Psalms* 60:10: עָלַי פְּלֶשֶׁת הִתְרוֹעָעִי [lit. 'over me, Philistia, conquer!'] which is obviously not meant to be a wish, but a threat: 'Go, ahead! *Now let Philistia dare triumph over me* — and let them see what I will do in return!; also a similar instance is found in *Lamentations* 4:21 *'Rejoice and exult O daughter of Edom . . .'* [which of course is not to be construed as a blessing but as a sarcastic remark as if to say: 'Rejoice while you can, because you will not escape punishment for your sins.']

The *Talmud* explains the first half of the verse [until וְדָע, *'but be aware'*] as being the words of the יֵצֶר הָרַע, man's Evil Inclination [urging him to sin]; the second half as being the words of the יֵצֶר הַטּוֹב man's Good Inclination [man's better nature]. According to Resh Lakish, the former refers to Torah study, the latter to good deeds [i.e. rejoice in your youth when you can

Infinite in holiness and purity . . . let him picture himself standing before Him as a mere insignificant being, worthless and despicable, and in actions unclean and repellent. Will he dare lift up his head? Will his mouth find words? When he will be asked: 'Where is your mouth now? Where is all the pride and glory you displayed in your world?' What will he answer, and how will he reply to such reproof?

your heart cheer you in the days of your youth; follow the path of your heart and the sight of your eyes — but be aware that for all these things God will call you to account. 10 *Rather, banish anger from your heart and remove evil from your flesh — for*

study, and apply your heart and eyes, i.e. your full understanding. But be aware that you will be judged for non-fulfillment of the commandments studied by you.] *(Shab. 63b).*

וִיטִיבְךָ לִבְּךָ ... בְּדַרְכֵי לִבְּךָ וּבְמַרְאֵה עֵינֶיךָ,—*Let your heart cheer you . . . your heart and the sight of your eyes* — [Reminiscent of the injunction (*Numbers* 15:39) וְלֹא תָתוּרוּ אַחֲרֵי לְבַבְכֶם וְאַחֲרֵי עֵינֵיכֶם *'and seek not after your own heart and your own eyes* — the *'eyes'* and *'heart'* used in this context being understood as the organs of desire.]

The similar phrase מַרְאֵה עֵינַיִם, *'what the eyes see'* denoting according to some: *'lustful gaze'* appears in 6:9. See *comm.* there.]

וִיטִיבְךָ לִבְּךָ — *Let your heart cheer you,* i.e. do whatever your heart desires *(Metzudas David).*

וְדָע — *But be aware* [lit. *'and know'*]

[The prefix ו, is to be understood here not as the conjunction *'and'* but as the preposition *'but'* which introduces the consequences which will follow such sinful behavior.]

כִּי עַל־כָּל־אֵלֶּה — *For all these things* — i.e. for rejoicing, following the heart and the sight of your eyes *(Ibn Ezra),* 'For there is no forgetfulness before His Throne of Glory' *(Sh'nos Chaim).*

The *Midrash* stresses כָּל, *'all':*

It may be likened to a man who used to steal. They arrested him and said to him, 'Give up what is in your possession.' He answered, 'Take whatever I have with me.' They retorted, 'Do you think that we will only extract what is with you at the present time? We demand from you all that is with you and all that you stole during the years you were a thief!'

Similarly, it is stated, 'But be aware that for *all* these things God will bring you into judgment.'

10. וְהָסֵר כַּעַס מִלִּבֶּךָ — *Rather banish anger from your heart* — i.e. banish anything that causes anger to God *(Rashi).*

Most commentators however, view this moralistically: man should avoid anger, because 'anger betrays the fool' *(Midrash).*

[Compare 7:9: *'Do not be hastily upset, for anger lingers in the bosom of fools.'*]

In the words of the *Talmud*: If a young scholar becomes enraged it is because the Torah [i.e. the tension of strenuous study] enflames him . . . Despite this, a man should train himself to be gentle, for it is said: *'Rather banish anger from your heart' (Taanis* 4a*).*

וְהַעֲבֵר רָעָה מִבְּשָׂרֶךָ — *And remove evil from your flesh* — i.e. do not pamper your flesh's evil desires *(Metzudas David).*

Let a man just for a moment envision this scene as it will, indeed, be enacted, and all pride will leave him forever (Mesillas Yesharim).

פרק יא כִּֽי־הַיַּלְד֥וּת וְהַשַּׁחֲר֖וּת הָֽבֶל׃

פרק יב
א־ב
א וּזְכֹר֙ אֶת־בּ֣וֹרְאֶ֔יךָ בִּימֵ֖י בְּחוּרֹתֶ֑יךָ עַ֣ד
אֲשֶׁ֤ר לֹא־יָבֹ֙אוּ֙ יְמֵ֣י הָֽרָעָ֔ה וְהִגִּ֣יעוּ שָׁנִ֔ים
ב אֲשֶׁ֣ר תֹּאמַ֔ר אֵֽין־לִ֥י בָהֶ֖ם חֵֽפֶץ׃ עַ֠ד אֲשֶׁ֨ר

כִּי־הַיַּלְדוּת וְהַשַּׁחֲרוּת הָבֶל — *For childhood and youth are futile* — the desires of man's youth are valueless. Therefore one must exercise great caution [and avoid these pitfalls] *(Metzudas David).*

[The word שַׁחֲרוּת is variously explained by the commentators as related either to שַׁחַר, 'dawn' — i.e. youth, the dawn of life *(Rashi; Metzudas David)*; or to שָׁחוֹר,'black' — i.e. the period of adolescence when one's hair is still dark *(Targum; Rashi).* In either case, the implied meaning is the same.]

The *Talmud* explains the word as 'black' and homiletically comments: 'The things a man does in his youth *blacken him* [i.e. with shame] in his old age' (*Shabbos* 152a).

Taalumos Chachmah explains this last clause as being the response to recalcitrant youths who query: 'Why should I forego the pleasures of my youth?' The answer is: *'Childhood and youth are futile'* [they are fleeting and pass away like a breath. see *comm.* to 1:2 s.v. הֲבֵל הֲבָלִים.]

XII

1. [This verse is closely related to the preceding one as indicated by its opening conjunction *'and'*. Having warned recalcitrant youth to *'be aware that for all these things God will call you to account'* (11:9) and that *'childhood and youth are futile,'* (11:10), Solomon continues that man should spend his vigorous youth in the service of his Creator.]

וּזְכֹר אֶת־בּוֹרְאֶיךָ — *So* [lit. *'and'*] *remember your Creator, and try* — in spirit and deed — to honor Him *(Sforno).*

[בּוֹרְאֶיךָ is spelled מָלֵא, full — with a י, *yud,* because the Deity is referred to in the plural as a sign of respect similar to להבדיל the royal 'we.' Compare, e.g., the spelling of אֱלֹהֶיךָ, *your God.*]

The *Jerusalem Talmud* quotes the dictum of Akaviah ben Mehalalel [in *Avos* 3:1]: 'Ponder well three things and you will not come into the clutches of sin: know from what you come — from a putrid drop; where you are going — to a place of dust, worm, and maggot; and before Whom you are destined to give an account and reckoning — before the Supreme King of Kings — the Holy One, blessed be He.' Rabbi Akivah expounded homiletically upon combinations of letters from the word בּוֹרְאֶיךָ in our verse

childhood and youth are futile.

XII
1 **S***o remember your Creator in the days of your youth, before the evil days come, and those years arrive of which you will say, 'I have no pleasure in*

to derive from it Akaviah's entire dictum: know: בְּאֵרְךָ, "your source", [from where you came] בּוֹרְךָ, "your grave" [where you are going]; and בּוֹרְאֶךָ, "your Creator" [before Whom you are destined to give an account and reckoning.] *(Yerushalmi Sotah 2:2).*

בִּימֵי בְּחוּרֹתֶיךָ — *In the days of your youth.* While in the possession of your strength *(Midrash).*[1]

Man should take advantage of vigorous youth to serve God, before old age sets in and service becomes more difficult *(Metzudas David).*

יְמֵי הָרָעָה — *The evil days* — The infirmities of old age *(Rashi).*

וְהִגִּיעוּ שָׁנִים — *And those years arrive,* the time of suffering.

אֵין־לִי בָהֶם חֵפֶץ — *I have no pleasure in them.* i.e. my desires no longer manifest themselves in them; I prefer death *(Metzudas David).*

Taalumos Chachmah explains the verse as follows: If you have sinned in your youth, remember your Creator while you are still a youth *before the evil days come* — i.e. before the days of punishment and retribution . . . But if one did not repent in youth, he should not fail to repent even when the days come when he will say, *'I have no pleasure'* — i.e. old age when you will rationalize and say: 'Of what avail is my repentance now that my desires are gone!' — No, do what is required of you even then, and repent.

M'lo haOmer perceives in this verse a reference to the verse [*Lev.* 19:32]: מִפְּנֵי שֵׂיבָה תָּקוּם [lit. *'before a man grey with age rise up'*] which the *Zohar* translates: *'before'* you reach *'old age, rise up'* and conquer your Evil Inclination and repent. Here, too, Solomon, exhorts man to conquer his passions *before* the feebleness of old age sets in.

2. [The following verses, as explained by the commentators, poetically conjure up an image of the fading of life as old age approaches. The allegory refers to the waning powers of the organs of the body, as will be explained.

The *Talmud* relates an incident in which an old man described his old age as follows: 'The mountain is snowy, it is surrounded by ice, the dog does not bark, and the grinders do not grind' [i.e. my head is snowy white, my beard likewise; my voice is feeble and my teeth do not function;] *(Shabbos* 152a).

1. [Obviously the verse is not to be construed to mean that man should 'remember God *only* in his youth. Surely man must serve his Creator throughout every period of his life. The inference, however, is that man should concentrate on God and repent from his evil ways es-

לֹא־תֶחְשַׁךְ הַשֶּׁמֶשׁ וְהָאוֹר וְהַיָּרֵחַ
וְהַכּוֹכָבִים וְשָׁבוּ הֶעָבִים אַחַר הַגָּשֶׁם:
ג בַּיּוֹם שֶׁיָּזֻעוּ שֹׁמְרֵי הַבַּיִת וְהִתְעַוְּתוּ אַנְשֵׁי
הֶחָיִל וּבָטְלוּ הַטֹּחֲנוֹת כִּי מִעֵטוּ וְחָשְׁכוּ
ד הָרֹאוֹת בָּאֲרֻבּוֹת: וְסֻגְּרוּ דְלָתַיִם בַּשּׁוּק
בִּשְׁפַל קוֹל הַטַּחֲנָה וְיָקוּם לְקוֹל הַצִּפּוֹר
ה וְיִשַּׁחוּ כָּל־בְּנוֹת הַשִּׁיר: גַּם מִגָּבֹהַּ יִירָאוּ

הַשֶּׁמֶשׁ וְהָאוֹר וְהַיָּרֵחַ וְהַכּוֹכָבִים — *The sun and the light, and the moon and the stars.* — The forehead, the nose, the soul, and the cheeks *(Midrash).*

According to *Targum:* The light of the face, the sparkle of the eyes, the cheeks, the eyeballs.

וְשָׁבוּ הֶעָבִים אַחַר הַגָּשֶׁם — *And the clouds return after the rain* — The eyesight which is weakened by weeping — [The weeping of old age, caused by trouble and sickness, destroys the eyesight; crying, puffy eyes, being compared to clouds *(Torah Temimah)*] *(Shabbos* 151b).

Ibn Ezra comments that the reference is to the world which is darkened for a sick, dying man, as though beclouded. For after a rain it appears to him that not sun, but clouds, appear.

3. שֹׁמְרֵי הַבַּיִת — *The guards of the house.* [Koheles compares the aged human body to a house in ruins]: The 'guards of the house' are the hands and arms which protect the body from threat and injury *(Ibn Ezra)* [but now are enfeebled.]

According to the *Talmud,* they are the sides and the ribs *(Shabbos* 152a) which protect the hollows [i.e. the internal organs] of the body *(Rashi).*

אַנְשֵׁי הֶחָיִל — *The powerful men* i.e. the legs which uphold the bodily structure *(Rashi)* [and which grow weak in old age.]

הַטֹּחֲנוֹת — *The grinders.* i.e. the teeth, which in old age have fallen out *(Rashi).*

[The Hebrew is in the feminine gender. A literal translation might be *'the maidens that grind'*].

הָרֹאוֹת בָּאֲרֻבּוֹת — *The gazers through the windows are dimmed.* i.e. the eyes *(Talmud,* ibid.*).*

[Here, too, the Hebrew is in the feminine gender and a more literal rendering would be: *'those ladies that peer through the windows.'*]

[Scripture often depicts women as modestly peering through windows). Comp. *Judges* 5:28; *II Sam.* 6:16; *II Kings* 9:30. In Jewish tradition modesty is a treasured, respected virtue in woman. It is considered to be a regal characteristic as in the verse כָּל־כְּבוּדָּה

pecially during the vigor of his youth when the allures of life are most tempting. Certainly, repentance of one's sins during youth — while man still has the capacity to sin — is more virtuous than repentance in old age when, as *Rambam* points out in *Hilchos Teshuvah* 2:1, he is no longer capable of doing what he had done, and when his desires have abated and the allures of sin no longer tempt him.]

them;'
2 *before the sun, the light, the moon and the stars grow dark, and the clouds return after the rain;*
3 *in the day when the guards of the house will tremble, and the powerful men will stoop, and the grinders are idle because they are few, and the gazers through windows are dimmed;*
4 *when the doors in the street are shut; when the sound of the grinding is low; when one rises up at the voice of the bird, and all the daughters of song grow dim;*
5 *when they*

בַּת־מֶלֶךְ פְּנִימָה, *'The king's daughter is all glorious within' (Psalms 45:14).*]

4. וְסֻגְּרוּ דְלָתַיִם בַּשּׁוּק — *When the doors in the street are shut.* This refers to the apertures of man which close *'when the sound of the grinding is low,'* i.e. on account of the stomach's failing to digest ['grind'.] *(Talmud* ibid; *Rashi).*

According to *Ibn Ezra,* 'doors' refers to the lips (as in *Job* 41:6: דַּלְתֵי פָנָיו מִי פִתֵּחַ *'who can open the doors of his face,* i.e. his lips;) because the teeth which give them needed support are lacking *(Metzudas David).*

Ibn Ezra continues to explain that in a metaphoric sense, the verse depicts a situation where the milling stops and there is no flour; the bakeries in the market-place then close their doors.

וְיָקוּם לְקוֹל הַצִּפּוֹר — *When one rises up at the sound of a bird* — even the chirping of a bird will wake the aged from sleep *(Talmud* ibid. ; *Rashi, et al).*

וְיִשַּׁחוּ כָּל־בְּנוֹת הַשִּׁיר — *And the daughters of song grow dim* — i.e. even the voices of singers sound to him like whispers [because of deafness] as Barzilai said to David: [*II Sam.* 19:36]: *'I am today eighty years old . . . can I hear any more the voice of singers?'*

Rashbam explains that *'the daughters of song'* refers to those who indulge in music and are fond of singing. But their art repels the aged who are frustrated by their deafness.

According to *Ibn Ezra* it refers to the throat which once produced beautiful song but which becomes *'stooped'* in old age and is incapable of singing.

[The condition of the aged is paradoxical: During the day the voice of singers sound low to him while at night he is awakened by the chirping of a bird!]

The *Talmud* (ibid.) continues: 'Regarding scholars, the older they grow the more wisdom they acquire;. . . but as for the ignorant, as they wax older they become more foolish.'

5. גַּם מִגָּבֹהַּ יִירָאוּ — *[When] they even fear a height* — even a small knoll looks to him like the highest of mountains *(Talmud* ibid.*);* and he is apprehensive that he is liable to stumble *(Rashi);* and he conjures

וְחַתְחַתִּים בַּדֶּרֶךְ וְיָנֵאץ הַשָּׁקֵד וְיִסְתַּבֵּל
הֶחָגָב וְתָפֵר הָאֲבִיּוֹנָה כִּי־הֹלֵךְ הָאָדָם
אֶל־בֵּית עוֹלָמוֹ וְסָבְבוּ בַשּׁוּק הַסּוֹפְדִים:
ו עַד אֲשֶׁר לֹא־יֵרָחֵק* חֶבֶל הַכֶּסֶף וְתָרֻץ
גֻּלַּת הַזָּהָב וְתִשָּׁבֶר כַּד עַל־הַמַּבּוּעַ וְנָרֹץ
ז הַגַּלְגַּל אֶל־הַבּוֹר: וְיָשֹׁב הֶעָפָר עַל־

* יֵרָתֵק ק׳

up exaggerated obstacles *(Rashbam).*

Ibn Ezra renders: 'For the aged no longer have the strength to climb heights.' When a man is invited someplace, he asks: 'Are there ups and downs on the way to it?' [He is always apprehensive of dangers — imagined or real.]

וְחַתְחַתִּים בַּדֶּרֶךְ — *And terror in the road.* When he walks on a road his heart is filled with fears *(Talmud).*

Fears of the journey fall upon him and he asks: 'Shall I go or not?' and decides not to go. Or he says: 'As far as such and such a place I am strong enough to go, but not as far as the place to which I was invited' [and he does not go] *(Midrash).*

The word וְחַתְחַתִּים is a form of חַתַת, 'fear' *(Ibn Ezra)* the plural form denotes 'excessive fear' *(Metzudas David).*

וְיָנֵאץ הַשָּׁקֵד — *And the almond tree blossoms.* This alludes to the whiteness of the hair in old age *(Ibn Ezra)* and since the fruit of the almond tree sprouts before any other tree it symbolizes old age which will quickly overtake him *(Rashi).*

According to the *Talmud* this refers to the coccyx [the lowest end of the vertebrae; the 'nut' of the spine *(Midrash):* The extreme weakness of old age causes it to 'blossom', i.e. protrude and move from its place, seriously impeding mobility.]

וְיִסְתַּבֵּל הֶחָגָב — *The grasshopper becomes a burden* [or: *'The grasshopper drags itself along'*.]

He will be so weak, that even if a grasshopper would alight upon him it would seem like a burden *(Metzudas David).* [Metaphorically depicting the frailties of old age.]

Rashi takes חָגָב as a form of עָגָב, *ardor,* and renders: 'even his ardor becomes burdensome to him.'

The *Midrash* translates: 'the ankles,' and following this, *Targum* renders: 'the ankles swell up' [and the old man thus drags himself along with difficulty] — an image of the awkward, bent-over way an old man walks *(Ibn Yachya).*

וְתָפֵר הָאֲבִיּוֹנָה — *And the desire fails* [This translation follows the *Talmud; Midrash; Rashi;* and *Metzudas David* who relate it to אבה, wish, and תַּאֲוָה, desire, which wanes in old age.]

[The word אֲבִיּוֹנָה is found in *Mishnah Maaseros* 4:6. It means literally *'caperberry'*, a fruit said to stimulate desire. In this context, then, this potent fruit is of no avail to the aged.]

Metzudas David offers an alternative rendering, relating it to בִּינָה, *wisdom.*

XII
6-7

even fear a height and terror in the road; and the almond tree blossoms and the grasshopper becomes a burden and the desire fails — so man goes to his eternal home, while the mourners go about the streets.

6 *Before the silver cord snaps, and the golden bowl is shattered, and the pitcher is broken at the fountain, and the wheel is smashed at the pit.* 7 *Thus the dust*

כִּי־הֹלֵךְ הָאָדָם אֶל־בֵּית עוֹלָמוֹ — *So man goes to his eternal home* i.e. the grave where he will dwell forever *(Ibn Ezra).*

The *Midrash* stresses the possessive *his* indicating that each man has his *own* eternal home: It may be likened to a king who entered a province accompanied by generals, commanders, and officers. Although they all entered through the same gate, each went and lodged in a place corresponding to his rank. Similarly, although all human beings experience death, each has a *'home'* for himself [according to his conduct in life.]

וְסָבְבוּ בַשּׁוּק הַסּוֹפְדִים — *While the mourners go about the streets* — often preparing their eulogies even before death has actually occurred *(Seder haYom).*

6. [The following verse also amplifies upon verse 1, exhorting man to repent before the oncoming of old age and offers another metaphor for the *final* dissolution of life.]

חֶבֶל הַכֶּסֶף — *The silver cord* — i.e. the spinal cord *(Rashi).*

וְתָרֻץ גֻּלַּת הַזָּהָב — *And the golden bowl is shattered* i.e. the skull *(Midrash);* the marrow *(Targum);* the *membrum virile (Rashi).*

Ibn Ezra interprets this as referring to the spinal column and the brain: when one is severed from the other, life ends.

וְתִשָּׁבֶר כַּד עַל־הַמַּבּוּעַ — *Or the pitcher is broken at the fountain.* This refers to the stomach *(Rashi; Midrash).*

הַגַּלְגַּל — *The wheel* — the eye *(Rashi)* the body *(Targum).*

[The metaphor, then, is as follows: The body — near death — is likened to the malfunctioning machinery of a well: cord, wheel and pitcher. The cord (spine) snaps; the skull shatters; the stomach breaks; and the body is smashed.]

7. וְיָשֹׁב הֶעָפָר — *Thus the dust returns* i.e. 'dust' refers to the body of man which was formed from dust [comp. *Gen.* 2:7 *'and God formed man from the dust of the earth'*] . . .

עַל־הָאָרֶץ כְּשֶׁהָיָה — *To the ground, as it was* [i.e. as it was at Creation]; it rejoins the earth from which it was formed *(Almosnino).*

As it is written [*Gen.* 3:19]: *'For you are dust and unto dust you shall return' (Midrash Lekach Tov).*

Only the bones remain — and even they eventually disintegrate *(Ibn Ezra).*

[The translation, *'to the ground'*

הָאָרֶץ כְּשֶׁהָיָה וְהָרוּחַ תָּשׁוּב אֶל־
ח הָאֱלֹהִים אֲשֶׁר נְתָנָהּ: הֲבֵל הֲבָלִים אָמַר
ט הַקּוֹהֶלֶת הַכֹּל הָבֶל: וְיֹתֵר שֶׁהָיָה קֹהֶלֶת
חָכָם עוֹד לִמַּד־דַּעַת אֶת־הָעָם וְאִזֵּן וְחִקֵּר
י תִּקֵּן מְשָׁלִים הַרְבֵּה: בִּקֵּשׁ קֹהֶלֶת לִמְצֹא

instead of lit. *'upon* the ground' follows *Metzudas Zion.*]

וְהָרוּחַ תָּשׁוּב אֶל־הָאֱלֹהִים... — *And the spirit returns to God Who gave it.* But the soul returns to its Source from which it was taken; unto God Who gave it at birth [as it is written (*Gen.* 2:7): *'And [God] breathed into his nostrils the breath of life'*]

The earthly portion returns to the earth; but the soul returns to God to give an account and reckoning [of its actions on this world] *(Sforno).*

This verse refutes those who claim that the soul came into existence coincidentally. An accident has no source to which to return *(Ibn Ezra).*

'רוּחַ' also signifies 'that which remains of man after his death and is not subject to destruction' *(Moreh Nevuchim).*

God says to man: 'I gave you a soul which is pure, return it to Me pure' *(Midrash).*

8. [Thus begins the epilogue of the Book.] Having discoursed on the life and trials of man, and described the vicissitudes which man experiences *'under the sun'* until death, Koheles reiterates the recurring refrain of his conclusions: 'All *is futile' (Rashbam; Kehillas Yaakov).*

הֲבֵל הֲבָלִים — *Futility of futilities!* 'Much futility do I observe in the world' said he in whom is assembled much wisdom; 'all that was created in the six days of Creation is futile' *(Rashi).*

Many commentators suggest that this verse is to be understood in the imperative: *'Abhor futilities!,* because everything is futile. [Comp. 1:2 where this opinion is quoted in the name of *Ramban* and *Metzudas David;* in our verse it is also concurred with by *Ibn Ezra* and *Taalumos Chachmah.*]

Having discussed death, I have verified all my conclusions just as I began my discourse: *'All is futile' (Akeidas Yitzchak).*

הַקּוֹהֶלֶת — *Koheles.* The Hebrew has the definite article ה, *'the* Koheles' because, as pointed out, Koheles is not a proper name but a title [see *comm.* to 1:1] *(Ibn Ezra).*

9. וְיֹתֵר שֶׁהָיָה קֹהֶלֶת חָכָם — *And besides being wise,* i.e. Solomon was even wiser than can be adduced from this Book *(Rashi);* and as the wisest of men his knowledge was not limited to what is recorded in this Book; he taught students from the great range of his wisdom and had a wide sphere of influence *(Rav Saadiah Gaon).*

עוֹד לִמַּד־דַּעַת אֶת־הָעָם — *He also imparted knowledge to the people.* i.e. he did not content himself with being wise — he actively imparted his wisdom to the public as well *(Metzudas David).*

... Unlike many geniuses who

returns to the ground as it was, and the spirit returns
to God Who gave it. 8 *Futility of futilities — said*
Koheles — All is futile!
9 *And besides being wise, Koheles also imparted*
knowledge to the people; he listened, and sought out;
and arranged many proverbs.

cannot distill their wisdom in a manner that the masses can comprehend, the verse stresses that Solomon, *'the wisest of all men'* [*I Kings* 5:11] was blessed with this ability, and he utilized it by publicly expounding his knowledge in popular form *(Rav Yaakov Chagiz).*

וְאִזֵּן — *He listened* [This translation of the word — which is un-duplicated in this form throughout Scripture — follows *Targum, Rashbam, Taalumos Chachmah:* i.e. He was attentive to the words of wise men who preceded him, sorting them out; giving his אֹזֶן, ear, and complete mind to this goal.]

Ibn Janach [also *Ibn Ezra*] relates it to מֹאזְנַיִם, scales, and translates: 'he weighed all matters and researched them.'

Ibn Ezra [as an alternative interpretation] and *Metzudas David* view it as a transitive verb: he caused [others] to listen, [i.e. he imparted instructions in a manner which the public found interesting.]

Metzudas Zion relates it to *Deut.* 32:1 הַאֲזִינוּ, *'incline your ear.* [which *S.R. Hirsch* a.l. explains that הַאֲזִין, *'to incline one's ear'* expresses a greater readiness to listen to what is being said that שְׁמַע, *'hear'.''*]

Rashi derives the word from 'handles,' אָזְנַיִם, as in the *Talmudic* comment [*Eruvin* 21b]: אָזְנַיִם לַתּוֹרָה 'handles to the Torah.' Handles make it easier to carry an object. Solomon instituted ordinances to help people avoid transgressions, thus making the Torah 'easier to carry.'

Harav David Feinstein explains Solomon's probable motivation for instituting ordinances:

Solomon transgressed two Biblical prohibitions: First, that a king not multiply wives that they may not turn his heart from the proper path; and second, that he not multiply horses that he not cause Israel to return to Egypt (in search of fine horses) [*Deut.* 17:16,17]. Solomon was convinced that his superior wisdom would prevent the threathened consequences from happening. He was wrong. Realizing from his errors that preventive ordinances cannot be taken lightly, he instituted preventive ordinances of his own, אָזְנַיִם לַתּוֹרָה, to keep others from sinning.

וְחִקֵּר — *And sought out.* Imparted to the public, methods of seeking wisdom *(Ibn Ezra).*

תִּקֵּן מְשָׁלִים הַרְבֵּה — [And] *he arranged many proverbs.* Following *Targum:* 'Inspired by a divine prophetic spirit, he composed books of wisdom and sensible proverbs.'

As it is written [*I Kings* 5:12]: *'And he spoke three thousand proverbs' (Ibn Ezra).*

The use of proverbs made his wisdom palatable and comprehensi-

דִּבְרֵי־חֵפֶץ וְכָתוּב יֹשֶׁר דִּבְרֵי אֱמֶת׃
יא דִּבְרֵי חֲכָמִים כַּדָּרְבֹנוֹת וּכְמַשְׂמְרוֹת
נְטוּעִים בַּעֲלֵי אֲסֻפּוֹת נִתְּנוּ מֵרֹעֶה אֶחָד׃
יב וְיֹתֵר מֵהֵמָּה בְּנִי הִזָּהֵר עֲשׂוֹת סְפָרִים

ble even to the most uneducated (*Torah Temimah*).

This implies that he composed *Proverbs* and *Song of Songs*, as well as *Koheles* (*Rav Saadiah Gaon*).

10. בִּקֵּשׁ קֹהֶלֶת לִמְצֹא דִּבְרֵי־חֵפֶץ — *Koheles sought to find 'words of delight'* i.e. Koheles sought in his quests to achieve supreme wisdom; he exerted himself to find Truth (*Ibn Ezra; Metzudas David*).

[The commentators explain that Solomon sought to comprehend God's government of the Universe.]

The *Talmud* elucidates: Koheles sought to be like Moses [and attain forty-nine gates of understanding] but a בַּת קוֹל, Heavenly Voice, said to him there are *'words of truth written properly'* [i.e. it is already recorded in the Torah (*Deut.* 34:10)]: *'There arose not a prophet again in Israel like Moses.'* The other said: Among the *prophets* there arose not, but among the *kings* there did arise (*Rosh Hashanah* 21b).

The *Midrash* comments that Solomon sought to discern the reward for the performance of the mitzvos and the study of Torah, and to fathom when the 'end' [i.e. the advent of Mashiach] would be. But God quoted from 'the Book of Truth' that these goals are beyond him.

וְכָתוּב יֹשֶׁר דִּבְרֵי אֱמֶת — *And words of truth recorded properly* — This refers to the Bible (*Rashi*).

Alshich renders: He sought to insure that people would find his proverbs to be a 'delight of God' and he later discovered that all his thoughts were already recorded in the Word of Truth [i.e. that his wisdom reflected the Truth of Torah.]

Some commentators translate the verse: *'Solomon sought to find felicitous language* — i.e. to put his words in beautiful, appealing form, *'and words of truth recorded properly,'* so that his written words should merit public acceptance for posterity (*Almosnino; Divrei Chefetz*).

11. דִּבְרֵי חֲכָמִים כַּדָּרְבֹנוֹת — *The words of the wise are like goads.* Used by shepherds to prod their animals (*Metzudas David*).

As *Rashi* explains: Just as the goad directs the heifer along its proper path, so do words of the wise lead men along the paths of life (*Chagigah* 3b).

The *Midrash* homiletically relates it to כַּדּוּר בָּנוֹת, a girl's ball. 'Just as a ball is thrown from hand to hand without falling, so Moses received the Torah at Sinai and delivered it to Joshua [intact], Joshua to the elders, the elders to the prophets, and the prophets delivered it to the men of the Great Synagogue' [*Avos* 1:1].

The *Midrash* adds: If a man makes a goad for his heifer, how much more should he make one for his Evil Inclination which seduces him from this world and the World to Come!

XII
10-12

[10] *Koheles sought to find words of delight, and*
words of truth recorded properly. [11] *The words of the*
wise are like goads, and like nails well driven are the
sayings of the masters of collections, coming from
one Shepherd.
[12] *Beyond these, my son, beware: the making of*

וּכְמַשְׂמְרוֹת נְטוּעִים — *And as nails well-driven* [lit. *'planted'*.] Just as a well-driven nail is permanent, so are the sayings of the 'masters of collections' *(Rashi; Metzudas David).*

— So are the words of Torah immutable and inviolate *(Alshich).*

בַּעֲלֵי אֲסֻפּוֹת — *Masters of collections* [or: *'assemblies'*] — These are the disciples of the wise who sit in manifold assemblies and occupy themselves with the Torah, some pronouncing 'clean,' some pronouncing 'unclean', some prohibiting and some permitting . . . should a man say: How, [in view of the contradictory opinions held by scholars] shall I learn Torah? — The verse therefore concludes: נִתְּנוּ מֵרֹעֶה אֶחָד, *coming from one Shepherd:* One God gave them [i.e. all the various opinions do not emanate from different 'Revelations,' but have their origin in the One Torah, given by the One God]; one leader [i.e. Moses; (as *Maharsha* explains that the term רֹעֶה, *Shepherd,* is used in the Bible to refer both to God — *Gen.* 48:15; *Psalms* 80:2 — and to Moses — *Isaiah* 63:11)] uttered them from the mouth of the Lord of all creation. Therefore make yourself like a hopper [which is funnel-shaped and more enters than issues from it; i.e. hear all commentaries and interpretations of the Torah; then discern the Truth] and develop a perceptive heart to understand the words of those who pronounce 'unclean,' and the words of those who pronounce 'clean,' the words of those who prohibit and the words of those who permit . . . *(Chagigah* 3b).

The word רֹעֶה, *shepherd, is used here in consonance with the metaphor of the shepherd's goad at the beginning of the verse (Ibn Ezra).*

The author of *Pele Yoetz* makes the following comment *apropos* to בַּעֲלֵי אֲסֻפּוֹת, masters of collections, homiletically referring to those who prepare anthologies:

How great a service was performed by the eminent Sages of every generation who prepared digests. Were it not for them, Torah would, God forbid, be forgotten. Especially during the most harried times when the average person hasn't the time to study many books — much less the means to acquire a sizable library — it is even more beneficial that they publish anthologized laws, *mussar* concepts and homiletics. There is no greater service than this for it benefits the very essence of the soul. Such works are obviously of the utmost importance — more than any others — and the authors, 'masters of collections' are to be commended.

12. וְיֹתֵר מֵהֵמָּה בְּנִי הִזָּהֵר — *Beyond these, my son, beware.* The verse is couched in a term of endearment [as

הַרְבֵּה אֵין קֵץ וְלַהַג הַרְבֵּה יְגִעַת בָּשָׂר׃
יג סוֹף דָּבָר הַכֹּל נִשְׁמָע אֶת־הָאֱלֹהִים יְרָא
יד וְאֶת־מִצְוֺתָיו שְׁמוֹר כִּי־זֶה כָּל־הָאָדָם׃ כִּי
אֶת־כָּל־מַעֲשֶׂה הָאֱלֹהִים יָבִא בְמִשְׁפָּט
עַל כָּל־נֶעְלָם אִם־טוֹב וְאִם־רָע׃

סוף דבר הכל נשמע את־האלהים ירא ואת
מצותיו שמור כי־זה כל האדם׃

if addressing a pupil] *(Metzudas David).*

Beyond the *'just words of Truth'* mentioned above, *'beware, my son'* to heed the words of the wise *(Rashi).*

In your deeds *'beyond these,'* i.e beyond what is required of you in published books *(Metzudas David).*

עֲשׂוֹת סְפָרִים הַרְבֵּה אֵין קֵץ — *The making of many books is without limit.* Let you say 'if it is necessary to obey wise men why are their words not published?' The answer is– *'the making of many books is without limit,'* committing everything to writing is impossible *(Rashi).*

Rav Yisroel Salanter, when discussing publishing books would homiletically cite this verse and say: King Solomon cautioned us that not everything that man thinks must he say; not everything he says must he write, but most important not everything that he has written must he publish.

Ibn Ezra relates עֲשׂוֹת to הִזָּהֵר and renders: *'Be careful about making many books without limit'* (as in *Exodus* 19:12: הִשָּׁמְרוּ לָכֶם עֲלוֹת בָּהָר, *'Take heed to yourselves that you do not go up to the mountain.' Ibn Ezra* also suggests that עֲשׂוֹת could also mean *'acquire'* [as in *Gen.* 12:5 הַנֶּפֶשׁ אֲשֶׁר עָשׂוּ בְחָרָן: and above 2:8: עָשִׂיתִי לִי שָׁרִים וְשָׁרוֹת] which is in the sense that the *Midrash* understands it. Thus: *'avoid acquiring books without limit.'*

The *Midrash* interprets this as an allusion against acquiring extra-canonical books: *'Beyond these'* [מֵהֵמָּה] — read מְהֻמָה 'confusion,' because whoever brings into his house more than the twenty-four Books of the Bible — and the *Talmud* and commentaries which explain Torah — introduces confusion into his house.

Interestingly, the *Targum* seems to interpret this verse in the positive sense: Be cautious to compose wise books without limit, to be engaged in the words of the Torah, and in the sayings of the wise.

וְלַהַג הַרְבֵּה יְגִעַת בָּשָׂר — *And much study is weariness of the flesh.* The total accumulation of Torah knowledge is more than man can absorb. If so, you may ask, 'Why indulge in so much wearying effort?' The answer is given in the following verse.

Since reading and memorizing many books is a hardship on most people, therefore, one should use his own common sense to avoid what should be avoided *(Metzudas David).*

many books is without limit, and much study is weariness of the flesh.

13 *The sum of the matter, when all has been considered: Fear God and keep His commandments, for that is man's whole duty.* 14 *For God will judge every deed — even everything hidden — whether good or evil.*

The sum of the matter, when all is considered: fear God and keep His commandments, for that is man's whole duty.

Similarly, one should always learn in the most concise manner *(Alshich).*

Man is enjoined in this verse against wasting his time in laboring over any books beside those of the Torah, because they cause unfulfilled weariness and waste man's precious time *(Rav Saadiah Gaon).*

Time should not be devoted to literature outside of Torah because man exhausts himself in its study; such weariness must be reserved for Torah-study *(Midrash; Almosnino).*

13. סוֹף דָּבָר הַכֹּל נִשְׁמָע — *The sum of the matter, when all has been considered* [lit. *'the end of the thing; all is heard'*] i.e. the upshot of all the discourses in this Book *(Ibn Latif).*

'Now that I have made you aware and you have heard all sides . . .' *(Ibn Ezra).*

[The *Midrash* translates literally: 'the end is a word']: The end of man's conduct is that all proclaim his deeds, saying, so-and-so was right-living; so-and-so was God-fearing.

הַכֹּל נִשְׁמָע — [lit.] *All is heard.* All has already been heard at Sinai: therefore, *'fear God. . .' (Sforno).*

Whatever man does is 'heard' in Heaven . . . therefore do not transgress any of His words *(Metzudas David).*

Solomon said: Although I have expounded many esoteric and difficult concepts in this Book, nevertheless סוֹף דָּבָר, *the summation of the Book,* הַכֹּל נִשְׁמָע, *is obvious to all* and unquestionable: *Fear God* with your every limb and organ, *for this is all of man (Derech Chaim).*

אֶת־הָאֱלֹהִים יְרָא וְאֶת־מִצְוֺתָיו שְׁמוֹר — *Fear God and keep His commandments. 'Fear God'* — in your heart; *'and keep His commandments'* by deed *(Ramban).*

Do your utmost [and direct] your heart to Heaven *(Rashi).*

כִּי־זֶה כָּל־הָאָדָם — *For that is man's whole duty* [lit. *'for this the whole man'*] It was for this that all men were created *(Rashi).*

This is the essence of man *(Ibn Ezra);* and 'the entire world was created only for such a man' *(Shabbos 30b).*

14. כִּי אֶת־כָּל־מַעֲשֶׂה — *For every deed:* that man does. The pause, according to the accented punctuation is after מַעֲשֶׂה [i.e. the word מַעֲשֶׂה is part of the beginning of the verse and does not attach to God's Name:

'for every deed,' and not: *for every deed of God] (Rashi).*

הָאֱלֹהִים יָבִא בְמִשְׁפָּט — *Will God judge* [lit. *'will God bring in judgment']*

עַל כָּל־נֶעְלָם — *Even everything hidden* — Even unwillful transgressions *(Rashi);* including those sins of which you are not even aware *(Ibn Ezra).*

— Even transgressions done in privacy [concealed from your fellow man and hence not punishable by human courts of law] *(Ralbag).*

This phrase refers to any misrepresentation on the part of the soul that might be hidden from us but is revealed to God *(Rav Saadiah Goan).*

אִם־טוֹב וְאִם־רָע — *Whether good or evil* i.e. whether the intent was good or evil *(Metzudas David).*

Whether the deed was good and deserving of reward; or evil and deserving of punishment *(Sforno).*[1]

An example of this is one who gives alms to a poor person publicly [an apparently good deed which is repugnant because it embarrasses the recipient.] . . . Rav Yannai once saw a man give a coin to a poor person publicly. He said to him: 'It would have been better had you not given him, than to have given him publicly and put him to shame' *(Chagigah* 5a*).*

סוֹף דָּבָר — *The sum of the matter* [It is customary, during public-readings of Koheles, to repeat verse 13 rather than end with the word רָע, *evil* in verse 14. We act similarly at the end of *Isaiah, Malachi* and *Lamentations,* and thus end these books on a positive note.]

תם ונשלם שבח לאל בורא עולם

מוצש״ק פ׳ שופטים תשל״ו
Brooklyn, NY

1. God rewards measure for measure . . . Trivial sins are weighed in the balance with the same care as the grave ones. Greater sins do not cause lesser ones to be ignored . . . In the same way that God allows no good deed — however insignificant — to go unrewarded, so He allows no evil deed — however trivial — to pass unjudged and unpunished. This should be a warning to those who delude themselves with the thought that God does not take into account matters of seemingly small importance, and does not include them in His reckoning . . .

It follows, therefore, that a man who wants to be perceptive will look for no pretexts to be remiss in the duty of watching his conduct and being meticulous to the last degree. If a man will take these suggestions to heart, he will surely acquire the trait of watchfulness, if he only has the purity of soul and intention *(Messilas Yesharim).*

King Solomon ע״ה composed the Book of Koheles essentially for the purpose of causing one to take to heart the idea that the world is futile and that it should be used for nothing except the service of the blessed Creator. This purpose he expressed in both the introduction and the conclusion. He begins *'Futility of futilities'*, said Koheles, *'futility of futilities, all is futile'*, concerning which the *Midrash* comments: If someone else would have said this, we would have said: 'He probably never had two cents in his life, and that is why he looks at the world as being futile' but Solomon, of whom it is written (*I Kings* 10:27): *'And the king made silver to be in Jerusalem as stones'* — Solomon may well say that the world is futile.

Similarly he concludes saying: *'The sum of the matter, all having been considered: Fear God and keep His commandments, for that is man's whole duty.' (Rabbeinu Yonah)*

Bibliography
of Authorities Cited in the Commentary

Italics are used to denote the name of a work. ***Bold italics*** *within the biography indicate the specific work of that author cited in the commentary.*

An asterisk (*) precedes the names of contemporary figures

Albo, Rav Yosef

Spanish philosopher of the fifteenth century. Author of ***Sefer ha-Ikkarim.***

Little is known about his life, and the dates of his birth (1380) and death (1444) can only be conjectured. He was a student of Rav Chasdai Crescas, and according to some historians, he was a student also of Rav Nissim Gerondi (The 'Ran').

His most famous work, ***Sefer ha-Ikkarim***, ('Book of Principles'), is an important treatise on Jewish philosophy and faith. The book is divided into four parts the first of which was originally intended to be an independant work. The other three parts which elaborate upon the first part, were added later. The entire work was completed in Castile in 1425.

The work was first printed in 1485, and having achieved great popularity, has been reprinted many times since.

Alkabetz, Rav Shlomo haLevi:

[b. 1505-Salonica; d. 1576 Safed]
One of the greatest Kabbalists and mystical poets of his day. Author of the Piyyut *'L'cha Dodi'* recited every Friday evening. He was a contemporary and friend of Rav Yosef Karo, author of *Shulchan Aruch.*

He is often cited by early commentators, by whom he is referred to in various ways: *'Rashba haLevi'; 'Rav Shlomo haLevi;' 'Harav ibn Alkabetz haLevi.'*

He wrote commentaries on most of the Bible, the Passover Hagaddah, on *Kabbalah,* and was a noted Paytan.

In his Piyyut, *'L'cha Dodi,'* he speaks of the sufferings of the Jewish people and their aspirations for Redemption. Probably no other Piyyut has reached the popularity of *'L'cha Dodi'*; it is recited every Friday evening by all Jewish congregations throughout the world.

Almosnino, Rav Moshe:

Distinguished Rav and commentator. Born in Salonica, 1516, died in Constantinople about 1580.

His family dwelt originally in Aragon. Rav Moshe's grandparents were burned at the stake during the Inquisition, and his parents escaped and settled in Salonica, where he was born.

He was Rav of the Neve Shalom Spanish community in that city, and later of the Livyas Chen community.

Rav Almosnino was famous for his erudition and knowledge in both Torah and secular matters. In 1565 he represented the Jewish community before their Sultan Selim II petitioning for the confirmation of their civil rights. After six attempts, the Sultan acceded to his request and issued a proclamation guaranteeing equal rights to Jews.

He published many works — both in Hebrew and Spanish. Some were published during his lifetime, some posthumously. Many of his works are extant in manuscript form, others have been lost.

Among his works are: *Tefilah l'Moshe* on *Chumash; Pirkei Moshe* on *Avos; M'ametz Koach,* a collection of sermons; *Regimento de la Vida* (Way of

Life) in Spanish. His commentary to the *Five Megillos* entitled ***Yedei Moshe*** was published in 1572.

Alshich, Rav Moshe:

[Also spelled Alshekh]

Rav, Posek and Bible Commentator. Born in Andrionople in 1508; studied Torah there in Yeshiva of Rav Yosef Karo. Settled in Safed where he spent most of his life and was ordained there by Rav Karo with the full *Semichah* re-introduced by Rav Yaakov Berav. Among his pupils was Rav Chaim Vital, whom he ordained in 1590.

He died in Damascus, where he was travelling, before 1600.

He wrote Commentaries on most of the Bible, and published a collection of 140 of his *halachic* Responsa.

His commentary to *Koheles, **Devarim Tovim*** was originally published in 1608. The abridged form of his commentary appearing in many editions of the Bible as ***'Kittzur Alshich'*** was edited by Rav Eleazar Tarnigrad, Amsterdam, 1697. Tarnigrad added much original material into this abridgement which he attributed to the Alshich but which cannot be found in the Alshich's commentary.

Alter, Rav Yitzchak Meir

(1789-1866)

Gerrer Rebbe; founder of the Gerrer Chassidic dynasty. Rav Yitzchak Meir was a disciple of the Maggid of Koznitz, and later of Rav Simcha Bunem of Pshyscha, and of Rav Menachem Mendel of Kotzk.

After the Kotzker's death in 1859, Rav Yitzchak Meir was acknowledged Rebbe by the majority of Kotzk Chassidim.

His influence was far-reaching. Although his leadership lasted only seven years, he had a formative influence on the development of Chassidus in Poland. Gerrer Chassidus became a powerful element in Orthodox Polish Jewry.

He is most famous for ***Chiddushei haRim,*** novellae on the Talmud and *Shulchan Aruch,* and was frequently referred to by the name of his work, "The Chiddushei haRim."

Alter, Rav Yehudah Aryeh Leib:

(1847-1903)

Gerrer Rebbe; known by his work 'Sefas Emes'.

His father, Rav Avraham Mordechai, a great but chronically ill man, died when Yehudah Leib was only 12 years old. His upbringing fell to his grandfather, the illustrious Chidushei haRim. Yehudah Aryeh would study eighteen hours a day as a youth. It became widely known that a fitting successor was being groomed for the Chiddushei haRim.

He was 19 years old when his grandfather died and, despite the pleas of the chassidim, insisted he was unworthy to become Gerrer Rebbe. Several years later, after the death of Rav Henach of Alexandrow, he acceded to their wishes and molded Ger into the largest chassidus in Poland.

A prodigious and diligent scholar, he nevertheless found time to counsel tens of thousands of disciples every year and to become an effective leader in Torah causes. His discourses were distinguished for profundity and originality.

Although he never wrote for publication, his writings were posthumously published as ***Sefas Emes***, separate volumes of novellae on Talmud, and chassidic discourses on Torah and festivals.

Altschuller, Rav Yechiel Hillel ben David

Bible commentator of 18th century.

In order to promote the study of the Bible Reb Yechiel Hillel's father, Reb David, planned an easy-to-read commentary of Neviim and Kesuvim (Prophets and Hagiographa) based on earlier commentators.

His commentary to *Psalms, Proverbs* and Job was published before he died in 1753.

Rav Yechiel edited his father's remaining manuscripts and completed the missing books himself. By 1780, the entire completed commentary was published. It consisted of two parts: ***Metzudas Zion*** which explains individual words; and ***Metzudas David*** which provides a running commentary to the text. Due to their simple and concise language, the dual commentaries have become almost indispensable aids in Bible-study. They have attained great popularity and have been reprinted in nearly every edition of the Bible.

Anaf Yosef

see *Rav Chanoch Zundel ben Yosef.*

Arama, Rav Yitzchak b. Moshe:

(1420-1494)

Spanish Rav, philosopher and preacher. He was Rav of Calatayud where he wrote most of his works. After the expulsion of the Jews from Spain in 1492, he settled in Naples where he died.

He is best known for his book ***Akeidas Yitzchak***, a collection of allegorical commentaries on the Torah. First published in 1522, it has been reprinted many times and has exercised great influence on Jewish thought.

Because of this work he is often referred to as the *'Baal Akeidah'* ['author of the *Akeidah'*.]

He also wrote a **Commentary on the Five Megillos** which was printed together with his *Commentary to the Torah* in Salonica, 1573.

He wrote *Yad Avshalom,* a commentary on *Proverbs,* in memory of his son-in-law, Avshalom, who died shortly after his marriage.

ARIzal

see *Luria, Rav Yitzchak.*

Avodah Zarah

Talmudic tractate in *Seder Nezikin.*

Azulai, Rav Chaim Yosef David:

Known by his Hebrew acronym CHIDA.

Born in Jerusalem in 1724; died in Leghorn in 1806. Halachist, Kabbalist, and bibliographer-historian, he possessed great intellectual powers and many-faceted talents.

He went abroad as an emissary and he would send large sums of money back to Israel. He ended his mission in 1778 in Leghorn where he spent the rest of his life.

His fame as a *halachist* rests on his glosses to *Shulchan Aruch,* contained in his *Birkei Yosef,* a work constantly cited by later authorities.

He was the author of the famous bibliographic work Shem haGedolim. Among his many works was the homiletical ***Nachal Eshkol*** on the *Five Megillos.*

Baal haTurim:

see *Rav Yaakov ben Asher.*

Bass, Rav Shabsai ben Yosef

Born in Kalisz 1641; died at Krotoschin, 1718.

His parents were killed *'Al Kiddush Hashem'* in the Kalisz massacres of 1655. He went to Prague where he excelled in the Yeshivah there. Possessing a fine voice he served as a member of the choir in the famous Altneuschul in Prague, hence his surname Bass.

Between 1674 and 1679 he travelled through Europe visiting libraries, and became profoundly interested in bibliographic studies. He established a publishing house in Breslau where his books were famous for their beautiful appearance. The first book he published was the then new commentary *'Beis Shmuel'* on *Even haEzer.*

In 1680 he published his own work,

Sifsei Yesharim, a well-arranged bibliographical listing of all books published till his time.

His most famous work is ***Sifsei Chachamim*** — a commentary on Rashi's interpretation of Chumash and Five Megillos — where he clarifies with admirable brevity the surface difficulties in Rashi's commentary, and which is an almost indispendable aid toward understanding and appreciating *Rashi.* It is printed alongside *Rashi's* commentary in most large editions of the Bible. It has also been condensed and appears in many editions as *Ikkar Sifsei Chachamim.*

Bava Basra:

Talmudic tractate in *Seder Nezikin.*

Bava Kamma:

Talmudic tractate in *Seder Nezikin.*

Berachos:

Talmudic tractate in *Seder Zeraim.*

Binyan Ariel:

see *Rav Shaul ben Aryeh Leib of Amsterdam.*

Rav Chanoch Zundel Ben Yosef

(d. 1867).

Rav Chanoch lived in Bialystock, Poland, where he devoted his life to writing commentaries on the *Midrash* and the *Ein Yaakov.*

He published two commentaries which appear side-by-side in the large editions of the *Midrash Rabba* and *Ein Yaakov*: *Eitz Yosef,* in which he strives to give the plain meaning of the text; and ***Anaf Yosef*** which is largely homiletical.

Rav Chanoch also published a commentary to *Pirkei Avos,* but his commentaries to *Yalkut Shim'oni* and the *Mechilta* are still in manuscript.

Chasman, Rav Yehudah Leib:

(1869-1935)

Born in Lithuania, he studied in Slobodka, Volozhin, and Kelm. He was strongly influenced by three of the *Mussar* giants of the era: Rav Simcha Zisel Ziev of Kelm; Rav Yitzchak Lazar of St. Petersburg — both of whom were among the foremost disciples of Rav Yisrael Salanter; and Rav Nosson Zvi Finkel of Slobodka.

Rav Chasman held several positions as Rav and lecturer of *Talmud.* He found his place in Shtutzin, Lithuania, where, after assuming the rabbinate in 1909, he established a Yeshivah that grew to 300 students. However, the destruction and dislocation brought about by World War I, destroyed the Torah life of the city.

After the war, Rav Chasman was a vital activist in rebuilding Torah life in the city.

The call to become *'mashgiach'* (Spiritual Guide) of the Hebron Yeshivah in Eretz Yisrael, gave him the opportunity to become a seminal figure in the development of the Torah Yishuv.

Ohr Yohel, published poshumously by his students, is a collection of his lectures and writings.

Chidah:

See *Azulai, Rav Chaim Yosef David.*

Chidushei haRim:

see *Alter, Rav Yitzchak Meir.*

Derech Hashem:

see *Luzatto, Rav Moshe Chaim.*

Dessler, Rav Eliyahu Eliezer:

(1891-1954).

One of the outstanding personalities of the Mussar movement. He was born in Homel, Russia.

In 1929 he settled in London. He exercised a profound influence on the teaching of Mussar, not only because of

the profundity of his ideas, but also on account of his personal, ethical conduct.

In 1941 he became director of the Kollel of Gateshead Yeshiva in England.

In 1947, at the invitation of Rav Yosef Kahaneman, he became *Mashgiach* of Ponovez Yeshiva in Bnei Brak, Israel, and there remained until his death.

His teachings reflect a harmonious mixture of Mussar, Kaballah, and Chassidus. Some of his ideas were published by his pupils in ***Michtav me-Eliyahu*** (3 vols. 1955-64).

Dubna Maggid:

See *Kranz, Rav Yaakov.*

Eidels, Rav Shmuel Eliezer ben Yehuda haLevi:

1555-1631.

(Known as Maharsha — 'Moreinu ha-Rav Shmuel Eliezer'.)

One of the foremost Talmud commentators, whose ***commetary*** is included in almost every edition of the Talmud.

Born in Cracow, he moved to Posen in his youth. In 1614 he became Rav of Lublin, and in 1625 of Ostrog, where he founded a large Yeshivah.

Eiger Chumash:

A medieval manuscript found in Prague containing a commentary to the Siddur and a short running commentary to ***The Five Megillos.*** Published in 1846.

Einhorn, Rav Zev Wolf:

Rav in Vilna, end of 19th century.

Author of ***Peirush Maharzu,*** comprehensive and well-detailed commentary to *Midrash Rabba* appearing in the Romm edition.

Rav Eliezer b. Yehudah of Worms:

[*Heb.* Eliezer of Germizah. Also known as *Baal haRokeach*].

1160-1237.

Scholar in the field of Halachah, Kaballah, and also a paytan (composer of liturgical poems) in medieval Germany. Student of Rav Yehudah haChassid the author of *Sefer Chassidim.*

Rav Eliezer is known primarily for his authoritative halachic work ***Sefer Rokeach,*** which is quoted extensively in the *Shulchan Aruch.*

His students were many, among them Rav Yitzchak of Vienna, author of *Or Zarua.* Among his exegetical works are *Shaarei Binah.*

Emunos v'De'os

see *Rav Saadiah Gaon.*

Epstein, Rav Baruch haLevi:

(1860-1940).

Born in Bobruisk, Russia. He received his early education from his father, Rav Yechiel Michel Epstein, author of *Aruch haShulchan.*

Rav Baruch later studied under his uncle, Rav Naftali Zvi Yehudah Berlin [the 'Netziv'].

He was the author of several works, but he is best known for a brilliant commentary to Chumash ***Torah T'mimah***, in which he quotes and explains the Halachic and Aggadic passages on the various verses. He also wrote ***Gishmei Bracha*** on the *Five Megillos.*

Eshkol haKofer:

See *Sava, Rav Avraham ben Yaakov.*

Eyebeschuetz, Rav Yonasan:

Rav, and one of the greatest Torah scholars of his generation.

Born in 1690 in Cracow; served as Rosh Yeshivah in Prague. Served as Rav of the 'Three Communities' — Altona, Hamburg and Wandsbek, until his death in 1796.

Rav Yonasan published extensively on *Halachah* and Bible. His most famous *Halachic works were Urim v'Tumim* on *Choshen Mishpat* (1775), and *Kreisi*

U'pleisi on *Yoreh De'ah*. His homiletic work, ***Yaaros D'vash***, published posthumously, was reprinted many times.

Because of his friendly relations with the government officials, he secured the right to reprint the entire Talmud — something which had been prohibited for centuries until that time.

Rav Yonasan's use of amulets sparked off a bitter controversary between him and Rav Yaakov Emden, repurcussions of which lasted even after Rav Yonasan's death. All who knew Rav Yonasan vouched for his righteousness, scholarship and sincerity.

Galanti, Rav Moshe ben

16th century Talmudist and Kabbalist. Rav Moshe was the brother of Rav Avraham Galanti (see bibliog. to ArtScroll ed. of *Eichah.)*

Rav Moshe received *Semichah* from his teacher, Rav Yosef Caro, author of the *Shulchan Aruch.* His teacher in *Kaballah* was Rav Moshe Cordovero.

From 1580 he served as Head of the Rabbinical Court in Safed.

He lived to over 90 and died after 1612.

He is the author of several halachic and esoteric works, including ***Koheles Yaakov***, a partly homiletic and partly kabbalistic work on Koheles (Safed, 1578).

Galico, Rav Elisha ben Gavriel:

Prominent Talmudist and Kabbalist of the early 16th century.

Rav Elisha was a student of Rav Yosef Caro, author of the *Shulchan Aruch,* and was a member of his Rabbinical Court in Safed.

Rav Elisha was the teacher of Rav Shmuel de Uzeda, author of *Iggeres Shmuel* and *Lechem Dim'ah* (see bibliog. in ArtScroll ed. of *Ruth* and *Eichah*).

Rav Elisha's halachic responsa are quoted in *Knesses haGedolah.* He published a commentary to all Five Megillos. His ***Commentary to Koheles*** was published in Venice, 1578.

Gans, Rav David.

(1541-1616).

Chronicler and mathematician.

Rav David was a student of the RAMA (Rav Moshe Isserles) and the MAHARAL of Prague (Rav Yehudah Loew), where he mastered his Talmudic studies.

He spent most of his life in Prague where he wrote many works, most of which have been lost.

Encouraged by the RAMA, Rav David published the historical work for which he is most famous: ***Tzemach David.*** The book is in two parts: one part deals with Jewish history; the other with general history.

This work has become a standard reference work for later chroniclers.

Gishmei Brachah:

see *Epstein, Rav Baruch haLevi.*

Heilprin, Rav Yechiel b. Shlomo:

(1660-1746).

Lithuanian Rav, Kabbalist and historian.

He was a descendant of RASHAL (Rav Shlomo Luria), and traced his ancestry back through Rashi to the Tanna, Rav Yochanan haSandlar.

He was Rav and Rosh Yeshivah at Minsk, where he studied Kabbalah and published several works.

He is most known for his ***Seder ha-Doros***, a history from Creation down to his own time.

He based his work on *Sefer haYuchsin* of Rav Avraham Zacuto; *Shalsheles haKaballah* of Rav Gedaliah ibn Yachya; and *Tzemach David* of Rav David Gans, as well as on an abundance of Talmudic and Midrashic references.

Hirsch, Rav Shamshon Raphael:

(1808-1888).

The father of modern German Orthodoxy. He was a fiery leader, brilliant writer, and profound educator. His greatness as a Talmudic scholar was obsured by his other monumental accomplishments. After becoming chief Rabbi and member of Parliament in Bohemia and Moravia, he left to revitalize Torah Judaism in Frankfort-am-Main which he transformed into a Torah bastion.

His best known works are the classic six-volume ***Commentary on Chumash*** noted for its profound and brilliant philosophical approach to Biblical commentary; his ***Commentary to Psalms***, and ***Horeb***, a philosophical analysis of the mitzvos.

Ibn Ezra, Rav Avraham:

(Born 1089 in Toledo; died 1164).

Famous poet, philosopher, grammarian, astronomer — and above all — Biblical commentator. He also wrote a ***Commentary on the Five Megillos***

In all his Bible commentaries he strived for the plain, literal meaning of the verse. His aim was to explain the etymology of difficult words within their grammatical context. Next to Rashi, his commentary on the Torah is most widely studied, and appears in almost all large editions of the Bible.

In France, he met Rav Yaakov Tam ['Rabbeinu Tam'] — grandson of Rashi, and a deep friendship between the two followed.

According to some, he married the daughter of Rav Yehudah haLevi, and had five sons.

Legend has it that he once met the Rambam and dedicated a poem to him on the day of his death.

Ibn Janach, Rav Yonah

Born in Cordova, c 985; died in Saragossa, first half of 11th century.

One of the foremost *'Baalei Dikduk'* (grammarians and philologists) of the early middle ages. Little is known of his life.

He published one of the first Biblical grammar books and dictionaries, the earliest to have come down to us in its entirety. It was originally written in Arabic and later translated into Hebrew by Rav Yehudah Ibn Tibbon. It is divided into two parts: *Sefer haRikmah*; and ***Sefer haShorashim***.

He is often quoted by later Bible commentators and Hebraists such as: Ibn Ezra; Ibn Daud; Kimchi; Mizrachi; Rambam.

The notable exception is *Rashi* who seems to have been unacquainted with his work (or who may have chosen not to quote him.)

Ibn Janach was also a physician and he published several treatises on medicine, which have been lost.

Ibn Yachya, Rav Yosef.

Bible commentator; member of the famous Ibn Yachya family of which many scholars were descendants.

He was born in Florence, Italy in 1494, his parents having fled to that country from Portugal.

He relates in his preface to his *Torah Or* that in her first month of pregnancy with him, his mother, under threat of being ravaged, had thrown herself off a roof in Pisa in order to preserve her modesty, and she was miraculously saved.

She then fled to Florence where he was born.

His ***Commentary to the Five Megillos,*** was published in Bologna, 1538. Two of his other works: *Derech Chaim* and *Ner Mitzvah* were consigned to flames at the burning of the Talmud in Padua in 1554.

Rav Yosef had three sons, one of whom was Gedaliah, the author of *Shalsheles haKabbalah.*

Rav Yosef died in 1534. Ten years after his death his remains were brought to *Eretz Yisrael. Rav Yosef Caro* arranged for his burial in Safed.

Kara, Rav Yosef

French Bible commentator, c1060-1130. [not to be confused with Rav Yosef Caro, 15 century author of *Shulchan Aruch*].

Rav Yosef was the student of his illustrious uncle, Rav Menachem Chelbo, whom he often cites in his commentary.

Rav Yosef resided in Troyes, the same city in which Rashi lived, and he frequented Rashi's house, where he made the acquaintance of Rashi's grandson, *Rashbam.*

Rav Yosef wrote a commentary on Torah — based upon Rashi's commentary which he enlarged and expanded upon. He also added glosses to Rashi's commentary which Rashi himself agreed with and later incorporated into his own manuscript.

Rav Yosef also wrote an independant commentary to most of Tanach, including ***The Five Megillos.***

In his commentaries he followed the general style of Rashi but was not as brief. Sometimes whole sentences are translated into French. He cares more for the sense of the whole sentence than for the grammatical dissection of a single word. Although he prefers peshat, the simple meaning of the text, he does not altogether hold aloof from haggadic interpretation — which he held was an adornment of the text and was necessary to 'render Torah great and glorious.'

Kedushas Levi:

See *Rav Levi Yitzchak of Berditchev*

Kimchi, Rav David:

French grammarian and commentator; known by his acronym 'RADAK'.

Born in Narbonne, 1160; died there in 1235.

His father, Rav Yosef, also a grammarian, died when Rav David was a child, and he studied under his brother, Rav Moshe, who had also published several volumes on grammar.

Radak's commentary on Prophets is profound, and is included in most large editions of the Bible.

Many have applied to him the saying from *Pirkei Avos*: 'Without *kemach* ['flour' i.e. *'Kimchi'*] there is no Torah; such was his great influence.

His main work was the ***Michlol,*** the second edition of which came to be known independently as *the Sefer ha-Shorashim* (not to be confused with a work by the same name by Ibn Janach).

In his commentary, he stressed the *derech ha'peshat,* the plain sense, wherever possible, striving for clarity and readibility, rather than the compression and obscurity of some of his contemporary commentators.

Kiflayim l'Sushiyah:

see *Landau, Rav Yitzchak Eliyahu ben Shmuel.*

Koheles Yaakov:

see *Galanti, Rav Moshe ben Mordechai.*

Kol Yaakov:

See *Kranz, Rav Yaakov.*

Kranz, Rav Yaakov:

(1741-1804).

Known as the 'Dubna Maggid.'

Born near Vilna; Rav Yaakov demonstrated his skill as a preacher at an early age, and was barely 20 years old when he became *darshan* in his city. He later became *darshan* in several cities, but he achieved his fame as preacher in Dubna where he served for 18 years.

He came into frequent contact with the Vilna Gaon, who, it is said, enjoyed his homiletical interpretations, stories, and parables.

The Dubna Maggid's works were printed posthumously by his son Yitzchak, and his pupil Baer Flahm. Among these works were: *Ohel Yaakov* on *Chumash*; ***Kol Yaakov*** on the *Five Megillos;* Commentary on the Passover *Haggadah;* and *Mishlei Yaakov,* a collection of his parables.

Landau, Rav Yitzchak Eliyahu ben Shmuel:

(1801-1876)

Lithuanian Rav, Maggid, and Bible commentator.

Little is known of him. He was born in Vilna; married the daughter of the wealthy and well-known Tzadok Marshalkovitch of Dubna and was thus relieved of financial cares. He spent most of his life compiling his books and sermons using the method of Rav Yaakov Kranz, the Dubna Maggid.

In 1868 he became the *Dayyan* of Vilna, a position he held until his death.

He published commentaries to many books of the Bible. Well-known is his commentary *Mashal U'Melitzah,* in which he explains the verses by using parables; and his exegetical commentary — printed alongside the *Mashal U'Melitzah* — entitled ***Kiflayim l'Sushiyah***, in which he translates difficult words and provides a running commentary, profoundly clearing up surface difficulties.

He also published commentaries to the *Tanna debe Eliyahu;* to *Mechilta; Pas'shegen haDas* on Torah; *Acharis l'Shalom* on the Pesach Haggadah; *Simlah Chadashah* on the *Machzor;* and several volumes of Talmudic commentaries.

Rav Levi ben Gershom:

(Known by his acronym RALBAG; also known as Gersonides).

Born in Bangols, France in 1288; died 1344.

One of the most important Bible commentators of his time, he was also a mathematician, astronomer, philosopher and physician.

He wrote commentaries to *The Torah; Job, the Five Megillos, Former Prophets, Proverbs, Daniel,* and *Nechemiah.*

His commentary to ***Koheles*** was written in 1328.

His Bible comments show the work of a profound philosopher; and he has a great skill in analyzing a text and extracting the ethical and religious teachings inherent in them.

His commentary to *Job* was one of the first books printed in Hebrew (Ferrara, 1477).

Rav Levi Yitzchak of Berditchev:

(1740-1810)

Chassidic Tzaddik and Rebbe. One of the most famous personalities of the third generation of the Chassidic movement.

He was born into a distinguished rabbinic family to his father, Rav Meir, who was Rav in Hoshakov, Galicia. It is said that at the moment of Rav Levi Yitzchak's birth the Baal Shem Tov remarked that a great soul had just descended from heaven which is destined to be the greatest intercessor of the Jewish people.

He was drawn to Chassidus by Rav Shmelke of Nicholsburg, and he became one of the foremost disciples of Rav Dov Ber, the Maggid of Mezeritch.

He succeeded Rav Shmelke in Richwal, and later became Rav in Zelechov, and was thus known as the 'Rebbe of Zelechov' by many of his Chassidim.

He ultimately moved to Berditchev in 1785, and served as Rebbe there until his death. His fame grew throughout the world as a Torah scholar and Tzaddik.

Under him, Berditchev became a great Chassidic center and many — including

great Torah Sages — flocked to consult with him.

His great love for every Jewish soul — always seeking the good side of every Jew, never the bad — permeated his very essence and he became the subject of many legends.

In his writings he notes that 'only he who admonishes Jewish people gently, elevates their souls and always extols them righteously, is worthy of being their leader.'

Although he did not found a dynasty, he had many pupils and left an indelible mark on Chassidim.

His most famous work is ***Kedushas Levi*** — a commentary on the Torah and some holidays. It was published during his lifetime in 1798. An expanded edition — supplemented by his sons from manuscript — was published posthumously in 1811.

Lorberbaum, Rav Yaakov ben Yaakov Moshe of Lissa:

(Polish Rav and Posek. Known as the 'Lissa Rav'; or 'Baal Nesivos').

(1760-1832).

He was the great-grandson of 'Chacham Zvi.' His father, Rav Yaakov Moshe, died before Yaakov was born, and his relative Rav Yosef Teomim brought him up.

He studied under Rav Meshullam Igra, and later became Rav in Kalish where he wrote most of his works.

After he published — at first anonymously — his *Chavas Da'as* on *Yoreh De'ah,* and *Nesivos haMishpat* on *Choshen Mishpat,* he became acknowledged as an outstanding *posek.*

His contemporaries said of him that his learning was so pure and *'lish'mah,'* that his halachic decisions were as acceptable and unquestionable as if 'from Moshe at Sinai.'

Together with Rav Akiva Eiger and the Chasam Sofer he vehemently attacked and opposed the *Maskilim* and Reformers.

In 1809 he responded to an invitation to become Rav in Lissa where he enlarged the Yeshivah to an enrollment of hundreds of students.

In 1822 he left Lissa due to community strife, and returned to Kalish where he spent his time publishing many more of his books.

Among his writings were *Imrei Yosher,* a comprehensive commentary on the Five Megillos, each published separately under different names. His profound commentary to *Koheles,* entitled ***Taalumos Chachmah*** appears in most large editions of the Bible.

Luria, Rav David:

(1798-1855; Known as RADAL).

Lithuanian Rav and *posek.* Student of Rav Shaul Katzenellenbogen of Vilna.

After the death of his mentor, the Vilna Gaon, Radal was considered one of the Torah leaders of his generation. His scholarly writings embrace almost all of Torah literature. Among his works is his commentary to the Midrash, ***Chidushei Radal***, printed in the Romm edition of the *Midrash Rabba.*

Luria, Rav Yitzchak:

(Known as ARI*zal [from the initials of ha**E**loki **R**abbi **Y**itzchak, **z**ichrono **l**ivrachah]*).

The fountainhead of modern *kabbalistic* thought.

Born in Jerusalem, 1534, to his father, Rav Shlomo Luria, a relative of Maharshal.

While still a child, he lost his father. His mother moved the family to Egypt, and he was brought up by his wealthy uncle Rav Mordechai Francis in Cairo.

He studied at the Yeshivah of Rav David

ben Zimra (Radvaz) who was his teacher, *par excellence* in *Torah* and *kaballah*. He was a student / comrade of Rav Betzalel Ashkenazi (author of *Shittah Mekubetzes*) who himself was a student of Radvaz.

ARIzal was beloved by his uncle, and at the age of fifteen, was given his cousin in marriage. He was thus enabled to continue his studies undisturbed.

His holiness manifested itself at an early age and students flocked to him, extolling his virtues and saintly qualities.

In 1570, at the age of 36, he moved to Eretz Yisrael and settled is Safed where he formed a circle of *kabbalists* among whom were Rav Moshe Cordovero (Ramak); Rav Shlomo Alkabetz; Rav Yosef Caro; Rav Moshe Alshich; Rav Yosef Chagiz.

His circle widened and his influence grew greatly. He was regarded by all who knew him as a profound Tzaddik who had the power to perform miracles.

He entrusted his kabbalistic teachings to his disciple Rav Chaim Vital, who, according to ARIzal possessed a soul which had not been soiled by Adam's sin.

After the ARIzal's death in 1572, Rav Chaim Vital collected notes which the ARIzal's students had made of their master's teachings, and published them. Among the works so published were: *Eitz Chaim; Hadras Melech; Marpei Nefesh; Tikkunei Shabbos; Commentary to Zohar Chadash;* and *Shulchan Aruch of the ARIzal* incorporating his halachic customs. These customs are quoted extensively by later Halachic authorities, and his influence is immense.

ARIzal revealed many of the sepulchres of Sages whose locations had been forgotten until his time. He is also credited with composing the Sabbath Zemiros: *Azamer Bish'vachin, Asader liSeudasa,* and *Bnei Haichala.*

He died in Safed, 1572, at the young age of 38.

Luzatto, Rav Moshe Chaim

(1707-1746)

Kabbalist; author of Mussar ethical works; and poet.

Born in Padua, Italy, Rav Moshe Chaim was regarded as a genius from childhood, having mastered *T'nach, Midrash* and *Talmud* at an early age. He later went on to delve into Kabbalistic and ethical studies.

He is most famous for his profound ethical treatise, ***Mesilas Yesharim*** ('The Path of the Upright') which has, alongside the *Chovos haLevavos* of Rav Bachya ibn Paquda and *Shaarei Teshuvah* of Rabbeinu Yonah, became the standard ethical-Mussar work.

Among his Kabbalistic works were: *Razin Genizin,* ***Megillas Sesarim;*** *Maamar haGeulah;* **Derech Hashem.**

In 1743, he emigrated to Eretz Yisrael. He lived a short time in Acre, and died there, with his family, in a plague.

Maharal:

see *Rav Yehudah Loewe ben Bezalel.*

Maharam Rothenburg:

see *Rav Meir b. Baruch of Rothenburg.*

Maharsha:

see *Eidels, Rav Shmuel Eliezer ben Yehudah haLevi.*

Mashal Umelitzah:

Collection of homiletic interpretations on the Torah by Rav Avraham Naftali Galanti. Published in New York City during the last generation. (Not to be confused with the Bible commentary of the same name by Rav Yitzchak Eliyahu Landau.)

Matanos Kehunah:

see *Rav Yissachar Berman haKohen.*

Me'am Loez:

A contemporary commentary by Rav Shmuel Yerushalmi a noted Israeli Torah scholar, following the style of the

18th century homiletical bible commentary in Ladino; the outstanding work of Judeo-Spanish literature. A commentary of encyclopedic nature begun by Rav Yaakov Culi (1685-1732), of whom the *Chidah* in *Shem haGedolim* speaks in the most superlative of adjectives. No work designed to instruct the Jewish masses ever proved so popular. Rav Yaakov Culi died in 1732 having published only *Breishis*. He left many unfinished manuscripts and his work was completed by others.

A Hebrew translation of the entire work -with many new additions, and entitled ***Yalkut Me'am Loez*** was undertaken by Rav Shmuel Yerushalmi in 1967. *Koheles* was published in 1975.

Megillah

[as differentiated from *'Megillas Esther'* — the Biblical Book of *Esther*.]

Talmudic tractate in *Seder Mo'ed*.

Megilas Sesarim:

See *Luzatto, Rav Moshe Chaim*.

Rav Meir ben Baruch of Rothenburg:

German Tosafist and Posek.

Known by his acronym *Maharam Rothenburg*. Maharam was born in Worms 1215 to a family of illustrious Torah scholars.

During his early years he was taught by his father.

One of his first teachers were Rav Yitzchak ben Moshe of Vienna (author of *Or Zarua)* and Rav Shmuel of Wurzburg. Maharam also studied at French Yeshivos under the eminent Rav Yechiel of Paris.

On his return to Germany, he quickly gathered around him a band of devoted pupils who were eager to study under so brilliant a teacher.

He officiated as Rav in the following communities: Kostnitz, Augsburg, Wurzburg, Rothenburg (where he spent the major part of his life), Worms, Nuremberg and Mayence.

He was recognized by his Ashkenazi contemporaries as the Torah giant of the generation and his halachic decisions were accepted as authoratative.

As a result of constant persecution, many German Jews emigrated abroad to Eretz Yisrael at the time. In 1286, Maharam was leading such a group when he was seized and thrown into prison in the fortress of Ensisheim, Alsace.

The King demanded an exhorbitant ransom for his release. The Jewish community was ready to raise the sum and liberate their leader, but Maharam himself prevented any such high sum being paid for his liberation lest the government use this as a precedent for imprisoning important men to extort ransoms. He therefore put the community welfare over his own and heroically spent the next seven years in prison — until his death in 1293.

He submitted to his fate in the thought that it was the will of God whose ways are always just. Even in prison he was occupied solely with studying and teaching. Several of his students were allowed to visit him there. It was there that his pupil Rav Shimshon ben Zadok compiled his 'Tashbetz.' He wrote, or revised a large part of his works; and his responsa now took the place of oral instruction.

He was a voluminous writer. He wrote Tosafos to various tractates of the Talmud; published various halacha codifications, and extensive amount of responsa and novellae.

Maharam had many distinguished disciples. Among them: Rav Asher ben Yechiel (*'Rosh'*), Rav Mordechai ben Hillel (The *'Mordechai'*); Rav Yitzchak Madura (*'Shaarei Dura'*).

Even after his death there was no peace. The King would not release his body, and his remains lay unburied for fourteen years until an exorbitant ransom was paid by a wealthy man, Reb Alex-

ander Wimpan, whose only request was that when he dies he be buried alongside Maharam. His request was fulfilled.

Mendlowitz, Rav Shraga Feivel:

(1886-1948).

Born and educated in Austria-Hungary, Rav Mendlowitz became principal and teacher in the Scranton Pa. *Talmud Torah*. In 1921 he came to Brooklyn, where he became principal of the then small *Yeshivah Torah Vodaath*. During his tenure, he built it into one of the world's leading Torah centers. With the holocaust, he launched a new effort to train great Torah scholars to replace those lost in the War.

Rav Mendlowitz was a visionary who brought many dreams to reality. He pioneered such concepts as *Kollel* by founding Beth Medrosh Elyon, summer learning camps by founding Camp Mesivta, and the Day School Movement through Torah Umesorah.

Totally unselfish, he was instrumental in helping establish many of the country's great Yeshivos. He was widely respected for his willingness to work for other institutions even when his own was in need.

His philosophy was that Torah, not any individual institution, is the main responsibility ot every Jew. Though he was ill and often in pain for the last twenty years of his life, his efforts were uninterrupted until his death.

A charismatic and inspiring teacher, his memory continues to be a beacon to hundreds of his students.

Mesillas Yesharim:

see *Luzatto, Rav Moshe Chaim.*

Michtav me-Eliyahu:

see *Dessler, Rav Eliyahu Eliezer.*

Michlol:

see *Kimchi, Rav David.*

Midrash:

see *Midrash Rabbah.*

Midrash Lekach Tov:

Midrash on various Books of the Bible attributed to ***Rav Toviah ben Eliezer*** 11th century. The work has achieved great popularity and is quoted by many *Rishonim* such as Rabbenu Tam, Rambam, Baal haIttur, *Or Zaruah, Shibolei haLeket.* Ibn Ezra also refers to it in his commentary.

This *Midrash* has been published at separate times on the various books of the Bible as the manuscripts have been re-discovered. ***Koheles*** was published together with *Eichah* in 1908.

Midrash Rabbah:

[Lit. 'The Great Midrash'].

The oldest Amoraic classical *Midrash* on the *Five Books of the Bible* and the *Megillos.*

[*Note: Throughout the commentary of this Book, whenever* 'Midrash' *alone is shown as the source, the reference is to* Midrash Koheles Rabba.]

Midrash Zuta.

Also called *Koheles Zuta* ('Minor Koheles'). This *Midrash* was probably compiled before the 10th century. It is quoted by the author of *Midrash Lekach Tov* which was written in the 11th century.

It was published by Buber from a Parma manuscript in 1894.

Miller, Rav Avigdor:

Contemporary Rav, noted lecturer and author. A major force on the American Orthodox scene. Rav in Brooklyn, New York. Author of ***Rejoice O Youth!; Sing You Righteous;*** *Torah Nation; Behold A People.*

Minchas Shay:

see *Rav Yedidiah Shlomo of Norzi.*

Moed Katan

Talmudic tractate in *Seder Moed.*

Rav Moshe ben Maimon:

Known by his acronym: RAMBAM; Maimonides.

(1135-1204).

One of the most illustrious figures in Judaism in the post-Talmudic era, and among the greatest of all time. He was a rabbinic authority, codifier, philosopher, and royal physician. According to some, he was a descendant of Rav Yehudah haNasi.

Born in Cordoba; Moved to Eretz Yisrael and then to Fostat, the old city of Cairo, Egypt.

At the age of 23 he began his *Commentary on the Mishnah,* which he wrote during his wanderings. His main work was ***Mishneh-Torah Yad-haChazakah,*** his codification of the spectrum of *Halachah* until his day. This was the only book he wrote in Hebrew, all his other works having been written in Arabic, a fact he is said to have regretted later in life.

He is also known for his profound and philosophic ***Moreh Nevuchim ('Guide for the Perplexed'),*** and for his many works in the field of medicine, hygiene, astronomy, etc.

Truly it may be said 'from Moshe to Moshe there arose none like Moshe.'

Rav Moshe ben Nachman:

Known by his acronym: RAMBAN; Nachmanides.

(1194-1270)

One of the leading Torah scholars and authors of Talmudic literature during the generation following Rambam; also a renowned philosopher, biblical commentator, poet and physician .

Born in Gerona to a famous rabbinic family, he is sometimes referred to, after his native town, as Rabbenu Moshe Gerondi. He spent most of his life in Gerona, supporting himself as a physician. He exercised extensive influence over Jewish life. Even King James I consulted him on occasion.

Already at the age of 16 he had published works on Talmud and Halachah.

Among his works were: *Milchemes Hashem,* in defense of the Rif against the 'hasagos' (disputations) of Rav Zerachiah haLevi in his Sefer haMaor; *Sefer haZechus,* in response to the 'hasagos' of the Ravad on the Rif; *Sefer haMitzvos; Iggeres haRamban; Iggeres haKodesh;* and his profound and encyclopedic ***Commentary on the Torah,*** which is printed in all large editions of the Bible.

In 1263 he was coerced by King James I into holding a public disputation with the apostate Pablo Christiani which resulted in a victory for the Ramban, but which aroused the anger of the church and resulted in his forced exile from Spain just in time to escape the death penalty. He then emigrated to Eretz Yisrael. In 1268 he became Rav in Acco, successor to Rav Yechiel of Paris.

He died in 1270; his burial site has not been definitely ascertained.

Nachal Eshkol:

see *Azulai, Rav Chaim Yosef David.*

Nachmanides:

see *Rav Moshe ben Nachman [Ramban].*

Nedarim:

Talmudic tractate in *Seder Nashim.*

Niddah:

Talmudic tractate in *Seder Tohoros.*

Ohr Yohel:

See *Chasman, Rav Yehudah Leib.*

Pesikta Rabbasi:

Ancient Midrash; a collection of discourses dating from the first half of the first century, C.E. Divided in *Piskas* [sections] and containing discourses on the holidays, festivals and special Sab-

baths. Several *piskas* are devoted to Tishah b'Av, the Destruction, and ultimate Comfort and Restoration.

Pirkei d'Rabbi Eliezer:

Ancient aggadic work attributed to the first century *Tanna,* Rabbi Eliezer ben Hyrcanos.

Poras Yosef:

see *Taitatzak, Rav Yosef.*

Pri Tzaddik:

See next entry.

Rabinowitz, Rav Tzadok haKohen:

(1823-1900)

Born in Kreisburg, Latvia, young Tzadok attracted attention as a phenomenal genius. Orphaned at the age of six, he was raised by his uncle near Bialystock. Such was the child's reputation, that Rav Yitzchak Elchanan Spektor of Kovno made a point of testing him when he happened to be near by.He prophesied that 'the boy will light a great torch of knowledge in Israel.

In later years, Rav Tzadok lived in Lublin where he became acquainted with Rav Leibele Eiger, a disciple of Rav Mordechai Yosef of Izbica. Rav Tzadok became their disciple, and, with their passing, became Rebbe of the Chassidim of Izbica. He became known far and wide as the 'Kohen of Lublin'. The breadth and depth of his thought were astonishing. Many considered him the greatest Torah scholar in all of Poland.

Pri Tzaddik, is a collection of his discourses on the weekly portion, and festivals. He was a very prolific writer. Although much of his works have been published, he left many unpublished manuscripts that were destroyed during World War II.

Among his other works are Responsa *Tiferes Zvi; Meishiv Tzaddik;* and ***Resisei Layla.***

Radak:

see *Kimchi, Rav David.*

Ralbag:

see Rav Levi ben Gershom:

Rambam:

see *Rav Moshe ben Maimon.*

Ramban:

See *Rav Moshe ben Nachman.*

Rashba haLevi:

see *Alkabetz, Rav Shlomo haLevi.*

Rashbam:

see *Rav Shmuel ben Meir.*

Rashi:

see *Rav Shlomo ben Yitzchak.*

Resisei Layla:

see *Rabinowitz, Rav Tzadok haKohen.*

Rottenberg, Rav Shlomo:

Noted contemporary teacher, lecturer and historian. His monumental series, ***Toldas Am Olam,*** unifies all Talmudical Midrashic sources on the history from the latter period of the First Temple.

Rav Saadiah (ben Yosef) Gaon

(892-942).

Rosh Yeshivah of Sura, and one of the most important figures of the illustrious Gaonic period.

Rav Saadiah was made Gaon by the Resh Gelusa (Exilarch) David ben Zakkai in 928, and the ancient acacemy in Sura, founded by Rav, then entered upon a new period of brilliancy.

He was a sage in every sphere of Torah knowledge, had a full grasp of the secular knowledge of his time, and was a dynamic leader, fighting a valiant battle against the growing influence of Karaism.

He published in many areas: Halachah, responsa, philosophy, grammar, but most of his works are lost or scattered among the genizas, waiting to be published.

Among the most important of Saadiah's works to have come down to us are his translation of and partial ***Commentary to the Bible,*** which was the first translation of the Bible from Hebrew into Arabic, and has remained the standard Bible for Arabic-speaking Jews; his *Siddur,* the first systematic compilation of prayers for the whole year; *Sefer haAgron,* on grammar; and his profound ***Sefer Emunos v'De'os,*** *(Book of Belief and Doctrines),* originally written in Arabic and translated in Hebrew by Rav Yehudah Ibn Tibbon. This major philosophic work is the earliest such work to have survived intact.

There is hardly a figure after him who does not pay generous and laudatory tribute to his pioneering work: the philologist Rav Menachem ben Yaakov (often quoted by Rashi); Ibn Janach; Ibn Ezra, all praise him in the greatest of superlatives.

Even Rambam who disagreed with Rav Saadiah on many fundamental points, states in his Iggeres Teiman: 'were it not for Rav Saadiah, the Torah would have well-nigh disappeared in the midst of Israel.'

Saba, Rav Avraham ben Yaakov.

15-16th Century Kabbalist, Bible commentator and Darshan.

Rav Avraham was among those expelled from Spain in 1492. He moved to Portugal where he wrote his commentary ***Eshkol haKofer*** to the *Chumash,* the *Five Megillos,* and *Pirkei Avos.*

In his youth, many of his works were lost, and he was forced to rewrite them later in life from memory.

His commentary to the *Chumash* was entitled *Tzror haMor.*

According to the *Shem haGedolim,* he died on board a ship on Erev Yom Kippur 1508.

Sanhedrin:

Talmudic tractate in *Seder Nezikin.*

Seder haDoros:

see *Heilprin, Rav Yechiel b. Shlomo.*

Seder Olam:

Early Midrashic-chronological work. *Seder Olam* is mentioned in the Talmud *(Shab. 88a; Yev. 82b et al.)* and is ascribed to the *Tanna* Rav Yose ben Chalafta.

Sefas Emes:

See *Alter, Rav Yehudah Aryeh Leib.*

Sefer Chassidim:

see *Rav Yehudah haChassid.*

Sefer haIkkarim:

see *Albo, Rav Yosef.*

Sforno, Rav Ovadiah.

(1470-1550).

One of the greatest Italian commentators and literary figures of the Renaissance period.

Little is known of Ovadiah's youth, except that he excelled in Torah studies and at an early age his halachic opinions were sought by many. His decisions are quoted by Rav Meir Katzenellenbogen (Maharam Padua) where he is referred to with great esteem.

Sforno studied medicine which profession he followed.

He finally settled in Bologna where he was a major force in organizing the religious life of the town and established a *bais medrash* which he headed to his death.

Sforno's great fame, however, rests with his Commentary to the most of the Bible, in which he tries to explain the text literally, usually regarding the verse as a complete entity rather than philologically dissecting it. He usually avoids esoteric or kabbalistic interpretations. His commentary to the Chumash was edited by his brother Chananel after his death. The ***Commentary to Koheles*** was first published in Venice in 1567.

Shabbos:

Talmudic tractate in *Seder Moed.*

Shaar Bas Rabim:

Scholarly and erudite anthology of commentaries on the Torah and *Megillos* by Rav Chaim Aryeh Leib Yedvavnah; late 19th century.

Shaarei Binah:

see *Rav Eleazar ben Yehudah of Worms.*

Rav Shaul ben Aryeh Leib of Amsterdam:

Born 1717 in Risha; died in Amsterdam, 1790.

Member of famous rabbinical family.

Served as Rav in many important cities, and upon the death of his father he replaced him as Rav of the prestigious Ashkenazi community of Amsterdam, where he served until his death.

He published many works on Bible, Talmud and Halachah, most famous of which was ***Binyan Ariel.***

When the Chidah visited Amsterdam, he stayed at the home of Rav Shaul and was so awed by his erudition and righteousness, that he praised him most flourishingly in his *Shem haGedolim.*

Shem haGedolim:

see *Azulai, Rav Chaim Yosef David.*

Rav Shlomo ben Yitzchok:

(Known by his acronym RASHI)

Leading commentator on the Bible and Talmud.

He was born in Troyes, France in 1040 — the year in which Rabbeinu Gershom M'or haGolah died. According to tradition, Rashi's ancestry goes back to Rav Yochanan haSandlar and to King David.

The summit of Rashi's commentaries was his commentary on the Talmud — an encyclopaedic and *brilliant* undertaking. Nothing can be compared to the impact this commentary has had upon all who study the Talmud. Rashi's commentary has opened to all what otherwise would have been a sealed book. Without his commentary, no one would dare navigate the 'Sea of Talmud.' Every word is precise and laden with inner meaning. Rashi's corrections of the Talmud text were, for the most part, introduced into the standard editions and became the accepted text.

Rashi's ***Commentary to the Bible***, too, made a similar impact — and virtually every printed Bible contains his commentary which is distinguished by its conciseness and clarity.

Many Halachic works from the 'School of Rashi' have come down to us: *Sefer haOrah; Sefer haPardes; Machzor Vitry; Siddur Rashi;* and responsa.

Rashi died on Tammuz 29, 1105. His burial place is not known.

Rav Shmuel ben Meir

(Known by his acronym RASHBAM).

Bible and Talmud commentator and Tosafist. Born in Northern France in 1080 to Rav Meir one of the first Tosafists and disciple of Rashi, whose daughter Yocheved Rav Meir Married.

Thus, a grandson of Rashi, he was the also the brother of the prominent Rabbeinu Tam,and a colleague of Rav Yosef Kara.

Rashbam studied under his father, but later was most influenced by his grandfather. They spent much time together in legal and exegetical discussions. In many instances *it is* noted that Rashi accepted his grandson's opinion in exegesis.

Rashbam lived a simple life. He would always pray that he might be privileged to perceive the Truth and to love peace.

He is most famous for his commentary to the Bible which is characterized by his extreme devotion to 'pshat'. He constantly refers to 'the profound literal meaning of the text. In many ways he considered his commentary as complementing that of Rashi; in many cases his commentary is exactly identical with his grandfather's.

He was also known as a Talmudic commentator. His commentary to portions of Pesachim and Bava Basra where Rashi did not manage to complete his own commentary, were annexed to Rashi's.

Sotah:

Talmudic tractate in *Seder Nashim.*

Taalumos Chachmah:

see *Lorberbaum, Rav Yaakov ben Yaakov Moshe of Lissa.*

Taanis:

Talmudic Tractate in *Seder Moed.*

Taitatzak, Rav Yosef:

c.1487-c1545.

Talmudist and kabbalist of 16th century Salonika. He was the teacher of such eminent disciples as Rav Shmuel Modina (Maharshdam); Rav Yitzchak Adarbi ('Divrei Rivos'); Rav Shlomo Alkabetz.

A renowned kabbalist, Rav Yosef may be regarded as one of the founders of the kabbalistic circle founded by his disciples in Safed. He spent over 18 hours a day immersed in Torah study, and it is related that he never slept in a bed for forty years apart from Shabbos. He was once addressed by Rav Yosef Caro in a halachic inquiry as 'the light and holy one of Israel, crown of the Diaspora,' etc.

He published a profound commentary to Koheles: ***Poras Yosef.***

Targum:

The ancient, authoritative translation of the Bible into Aramaic.

Teitelbaum, Rav Moshe:

(1759-1841). Founder of the Sigheter dynasty. A pupil of the Chozeh of Lublin. A renowned Tzaddik, he was among the first to spread Chassidus in the Northern and Central districts of Hungary in his capacity as Rav of Vjhely. Author of ***Yismach Moshe,*** considered one of the classic works of Chassidus.

Toldos Am Olam:

See **Rottenberg, Rav Shlomo.*

Torah T'mimah

See Epstein, *Rav Baruch haLevi.*

Tuv Taam

Commentary to the Five Megillos by *Rav Yeshayah Hammer;* Cracow, 1897.

Tzemach David

See Gans, *Rav David.*

Rav Yaakov ben Asher

(1270-1340)

Posek and codifier; 'Baal haTurim'.

Son of Rav Asher ben Yechiel (the 'ROSH') under whom he studied. He was born in Germany, and in 1303 he accompanied his father to Toledo, where he lived in great poverty, and devoted his life to Torah.

Rav Yaakov's enduring fame rests on his encyclopedic Halachic codification *Arbaah Turim,* which is the forerunner of our *Shulchan Aruch* today, and as a result of which he is referred to as the "Baal haTurim."

The arrangement and wealth of content made it a basic work in halachah and it was disseminated greatly through the Jewish world. It became so widely accepted, that when Rav Yosef Caro wrote his major work, *Bais Yosef,* , he decided to base it upon the *Turim* "because it contains most of its views of the *Poskim.*"

Rav Yaakov also wrote a comprehensive commentary on the Chumash anthologizing the literal explanations *(p'shat)* by earlier Bible commentators. To the beginning of each section he added "as a little appetizer, *gemmatrios* and explanations of the *Masorah,* in order to attract the mind." Ironically the whole work was printed only twice. It was just these "appetizers" that were popularly published alongside most editions of the Bible under the title ***Ba'al HaTurim.***

Among Rav Yaakov's students was Rav David Abudarham.

According to *Shem haGedolim* Rav Yaakov died en route to Eretz Yisrael.

Yalkut Shimoni

The best known and most comprehensive Midrashic anthology covering the entire Bible.

It is attributed to Rav Shimon ha-Darshan of Frankfort who lived in the 13th century.

The author collected *Midrashim* from more than 50 works, arranging them into more than 10,000 statements of *Aggadah Halachah* according to the verses of the Bible.

Rav Yedidiah Shlomo of Norzi

Rav and Commentator.

Born in Mantua 1560; died in 1626. Became Rav in Mantua in 1585.

Rav Yedidiah consecrated the greater part of his life to studying the *Masorah* of the Bible — and by studying every previously printed *Masorah* text, comparing the various readings scattered through *Talmudic* and *Midrashic* literature, as well as in published and unpublished manuscripts.

The resulting work was entitled *Geder Poretz,* but was published under the name ***Minchas Shai.***

This work, which was as perfect as thorough learning and conscientious industry could make it, has become the most accepted work in establishing the *Masorah*. The ***Minchas Shai*** is printed in the back of all large Bibles.

Rav Yehudah (ben Shmuel) haChassid:

(c.1150-1217).

One of the main teachers of the 'Chassidei Ashkenaz' and one of the most profound ethical teachers to have lived.

Author-editor of ***Sefer Chassidim***, a profound ethical / halachic treatise which has come down to us in two separate editions. The book has achieved great popularity and was reprinted many times.

Rav Yehudah's father, Shmuel, was a renowned Rosh Yeshiva in Speyer, and Rav Yehudah studied under him. His saintly life was revered by all.

Among his illustrious students were: Rav Eliezer of Worms (*Baal Rokeach*); Rav Yitzchak of Vienna (*Or Zarua*).

His contemporaries said of him: 'Had he lived in the time of the prophets, he would have been a prohet; in the time of the Tannaim, he would have been a Tanna; in the time of the Amoraim, an Amora ...'

Rav Yehudah Loewe ben Bezalel.

Known as the MAHARAL of Prague.

One of the seminal figures in the last 500 years of Jewish thought, Rav Yehudah was born c. 1512 and died in Prague in 1609. His genealogy can be traced to King David.

Although he was universally acknowledged as one of the rabbinic greats of the era, his life was not an easy one. He delayed his marriage for 20 years due to financial difficulties. He was Chief Rabbi of Moravia, residing in Nikolsburg, for 20 years.Then, in 1573, he transferred his yeshiva to Prague, the Torah metropolis of Europe. Upon two different occasions, he accepted the rabbinate of Posen in order to settle communal strife.

He was elected Chief Rabbi of Prague in 1597 as a very old man. It appears that the position had been denied him up to then because of his outspokenness in attacking social evils and religious laxity.

Though commonly known as a folk hero and miracle worker, his greatest contribution was his formulation of a self-contained system of Jewish thought. His many books and lengthy sermons formed the basis for much of the significant writing of succeeding centuries.

Among his many erudite works were: *Novellae* on *Shulchan Aruch Yoreh Deah;* ***Gur Aryeh*** on the Torah; *Be'er*

haGolah on the *Passover Hagaddah; Derech Chaim; Netzach Yisrael; Nesivos Olam,* etc. Many of his works are extant and were recently republished in an 18-volume set: *Sifrei Maharal.*

Yerushalmi, Peah

Tractate *Peah* in the Jerusalem Talmud.

Yevamos

Talmudic tractate in *Seder Nashim.*

Yismach Moshe:

see *Teitelbaum, Rav Moshe.*

Rav Yissachar Berman haKohen

Known as Berman Ashkenazi.

16-17th Century commentator on the Midrash.

Very little is known about him except that he was born in Sczebrzesyn, Poland, and that he was a student of the Rama (Rav Moshe Isserles).

He is the author of the famous commentary to the Midrash Rabba, ***Matanos Kehuna,*** first published in 1584, and appearing subsequently in nearly every edition of the Midrash.

Rav Yissachar makes it very clear in his introduction that he was very concerned with establishing the correct text for the *Midrashim,* basing his text upon all the various printed editions up to his time and on various manuscripts.

Yoma

Talmudic tractate in *Seder Moed.*

Rabbeinu Yonah of Gerona:

Spanish Rav and Moralist of the thirteenth century.

Rabbeinu Yonah was a cousin of

Rabbeinu Yonah was one of the people who banned the Rambam's (Maimonides) *Moreh Nevuchim* out of fear that philosophical influences — rampant at the time — would cause untold harm to the religiosity of the people. But when he saw that this anti-Rambam controversy was getting out of hand — and even resulted in the public burning of the Talmud in the same place where the philosophical writings of Rambam had been destroyed — Rabbeinu Yonah publicly admitted that he was wrong in all his acts against the works of Rambam. In his repentance he vowed to travel to Eretz Yisrael and prostrate himself over the grave of the great teacher and implore his pardon in the presence of ten men for seven consecutive days.

He left France with that intention, but was detained — and died before he was able to fulfill his plan, in 1263.

Rabbeinu Yonah wrote many works, among them commentaries on portions of Tanach; commentary of Avos; Chiddushim on several tractates of the Talmud; and his famous Mussar works, later reprinted: *Iggeres haTeshuva;* ***Shaarei Teshuvah;*** and *Sefer haYirah.*

Rabbeinu Yonah established Yeshivos. Among his most prominent pupils were Rav Shlomo Adret (Rashba).

He stayed in close contact with his cousin, Ramban, and Ramban's daughter married Rabbeinu Yonah's son. When Rabbeinu Yonah died, his daughter was pregnant. When she gave birth to a son, Ramban told her to name the child Yonah so that he will assuredly excell in Torah and piety.